COMETS AND THE HORNS OF MOSES

THE SECRET HISTORY OF THE WORLD
VOLUME II

BOOKS BY LAURA KNIGHT-JADCZYK

Amazing Grace – An Autobiography of the Soul
The Apocalypse: Comets, Asteroids and Cyclical Catastrophes
The Noah Syndrome
The Secret History of the World and how to get out alive
High Strangeness: Hyperdimensions and the Process of Alien Abduction
9/11: The Ultimate Truth

THE WAVE SERIES:

Riding the Wave
Soul Hackers
The Terror of History
Stripped to the Bone
Petty Tyrants
Facing the Unknown
Almost Human
Debugging the Universe

Laura Knight-Jadczyk

COMETS AND THE HORNS OF MOSES

THE SECRET HISTORY OF THE WORLD
VOLUME II

Red Pill Press
www.redpillpress.com

First edition.
Copyright © 2013 Laura Knight-Jadczyk.
Research Sponsored by Quantum Future Group, Inc.
P. O. Box 5357 Baltimore, MD 21209
U.S.A.

ISBN 978-1-897244-83-8

Cover design by Mark Andersen, Jonathan Soper and Robert Bakos,
based on the image from the book *Theatrum cometicum* by Stanislas Lubieniczki (1681).

He who learns must suffer,
And even in our sleep pain that cannot forget
Falls drop by drop upon the heart,
And in our own despair, against our will,
Comes wisdom to us by the awful grace of God.

— Aeschylus, *Agamemnon.*

TABLE OF CONTENTS

ACKNOWLEDGEMENTS

I must first acknowledge the Quantum Future Group, Inc. and all those who contribute to QFG and its projects for the needed support; without this help, the research and writing of this book and those that follow would not have been possible.

Secondly, I want to thank the members and participants of the QFG-sponsored Cassiopaea online Forum for research help, discussion and critique. No one person can do all the reading necessary for a book like this - life just isn't long enough – so thank you all for wading through so much and synopsizing so my energies could be conserved!

Thirdly, I want to thank my gifted writing assistant, Pierre Lescaudron for his enthusiastic participation in our cunning plans to suss out history and his invaluable knowledge in critiquing and rewriting certain technical sections. And, in the same breath, I want to thank Joseph Quinn for doing the dirty work on the manuscript – straightening out awkward sentences, cleaning up the references, and making sure I make sense on topics that are often difficult to be coherent about!

Lastly, I want to thank my husband, Ark, for his constant support, and my family for keeping me fed and happy so I can work long hours day after day and for being breakfast table sounding-boards for ideas and developments!

Oh, I should also mention the critics, defamers and assorted individuals who absolutely hate my work: thanks for making me stronger and developing my knowledge of psychopathology; I could never have figured some things out without you!

INTRODUCTION

This book, and the volumes to follow, have been a long time coming. Back in 2003, I confidently assured the readers of my lengthy (700 pages) tome, *The Secret History of the World*, that a companion volume was as good as written in my head and it was just a matter of putting it all down in writing. Famous last words, as they say. The problem was that, when I began to put it down in writing, it quickly became clear to me that more research was needed. It's one thing to more or less rehash accepted historical 'fact' and myth and include one's own interpretation or 'spin' on them, it's quite another to begin the process of questioning whether 'official' history is actually fact-based at all, and to take another look at what has been accepted as mere myth. In fact, based on the information you are going to read in this book and the subsequent volumes, you may end up coming to the same conclusion I have: that very often 'myth' provides a closer representation of 'what really happened' than what passes for historical 'fact'.

In this book, the second volume of a series that begins with *The Secret History of the World*, I am going to present material that will be foundational to understanding the subsequent historical chronicles in the next volumes. As we explore the details of many different histories, myths and personalities, the reader should keep in mind that there is a line of force running through all of what you will read: how cyclical cosmic cataclysms, specifically cometary events, have periodically punctuated the rise and fall of civilizations, and have had a direct and serious influence on human history and how it has been recorded (or not recorded, as the case may be). In addition, you will discover how the human population may exert a crucial influence on those cyclical cometary events and how, and why, over the course of history, this crucial knowledge was progressively twisted and ultimately erased from human memory.

To follow and understand this line of force, we'll intertwine four seemingly unrelated, though highly complementary, fields of research: history, myths and religions, psychology and hard science. While this is a journey

11

back through time, we will also be taking much cutting-edge research with us as we explore diverse topics to untie the Gordian Knot of history.

The topics will include some of the early ideas I had about Moses and his relationships to other key mythological figures and a possible connection to a key historical person. We will look at the Bible, treating it alternately as history and literature, then examine modern cognitive psychology to understand why there are such widely variant views of 'what really happened' when history is supposedly 'set in stone'.

Through an analysis of Sumerian, Mesopotamian, Hittite, Celtic, Babylonian, Egyptian, Mayan, Etruscan and Greek history, we'll learn how history appears to dramatically repeat itself and see just how uncanny it is for so many important historical episodes to be carbon copies of others before them.

We will also attempt to understand how 'history' got into such a mess, why we don't know our true history, and how, possibly, we might begin to recover it. Our study of myth and religions will show how the very real and regular threat to all life on Earth from comets and comet fragments was once fully understood, but was progressively transformed, first into 'gods' fighting in the sky that would periodically 'smite' humans, then into more aloof gods who had little interaction with humanity, then into human mythical heroes and ultimately into a unique, benevolent, sun-like God with a capital 'G'. We will then examine evidence that, in more recent times, history and the history of religion was rewritten in such a way that certain well-known religious persons were projected back in time in order to lend legitimacy to today's accepted 'history' of the modern monotheistic religions, which maintain a spiritual stranglehold on most of humanity today. This in turn will set the stage for how we have ended up with a scientific, uniformitarian, Newtonian cosmogony, where celestial bodies are governed by immutable laws and follow harmonious, predictable trajectories with humans as mere spectators of benign celestial revolutions that have no influence on us, and thus, are of little real interest.

I'm a firm believer in the saying, 'Those who do not remember history are doomed to repeat it'. I think it is safe to say that there are some horrors in the history of humanity that we do not want to repeat.

There is going to be science – the science of comets – and some speculations about legends of werewolves and vampires and their possible relation to comets (along with a selection of other myths and legends). We will learn about the origins of astrology – it is definitely not what is promulgated – as well as the origins of religions as we understand 'religion' today.

The subject of psychology, specifically cutting-edge psychological research, will help us understand why the secular and clerical elites throughout history have deprived the population of crucial knowledge, why the population accepted narratives that were (and are) so remote from truth and why certain forms of psychological deficiencies affecting some leaders can and do repeatedly affect whole populations and these mass actions may, in fact, trigger cosmic reactions.

Hard science will help us understand why the way our ancestors depicted cometary events was accurate, why cyclical cometary events occur, why they can leave so little in the way of evidence, what the origin and nature of comets are, and how they can interact with our planet, its climate and its tectonic activity.

In short, this volume is going to be a potpourri of indispensable concepts woven through historical accounts of 'what really happened'. I've taken the time and trouble to follow each thread as far as possible for these present purposes and to evaluate the sources. In most cases, I will quote directly from them so that you, the reader, can make your own decision regarding their reliability. Obviously, I can't include everything, but I've tried to cover a wide enough range and provide citations so that if anything interests you in particular, you can follow it up. In the instances where a book is rare, expensive, or otherwise difficult to get, I have quoted *in extenso*.

Volumes III, IV and V will contain some explosive new material so it will be important for you to have all the information that is packed into this book under your belt and at your neuron-tips by the time we get there. I can tell you that re-examining history and untangling the threads so as to make it clear – and even entertaining – is a difficult challenge. But it is true that if one just takes things one step at a time, stops at any given point and looks all around to find the clues, it can be done.

So, let's get going – we have millennia to cover and time's a-wasting!

CHAPTER ONE

THE MOSES MYTH
IN HISTORY

When I first attempted to sort out the problem of Moses many years ago, I began with some sort of nonsense such as "Moses is undoubtedly the best-known figure in human history whose influence affects every single one of us right down to the present day. This is problematical since nobody really knows who Moses was or if he was even a real person."

It could be said that this was true enough, and of course, I was planning on revealing exactly who he *really* was – a fact as yet unknown to all the world – and precisely when he lived and prob-ably what he really did, histori-cally speaking. Hubris, I know.

Moses showing the Ten Commandments.
Engraving by Gustave Doré (1865).

The plan of the book was to list the various theories about Moses and ideas about the historicity of the events of his life, so that I could, one by one, de-compose and compare these ideas and their relative strengths and weak-nesses, preparatory to revealing my own ideas and the proofs I had assem-bled; it was a cunning plan!

But cold reality set in after I had written the first few sentences along that same line; I stopped and asked myself: is it really true that everyone on the planet has heard of Moses and that nobody really has a clue who he was (assuming he was a real person)?[1] Is there anything that would absolutely contradict my own theory? Is there anything I've missed?

The effects of Mosaic doctrine on the world are pretty much self-evident. Moses created Judaism, Judaism was foundational to Christianity, Christianity drives Western Civilization, and Western Civilization 'rules the world', at least for now, as Jared Diamond[2] and Ian Morris[3] describe. But can all of that really be attributed to a single individual and his dramatic encounter with a god? I was certainly aware of the major ideas bruited in theological circles, most of which were based on circular reasoning: the Bible underwriting its own historicity because there was nothing else, or very little, to confirm or contradict it.

Opposing the theological point of view were the increasing scientific studies based on archaeology, most of which said there was no Exodus, thus no Moses, full stop![4, 5, 6, 7, 8, 9, 10] But this didn't stop the true believers. There were still 'biblical archaeologists' making creative interpretations using less than shreds of evidence based on their *a priori* beliefs, but their arguments were never convincing.

There was also the popular media and alternative history: books, articles, videos, all of which were based on the same fundamental error: that the Bible was history and it only needed to be interpreted properly which really amounted to writing fiction. Everybody had a theory about who Moses really was, what the Ark of the Covenant was, what actually happened to the Ark of the Covenant, missing treasures allegedly found by this or that secret organization in the ruins of Solomon's Temple, the very existence of

---

1. That Moses has had a profound influence on our Western civilization is undeniable, in my opinion, so that wasn't the issue that gave me pause.
2. Professor of Geography at the University of California, Los Angeles, author of *The Third Chimpanzee* (1991/2004), *Guns, Germs, and Steel* (1997), and *Collapse: How Societies Choose to Fail or Succeed* (2005).
3. Morris (2010), *Why the West Rules – For Now: The Patterns of History, and What They Reveal About the Future*.
4. Sand (2009), *The Invention of the Jewish People*.
5. Walton (2003), 'Exodus, date of', in Alexander & Baker, *Dictionary of the Old Testament: Pentateuch*.
6. Van Seters, John (1997), 'The Geography of the Exodus', in Silberman, *The Land That I Will Show You*.
7. Lemche (1985), *Early Israel: Anthropological and Historical Studies*.
8. Finkelstein & Silberman (2001), *The Bible Unearthed*.
9. Whitelam (2006), 'General Problems of Studying the Text of the Bible...', in Rogerson & Lieu, *The Oxford Handbook of Biblical Studies*.
10. Gmirkin (2006), *Berossus and Genesis, Manetho and Exodus: Hellenistic Histories and the Date of the Pentateuch*.

David and Solomon and the temple, and more, all of which related, in one way or another, to Moses. And certainly, since the texts of ancient times that have come down to us have been edited and altered many times, it left a lot of room for speculation. I don't think any scholar of ancient texts disagrees that the edits, changes, additions, and more, are present in those texts; there is just a range of interpretations as to why it happened and who did it.

Since I had noted that strange confluence of factors in comparing the stories of Moses and Abraham and Sarai in Egypt, and the life and reign of Akhenaten mentioned in the first book in this series, *The Secret History of the World*, what I wanted to know was: other than that, is there *any* solid, external evidence of a material nature for Moses and his deeds and if so what does it suggest about what really might have happened, and to whom? What was the historical seed that can be confirmed by some sort of evidence *outside of the Bible*?

Like so many others, I wasn't quite ready to give up the idea that there was at least *some* truth in the Bible. The only thing that made my approach at all different from any other 'true believer' or 'alternative history' author was that I was compelled to search for a factual, real piece of external evidence that was not contaminated by the influence of the Bible itself, and to then use that as a lynchpin and work from there. That certainly makes the task more difficult, but it also means that there is the possibility of getting close to what may have 'really happened' in the past – assuming that there is anything to be found after so many years.

Of course, I initially thought I had that piece of hard data – the evidence of the existence of the Amarna period[11] which had been unknown for so many years to Western society and which appeared to validate those passages in the Bible about Abram and Sarai[12], and that this surely implied knowledge within the Bible of something that had been hidden in the mists of the ages. But still, I felt strongly that there was something wrong with even that picture. I knew I hadn't actually found the 'smoking gun' even if I thought I had heard the shot! I decided I had better spend a little more time digging. Surely there is something out there, some bit of epigraphic or ar-

---

11. The Amarna Period was an era of Egyptian history during the latter half of the 18th Dynasty when Amenhoteop/Amenophis IV aka Akhenaten moved the royal residence and court to a newly built city called Akhetaten ('Horizon of the Aten') in what is now modern-day Amarna.

12. As part of Abram's covenant with 'The Lord', he and Sarai got a name change and were henceforth to be known as Abraham and Sarah. I will be using these pairs of names interchangeably.

chaeological evidence to be found? Surely, if my idea is correct, something must still exist that will nail it down incontrovertibly?

That was nine years ago. I can tell you in advance, there is no 'smoking gun'. But what I found along the way is a pile of circumstantial evidence that the Moses myth has had a far greater influence on our world than even I suspected. And, along the way, I may have found bits of evidence that reveal what really happened during the Amarna period; who Nefertiti was, what may have happened to her, and so on.

There is a mountain of material to pick through looking for solid data. Even when dealing with archaeology, which is supposed to be based on facts – things that ought to be pretty solid – one has to appreciate that there are biases operating in the individuals analyzing the artifacts and to navigate around that requires a good grasp of *psychology* and patience. Working this way means that it takes a lot of time – and money[13] – to get to the bottom of things. Academic books, journals and papers on these topics are not always cheap or easily available to the lay researcher. The best sources are often difficult to obtain, much less interpret due to the tendency of insiders in the various fields to use their own jargon which makes their findings opaque not only to the non-expert, but to experts in other fields! Not only that, quite often, a given worker in the field will write a paper with his opinion about what he has found and withhold the site data. Sometimes, other experts have to wait for years to have access to the first-hand material. No wonder science is in such a deplorable state!

Though I didn't focus *exclusively* on Moses per se, for *all* of these years, nearly everything I have read and/or written during that time has been, at most, only a few degrees away from the core elements of the topic: the influence of the Mosaic doctrine on our world. I became increasingly aware of how crucial knowledge of this important figure who dominates our existence, both consciously and unconsciously, actually is. I came to realize that even atheists in modern times are profoundly influenced by the Bible – centered on Moses, allegedly – because it dominates the entire foundations and discourse of our Western civilization! Consider, for example, the extent to which the idea of a Christian 'god' dominates the politics of the USA and the hold that idea has on the minds of the vast majority of people, be they true believers or not. The words 'in God we trust' are written on every single US coin and bank-note in circulation, and that term is also the official motto of the USA. There would be no 'god' in this context without Moses.

---

13. This book has probably cost about € 20K in obtaining the necessary books, journals and papers, so you are definitely going to be getting way more than your money's worth!

Something else that will become apparent as we go through this material is that monotheistic Judaism (via Christianity and its discontented offspring), is the father of scientific materialism, a fact that might shock many true believers. This process is most clearly explicated in the work of psychologist, Bob Altemeyer, in his books *Amazing Conversions: Why Some Turn to Faith and Others Abandon Religion*[14] and *Atheists: A Groundbreaking Study of America's Nonbelievers.*[15] What happens to an individual who is brought up to believe that truth (God's word) is the highest value and there is only one truth (one true God)? As Altemeyer shows with scientific studies, there are some individuals of relatively higher intelligence and strong internal morality who have taken a very serious look at their Christian beliefs. Their intelligence and observational skills induce them to notice that the Bible itself cannot be true, and their conviction that Truth is important forces them to submit the 'word of God' itself to analytical study. The result is invariably the conclusion that there is nothing true or holy about the Bible, which then confronts them with the choice of living a lie or abandoning their faith. There is another type of individual who may be born and raised in a non-religious family, yet yearns for an authority to follow to ameliorate the stress of life and to solve their problems for them. They are generally of lesser intelligence (which is probably why they can't solve their problems on their own and become overwhelmed) and so they are easy converts to 'official Biblical history'. This is the Authoritarian Follower personality type that we will discuss in more detail further on.

At the present moment, I cannot say that the research lines opened as a result of my inquiry into the 'Life of Moses' are anywhere near reaching *final* conclusion, though I have certainly made much headway in realizing how little I know and how much there is yet to learn. Unsurprisingly, there are some pieces of data that surprised me when I found them. What I can say is that, even at this preliminary stage of what could take a few more lifetimes to fully plumb, it is *now time* to get as much of it into written form as possible for two main reasons. The first reason is that there does seem to be a tantalizing glimmer of light at the end of this dark, nine-years-long tunnel, and I hope that presenting what I have found may inspire others who may know about, or have, additional pieces of the puzzle. The second reason is actually more pressing: *time.* Time passes and human beings get older and duller and I'm no exception. I'm now almost ten years older than I was when I so blithely promised the next volume of my *Secret History* series and

---

14. Altemeyer (1997).
15. Altemeyer (2006).

it has been 13 years since I first had the thoughts that led to my central idea: that maybe, just maybe, Moses and Abraham (and possibly others) were either one and the same person, or different people assimilated to the same mythical archetype or, in the case of the Amarna period, part of a scandalous episode of the past, the knowledge of which spread like wildfire around the ancient world, coloring and informing numerous myths and legends. With the possibility that someone else may have pieces of the puzzle (no one person can ever parse enough material in one lifetime), I don't want to take the risk that all the work I have done (with a lot of help from my friends) might be lost if I am unable to complete it.

Thus, I am going to attempt to bring some small insight to a wide array of topics in the hopes that some clue, some obscure reference, might be just the thing that some other researcher will need to make a connection that adds to the picture and/or is the smoking gun evidence that nails it all down. I also hope that, by the effort of untangling the knots, laying the threads of history out straight and writing everything down, I myself may actually find my way out of the maze of mystification erected around that well-known, yet totally unknown, giant of history: Moses.

The Moses Story In A Whole New Light

As a child, I was impressed and terrified by an image of Moses that was in my mother's Bible. Of course I wanted to know the story. A guy is chosen by God to do a whole raft of heroic things, including getting to chat with God Almighty face to face. During the chat, God gives him a list of important rules – actually writes them Himself – and then the guy comes down the mountain and sees everyone playing around while he was up there being serious. He then has a fit of rage and breaks what God Himself, gave him. Obviously, Moses didn't think much of God's effort.

My next question was, of course, what did God do about that? It puzzled me to no end that God didn't strike him dead on the spot. When I found out that God actually approved of this behavior because he was a "jealous god", and helped Moses replace the broken tablets, I lost a lot of respect for God.

That wasn't the only bad thing Moses did; he was also a murderer[16] and a coward and a whiner.[17] But despite all this, he was still God's top man. Even

---

16. [Moses] looked this way and that, and when he saw there was no one around, he struck down the Egyptian and hid him in the sand." (Exodus 2:12)

17. When God asks Moses to guide the people of Israël, the following exchange occurs: Moses said to the Lord, "Pardon your servant, Lord. I have never been eloquent, neither

so, God was strangely fickle in respect of his top-man. Moses wasn't allowed to go to the Promised Land because he again got angry and struck a rock instead of coaxing it sweetly as he was told to do. Even more bizarrely, after this incident, Moses begged for forgiveness and asked God to let him in, but God stubbornly refused. All his years of service and devotion to this god apparently counted for nothing; so the story goes.

In short, for me, Moses was not a very attractive character. Noah was much more interesting. And in fact, this present study of Moses and his 'Ark of the Covenant' actually began with Noah and his Ark almost 30

Moses and the Ten Commandments.
Engraving by Gustave Doré (1866).

years ago. Well, actually, it all began with Adam and Eve in the Garden of Eden and the appearance on the scene of evil in the form of a serpent. The short version is that in pondering the Biblical explanation for the existence of evil in our world, the eschatology of the Bible took center stage. I focused on the topic of End Times prophecies of the Book of Revelation and the connected alleged saying of Jesus in Matthew 24 where he was describing the End Times being "as it was in the days of Noë (Noah)." So, I read a lot of books about theories (scientific and pseudo-scientific) that were supposed to explain the Great Flood of Noah. (If there was really a flood, then there was something historical in the Bible, right?)

During the course of exploring questions about end-of-the-world scenarios and so forth, I encountered Immanuel Velikovsky and his book *Worlds in Collision*[18], which dealt mainly with the Exodus and Moses. I wasn't too interested in Moses at the time since, as mentioned, I was on the trail of Noah and the description of that event being the model for some future event as

---

in the past nor since you have spoken to your servant. I am slow of speech and tongue."
The Lord said to him, "Who gave human beings their mouths? Who makes them deaf or mute? Who gives them sight or makes them blind? Is it not I, the Lord? Now go; I will help you speak and will teach you what to say." But Moses said, "Pardon your servant, Lord. Please send someone else." (Exodus 4:10-13)

18. Velikovsky (1950).

supposedly predicted in Revelation and Matthew 24.

It was in Velikovsky's work that I saw that his blow-by-blow account of the events of the Exodus, created by juxtaposing the Biblical account with the account recorded in the *Ipuwer Papyrus*[19] and interspersed with his analysis of what must have actually been taking place, was nearly point-by-point identical with what was written in Revelation[20] which was already con-

Depiction of Moses on Mount Sinai.

nected to the great Flood of Noah by Matthew 24. I casually discarded the fact that Velikovsky was writing about the Exodus exclusively because right there in the Bible it told me that the end-time event should be compared to the Deluge, *not* the alleged Exodus event.

At that moment, I actually had an inkling that Moses was just Noah redux, that some event with a few similarities to the Great Flood had occurred at some later point, and the already existing legends of Noah were adapted to underpin a new hero who may or may not have existed. I had read a number of articles about scientific studies that declared that the Exodus never happened because there was no evidence for it, so I just assumed that the *Ipuwer Papyrus* was about the Noachian event and that Velikovsky was off by a few (thousand) years and had mislabeled the event. But it was thanks to the Moses Story that a story of the Flood was actually brought to my attention. I thought we could now have an idea of what might have happened during the time of Noah and that that was the sort of thing that John was ranting about in Revelation: not really the end of the world in the sense of a global flood, but certainly catastrophic events almost guaranteed to bring civilizations to their knees.

Of course, I didn't completely discount some sort of Exodus from Egypt, such as the Hyksos leaving *en masse*, and somewhere in there was the erup-

---

19. The *Ipuwer Papyrus* is an ancient Egyptian poem which has been interpreted by some as an Egyptian account of the Plagues of Egypt and the Exodus in the Old Testament.
20. Leave aside for the moment the idea that Revelation may have been written to describe a political situation current in the 1st century which is one theory. At the time, I was considering that it was entirely possible that it was a prophecy about the End of the World and I was rather shocked to note the similarities between Revelation and Exodus. What this factor implied, to me, was that both events were cataclysmic – not necessarily caused by any divine being – and certainly not the END of the world.

tion of the Santorini volcano [21], Thera, which probably added a few stories to the mix. But still, I wasn't terribly interested in Moses in relation to prophecy or eschatology – he became, to me, just a Johnny-come-lately Noah-wannabe. Noah and the ark were what 'floated my boat', to use an apt metaphor. My view of Moses and the Exodus at the time, gave more weight to the experience of some small group of people escaping Egypt, probably during the course of the Theran eruption, than to the figure of Moses himself. I wrote (rather naïvely) in my book *The Noah Syndrome*:

> The events of the Exodus had such an incredible impact upon the Jewish people that it is mentioned dozens of times throughout the scriptures. It could be said to be the single most important event in the long history of these beleaguered people. It was the Exodus which saved them, as a nation, from assimilation, annihilation, and historical obscurity. It was the Exodus which planted the seeds of chosenness and knitted threads of national identity into bonds strong enough to withstand centuries of oppression and dispersion. And, since their national identity was created by this event – while the identities of many other peoples were obliterated from the face of the earth by the same event – who are we to say that this was not part of a great and noble intent on the part of the intelligence of the cosmos? [22]

Along the way I came upon the work of Walter and Luis Alvarez (a geologist and physicist respectively) and their comet/asteroid-impact theory that explained the extinction of the dinosaurs.[23] This then led to the ideas of cyclical 'dyings' [24] – all of which were projected so far into the past or future that we really didn't need to worry about it at all. But obviously, the demise of the dinosaurs happened so long ago that it could not have been part of human memory, so there must have been at least one other event since then: the one recorded in the *Ipuwer Papyrus* and the Bible – which took the idea from other ancient legends of Mesopotamia – as the Exodus, not to mention hundreds, if not thousands, of similar legends the world over. That opened the door to wondering if such events happen a bit more often than the Great Dyings would indicate, and are perhaps, in some cases, more localized? That is, science came around to catastrophism, finally, but in a very reserved and particular way: sure, it can happen, but only by an asteroid and

---

21. Volcano located in the Aegean sea between Greece and Turkey.
22. Knight-Jadczyk (2012).
23. Alvarex (1980), 'Extraterrestrial Cause for the Cretaceous-Tertiary Extinction: Experiment and Theory'.
24. Raup & Sepkoski (1984), 'Periodicity of extinctions in the geologic past'.

it is very, very rare – like millions of years rare! But that's not what the myths and stories claim.

The two big problems were evidence and causation for the more frequent and less world-destroying events. Was there evidence and if there was, what was the true cycle? And if one had some idea of the true cycle of catastrophes, could this be related in any way to a regular cause, something that occurs in our solar system like clockwork?

After reading many, many books about what are called OOPARTS[25] I finally decided that there did, indeed, seem to be evidence of numerous such catastrophic events, though getting any kind of real dating so as to be able to deduce a cycle was problematical. So I weaseled on the issue of the actual cycle and tried to look for a cause to see if it would give me a hint as to the cycle. Given that the Sun is the central element of our solar system, it seemed to me that it probably played a central role in any cyclical cataclysmic events involving the planets of our solar system. I read a lot about the Sun and its cycles of activity and theorized that maybe it had mega and mega-mega cycles.

Velikovsky had written about Venus being a giant comet that came careening into the solar system, but that seemed a bit too iffy to me to fit in with the idea of cycles, so I discarded the 'Venus as giant comet' idea and instead speculated that, perhaps, at long cycles, the Sun sends out so much electricity into the Solar System that planets which are normally not endowed with magnetic fields acquire them, while the ones that have magnetic fields become highly charged, and they all begin to move around in erratic ways, such as changing their orbits, rather like electrons jumping from one energy level to another. These motions resulted in exchanges of energy between planets, and possibly exchanges of matter. I even allowed for the possibility that this super-charging of the bodies of the solar system could attract comets from the Oort cloud into our inner solar system.[26]

The final ideas I came to in writing *The Noah Syndrome* were that indeed, as Velikovsky had written, the Solar System is rather like a giant atom and the key to the great dyings was *macrocosmic quantum jumps resulting in metamorphosis.*

> When physicists came upon the idea that the atom is built like a solar system, the atoms of various chemical elements differing in the mass of their suns (nuclei) and the number of the planets (electrons) the notion was looked

---

25. Out Of Place Artifacts
26. Spherical cloud of comets, asteroids and dust surrounding the Solar System.

upon with much favor. But it was stressed that an atom differs from the solar system by the fact that it is not gravitation that makes the electrons go around the nucleus, but electricity.

Besides this, another difference was found: an electron in an atom on absorbing the energy of a photon (light), jumps to another orbit, and again to another when it emits light and releases the energy of a photon. Because of this phenomenon, comparison with the solar system no longer seemed valid. 'We do not read in the morning newspapers that Mars leaped to the orbit of Saturn, or Saturn to the orbit of Mars,' wrote one critic. True, we do not read it in the morning papers; but in ancient records we have found similar events described in detail, and we have tried to reconstruct the facts by comparing many ancient records. The solar system is actually built like an atom; only, in keeping with the smallness of the atom, the jumping of electrons from one orbit to another, when hit by the energy of a photon, takes place many times a second, whereas in accord with the vastness of the solar system, a similar phenomenon occurs there once in hundreds or thousands of years.

If the activity in an atom constitutes a rule for the macrocosm, then the events described... were not merely accidents of celestial traffic, but normal phenomena like birth and death. The discharges between the planets, or the great photons emitted in these contacts caused metamorphoses in inorganic and organic nature.[27]

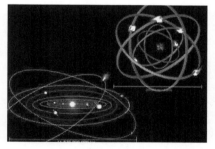

Solar system / atom analogy.

And just as quantum phenomena on the small scale were only statistically probable, so it was with the so-called 'End of the World'. As you notice from my remarks above, I also developed a rather primitive idea of an electric Sun and Solar System years before I was aware of plasma cosmology. I also came to think that psychic/paranormal phenomena had certain electrical and quantum probabilistic features which indicated their nature as a sort of bridge between the information/quantum and classical worlds (we'll come to that in the next volume). In short, the 'Second Coming of Jesus', the so-called 'End of the World', was really going to be just a cyclical planet-to-planet or comet-to-planet interaction, and the image of Jesus coming in the heavens on clouds of glory was a description of macrocosmic quantum phenomena.

---

27. Velikovsky (1950), *Worlds In Collision*.

So, I wrote all this down and was pretty pleased with myself; glad to have that settled! There was no longer any necessity for obsessing over either Noah or Moses; I had a hypothesis that pretty much included all the data points. All I had to do was keep my eyes open for more data and evidence, and just plug it into the correct categories when I found it because, of course, the actual cycle was not yet determined and a probabilistic 'when' became the important question. Also, realizing that I was dealing with a macrocosmic phenomenon suggested that the 'signs' might be a bit difficult to put together because some of them would manifest over much longer periods of time than most peoples' lives. I pictured the process as something similar to a phase transition. You can expose water to gradually decreasing temperatures over an indefinite period of time, but when you reach 32°F (or 0°C), the water suddenly begins to freeze – a phase transition. It may take a little time for all of it to turn to ice, depending on the volume, but as soon as every molecule is at that temperature, all of that water will stop being liquid and will become solid. To my mind, a macrocosmic quantum transition might begin to manifest years in advance, an accumulation of things that would amount to something like collecting energy, cooling, or heating, preparatory to a then fairly sudden transition that would fall like dominoes. So, trying to figure out what the signs might be became important. Indeed, the signs were listed in Matthew 24:

> And as he sat upon the mount of Olives, the disciples came unto him privately, saying, Tell us, when shall these things be? And what shall be the sign of thy coming, and of the end of the world?...
>
> [Jesus answered] ye shall hear of wars and rumours of wars... For nation shall rise against nation, and kingdom against kingdom: and there shall be famines, and pestilences, and earthquakes, in divers places. ... then shall many be offended, and shall betray one another, and shall hate one another. And many false prophets shall rise, and shall deceive many. And because iniquity shall abound, the love of many shall wax cold... For then shall be great tribulation, such as was not since the beginning of the world to this time, no, nor ever shall be ... For as the lightning cometh out of the east, and shineth even unto the west; so shall also the coming of the Son of man be ... Immediately after the tribulation of those days shall the sun be darkened, and the moon shall not give her light, and the stars shall fall from heaven, and the powers of the heavens shall be shaken: And then shall appear the sign of the Son of man in heaven: and then shall all the tribes of the earth mourn, and they shall see the Son of man coming in the clouds of heaven with power and great glory. And he shall send his angels with a great sound of a trumpet, and they shall gather

together his elect from the four winds, from one end of heaven to the other. Now learn a parable of the fig tree; When his branch is yet tender, and putteth forth leaves, ye know that summer is nigh: So likewise ye, when ye shall see all these things, know that it is near, even at the doors.[28]

Mythology and the History of Religion

Regarding my perception of the Bible as a historical document: how could I not think so, having been raised on the idea that it was not just true history, but was the word of God about history and humanity itself?! After Velikovsky, I gave up the 'word of God' bit, but I remained open to the idea that the authors were inspired by distorted understandings of amazing events in their world which might help us understand our own reality and future. I was convinced that if we could know the truth about our past, we would have some idea of our future. Thus, I spent a lot of time reading the Bible itself and books about the Bible. It seemed to me that using analyses such as Velikovsky's would go a long way toward helping modern scholars to better interpret the text. I later learned that astronomer Fred Hoyle and others had much the same idea.[29]

I combed through the material with great care, looking for evidence that the history the Bible recounted was reliable. I was engaged in this for over 15 years before I wrote *Secret History*, where I cover this topic at length in a section entitled 'Who Wrote The Bible'. There my focus was the 'Documentary Hypothesis', which proposes that several widely divergent sources (J = Yahweh), E (lohim), D(euteronomy) and P(riestly) were combined into one by a final editor who added his own touches, and that even this was done at different times and in different ways. Each of the sources is said to be clearly identifiable by characteristics of language and content. To some extent, I have revised my view of the documentary hypothesis which the reader will discover as we go along.

There were parallel lines of research that could more or less be described as Anthropology of Religion and History of Religion which, naturally, included mythology. In my pursuit, I encountered the works of Mircea Eliade and the books that stand out for me are: *Shamanism: Archaic Techniques of Ecstasy* and *The Myth of the Eternal Return*. There were two critical concepts here: cyclical time and the mythicization of historical events and persons; these topics are discussed at length, in the first volume of my *Secret History*.

28. Matthew 3-33, excerpts.
29. Hoyle (1993), *The Origin of the Universe and the Origin of Religion*.

The examples that Eliade gave of almost real-time mythicization proc-esses[30] were quite interesting to me because I had actually observed simi-lar, smaller-scale processes among my own acquaintances and family (urban myths are a good example). Since that time, I have spent years researching cognitive science and the processes involved seem to be almost universal in human beings.[31] There is really nothing mystical about it, it's just the brain-as-a-pattern-seeking device doing its ordinary job 'explaining the order of the universe' in ways that allow the individual to relieve stress and conserve energy. The brain doesn't like stress and it tends to be lazy and the same is true for the brains of scientists unless great care is taken to calibrate for bi-ases which scientists often refer to as a heuristic approach to solving a problem.[32] Indeed, heuristics are es-sential, but one has to understand that so-called 'common sense' and 'rules of thumb' can be powerfully in-fluenced by early conditioning via the family and/or culture. A fish born and raised in dirty water doesn't even imagine that clean water exists.

Moses found. Oil on canvas by Rembrandt (1635).

Another book that came along in that period was Georgia Sallaska's *Three Ships and Three Kings*. Though fiction, this entertaining book expanded on the idea that a single historical person could appear in many guises under different names, each important act or change of status in their lives being depicted as a singular, mythic event with the name changing according to various mythic norms as described

---

30. In one striking example, Eliade describes how a Romanian folklorist recorded a ballad describing the death of a young man bewitched by a jealous mountain fairy on the eve of his marriage. The young man, under the influence of the fairy was driven off a cliff. The ballad was filled with "mythological allusions, a liturgical test of rustic beauty." The folklorist, having been told that the song concerned a tragedy of "long ago," discovered that the fiancée was still alive and went to interview her. To his surprise, he learned that the young man's death had occurred less than 40 years before. He had slipped and fallen off a cliff; in reality, there was no mountain fairy involved.
    Eliade notes that "despite the presence of the principal witness, a few years had sufficed to strip the event of all historical authenticity, to transform it into a legendary tale."
31. See *Strangers to Ourselves* (Wilson, 2004) and *Thinking, Fast and Slow* (Kahneman, 2011) for one side of this question: how the brain is actually wired to work.
32. Where an exhaustive search is impractical, heuristic methods are used to speed up the process of finding a satisfactory solution. Examples of this method include using a rule of thumb, an educated guess, an intuitive judgment, or common sense.

by Eliade. One example is the change of the names of Abram and Sarai to Abraham and Sarah, or the 'Moses in a basket' story which was told about Sargon of Akkad[33] long before the Bible was ever imagined. Alternatively, the main character in a re-told story might be given the name of a revered ancestor of a particular group or tribe, thus assimilating deeds done by someone else's ancestor to their history. The actions of local heroes could be added to the list of deeds done by a mythic hero, or vice versa. In these ways, the life story of a single heroic – or at least interesting or scandalous – person could be divided up into separate events, each assigned to a mythical exemplar or tribal an-

David with the head of Goliath. Oil by Caravaggio (1610).

cestor. Conversely, the deeds of many different heroic individuals could be gathered together and told as the single story of a single hero, mythical or real. There were endless permutations of how the brain in its function as a pattern-recognition 'machine', could arrange things observed or experienced; and all in the effort to relieve stress on the 'machine' or save energy. It truly is a fascinating study. By now you can probably understand why this book will be informed by the study of psychology, including psychopathology.

After reading *Three Ships and Three Kings*, what struck me was the similarity of the story of David and Goliath to the story of Perseus and the Gorgon. Just as Perseus slew the Gorgon and cut off her head, David slew the giant, Goliath. They both had 'wallets'[34], and 'stones' were important elements of both stories. David was 'adopted' into the royal court because he was a famous harpist and singer in the manner of Orpheus. Like Hercules and other Greek heroes, David was a rebel and freebooter, and like Paris stole Helen, he stole another man's wife, Bathsheba. He also conquered the great citadel of Jerusalem and a vast empire beyond. In the 5th century BCE, the Greek poet, Pindar, assigned Perseus's encounter with Medusa to Hyperborea – assumed to be ancient Britain – where Stonehenge was known as the 'Giant's dance'. Stones, pouches, cutting off heads, giants... I wondered if a Greek myth had been 'historicized' with the fantastic elements removed to make it seem as though it really happened; or if the Bible recorded an orig-

---

33. Akkadian emperor who conquered the Sumerian city-states in the 23rd and 22nd centuries BCE.
34. Reference to the magic bag in which Perseus put Medusa's head and of course to the bag where David kept the stones for his slingshot: "David put his hand in his bag, and took thence a stone, and slang it" (1 Samuel 17:49).

inal event that was later mythicized into the Perseus story? Or, was there an original exemplar from which both sources drew? Another thing I noted was that the story of David and Goliath was very similar to the story of Nestor fighting the giant Ereuthalion [35] in the *Iliad*. Was this the exemplar from which these stories were drawn, I wondered? Which came first: Greek myths or the Jewish tales? It seemed important to me to figure out this point, to find some evidence. If it was the former, that would mean that the authors of the Jewish stories had taken Greek myths and 'historicized' them and for a couple of millennia, Western man had been basing his history on second-hand, displaced myths that were stolen from the Greeks by the Hebrews, making figuring out what really happened all the more difficult. [36] I should note here that this is the approach taken by a number of 'alternative history writers' who are conditioned to assume that the Bible is the oldest history in the world. But they should know better. That assumption only exists thanks to the

Perseus with the head of Medusa. Bronze statue by Cellini.

claims of the authors themselves, supported later by the Christian historian, Eusebius. In short, even that assumption must be subjected to study!

The similarity of the story of David to Greek myths piqued my curiosity to no end and I wanted to know every detail about the life of David just to check for any other correspondences. As it happened, I had several versions of the Bible in a searchable program on my computer, so I decided to use it. I guess it would have been alright if I had just searched for the name 'David' but I was being thorough and also searched using 'giant(s)' and 'Goliath'. There I learned something very interesting. It seems that the Bible text is a little confused about who actually killed Goliath: David, or some guy named Elhanan (Eleanan in the Septuagint [37]), a name that is strangely similar to

---

35. Each giant has a distinctive weapon (bronze spear for Goliath, iron club for Ereuthalion), each giant wears an armor and defies the whole army and each hero is told that he's too inexperienced by an elder (David's patron, Nestor's father).

36. The problem was actually deeper and wider than this, as I eventually discovered in the works of Hoyle, Baillie, Clube, Napier & Bailey and more. But we will come to that.

37. Translation of the Hebrew Bible and some related texts into Greek; we will discuss this further on.

Ereuthalion (the giant killed by Nestor). This hinted at a multiplicity of versions, even among the early Hebrews, and that led to the idea that the global repetition of these stories in the Middle East were based on an historical exemplar: some place, at some time, a green young man went up against a big, powerful opponent, with primitive weapons, and defeated him; the young man may have become king, thereby. We will soon see that even this assumption of mine was wrong. The only good thing about following this process was that I was, bit by bit, divesting myself of illusions in respect of the Bible. Funnily enough, in retrospect, it was like Inanna descending to the Underworld and having to remove her clothing piece by piece, although in my case it was 'clothing of the mind'.

This comparison that I made at the time actually turned out to be somewhat predictive of what I was to learn later. The reason Inanna gives to the gatekeeper for visiting the underworld is that she wants to attend the funeral rites of Gugalanna, the first husband of the goddess of the underworld, Ereshkigal. Gugalanna was the *Bull of Heaven* in The Epic of Gilgamesh. Gugalanna was sent by the gods to take retribution upon Gilgamesh for rejecting the sexual advances of the goddess Inanna. Gugalanna, whose feet *made the earth shake*, was slain and dismembered by Gilgamesh and Enkidu. Inanna, from the heights of the city walls looked down, and Enkidu took the haunches of the bull shaking them at the goddess, threatening he would do the same to her if he could catch her! For this impiety, Enkidu later dies. To further add to the confusion, Ereshkigal's husband is typically the *plague god*, Nergal. All of these elements will shortly come into play in our discussion. I just find it fascinating that coming to an understanding of the topics of this book should have been related in my mind to the strip-tease of Inanna in the Underworld!

One very familiar character in the story of King David was Bathsheba, the wife David stole from one of his generals, Uriah the Hittite. David was on the roof of his palace and looking down, saw Bathsheba bathing and was smitten. He immediately sent her husband, Uriah, off to war so he would get killed. I started wondering about that situation in respect of Helen of Troy, stolen away by Paris from her husband, Menelaus, which got the whole Trojan War going. That, of course, took me in a quick circle back to the *Iliad*, the possible source of the 'David and Goliath' story. Then, of course, there is Solomon and the Queen of 'Sheba' to compare to 'Bath*SHEBA*' where 'bat' means 'daughter of' in Hebrew. Was there a little duplication of stories going on here?

Thinking of beautiful women who caused wars in relation to Hittites cued up Abraham. Abraham conducted negotiations with some Hittite residents of Palestine for a burial cave for his wife; the same wife that he asked to pretend she was his sister when they went to Egypt because she was so beautiful he was afraid that the Egyptians would kill him to take her which, of course, circled right back around to David who had done exactly that regarding Bathsheba: he had her husband set up to be killed so he could snag her. There was the 'beautiful woman in relationship to war' theme which reminded me of Abraham's reputation as a war-lord in relation to the detail of the Abram/Sarai-in-Egypt story: the plagues that fell on the house of Pharaoh and caused him to tell Abram to take his wife and go away!

> Now there was a famine in the land, and Abram went down into Egypt to live temporarily, for the famine in the land was oppressive (intense and grievous). And when he was about to enter into Egypt, he said to Sarai his wife, "I know that you are beautiful to behold. So when the Egyptians see you, they will say, 'this is his wife'; and they will kill me, but they will let you live. Say, I beg of you, that you are my sister, so that it may go well with me for your sake and my life will be spared because of you."
>
> And when Abram came into Egypt, the Egyptians saw that the woman was very beautiful. The princes of Pharaoh also saw her and commended her to Pharaoh, and she was taken into Pharaoh's house. And he treated Abram well for her sake; he acquired sheep, oxen, he-donkeys, menservants, maidservants, she-donkeys, and camels.
>
> But the Lord scourged Pharaoh and his household with serious plagues because of Sarai, Abram's wife. And Pharaoh called Abram and said, "What is this that you have done to me? Why did you not tell me that she was your wife? Why did you say, 'She is my sister', so that I took her to be my wife? Now then, here is your wife; take her and get away [from here]!" And Pharaoh commanded his men concerning him, and they brought him on his way with his wife and all that he had.[38]

The 'she's my sister' gambit actually played out more than once in the Bible: it's one of the problematical doublets (and triplets). Doublets are duplicate narratives of the same story which scholars think can be explained by the idea that the story was re-told by different authors living in different periods, which were then all patched in together by a later editor (the documentary hypothesis). So much for the absolutely true 'word of God'!

The story of Abraham's 'half-truth' (Sarah was his half-sister, allegedly), occurs twice in Genesis (12:10-20 and 20:1-18), and then, amazingly, the same thing happens to his son, Isaac in respect of his wife, Rebekah![39] Are

---

38. Genesis 12:10-20.
39. Genesis 26:6-11.

we seeing shades of father David and Bathsheba and son Solomon and the Queen of Sheba here?

Since it is fun, let's stop here and take a look at some comparisons of the stories arranged in a table with the Abraham stories first:

GENESIS 12:10-20 ABRAM (ABRAHAM)	GENESIS 20:1-18 ABRAHAM
Abram goes to Egypt because of a famine (v. 10)	There is no reason given for Abraham's journey to Gerar
Egypt and Pharaoh	Gerar and Abimelech [40]
Pharaoh was told of the beauty of Sarah (v. 14-15).	Abimelech was not told of the beauty of Sarah (v. 2)
Pharaoh gave Abram gifts before discovering that Sarah was his wife (v. 16)	Abimelech gave Abraham gifts after discovering that Sarah was his wife (v. 14-16)
Pharaoh determines the truth when investigating the cause of the plagues (v. 18)	God reveals the truth to Abimelech in a dream (v. 3)
The plagues are unspecified (v. 17)	God closes the wombs of the household of Abimelech (v. 18)
Pharaoh does not call a meeting with his servants	After awaking from his sleep, Abimelech, calls a meeting with all the servants of his household (v. 8)
Pharaoh confronts Abram but his reasons are not recorded	Abimelech confronts Abraham who explains his reasons (v. 11-13)
No mention of Abram interceding for Egypt	Abraham's prayer is instrumental in lifting the curse (v. 17)
Pharaoh expels Abram from Egypt (v. 20)	Abimelech allows him to remain and offers him to settle wherever he wishes (v. 15)

Now, let's look at Abraham's event compared to Isaac's:

GENESIS 20:1-18 – ABRAHAM	GENESIS 26:1-11 – ISAAC
Abraham journeys to Gerar (v. 1)	Isaac lives in Gerar (v. 6)
Gerar and Abimelech	Gerar and Abimelech
Abimelech was not told of the beauty of Sarah (v. 2) →	Rebekah is known for her beauty (v. 7) →

---

40. Abimelech was the king of Gerar, a philistine town in Palestine.

GENESIS 20:1-18 – ABRAHAM	GENESIS 26:1-11 – ISAAC
→ Abraham claims Sarah as his sister out of fear for his personal safety (v. 2)	→ Isaac claims Rebekah as his sister out of his fear of personal safety (v. 7)
Abimelech gave Abraham gifts after discovering that Sarah was his wife (v. 14-16)	There was no record of gifts given to Isaac
God reveals the truth to Abimelech in a dream (v. 3)	Abimelech discovers the truth by observing Isaac (v. 8)
God closes the wombs of the household of Abimelech (v. 18)	There is no record of a curse on Abimelech's household.
After awaking from his sleep, Abimelech, calls a meeting with all the servants of his household (v. 8)	Dream not involved in this version.
Abimelech confronts Abraham who explains his reasons (v. 11-13)	Abimelech confronts Isaac who explains his reasons (v. 9)
Abraham's prayer is instrumental in lifting the curse (v. 17)	No curse needed to be lifted.
Abimelech allows him to remain and offers him to settle wherever he wishes (v. 15)	Abimelech sends Isaac away from his people as Abram had been sent away from Egypt. (Gen 26:27)

Those who wish to believe that the Bible is the word of God and that every word is true; try to argue that these differences indicate three actual separate events. So, unlikely as it is for two nearly identical episodes to happen in the life of one man, and another almost identical episode to happen in the life of his son, even including many of the same individuals, this is their story and they stick to it! More intellectually mature (or sane) scholars argue that this is just evidence for the documentary hypothesis. I, of course, wonder about the core of the story here: a beautiful woman and a cuckolded husband.[41]

---

41. The term derives from an old French word for a cuckoo ('coucou'). The females of some species of cuckoo lay their eggs in other birds' nests and leave them to bring up the offspring. A cuckolded man might raise a child that is not his. That's the simple explanation. But what about the horns representing a cuckolded husband? One of the earliest explanations comes from the old Roman Empire. Back then, returning soldiers were given horns, symbolising success on the battlefield. But the horns also represented the fact that the soldier had been absent and could he be sure that his wife had been faithful? Another theory is the 'capon' explanation. Apparently, in old France, there was a

A Beautiful Woman

It was about this time that I was reading Geoffrey Ashe's *The Book of Prophecy*, specifically the chapter entitled 'Prophetic Israel':

> The theme [of the Old Testament] is the relationship between the God of Israel – Yahweh, the Eternal, the Lord – and the world and its people, especially his Chosen People, the ancient Israelites and their Jewish descendants. Why Chosen? Not because of their numbers, importance or cultural distinction, and certainly not because of a supposed racial superiority. ...
>
> Genesis, the first of these books, gives the account of the tribes' origin that was developed by their leaders. They had a common ancestor, **Abraham**, who lived in the Mesopotamian city of Ur, a real and important place, about a thousand years previously. ... God summoned him to leave Ur with his family and household... "Israel" was a name divinely bestowed on his grandson **Jacob**.
>
> In a crucial passage (13:14-17) God promises to give Canaan to Abraham's descendants. [...] This is the Lord's ... covenant.[42]

Next came Moses and his special relationship with God where he went up onto a mountain and allegedly talked with God face to face and God gave him the Law and sent him on the road to the Promised Land – the final fulfillment of the covenant with Abraham which was later reaffirmed to Jacob, Abraham's grandson, through his 'miracle baby', Isaac (who also had a dream-visit from God).[43] Ashe points out about the covenant:

> Two points are vital and remain so. One is the *territorial claim*. The Promised Land is central to Israelite religion and to the Judaism that later evolved from it. The other point is the nature of the God who has made the gift. The first chapter of Genesis presents him as the creator of the world. ... He never figures in the Bible as a mere tribal deity among other tribal deities. In the eyes of its authors, he is always the only Higher Power to matter. Other gods have a sort of reality but an infinitely inferior reality; they are hardly more than idols, and they dwindle as

---

custom of cutting the spurs from cockerels when they were castrated and implanting them in the comb where they would grow into hornlike protrusions making it easy to pick out the capons in the flock. Thus, the mark of the capon's castration was taken to represent the symbolic castration of the cuckolded man. Obviously, the question remains: would spurs cut from the legs of a cock grow on the root of an excised crown and were people of that time capable of performing such an operation so easily?

42. Ashe (1999).
43. Genesis 26: 3-5 and 24.

Israelite ideas mature. God's decisions are, therefore, absolute and unchallenge-able, and they include the granting of the Promised Land to his Chosen People.[44]

THE PROMISED LAND BY THE EXCLUSIVE GOD

ABRAHAM	ISAAC	JACOB	MOSES
Now the LORD had said to Abram, Depart from your country, and from your kindred, and from your father's house, to a land that I will show you: And I will make of you a great nation, and I will bless you, and make your name great; and you shall be a blessing: And I will bless them that bless you, and curse him that curses you: and in you shall all families of the earth be blessed. (Gen. 12: 1-3)	Sojourn in this land, and I will be with you, and will bless you; for unto you, and unto you seed, I will give all these countries, and I will perform the oath which I swear unto Abraham your father; And I will make your seed to multiply as the stars of heaven, and will give unto your seed all these countries; and in your seed shall all the nations of the earth be blessed; Because that Abraham obeyed my voice, and kept my charge, my commandments, my statutes, and my laws. (Gen. 26:3-5) And the LORD appeared to him the same night, and said, I am the God of Abraham your father: fear not, for I am with you, →	Therefore God give you of the dew of heaven, and the fatness of the earth, and plenty of corn and wine: Let people serve you, and nations bow down to you: be lord over your brethren, and let your mother's sons bow down to you: cursed be every one that curses you, and blessed be he that blesses you. (Gen. 27:28-29) And your seed shall be as the dust of the earth, and you shall spread abroad to the west, and to the east, and to the north, and to the south: and in you and in your seed shall all the families of the earth be blessed. And, behold, I am with you, and will keep you in all places where ever you go, and will bring you again →	So God heard their groaning, and God remembered His covenant with Abraham, with Isaac, and with Jacob. (Ex. 2:24) Now Moses was tending the flock of Jethro his father-in-law, the priest of Midian. And he led the flock to the back of the desert, and came to Horeb, the mountain of God. And the Angel of the Lord appeared to him in a flame of fire from the midst of a bush. So he looked, and behold, the bush was burning with fire, but the bush was not consumed. Then Moses said, "I will now turn aside and see this great sight, why the bush does not burn."... God called to him from the midst of the bush and said, "Moses, Moses!" And he said, →

---

44. Ashe (1999), pp. 25-26, excerpts.

ABRAHAM	ISAAC	JACOB	MOSES
	→ and will bless you, and multiply your seed for my servant Abraham's sake. (Gen. 26:24)	→ into this land; for I will not leave you, until I have done that which I have spoken to you of. (Gen. 28:14-15)	→ "Here I am." … He said, "I am the God of your father – the God of Abraham, the God of Isaac, and the God of Jacob." … Go and gather the elders of Israel together, and say to them, 'The Lord God of your fathers, the God of Abraham, of Isaac, and of Jacob, appeared to me, saying, …I will bring you up out of the affliction of Egypt to the land of the Canaanites and the Hittites and the Amorites and the Perizzites and the Hivites and the Jebusites, to a land flowing with milk and honey." (Ex. 3, excerpts.)

THE COVENANT

ABRAHAM	ISAAC	JACOB	MOSES
This is my covenant, which you shall keep, between me and you and thy seed after you; Every man child among you shall be circumcised. And you shall circumcise the flesh of your foreskin; →			And Moses took his wife and his sons, and set them upon an ass, and he returned to the land of Egypt… And it came to pass by the way in the inn, that the LORD met him, and sought →

ABRAHAM	ISAAC	JACOB	MOSES
→ and it shall be a token of the covenant between me and you. … and my covenant shall be in your flesh for an everlasting covenant. And the uncircumcised man child whose flesh of his foreskin is not circumcised, that soul shall be cut off from his people; he has broken my covenant. (Gen. 17:10-15)			→ to kill him. Then Zipporah took a sharp stone, and cut off the foreskin of her son, and cast it at his feet, and said, Surely a bloody husband art thou to me. So he let him go: then she said, A bloody husband thou art, because of the circumcision. (Ex. 4:29-31)

Notice the oddness of the story about Moses passing by Mt. Horeb where there was a burning bush in comparison to Moses and Mt. Sinai where there was a 'pillar of fire'. In both instances, God talks to Moses out of the fire and smoke associated with a mountain. Also, notice the oddness of the story of Zipporah circumcising the son of Moses. They are traveling toward Egypt to announce the coming plagues to the pharaoh. The standard explanation for this bizarre episode is that God wanted to kill Moses because he had failed to circumcise his son. However, I would like to point out the similarity to the story of Jacob wrestling with the angel.[45] Note also that, in the story of the burning bush, there is an angel at first, and then God speaks. Abraham, too, is visited by three 'angels' and then, as soon as they travel on to destroy Sodom and Gomorrah, Abraham has a casual conversation with God himself, arguing about whether or not total destruction is really advisable. Moses being associated with a burning bush, then the circumcision of Moses' son to save Moses' life, reminds one of the almost sacrifice of Abraham's son. He was or-

---

45. "Your name will no longer be Jacob, but Israel, because you have struggled with God and with men and have overcome." Jacob said, "Please tell me your name." But he replied, "Why do you ask my name?" Then he blessed him there. So Jacob called the place Peniel, saying, "It is because I saw God face to face, and yet my life was spared." Genesis 32:28-30.

dered to go to a *mountain* where he had gotten everything ready and was about to do the deed when the angel stopped him saying:

> ...now I know that thou fearest God, seeing thou hast not withheld thy son, thine only son from me...[46]

The angel is obviously having a bit of an identity crisis. Anyway, following this incident, the terms of the covenant are repeated yet again, announced by another angel who somehow turns into God almighty in mid-sentence:

> ...I will bless thee, and in multiplying I will multiply thy seed...[47]

Oddly enough, in one of the covenant-with-Abraham repetitions, a curious incident takes place:

> And he said unto him, I am the LORD that brought thee out of Ur of the Chaldees, to give thee this land to inherit it. And he said, LORD God, whereby shall I know that I shall inherit it? And he said unto him, Take me an heifer of three years old, and a she goat of three years old, and a ram of three years old, and a turtledove, and a young pigeon. And he took unto him all these, and divided them in the midst, and laid each piece one against another: but the birds divided he not. And when the

Destruction of Gomorrah.
Van Leyden (1520).

fowls came down upon the carcasses, Abram drove them away. And when the sun was going down, a deep sleep fell upon Abram; and, lo, an horror of great darkness fell upon him.

... And it came to pass, that, when the sun went down, and it was dark, behold a smoking furnace, and a burning lamp that passed between those pieces.[48]

---

46. Genesis 22:12, excerpts.
47. Genesis 22:17, excerpts.
48. Genesis 15:7-15, excerpts.

So we have burning bushes on fire and bushes with rams caught in them, pillars of fire, smoking furnace and burning lamps, torches, sacrifices, sons, altars on mountains ... are we getting a hint of a theme here?

Having the three (actually four, including Isaac) main characters of the Old Testament, Abraham, Jacob and Moses, connected with this issue – the covenant promising a specific land to a people with repeating similar elements – made me stop and think: just how many people actually were parties to having face-to-face chats with a somewhat hostile God? Obviously Abraham did when he argued with God about Sodom and Gomorrah. Jacob, after wrestling with an 'angel', called the place Peniel, saying, "it is because I saw God face to face, and yet my life was spared." [49] Obviously, Moses could have said the same thing when his wife saved him by the pseudo-sacrifice of his son's foreskin. Later, of course, God tells Moses "You cannot see my face, for no one may see me and live." [50] Jacob obviously did live after the experience, though he was said to have been crippled by it. But then, there is the story of the 'Horns of Moses' which I wrote about in the first volume of *Secret History* as follows, and where I reference the Priestly text [51] of the documentary hypothesis:

> The author of P also tells his own version of the revelation at Mount Sinai. P adds a detail at the end of the story that is, up to that point, very similar to the original. This detail is that there was something very unusual about Moses' face when he came down from the mountain. When people looked at him, they were afraid to come near him, and he was forced to wear a veil. According to P, whenever we think of Moses for the last 40 years of his life, we are supposed to think of him wearing a veil.
>
> What is it about Moses' face? The meaning of the Hebrew term is uncertain, and for a long time, people thought that it meant that Moses had **acquired horns**. This resulted in many depictions of Moses with horns in Medieval art. Another interpretation was that something was wrong with Moses' skin – that light beamed out from his skin. So many translations and interpretations go along with this idea and teach that there was "glory" shining from Moses' face that hurt the eyes of the beholders. I was taught this version myself.
>
> In more recent times, biblical scholar, William Popp, has assembled an array of evidence that suggests that the writer of P was telling his audience

---

49. Genesis 32:30.
50. Exodus 33:18-20.
51. Refers to material that priests allegedly incorporated in the Hebrew Bible during or soon after the Babylonian exile (c. 600-400 BCE).

that Moses was disfigured in the sense that he is so horrible to look upon that the people cannot bear to see him. The text does tell us that the "glory of Yahweh" is like a "consuming fire" and this suggests that the flesh of Moses' face has been eaten away making him a specter out of your worst nightmare. If this was an understood colloquialism of the time, then it is a masterly touch of manipulation by the author of P. He hasn't denigrated Moses, but he has created an image of horror that no one will want to contemplate!

However, I believe that there is a different reason for this allusion. ... the symbolism of the Old Babylonian god Huwawa (Humbaba). Huwawa appears in the Gilgamesh stories as Enlil's guardian of the Cedar Forest, and we have some idea that cedar wood was very important to the god of Moses as presented in the P text. ...

Was the relationship of the terrible face of Moses, in comparison to the terrible visage of Huwawa, the guardian of the cedar forest, understood by the people? Huwawa was described as a giant protected by seven layers of terrifying radiance. He was killed by Gilgamesh and Enkidu in a story that is quite similar to the slaying of Goliath by David and Medusa by Perseus. ...

Melam and *ni* are two Sumerian words which are often linked. Strictly speaking, *ni* seems to denote the effect on human beings of the divine power melam. The Babylonians used various words to capture the idea of *ni*, including *puluhtu*, "fear." The exact connotation of *melam* is difficult to grasp. It is a brilliant, visible glamour which is exuded by gods, heroes, sometimes by kings, and also by temples of great holiness. While it is in some ways a phenomenon of light, *melam* is at the same time terrifying, awe-inspiring. *Ni* can be experienced as a physical creeping of the flesh. Gods are sometimes said to "wear" their *melam* like a garment or a crown, and like a garment or a crown, *melam* can be "taken off." While it is always a mark of the supernatural, *melam* carries no connotation of moral value since demons and terrifying giants can "wear" it too.

So, it seems that this is very likely the point that the writer of P was trying to make about Moses. Moses was being compared to Huwawa/Humbaba, the horrible guardian of the cedar forest, a variation on the sun-god whose face is so brilliant that it must be "veiled"; following which Huwawa/Yahweh demanded that his sacrifices contain cedar, and his house be built of cedar! ...

In all of P there are only three stories of any length that are similar to JE: the creation, the flood and the covenant with Noah (excluding the sacrifice after the flood), [and] the covenant with Abraham, (excluding his almost sacrifice of Isaac). He also added a story that is *not* present in the older documents: the story of the death of Aaron's sons Nadab and Abihu which is presented to instruct the people that the sacrifice must only be performed as commanded by god, even if it is performed by bloodline Levites! ... The P writer seems overwhelmingly concerned with Sinai and the giving of the law, since half of Exodus, half of Numbers, nearly all of Leviticus, are concerned with the Levite law.

There is another story that P presents that has no parallel in the older accounts, so is thought to be entirely made up: the story of the cave of Machpelah. This story gives a lengthy description of the negotiations between Abraham and a Hittite over a piece of land with a cave on it which Abraham buys as a burial place for his family. Why does the P source, which leaves out so many fun facts and stories, divert to mention this mundane piece of business? Friedman believes that it is to establish a legal claim to Hebron, an Aaronid priestly city. But if that were the case, it could have been done any number of other ways. My thought is that maybe the story is not made up. ... maybe this tradition of Abraham being a "Great Prince" of the Hittites wasn't just blowing smoke because it does, indeed, indirectly point us in the direction of Huwawa! [52]

So, according to this idea, Moses had a terrible visage after his encounter with God. That relates him to Humbaba and, I eventually learned, to some other great characters of mythology in a very particular context. But, I hadn't gotten there yet. I was still working my way through what was available at that time. When I connected Abraham and Moses in the same thought, a whole lot of other connections between the two of them started falling into slots like the tumblers in a combination lock when the dial is turned correctly. What is more, at that moment I realized that, while Moses was supposedly born in Egypt, set adrift in a basket on the river exactly like Sargon the Great of Mesopotamia, and Abraham arrived on his anachronistic camels,[53] *both Moses and Abraham left Egypt under very similar circumstances: plagues fell on the land of Egypt and pharaohs told each of them "take your people/wife and GO!"*

MOSES LEAVES EGYPT	ABRAHAM AND SARAH LEAVE EGYPT
And I will give this people favour in the sight of the Egyptians: and it shall come to pass, that, when ye go, ye shall not go empty: But every woman shall borrow of her neighbour, and of her that sojourneth in her house, jewels of silver, and jewels of gold, and raiment: and ye shall put them upon your sons, and →	[And pharaoh] treated Abram well for her [Sarai's] sake: and he had sheep, and oxen, and he asses, and menservants, and maidservants, and she asses, and camels. And the Lord plagued Pharaoh and his house with great plagues because of Sarai Abram's wife. And Pharaoh called Abram and said, What is this that thou hast done unto →

---

52. Knight-Jadczyk (2004), pp. 581-582, excerpts.
53. Camels were domesticated around the 11th century BCE while Abraham is estimated to have lived many centuries earlier.

MOSES LEAVES EGYPT	ABRAHAM AND SARAH LEAVE EGYPT
→ upon your daughters; and ye shall spoil the Egyptians. (Ex. 3:21-22) And the Egyptians were urgent upon the people, that they might send them out of the land in haste; for they said, We be all dead men. …And the children of Israel did according to the word of Moses; and they borrowed of the Egyptians jewels of silver, and jewels of gold, and raiment. And the LORD gave the people favour in the sight of the Egyptians, so that they lent unto them such things as they required. And they spoiled the Egyptians. (Ex. 12: 33-36)	→ me? Why didst thou not tell me that she was thy wife? Why saidst thou, She is my sister? So I might have taken her to me to wife: now therefore behold thy wife, take her, and go thy way. And Pharaoh commanded his men concerning him: and they sent him away, and his wife, and all that he had. (Gen. 12:16-20) And Abram went up out of Egypt, he, and his wife and all that he had, and Lot with him, into the south. And Abram was very rich in cattle, in silver, and in gold. (Gen. 13:1-2)

Is it possible, I asked myself, that Abraham and Moses were one and the same person? And then the other clue fell into place, the name of Akhenaten's queen: Nefertiti: 'A Beautiful Woman Has Come' bears striking resemblance to Sarai's arrival, her extraordinary beauty, and the cuckolding of Abram. Was Abram really Moses and was it Moses who had been cuckolded? In many countries, 'horns' are a metaphor for suffering the infidelity of the partner. Was the reference in the Bible to the 'Horns of Moses' a hidden clue? As we will see, it's actually more interesting and complex than that, but it was one of the things that got me thinking out of the box.

What occurred to me, after thinking about it in terms of Eliade's mythicization of history principle was that the documentary hypothesis was probably somewhere close to the truth: the same story was retold by different groups or people with variations of characters and location which suggests strongly that there is a seed event. Whatever this event was, it was obviously a very popular story because there were several versions of it in the Bible alone!

And that is what really got me thinking. If this event (or the seed of it) was so well-known in the ancient Middle Eastern world, it must have been a serious scandal of the time. And that's when I started thinking about Nefertiti and Akhenaten from a different perspective and wondering if it was just possible that this odd little tale in the Bible that was repeated three times was actually a confabulated tale wrapped around the seed of the scandalous Amarna episode in Egypt. Was the story of Paris and Helen and the Trojan War somehow related? So many dangling threads and so little time in the life of one human being!

I knew already that Nefertiti's name meant 'a beautiful woman has come' or 'the radiant one has come , that her origins and fate are still a mystery (despite the many claims to having 'solved' the puzzle of her identity and parentage[54]) and that the Amarna period was so hated by the Egyptians (thus scandalous) that they tried to erase it from their history and memory completely. I knew that the evidence showed that something very bad must have happened to end Akhenaten's dream, that members of his family were dying: daughters, grandchildren, his mother, perhaps Nefertiti and Akhenaten himself; I knew that the Amarna letters[55] talked about a plague spreading throughout the Middle East at the time; I was familiar with the stories told by Manetho[56] about a plague being related to the origins of the Jews, a priest who led a group of diseased people out of Egypt. All of this coalesced in my mind with the question: is it possible that the Bible recorded a memory of the Amarna period in the stories of Abraham and Moses? And if so, did that mean they were one and the same person? And if that was the case, did the Biblical version include any data that was even remotely accurate about the Amarna events? Did Akhenaten take someone else's wife for a rather long period of time (in which case, she didn't object) like Paris and Helen, and then, when things went bad, did she escape with her original husband and did they run away to Palestine? Or, was the Bible story just completely made up of odd elements taken from various sources, with a dash of the Amarna scandal thrown in?

Obviously, this was a real can of worms.

Genealogical Placeholders?

Having become interested in genealogy some years before this, I had spent many hours working on my own family tree. I knew about 'place-holders' – someone you know nothing about, but you know he or she existed and that he or she is a bridge between generations, so you give them a name or other designation and put them in the tree without any real data. I began to wonder about the genealogies in the Bible that were placed between Abraham and Moses. Were they just 'placeholders between stories'? What about Isaac, the miraculous son of Abraham and Sarah who connects them via a bridge to the founders of the 12 tribes? What about Hagar, the *Egyptian* servant of

---

54. This will be examined in detail in the final volume of this topic.
55. Correspondence on clay tablets, mostly diplomatic, between the Egyptian administration and its representatives in Canaan and Amurru during the New Kingdom.
56. Egyptian historian and priest. His writings are used as evidence for the chronology of the pharaohs.

Jacob and Rachel at the well, by Giordano (1690).

Sarah who became the mother of Ishmael? Was she the same as Moses' Midianite wife?

Speaking of Isaac, we are reminded that he acquired his wife (via a servant who went to find one for him) in association with water as David had, though it was a well and not a bathing pool as in the case of Bathsheba. Rebekah brought her water jar to fill right after Abraham's servant had arrived. She gave the servant a drink and his camels also. It turned out that she was the granddaughter of Abraham's brother. How amazing! (This is going to be another repeating theme, so the *consanguinity* of the marriage partner appears to be significant, which reminds us of the practice of brother-sister marriages during Egypt's 18th Dynasty.[57])

Water and a well was central to Jacob's story too. He was *fleeing the murderous wrath of his brother*, who he had cheated (with the help of his beautiful mother, Rebekah). On his journey, he had a dream about the Stairway to Heaven[58] and God Almighty cheered him up with promises and rewards for

---

57. The 18th dynasty is the first dynasty of the New Kingdom. It includes some of the most famous pharaohs like Tutankhamun and, of course, Akhenaten.
58. While sleeping, Jacob dreamt of "a ladder…with its top reaching to heaven; and…the angels of God…ascending and descending on it" (Genesis 28:12).

Moses at the Well, by Botticelli (1481).

being a liar and a cheat. He continued on his approximately *400 mile journey*, arrived and stopped by a random well in a field, and Rachel came to water the sheep. Jacob played 'He-Man' by removing the stone covering from the well so she didn't have to wait, and shortly discovered that Rachel was the daughter of his mother's brother. Again, how amazing! (Not to mention consanguineous.)

Bizarrely (is anything about this still surprising?), a similar scenario had played out with Moses himself, who was *fleeing the pharaoh* because he had committed murder (shades of Jacob fleeing his brother). He sat down by a well, along came the lovely maidens to water the flocks; they are immediately subjected to harassment by some rough shepherds and Moses got to play the hero this time. Shortly, the father of the young ladies invited him for dinner; he stayed and married one of the girls, Zipporah.

Pulling on that thread brought me to the fact that, according to the Bible, Zipporah's father was a priest of Midian named Reuel who is also called 'Jethro' in several places; maybe that's because 'Reuel' may have been a son of Esau, Jacob's brother who may have figured in the original story (considering the amazing familial relationships of the brides of the other characters under consideration), but was changed to conceal Moses' true identity. Maybe the genealogies were real, they just weren't a long tree, vertical in time, but rather should be placed side by side, in a more shortened time frame? Of course, they could be entirely made up since, as Egyptologist Donald Redford[59] points out, very often *names in the genealogies are actually names of tribes or cities*.

The bottom line is that the story of Moses is centered around the fact that he was present in Egypt during a time when plagues were falling hard and fast as happened when Abram and Sarai were there. The extended Exodus story of planetary cataclysm as depicted in the *Ipuwer Papyrus* is woven in, and then Pharaoh (after being stubborn for a very long time) finally said 'get out from among my people... take your flocks and your herds and be-

---

59. Redford is a Canadian Egyptologist and archaeologist, whose extensive studies show that most of the toponymic features in Exodus reflect conditions *not older than* the 7th century BCE.

gone!' The Egyptians were so anxious to see the last of Moses and his crew that they gave them piles of loot. Then Moses escorted his people out of Egypt. Pharaoh chased after them and he and his army were drowned in the sea and so on. Likewise, Abraham and Sarah left with lots of goods that had been acquired by Pharaoh's favor during their sojourn. One is also reminded of Rachel's theft of her father's "household gods" when she and Jacob flee with Laban in hot pursuit. This was following many years of Jacob's servitude to his father-in-law to "earn" his wives. So, somehow, the theft of goods appears to be another sub-theme.

All of the above speculations raced through my mind in the course of about half an hour of thinking after reading that passage in Ashe's book about the Covenant of the Promised Land.[60]

The Murder of Moses

In addition to theft, the repeating references to a murder or murderous intent was floating around in the background of all these stories. I spent quite a bit of time reading some books that were about the problem of where the real Mount Sinai is. Obviously, this meant that I had to do word searches on the topic, examining every story about anybody going up on a 'mountain of God'. This got me to thinking about that Horns of Moses thing again: Moses coming down from the mountain with his face covered by a veil. Even though I thought I had sorted it, I decided to come at it again from a different angle: the Sherlock Holmes method. That detail was just so bizarre that it annoyed me. As it happens, Moses apparently went up the mountain to talk to God *a few times* and he even went up the mountain once with his brother Aaron who was apparently 'taken' (killed) by God on that trip and didn't come back down! The story includes the detail about Aaron being stripped of his garments which were then put on his son Eleazer (who also went up with them).

There were a lot of other mysterious details about the relations between Moses and Aaron and strange happenings around the whole relationship, not to mention so many other 'brotherly relationships' in the Bible, so I was thinking about that. I asked myself: if we strip away the miraculous details about Moses going up a mountain and talking to God – which obviously didn't happen – then why would he come down wearing a veil over his face? What about the other story of him going up the mountain with Aaron and Eleazer and only Moses (and Aaron's son) coming back down – because Aaron 'died there'. What do we have here? If Sherlock Holmes were think-

---

60. See subchapter: 'A Beautiful Woman'.

Moses wearing a veil. Stained glass window.

ing about this problem, what would he say? "When you have eliminated the impossible, whatever remains, however improbable, must be the truth."[61]

Well, I think we can eliminate the idea that God killed anybody. And whoever came back down wore a veil over his face for the rest of his life. If we eliminate that nonsense about his face glowing or looking like he'd been burned by radiation, the only reason I could see for somebody to cover their face for the rest of their life was to conceal identity; that is, it wasn't Moses who came down. Did Moses, Aaron and Eleazer go up that mountain and did Aaron and Eleazer murder Moses? Did Aaron then cover his face with a veil and pretend to be Moses for the rest of his life?

Well, of course, that's an interesting theory if one assumes that the stories are real – if garbled – history. But it stuck in my mind and I later learned that I wasn't the first person who had the idea that Moses had been murdered. Biblical scholar, Ernst Sellin, was certain that he had found traces of a tradition that *Moses met a violent end in a rebellion of his people.*[62] The true religion of Moses was then abandoned and replaced by an Aaronic/Levitical religion of rules and priests. According to Sellin, this tradition is not just evident in the book of Hosea[63]: it appears in the writings of most of the later Prophets. Sellin was convinced that the true Mosaic religion included the goddess Asheroth, or 'God's wife', and in fact, later archaeological finds support this view.

Supposedly, Freud picked up on the work of Sellin and went off on his own theory in *Moses and Monotheism*, that the deed was an example of oedipal violence and primal scene trauma then drawing an analogy between Israelite history and the typical course of an obsessive-compulsive neurosis.[64]

---

61. Doyle (1890), *The Sign of the Four*, chapter 6.
62. Hosea 9:7-13; 12:14-13:4; 5:2; 4:4-5; 11:3. Exodus 32:32 compared to Hosea 9:7; Numbers 11:12; 25:6 compared to 12:1; Deut. 34:1; II Kings 9:31; Amos 5:13; Deutero-Isaiah Ch. 53, the Suffering Servant chapter; Jeremiah 2:30; Deutero-Zachariah 10:12; 11:4-14; 13:7.
63. The Book of Hosea is one of the books of the Hebrew Bible. It stands first in order among what are known as the twelve Minor Prophets.
64. Paul (1994), 'Freud, Sellin and the Death of Moses'.

In *Moses and Monotheism*, Freud contradicts the Biblical story of Moses with his own retelling of events claiming that Moses only led his close followers into freedom during an unstable period in Egyptian history after Akhenaten and that they subsequently killed Moses in rebellion and later combined with another monotheistic tribe in Midian based on a volcanic God. Freud explains that years after the murder of Moses, the rebels regretted their action thus forming the concept of the Messiah as a hope for the return of Moses as the Saviour of the Israelites. Freud said that the guilt from the murder of Moses is inherited through the generations; this guilt then drives the Jews to religion to make them feel better.[65]

That wasn't exactly how Sellin had viewed the matter. He wrote:

Moses also became important for the religion of his people through his personal fate.[66] His interaction with God was seen increasingly as unique; only he had seen God face to face, only with him did God speak mouth to mouth. … He was massacred by those from his own people as a martyr to his faith, [and] that also remained unforgotten in the circles of his followers. While Hosea still simply took the view that this unexpiated crime was the pinnacle of all Israel's sins, that it would now inevitably bring judgment …, a concept was developing that Moses, the mildest of all people, … freely offered himself as a sin-offering, and from that arose the idea with Deutero-Isaiah of the salvation of the people through him, the hope of his return as a teacher of the Torah for the peoples of the earth … And it remains true: with him, a great one passed through history who won not only a significance for his people, but for all of humanity, one far wider than most people could even dream.[67]

Naturally, Sellin's (and Freud's) arguments were completely rejected by Jewish *and* Christian scholars despite the fact that Sellin was an eminent biblical scholar and archaeologist[68] (and Freud was promoted as the guy who figured out everything regarding the dark subconscious of all humanity; he was supposedly right on everything else, just wrong on this one thing!) Many of them claimed that Sellin, himself, had repudiated his own idea either 7 or 10

---

65. See: http://en.wikipedia.org/wiki/Moses_and_Monotheism
66. Sellin means Moses' murder at the hands of the Israelites.
67. Sellin (1924), *Geschichte des israelitische-jüdischen Volkes*, p. 94.
68. Freud's collaborator and biographer Ernest Jones describes Sellin as "one of the most distinguished Hebrew and Arabic scholars." He is perhaps most famous for his archaeological work including the excavation of Jericho, which he described in *Jericho, die ergebnisse der ausgrabungen dargestellt, Sellin und Watzinger* (1913).

Akhenaten offering to the handed sky-god Aten. Panel in painted limestone at Tell el-Amarna.

years later. In fact, Sellin published another book *13 years later* stating that he not only still held his views, but that he had found in the writings of other prophets further confirmation that a murder had occurred.

Putting murder into the mix with Moses and Aaron also brings to mind the Heresy of Peor. In this story, we have the prophet Balaam going to the top of a mountain (instead of Moses) and pronouncing a blessing on the Israelites he sees on the plain below him. The scene then switches rather suddenly to what is going on among the Israelites which is "whoring after the Moabite gods" and "joining themselves to Baal Peor" (associated with Mount Peʼor). This sounds exactly like the scene where Moses went up on the mountain to get the tablets and came down to find the Golden Calf taking center stage.

Yahweh orders Moses to hang the idolaters (instead of holding up a brass serpent, as the solution is prescribed in a similar story). At this point, Midianites (remember Zipporah, Moses' wife? A Midianite.) suddenly replace Moabites as the people of concern and a scenario is described where the Israelite, Zimri [69], brings a Midianite woman, Cozbi, into the camp in full view of Moses with all the people weeping all around for some reason that is not explicit. He takes her into a chamber – possibly the tabernacle – and the two of them are followed by the grandson of Aaron, Phinehas, who spears the both of them at once, suggesting that they went inside to copulate before the altar. [70]

The Talmud relates the word *Peʼor* to a Hebrew stem word meaning 'open'

---

69. The name 'Zimri' occurs 12 other times in the Bible; he was, apparently, a servant who killed Asa, king of Judah and then reigned for 7 days before Omri, the commander of the Army, was elevated to the kingship and went after him. Zimri then "went into the stronghold of the king's house and burned the king's house over him with fire and died." See I Kings 16:9-20, II Kings 9:31, and I Chronicles 8:36, 9:42, and Jeremiah 25:25 where it appears that Zimri is a tribe.

70. Numbers 25:1-15. Back references to the event occur in Numbers 25:18 and 31:16, Deuteronomy 4:3, Joshua 22:17, Hosea 9:10 and Psalm 106:28. A later reference is found in the New Testament, 1 Corinthians 10:8.

as in the mouth or bowels, and then it launches on a whole rant about how the worshippers of Baal Peor would defecate at the altar and perform other disgusting rites which probably amounts to defamation of the opposition, a fairly common tactic. (This story will take on more importance in the next volume when I deal with the Eleusinian mysteries.)

Balaam, the prophet who went on top of the mountain, is described as a 'son of Beor' and the phonetic similarity makes one think that he was a prophet or priest of *Baal Peor*. In 1967, archaeologists discovered an ancient inscription in Dier Alla, Jordan, with an extract from a *Book of Balaam*. In this narrative, Balaam is revealed as a 'son of Beor' and this is related to the sun god, Shamash.[71] Shamash was the sun god in the Akkadian, Assyrian and Babylonian pantheons; the god of justice and salvation. It was Shamash's favor for Gilgamesh that enabled him to defeat Huwawa/Humbaba. Shamash gave Gilgamesh three weapons, an axe, a sword, and a bow. As the god of salvation, he was the one who released sufferers from the grip of demons and demons were generally held to cause certain illnesses. The hymns to Shamash reveal that he was the one the sick man appealed to for relief from unjust suffering.

So, again, we have a combination of elements: going up a mountain, people on the plain below engaging in sinful activities, somebody coming along (down from the mountain?) and expressing terrible rage (breaking tablets/ spearing man and woman together; again, wait for the next volume on this topic!). Plus the element of hanging the sinners versus holding up a brass serpent, which was supposed to cure the wandering Israelites of snake-bite. Added to that, there is the hint of sickness, i.e. plague.

I wondered if it might not have been Zimri who was killed in the tabernacle/chamber performing a strange rite of unification with the goddess, but Moses instead? The connection to Moses-as-the-victim is suggested by the fact that he was married to a Midianite and the Israelite in the tent was murdered with a Midianite woman.

There are, apparently, Jewish traditions about Moses having been killed, as well as material in the Jewish midrash[72] that lend credence to Sellin's argument. But of course, all this circles around the issue of whether or not the Bible is history. There are hard-core minimalists we are going to meet soon who think that absolutely nothing in the Bible should be accepted as history unless there is clear, unequivocal, supporting archaeological evidence (none of which has been found). Certainly the Bible is a literary construction, but just as any literary source tends to record actual events even if un-

---

71. McCarter (1980), The Balaam Texts from *Deir 'Alla: The First Combination.*
72. Jewish texts interpreting the Bible.

consciously, so we might consider the Bible as having some bits and pieces of real events collected throughout the lifetime of the authors.

I was pretty excited to realize that I had come to this idea on my own, by a rather circuitous route, which began with the puzzle of why a man would wear a veil over his face for the rest of his life; the answer being that he wasn't who he claimed to be: Aaron and his son murdered Moses and then Aaron masqueraded as Moses for the rest of his days. But there is obviously more to the story and I wondered about it in relation to the story of Abraham *almost* sacrificing his son Isaac[73], Jacob wrestling with the angel, God wanting to kill Moses after the burning bush episode, and so on. What was significant to me is that it seems that *there was a tradition that Moses was murdered*, and whoever came along and put the stories together that make up the Bible, did their best to cover this up and turn Moses into a towering hero. And whoever they were, they must have known what they were doing. Sellin's idea that the Suffering Servant chapter in Isaiah is in reference to Moses, and was then taken retrospectively as a substitute sacrifice for his people, has certain implications, not the least of which that these ideas must also have been in the awareness of the authors of the New Testament who utilized it freely in their theological propaganda.

That the story/tradition existed and that it was an uncomfortable one that required re-interpretation, suggested that there was someone who was 'like' Moses, and he may have lived in Egypt or in Palestine – or both or even elsewhere – and he was murdered and it was a sufficiently big scandal to have spread over the Mediterranean world and been commemorated in stories, first oral, then written. The question that appeared at that moment was: could it have been Akhenaten who was murdered, and these stories shaped around the character of Moses were hints in that direction?

Beauty and the Plagues

So, I wandered around doing name searches and story comparisons and discovering all kinds of inconvenient bits of evidence that something really fishy was going on. All the while I was asking myself: was there any single thing out of all these elements that was matched by any – however remote – outside verification, like some sort of historical event recorded by any of the high civilizations that surrounded Palestine (which was a rural backwater) during any period that might make it relevant to the foundation myths of Israel?

---

73. Right there, we have evidence that, at least on occasion, Yahweh wanted human sacrifice.

And I kept coming back to that single, dangling thread of possible outside verification of a historical seed within the Bible: the story of Abraham and Sarah in Egypt juxtaposed against Akhenaten and Nefertiti.

In all of Egyptian history, nothing is as mysterious as the strange life of Akhenaten and the odd appearance and equally mysterious disappearance of his queen, Nefertiti. We notice in the above account that the Lord plagued Pharaoh and his house with great plagues because of Sarai. This reminds us of the plagues at the time of the Exodus. We also notice that the Pharaoh told Abraham, 'take your wife and go'. This strangely mirrors the demand of Moses, 'Let my people go'. But according to all the 'experts', Akhenaten and Nefertiti lived at the wrong time; they could not be correlated to the Exodus. But still, there it was: a beautiful woman has come. And all hell broke loose in Egypt, apparently; that was an archaeological fact.

On the one side, we have a very beautiful woman (Sarai/Sarah) married to Abraham, the original patriarch of an innovative religion, and both of them went to Egypt. On the other side, we have a very beautiful woman (Nefertiti) married to Akhenaten and he also founded an innovative religion.

Coincidence?

I'm not saying that Moses and Akhenaten are one and the same. I don't actually think that at all. Nor do I think that the Jews are descended from Egyptians. What I see here are a couple of dangling threads that are begging for attention; an idea that there may be some clues somewhere that can tell us more, though until we explore them, we cannot have any preconceived notions of what we will find.

What stands out and screams for attention is the presence of a very beautiful woman who was involved with a man who established a new, monotheistic, religion that was, apparently, a scandal across the Mediterranean world at the time. What is more, our Western civilization didn't know about Akhenaten and his beautiful wife until long after the Bible was written, published, and had become well known around the world. That is: the case of Akhenaten and Nefertiti might just qualify as an important, outside verification that at least something in the Bible was based on a seed of truth even if it was only a literary production: someone borrowed a well-known story and used it to write a 'life of Abraham' while Abraham and Sarah may not actually have existed at all.

Is it possible that the stories created about Moses and Abraham included elements that were based on events that occurred in Egypt? Is it possible that Sarai was modeled on the legendary Nefertiti? Is it possible that the apparently extraordinary reign of this Pharaoh, whose memory was so hated by the Egyptians that they erased every hint of his existence, is the key to unlocking the story of Moses? In short, were the horns that were put on Abraham when he was cuckolded by Pharaoh in a story, transformed into the Horns of Moses?

I was just getting warmed up.

CHAPTER TWO

PERCEPTION, REALITY AND RELIGION

Having formulated the idea that there was something about the reign of Akhenaten and Nefertiti reflected in the stories of Abram and Sarai, David and Bathsheba, Isaac and Rebekah, and Jacob and Rachel, and that the story of Moses could have been created using these features in creative ways, it was time to look at the cataclysmic elements (there *are* cataclysms in the story of Abram: Sodom and Gomorrah, that match the cataclysm of the Exodus). I began to think about the implications and problems of sorting it all out.

I knew that I wasn't the first person who had drawn a connection between the Exodus and Akhenaten. Ahmed Osman, an Egyptian writer wrote a book (several, in fact) about this topic. He theorized that Yuya, the father-in-law of Amenhotep III, grandfather to Akhenaten (Amenhotep IV), was the Patriarch, Joseph, who was sold into slavery in Egypt and became a power in the land. Based on this, he then iden-

tifies Akhenaten as Moses, and Tutankhamen as Moses' right-hand man, Joshua. While Osman may have had a good idea connecting Moses to Akhenaten in some way, in my opinion his main problem is that he decided *a priori* that the Bible stories were historical in and of themselves (even if encoded), and he sought to re-write history based on the Bible rather than looking at the known history based on archaeology to see if there was anything there that could tell its own story. It is true that Yuya may or may not have been a foreigner

Funerary mask of Yuya, Museum of Cairo.

and there are some mysteries to be solved, but Osman's apparent agenda is clear: to show that Monotheism is an Egyptian phenomenon, that Judaism and, ultimately, Christianity are just off-shoots of an original Egyptian religion, and that Islam is the purest form.

Prestidigitation and Numerology

Of course, it's fairly easy for people like Osman, and many others, to come up with these ideas because the truth is, the Bible is a huge muddle of mixed up stories and anachronisms which, until fairly recently, Western scholars fatally considered to be history. It's no wonder that so many alternative theorists think the Bible is history and start searching for things like the Ark of the Covenant because the Bible said it existed and belonged to the Jews after Moses created it. They never stop to ask the most important questions: What if Moses as a Jewish liberator (or any other ethnicity) never existed? What if he was made up from a composite of other stories belonging to other peoples? What if the Ark of the Covenant is just made up? Or, if there is a seed of truth, what if the Ark was something else and belonged to some other group's history? What if Solomon, as a Jewish king, never existed? Or, if there is a seed of truth, what if he was king of some other nation, somewhere else? What if the stories about him are just composites pieced together from stories originating in numerous other cultures that predate the creation of Israel? All of these are valid questions to be asking before accepting the Bible as a 'history of the Jews'. Regarding the use of the Bible as a historical source, my favorite quote on that topic is written by Donald B. Redford:

> For the standard scholarly approach to the history of Israel during the United Monarchy[74] amounts to nothing more than a bad attack of academic 'wishful thinking'. We have these glorious narratives in the books of Samuel and 1st Kings, so well written and ostensibly factual. What a pity if rigorous historical criticism forces us to discard them and not use them. Let us, then, press them into service – what else have we? – and let the burden of proof fall on others. [...]
>
> While one might be unwise to impute crypto-fundamentalist motives, the current fashion of treating the sources at face value as documents written up in large part in the court of Solomon, arises from an equally misplaced desire to rehabilitate the faith and undergird it with any arguments, however fallacious. [...]

---

74. 1025-928 BCE, when Saul, David and then Solomon were kings of the united kingdom of Israel.

Such ignorance is puzzling if one has felt inclined to be impressed by the traditional claims of inerrancy made by conservative Christianity on behalf of the Bible. And indeed the Pentateuch and the historical books boldly present a precise chronology that would carry the Biblical narrative through the very period when the ignorance and discrepancy prove most embarrassing. [...]

Such manhandling of the evidence smacks of prestidigitation and numerology; yet it has produced the shaky foundations on which a lamentable number of "histories" of Israel have been written. Most are characterized by a somewhat naive acceptance of sources at face value coupled with failure to assess the evidence as to its origin and reliability. The result was the reduction of all data to a common level, any or all being grist for a wide variety of mills.

Scholars expended substantial effort on questions that they had failed to prove were valid questions at all. Under what dynasty did Joseph rise to power? Who was the Pharaoh of the Oppression? Of the Exodus? Can we identify the princess who drew Moses out of the river? Where did the Israelites make their exit from Egypt: via the Wady Tumilat [75] or by a more northerly point?

One can appreciate the pointlessness of these questions if one poses similar questions of the Arthurian stories, without first submitting the text to a critical evaluation. Who were the consuls of Rome when Arthur drew the sword from the stone? Where was Merlin born?

Can one seriously envisage a classical historian pondering whether it was Iarbas or Aeneas that was responsible for Dido's suicide, where exactly did Remus leap over the wall, what really happened to Romulus in the thunderstorm, and so forth?

In all these imagined cases none of the material initially prompting the questions has in any way undergone a prior evaluation as to how historical it is! And *any scholar who exempts any part of his sources from critical evaluation runs the risk of invalidating some or all of his conclusions.* [...]

Too often "Biblical" in this context has had the limiting effect on scholarship by implying the validity of *studying Hebrew culture and history in isolation.* What is needed rather is a view of ancient Israel within its true Near Eastern context, and one that will neither exaggerate nor denigrate Israel's actual place within that setting.[76] (Emphases, mine.)

Please take careful note of Redford's comment: "any scholar who exempts any part of his sources from critical evaluation runs the risk of invalidating some or all of his conclusions." The seriousness of this cannot be overem-

---

75. Defunct tributary of the Nile delta.
76. Redford (1992), *Egypt, Canaan, and Israel in Ancient Times*, pp. 301, 258, 260-1, 263.

phasized. You see, people have died by the millions because of this book called 'The Bible' and the beliefs of those who study it. And they are dying today in astonishing numbers for the same reasons! For over 2,000 years, Moses and his horns have dominated Western Civilization with horrifying consequences and we need to think about this very carefully and consider the 'fruits of the tree'.

The problem with using the Bible as history is the lack of secondary sources. There is considerable material from the various ancient libraries prior to the 10th century BCE, 'grist for the historian's mill', but these sources fall silent almost completely at the close of the 20th dynasty[77] in Egypt. Thus, the Bible, being pretty much the only source that claims to cover this particular period, becomes quite seductive; never mind that the archaeology doesn't really fit, or can only be made to fit with a large helping of assumption or closing of the mind to other possibilities.

The person who is using the Bible as history is forced, when all emotional belief is taken out of the picture, to admit that he has no means of checking the historical veracity of the Biblical texts. As Donald Redford noted above, the scholars who admit, when pressed, that rigorous historical criticism forces us to discard the Biblical narratives, use them anyway saying 'what else do we have?' I say that *nothing* would be better than a pack of lies; consider what your acceptance of that particular text has done to the entire planet.

In older times, we know that the many books written about the Bible as history were inspired from a fundamentalist motivation to confirm the religious 'rightness' of Western Civilization. In the present time, there is less of this factor involved in Biblical Historical studies. Nevertheless, there is still a tendency to treat these sources at face value by folks who ought to know better, including a whole raft of 'alternative history' authors!

The Copenhagen School

I escaped from the clutches of the New Age historical revisionists thanks to several factors, including that my search for the historicity of the Biblical accounts in archaeological studies gave negative results for the most part. There were also glaring errors in many of the alternative histories; they accuse mainstream scholars of cherry-picking data and leaving out what is not convenient, and then they do it themselves! Sometimes it is worse because they discover a few interesting items and assume that the scholars are un-

---

77. The Pharaohs of the 20th dynasty ruled from c. 1187 to 1064 BCE. The last Pharaoh of the 20th dynasty was Ramses XI.

aware of them and write breathless fiction as though they had just invented the wheel. Yet, not unlike them, I was (and still am to some extent) holding on to the idea that there was *some* seed of history there. It just boggled the mind to think of anybody making all that up! But we need to keep in mind that this is purely a bias – my bias – inculcated in me and most other people, as a consequence of cultural and familial beliefs. Anybody who seeks to do research of any kind needs to always keep their own biases in mind and make efforts to calibrate their perceptions accordingly.[78] That is why, when I first began to write this book some years ago, I still felt uneasy. What I have learned since then certainly justified staying my hand from writing and getting them dirty by choosing to first engage in the hard work of wading through every available bit of material I could locate. This led me, inevitably, to the work of what is known informally as the Copenhagen School[79] of Biblical criticism, or 'Biblical Minimalism'.

What minimalism amounts to, in essence, is taking a *scientific* approach toward the study of ancient texts, *including* the Bible. That is, it is a cognitive style where no source is considered privileged, *a priori* and everything must be subjected to analysis and verification. What a concept! Needless to say, I was overjoyed to discover that somebody, finally, was doing this! I fell in love with the work of Giovanni Garbini, John Van Seters, Thomas L. Thompson, Niels Peter Lemche, Philip Davies and others. What has been shocking to discover is exactly how much is known among the scholars – *including* the fundamentalist true-believer critics of the minimalists – that is not known by the general public. I suppose I shouldn't be surprised since I have discovered this to be true in other fields, but when the subject is the foundation of religion – stuff people believe in and stake their lives on – well, it's pretty bad.

Judaism supposedly created Israel, and Judaism is also the parent of Christianity and Islam, so the origins of Judaism and Ancient Israel, from which it supposedly emerged, are not trifling topics. The fact is, as a growing body of scholarship within the minimalist school demonstrates, using a powerful set of critical algorithms, there was no *ancient* Israel. The Hebrew Bible is not, by any stretch of the imagination, a historical document, and trying to understand the history of *Palestine* by reading the Bible is like trying to understand Medieval history by reading the historical novel *Ivanhoe*.

---

78. If you think that you have no biases, you are suffering from a particular bias! Please read *Strangers to Ourselves* by psychologist Timothy Wilson and *Thinking, Fast and Slow* by Daniel Kahneman.
79. A movement in biblical scholarship started around 1990 by scholars of the Cophenaghen School and other universities.

The 'maximalists', of course, are true believers, and they are the ones who have controlled the study of the Bible for a very long time; they are the ones who created archaeology for the sole purpose of proving that the history in the Bible is true; but archaeology is, little by little, becoming more scientific, and as it has done so, as it has freed itself from the control of True Believers, it has revealed that the Bible is not a historical source.

So now we have to ask the question: why is there this conflict between minimalists, maximalists, believers, non-believers and so forth? After all, if reality is real, shouldn't it be generally understood in the same way by everybody?

Dark Interlude

I would like to ask the reader a question to set the stage for what I want to convey here. Have you ever, as a child, been accused of something you didn't do, either by your parents, teachers or other 'authorities'? And if so, were you punished unfairly for this something you didn't do? Do you remember how it felt?

As you remember, can you feel the frustration, the helpless anger and resentment that you *told the truth and no one believed you*? *You* know what you did or did not do, and no one can take that away from you. But they have taken away from you the right for that truth to be known by others, which means they have taken away the right of others to know the truth about you. You have been slandered and punished, and there is *no way* you can ever prove that it was wrong and unjust, and all the other people will have a 'history' of you that is false. In fact, this knowledge that others will have false memories of you, will have false ideas about what you did until they die, hurts almost worse than the punishment. What is more, in a vague way, you can perceive that those who believe the lie have been deprived of something valuable about you, a sharing of the real you: the truth that you did not do what you were accused of doing, and that you did tell the truth. A barrier has been erected between you and the others – the barrier of a lie.

Now expand that concept just a little bit. Imagine that such false accusations, false stories, *are being told about history at large*, the history that defines your origins. The only difference is that it is not a personal lie against you, and you do not therefore have the advantage of knowing that it is certainly a lie. Instead, it is a social lie, a lie about your origins and what is real and what is not, that has been widely disseminated and accepted as truth by most people.

Imagine that people are born, live their lives, and die believing lies about where they came from and how they got where they are, and the reasons for all that exists in the world around us. Just like the people who believed the lies about something you didn't do, people have been separated from the truth by the barrier of lies.

As you probably know, the event from your childhood may have been small in terms of your entire life history, but still, there are those who judge you based on that lie, and all your subsequent history follows from those beliefs about you. Now you, and everyone else who believes those lies, judge the world and other people based on the lies about human origins and what is real. And the result is very, very bad.

Regarding religion, and most particularly the religions that hold sway over our world such as Christianity born of Judaism, we simply cannot overstress the importance of deep and serious study. We cannot ignore the question of whether or not Christianity and Judaism and Islam are true, and if they are *not*, then why have they spread and persisted? And if they are not true, we need to evaluate a proper response to them.

Let us just say that in examining this process of the development of the 'Holy Scriptures' and Christianity itself, I have found nothing of the 'Holy Ghost' in there. That's the plain fact. And a lot of people in the business of religion know it.

Nevertheless, our institutions of higher learning generally have a special faculty allotment for the teaching of theology, *financed by the taxpayer*, whether Christian or Jew. One assumes that the students who study this theology are also given exposure to other studies, such as math, languages, science, and so forth. The question then becomes: what kind of strange distortion, what incomprehensible corruption takes place in the minds of human beings, so that they so completely separate their academic training and knowledge from what they hear preached at them from the pulpit? What kind of brainwashing can so effectively cause the simplest of facts to be forgotten? How does this happen?

It is literally staggering to a logical, intelligent human being, that the fairy tale of the Bible – as God's word – has endured so long. There is nothing to which we can compare this in the entire seven thousand years of human history of which we are aware. Calling it all a pack of lies seems rather harsh, but it is increasingly evident that it is certainly intentionally misleading. And, in that case, what shall we call it?

Naturally, all of these problems have led to many interesting theological solutions. It is amazing how creative true believers can be when faced with facts that this or that idea they have held for a long time is no longer tenable.

Obviously, in general, human beings are not genetically programmed to be members of one or another specific social group with a specific set of beliefs, though there may be some genetic implications as twin studies would indicate. Back in 1986, an Australian geneticist, Nick Martin, published a paper based on observations he had made while doing epidemiology studies on twins.[80] He noted that, of 4,500 pairs of fraternal and identical twins, it appeared that genetic factors played a larger role in the transmission of social attitudes than socio-cultural factors. Twenty years later, another group of geneticists in the United States took up the subject. Their survey concluded that between 40% and 50% of variation in political attitudes and ideologies was genetic and almost none of it due to parental influence. However, when they looked at specific questions regarding political party affiliation, the results were almost reversed: shared environment was the key.[81]

Not surprisingly, the paper generated vehement opposition from some quarters. However, those objections do not seem to hold up and the ones I have read are poorly founded, and consist mainly of emotional objections and polemic rather than coherent arguments and evidence.[82] And, of course, the cry of 'eugenics' is raised; clearly, after Hitler took eugenics the wrong way and made it a justification for genocide, it is difficult to be rational about the topic.[83]

What is Reality?

On the other side of the divide: in the book *The Social Construction of Reality*, the two authors, Peter Berger and Thomas Luckmann, write that how we perceive and interpret reality is a *social* construct. They say that the elements that shape a person's thinking are language, institutions (religion, government, school) and socialization practices. They do say there is a difference between objective and subjective reality but that both are powerfully influenced in their structure by the culture in which we are born. According to this social constructionist framework, 'truth' can be variable and what is true in one society can be false in another. This is an obviously valid observation.

---

80. Martin (1986), 'Transmission of social attitudes'.
81. Alford & Hibbing (2005), 'Are Political Orientations Genetically Transmitted?'
82. My assessment is not that of an expert, merely a well-educated researcher who attempts to read everything with an open mind. I am also, probably, a genetic 'conservative liberal'. I would advise the curious reader to search out the papers and books on both sides of the question.
83. Read, for example, Alford, Funk & Hibbing (2008), 'Twin Studies, Molecular Genetics, Politics, and Tolerance: A Response to Beckwith and Morris'.

According to Berger and Luckmann, culture is the conveyor of what are defined as 'facts' and that is the *filter* through which people get impressions about the world around them and upon which they build their knowledge. In one culture (the one I grew up in), the Earth is round and Catholics are damned for idolatry and will never go to heaven, only women have babies, and the bite of a poisonous snake can kill you. In a Catholic culture (that of my cousins), the Earth is round and Protestants are damned and will never go to heaven, only women have babies, and the bite of a poisonous snake can kill you. (Interestingly, many years later, my Catholic cousins converted to Protestantism after moving to an area where there were no Catholics.) In still another culture, the Earth is flat and sacrificing virgins will appease the gods and bring peace and plenty, only women have babies, and the bite of a poisonous snake can kill you. All three of these samples reveal that some cultural knowledge is true in an objective sense, without reference to a specific culture, and some is not, e.g. only women have babies and the bite of a poisonous snake can kill you, and in two of them, the Earth is round. The religious beliefs, on the other hand, are the major differences. And religious beliefs generally underpin many other socio-cultural ideas and practices, so the capacity for creating divisions between peoples via religion are manifold.

At the same time, this little example suggests to us strongly that there is an objective reality 'out there' and if we could only emerge from the cocoon of our culturally imposed perception restrictions, we could know what it is. For example, the Earth is round (more or less) and remains round no matter what different cultures through time have believed about it being flat. In his book *The New Skepticism*, Paul Kurtz writes:

> ...There is a real world out there, but we interact, modify, or interpret it in different ways in terms of our contexts or fields of behavior. But the world does not evaporate into, nor is it totally assimilated by, a person's action. Reality is not equivalent to activity; activity presupposes a real world independent of oneself. It is that which exists and causally interacts with other things, separate and distinct from an intersubjective community of observers. And it is that which endures and functions in some sense independent of my activities... The real is that which exists or would exist if I were not around, but I could say little about it if I did not observe, study, probe, manipulate, or use it.[84]

In respect of Berger, Luckman and Kurtz's views, psychologist, John Schumaker writes:

---

84. Kurtz (1992), *The New Skepticism: Inquiry and Reliable Knowledge.*

According to truly objective reality, the earth is round in shape. The objective reality of which Berger and Luckmann spoke should be again understood as the culturally influenced perception or interpretation of objective reality. It is hardly more stable that the subjective reality to which they also made reference. As Kurtz also realizes, there is an important difference between knowledge and impressions, and between knowledge and belief. It is not sufficient to equate belief with knowledge. Instead, in Kurtz's view, there are objective "anchors" in the real world that exist independently of beliefs, imaginations, dreams, fantasies, and so forth. It is even possible to judge the veracity of these mental constructions in terms of their alignment or misalignment with the objective "anchors" to which Kurtz refers.

In contrast with some prevailing schools of thought in sociology and anthropology, the fields of psychology and psychiatry have long histories of recognizing a stable reality that can be used as a touchstone by which to assess the personal reality of individuals. There would be no hesitation in saying that someone deviated from "real" reality if, for instance, that person claimed that he/she was Napoleon. Conversely, I know of no sane mental health professional who would take the position that such a person was Napoleon because this particular belief was an aspect of the personal reality of that person.[85]

Schumaker then goes on to say (and I will quote *in extenso* for clarity of this important topic):

Primary reality is reality as it would present itself if only that information or data available to the person were used as the building blocks of reality. This does not, however, mean that primary reality would necessarily be the result of rational modes of mental activity, such as critical and analytical thinking, reasoning, and so forth. Nor does it refer to "ultimate" reality in the sense that everything is known about an event or object. Instead, **primary reality is uncorrupted and unbiased because the creature does not modify, translate, or otherwise distort incoming information.**

Virtually all nonhuman animals operate within primary reality. Consider the squirrel. With no added bias from higher-order distortive mechanisms, the reality of a squirrel is a comparatively stable primary one wherein things are as they are. An acorn always remains something to eat or to stick into the hole of a tree. In the absence of the cerebral apparatus to misinterpret an acorn, squirrels never have acorn gods, nor do they ever develop acorn phobias. When an-

85. Schumaker (1995), *The Corruption of Reality: A unified Theory of Religion, Hypnosis, and Psychopathology.*

other squirrel dies, decomposes, and disappears, the remaining squirrels have no ability to alter the empirical data about the squirrel's death. When the dead squirrel is gone, it is gone. The primary reality of a squirrel does not permit a squirrel heaven or a happy acorn ground in an afterlife. Quite simply, there are no data to indicate, either to a squirrel or to ourselves, that there exists an afterlife.[86] Because of its brain design, the squirrel is prevented from reinterpreting empirical data, which gives it exclusive access to primary reality.

On the other hand, human beings have only one cerebral foot on the ground. They possess a talent that automatically banishes them from primary reality, at the same time offering endless other possibilities over the squirrel and all other nonhuman creatures.

But a point of clarification is essential here. While I agree that nonhuman animals have a generally stable reality by comparison with human reality, Berger and Luckmann ignore an important fact in arriving at their conclusion. It is that a large proportion of nonhuman animal behavior is acquired through social learning, in much the same way that it is done for human beings. Even the humble squirrel must learn that it is to eat acorns, and that a certain squeal from its mother means to scamper up the tree to safety. Furthermore, the Berger and Luckmann model discounts the ways in which *some dimensions of human behavior are locked into biologically determined patterns.* These may not be as obvious as those appearing in other species, but they do exist.

We might even go to the heart of the matter about reality and ask why it is that human beings, in all cultures, construct for themselves a reality that is not strictly empirical in nature. Why, all throughout our history, have we harbored irrational and often wildly false notions about the empirical world and our place in it? It is said that Socrates frequently began his speeches by imploring his listeners not to be angry with him if he tells them the truth. One gets the sense that Socrates definitely knew that falsehoods and errors held a central place in the human mind ...

Yet human beings are also capable of arriving at what Kurtz terms reliable knowledge. It is well *within our abilities* to process incoming information in order that our mental constructions correspond to primary reality. The fact that we so often miss the mark in this regard is owing to our tandem ability to *regulate reality* to suit our ends. ... as a consequence of our unique brain design, there is a highly fluid quality to human reality...

To the human being, acorns can be little bombs planted by aliens from outer space (an aspect of the reality of a paranoid person). Or they can be the source

---

86. While everything else that Schumaker writes is on target, this point is debatable as will be discussed extensively in a subsequent volume.

of powerful magic, capable of ensuring the immortality of a dead person if the corpse is dusted with burnt acorn powder prior to burial (an aspect of the reality of certain former religious beliefs). Or an acorn can be merely an acorn. Many options are open to members of our species, and we naturally try to avail ourselves of them for purposes of social, psychological, and physical survival.

Culture usually specifies the alternatives to a strictly empirically based reality. But, in our species, the reality of the person never overlaps completely with reality as it would be constructed with empirical or factual data only. This is true in "normal" as well as "abnormal" individuals. Also not exempt are the existential pathfinders who consider themselves to be at the front lines of the truth. Their personal reality is also skewed and biased, albeit with superficial differences in the appearance of that bias.

It must be conceded, however, that primary reality could also be false as it reveals itself to us. Take the acorn once more. It may be that acorns are little bombs, or that their burnt dust is the bestower of everlasting life. But in using empirical data to define real reality, one is proceeding on the basis of available data and probabilities and/or improbabilities. Therefore, it is highly improbable, in light of empirical data, that an acorn is an alien's bomb or that burnt acorn dust defeats the problem of mortality.

Religion cannot be given special consideration if we are to understand the principles of reality regulation. So, similarly, it must be said that, in all likelihood, *religious beliefs are examples of adaptive cognitive errors*. They are probably false because they are constructed in defiance and ignorance (in the sense of "ignore") of available empirical data. Thus they are deviations from primary reality.

We know that this is largely the case, since the thousands of religions in the world contain beliefs that directly contradict one another, thereby canceling out their credibility. For example, it cannot both be true that a bird-god gave birth to this planet four million years ago in the form of an egg, and also that the planet was born six thousand years ago when, over the course of six days, a different god created the earth one step at a time. Even so, there is no way of knowing that all religious beliefs are inaccurate, since their premises are not circumscribed by empirical evidence. Yet, with the aid of simple logic, we can safely say that *most religious beliefs are probably false*. ...

In short, personal reality defines itself by its deviation from primary reality, even though personal reality partially overlaps with primary reality. ...

One can only speculate about the degree of bias that features in personal reality. Ernest Rossi, an Ericksonian hypnotherapist, estimated that *at least 80 percent of the information contained in the human mind is false*. What makes this estimate more remarkable is that Rossi was referring to the vast quantity of error that is entertained, not as a result of formal hypnosis, but during the normal waking state. And here we are not talking about an animal with insufficient brain power to get things right. Instead, we are dealing with the creature with the most highly developed cerebral cortex. Yet, despite our cerebral talents, it seems that the mental world of the human being is often at odds with the true nature of things. Not only that, we will fight to preserve what is false. We do this while also, paradoxically, apprehending the world with astonishing precision. As a result, any useful theory about human behavior must explain the fundamental contradiction which is our capacity simultaneously to construe and misconstrue the world about us.

Whatever the actual extent of our cognitive error, it should be remembered that the generation of this error is the consequence of intricate cerebral processes that safeguard the integrity of the entire nervous system. Also, attempts to estimate the proportion of error in personal reality ignore the fact of *individual differences*. We should expect a substantial amount of variation regarding the distortive component of personal reality. These are reflective of *situational, constitutional, and sociocultural* factors that weigh differentially upon people. The actual content and emotional valence of the error contained in personal reality determines whether we describe that error as religion, psychopathology, or something else.

The inclusion of a category with the label "cultural reality" reinforces what was said previously about the "social construction" of reality. The reality of the individual is to some extent the result of constructions that are fabricated and propagated by culture. We are all tattooed from birth with indelible beliefs and understandings as they are served up to us by the culture into which we are born. However, this does not necessarily imply that all people rally around a single culture which manufactures a single set of messages, or suggestions. Granted, in many instances, the vast majority of those born within a specific culture will endorse the dominant core of that culture. For example, most adult people in contemporary Western culture would not feel threatened at the prospect of allowing their children to receive an education. Indeed, the majority would probably see it as a positive and worthwhile undertaking. But certain individuals are also subject to the influence of any number of subcultures which, together, make up the composite culture. Even with regard to the matter of the desirability of education, one could point to significant Western subcultures wherein education is viewed with fear and suspicion (e.g., the Amish and Mennonites). Therefore, our approach to the concept of culture must be flexible enough to include the shaping forces of subcultures, as well as those of the mainstream culture. As a result, we need to define cultural reality broadly *as the constellation of externally delivered suggestions that are normalized on the basis of group endorsement.* The term "normalized" as it is used here means normal both in the sense that a suggestion has achieved normative status, and that it is experienced as normal by the person.

The above definition allows for the possibility that a suggestion can be normalized by a subculture, sometimes even if it lacks majority endorsement in that society as a whole. One question that immediately arises is this: How large and/or cohesive must a group be for it to be capable of normalizing a suggestion? There is no simple answer that will apply to all individuals across all cultural contexts. While not trying to beg the question, it can only be said that a cultural suggestion becomes an element of the reality of a person when the group is, in fact, sufficiently large and/or cohesive for the person to perceive that suggestion as normal, or normative.

We see, therefore, that *cultural reality refers to reality that is shared, or agreed upon, at the group level,* even if that group is only one portion of the total population. Of course, conflicts can arise between the reality of the dominant culture and that of a subculture. For instance, some Amish children are quite literally presented with two opposing cultural realities on the issue of education, progress, technology, and so forth. As a result, conflict situations can arise later when educational and lifestyle decisions become necessary...

In a sense, culture is the central bank of cognitive distortions that provide individual members the means by which to translate empirical reality into a more acceptable form. The mass biasing of empirical reality often carries the label "religion," even though this process spills over into other terminological categories.

There may be some truth to the adage that the job of the old is to lie to the young. Likewise, Ernest Becker may have been justified in describing culture as a "macro-lie." In addition to normalizing errors, culture also transmits a great deal of vital data that is in close accord with primary or empirical reality. This has the obvious advantage of delivering information that is essential for survival. But cognitive error is also a requisite for survival; therefore, cultural reality must be viewed as an intentional and necessary blend of information and misinformation.[87]

Each social group creates its own constraints and imposes them on its members. This means that there is a lot of diversity to be noted between different social groups, but within any one group, diversity is not tolerated very well. If you move from being a member of one group to another group, you

---

87. Schumaker (1995), op. cit.

must change all your thinking and adapt to a different set of constraints that are imposed on you by the group you live among.

Of course, some people can move from the social group in which they are born into another quite easily because they are *born with the genetic tendencies that underpin the mindset that is normative for that group.* What this means is that there is a genetic potential for diversification regarding thought and conduct born into every single human being, a potential that permits growth in circumscribed directions that can be inhibited and/or enhanced by society. These characteristics have been explored extensively by Canadian psychologist, Bob Altemeyer.

The Authoritarians

Modern cognitive psychology has provided much new data that help us to understand that, just as Georges Gurdjieff said repeatedly, *man is a machine.*[88] There are people – and they seem to be a very large segment of societies everywhere – who are what Altemeyer calls 'Authoritarians'.[89] These are people who have what are clearly genetic tendencies to follow authority and never question it. The reason for this seems to lie in the way the brain works, as described by yet another psychologist, Daniel Kahneman. The basic idea is that the brain protects itself from stress and seeks always to conserve energy. What's more, when your brain learns at an early age how to shut out unpleasant sensations and create an 'alternate view' of things, usually in a lazy way, it sets up a pattern that you then continue to follow because it relieves stress.

Once you abandon rationalism in one domain, it is all too easy to be irrational in another one. The default setting of the human brain is to seek causes for effects; this was evolutionarily adaptive because the creature that can read the signs of the environment correctly, and anticipate future events that might be fatal, survives. If you add that evolutionary tendency to self-awareness, interesting things happen. Human beings are able to remember past mistakes and, with this ability to recognize patterns, anticipate how things could go wrong in the future; they can also conceive of their own death in the future. Being wired to figure out a solution, a defensive response, and

---

88. "Man such as we know him, is a machine", in Ouspensky (1949) citing G. I. Gurdjieff in *In Search of the Miraculous*, p.72.

89. See: Altemeyer (1981), *Right-Wing Authoritarianism*; (1988), *Enemies of Freedom: Understanding Right-Wing Authoritarianism*; (1997), *Amazing Conversions: Why Some Turn to Faith and Others Abandon Religion*; (2006), *Atheists: A Groundbreaking Study of America's Nonbelievers.*

also to conserve energy, religious belief becomes the path of least resistance.[90] Disbelief and facing hard truths or painful realities, on the other hand, requires effort and causes mental pain. Studies have shown that trauma – generally associated with fight, flight, or freeze responses – can activate this circuit in a powerful way, and that is where things get sticky. You see, religion can be easily inculcated in an individual or group by an individual (or more than one) who desires to establish and maintain control. The less control an individual feels that they have over their life, the more likely they are to follow a leader who promises certainty of resolution and safety. This is the Authoritarian Personality. I want to pause a moment and define this personality type based on the latest research, since we are going to be meeting a lot of them.

> **Authoritarian personalities** *n.* Authoritarian has two main meanings. First, it means believing in submitting to authority. Second, it means being dictatorial or tyrannical. So people who strongly believe in submitting to authority could be called authoritarians. And so could tyrants who insist that everyone obey them – which is the sort of thing you usually get from tyrants. [...]
>
> This personality trait consists of authoritarian submission, a high degree of submission to the established authorities in one's society; authoritarian aggression, aggression directed against various persons in the name of those authorities; and conventionalism, a strong adherence to the social conventions endorsed by those authorities. Why do psychologists call authoritarian followers "right-wing" authoritarians (RWAs)? Are they all members of a conservative political party? No. Right-wing is used here in a psychological sense, meaning wanting to please established authority. One of the original meanings of the adjective right (riht in Old English) was "lawful, proper, correct," which in those long ago days meant doing what your local lord and the king wanted.[...]
>
> In North America, where this research has mainly been done, persons who get high RWA scale scores quite readily submit to the established authorities in their lives and trust them far more than most people do. [...]
>
> High RWAs also are relatively willing to let authorities run roughshod over civil liberties and constitutional guarantees of personal freedom. They seem to think that authorities are above the law. They also hold authorities relatively blameless when the latter unjustly attack someone.[...]
>
> Right-wing authoritarians show a chilling inclination, compared to most people, to help the government persecute any group it targets. Also, if asked

---

90. See: Kahneman (2011), *Thinking, Fast and Slow*. Also: Wilson (2004), *Strangers to Ourselves: Discovering the Adaptive Unconscious.*

to play the role of judge, they will sentence convicted defendants to longer prison terms than most people will – unless the defendant is an authority or has attacked someone the authoritarian follower would like to see attacked. High RWAs favor capital punishment. As well, they deliver stronger electric shocks in "punishment" learning experiments. In general they believe that a good thrashing "works." But they also admit they get personal pleasure from punishing others and seeing wrongdoers get "what's coming to them." Finally, right-wing authoritarians tend to be highly prejudiced against most racial groups, feminists, homosexuals, people with different language backgrounds, and those with different religious views. Speaking of religion, the authoritarian follower's family religion produces a lot of his/her conventionalism. High RWAs tend to be fundamentalists in whatever religion they belong to, and fundamentalist churches are not shy about insisting everyone follow their beliefs about what is right, wrong, and normal. Those who walk other paths are often considered immoral and repugnant. Right-wing authoritarians also absorb the beliefs and teachings of the nonreligious authorities in their lives. [...]

Authoritarian followers thus appear to be, indeed, submissive, aggressive, and conventional. Further research with the RWA scale has uncovered a lot more about them, such as that they have weak reasoning skills and are gullible when people tell them what they want to hear; they fall back on dogmatism and social support when challenged, since they have little else to back up their beliefs; they are profoundly ethnocentric, identifying with their narrow in-groups, to which they give strong loyalty and in which they expect great cohesiveness; they are zealous in their causes and given to proselytizing; and they tend to be political and economic conservatives. "Deeper down," they use a lot of double standards in their judgments and often behave hypocritically; they are fearful and self-righteous, defensive, and unaware of themselves. Deep, deep down inside they seem to harbor secret doubts about the things they say they believe in most. So the picture of authoritarian followers after all these years of research is far from flattering – unless you are a potential dictator. If you are, these narrow-minded, closed-minded, easily fooled, zealous bigots looking for a man on horseback are exactly the kind of people you're looking for.

Who are the potential dictators? Most of all, they seem to be power-hungry individuals who live their lives according to the law of the jungle. They believe either you dominate others or you will be dominated instead. Thus they score high on the Social Dominance Orientation scale, which is the main way of identifying them. High dominators purposely make others afraid of them, believe in vengeance and using power however they must to get their way, and will try to crush whoever opposes them. They also tend to be believe that right and wrong do not matter at all, that people are objects to be manipulated, and that deceit and treachery are justified if they get you to the top... . They too are highly prejudiced and favor conservative political parties and economic philosophies. But most social dominators are not really religious, and their amorality would turn off most high RWAs. However, a non-religious but skilled social dominator has little difficulty persuading authoritarian followers that he/she shares their beliefs, and some social dominators are in fact religious and seem to have an especially good chance of heading an authoritarian movement. Experiments have found that when social dominators become leaders of groups of right-wing authoritarians, this "lethal union" produces aggression and exploitation in laboratory settings – just as it does in the real world.[91]

Authoritarian leaders and followers appear to constitute a goodly proportion of humanity and more and more researchers are coming to the conclusion that such tendencies are genetic. This is discussed in books such as *The Authoritarians* by Bob Altemeyer[92], *Without Conscience*[93] by Robert Hare and *Political Ponerology*[94] by Andrzej M. Lobaczewski.

Some of the scientific studies being done in cognitive science are terrifying in their implications for society considering the fact that the tendencies they reveal are rather widespread. For example, many people believe that when there are intimations of danger they have some sort of automatic system that will kick in and protect them and if they don't feel that 'fight or flight' response, everything must be okay. But that isn't true. There is a tendency to normalize even the most terrifying dangers; the brain can't tolerate the pain or the effort, so it basically shuts down. The truth seems to be that, when warned of danger, most human beings do *not* do things necessary for their survival. John Leach, a psychologist at the University of Lancaster who studies freezing under stress, says that about *75% of people find it impossible* to reason during a catastrophic event or impending doom. The 15 or so percent on either side of the bell curve react either with unimpaired, *heightened* awareness or blubbering, confused panic. *Normalcy bias* is freezing or stalling during a crisis and pretending everything will continue to be normal.

---

91. Matsumoto (Ed.) (2009), *Cambridge Dictionary of Psychology.*
92. Bob Altemeyer, University of Manitoba. Book available online: http://home.cc.umanitoba.ca/~altemey/
93. Hare (1999), *Without Conscience: The Disturbing World of the Psychopaths Among Us.*
94. Lobaczewski (2007), *Political Ponerology: A Science on the Nature of Evil Adjusted for Political Purposes.*

Much of your behavior is an attempt to lower anxiety. You know you aren't in any danger when everything is safe and expected. Normalcy bias is self-soothing through believing everything is just fine. If you can still engage in your normal habits, still see the world as if nothing bad is happening, then your anxiety stays put.

Normalcy bias is a state of mind out of which you are attempting to make everything OK by believing it still is. Normalcy bias is refusing to believe terrible events will include you even though you have every reason to think otherwise. The first thing you are likely to feel in the event of a disaster is the supreme need to feel safe and secure. When it becomes clear this is impossible, you drift into a daydream where it is. ...

All the tools of pattern recognition, all the routines you've become accustomed to are rendered useless in a horrific event. The emergency situation is too novel and ambiguous. You have a tendency to freeze not because panic has overwhelmed you but because normalcy has disappeared. Ripley calls this moment when you freeze "reflexive incredulity." As your brain attempts to disseminate the data, your deepest desire is for everyone around you to assure you the bad thing isn't real. You wait for this to happen past the point when it becomes obvious it will not. The holding pattern of normalcy bias continues until the ship lurches or the building shifts. You may remain placid until the tornado throws a car through your house or the hurricane snaps the power lines. ...

The solution, according to Mikami, Ikeda, and other experts, is repetition on the part of those who can help, those who can see the danger better than you. If enough warnings are given and enough instructions are broadcast, then those things become the new normal, and you will spring into action.

Normalcy bias can be scaled up to larger events as well. Global climate change, peak oil, obesity epidemics, and stock market crashes are good examples of larger, more complex events in which people fail to act because it is difficult to imagine just how abnormal life could become if the predictions are true.

Regular media over-hyping and panic-building over issues like Y2K, swine flu, SARS, and the like help fuel normalcy bias on a global scale. Pundits on both sides of politics warn of crises that can be averted only by voting one way or the other. *With so much crying wolf, it can be difficult to determine in the frenzied information landscape when to be alarmed, when it really is not a drill.*

The first instinct is to gauge how out of the norm the situation truly is and act only when the problem crosses a threshold past which it becomes impossible to ignore. Of course, this is often after it is too late to act.[95] (Emphases, mine.)

---

95. McRaney (2012), *You Are Not So Smart.*

The Social Contract Theory of Human Society?

One theory of human society is that of the 'social contract', which posits that a group of individuals get together and draw up an agreement to their mutual advantage by which they will all abide, and a 'society' is thus formed. The problem with this theory is that it relies on circular reasoning. It presupposes the very thing it purports to explain already exists: that human beings are already constrained by some values that allow them to get together to draw up this alleged contract. Such a group must already be able to conceptualize a situation in the future where they will benefit from being bound to these other people in a contract. Ernest Gellner outlines the basic theory of anthropology regarding how societies are formed. He writes:

> The way in which you restrain people from doing a wide variety of things, not compatible with the social order of which they are members, is that you subject them to ritual. The process is simple: you make them dance round a totem pole until they are wild with excitement and become jellies in the hysteria of collective frenzy; you enhance their emotional state by any device, by all the locally available audio-visual aids, drugs, dance, music and so on; and once they are really high, you stamp upon their minds the type of concept or notion to which they subsequently become enslaved. Next morning, the savage wakes up with a bad hangover and a deeply internalized concept. The idea is that the central feature of religion is ritual, and the central role of ritual is the endowment of individuals with compulsive concepts which simultaneously define their social and natural world and restrain and control their perceptions and comportment, in mutually reinforcing ways. These deeply internalized notions henceforth oblige them to act within the range of prescribed limits. Each concept has a normative binding content, as well as a kind of organizational descriptive content. The conceptual system maps out social order and required conduct, and inhibits inclinations to thought or conduct which would transgress its limits.

I can see no other explanation concerning how social and conceptual order and homogeneity are maintained within societies which, at the same time, are so astonishingly diverse when compared with each other. One species has somehow escaped the authority of nature, and is no longer genetically

Zulu cultural dance.

programmed to remain within a relatively narrow range of conduct, so it needs new constraints. The fantastic range of genetically possible conduct is constrained in any one particular herd, and obliged to respect socially marked bounds. This can only be achieved by means of conceptual constraint, and that in turn must somehow be instilled. Somehow, semantic, culturally transmitted limits are imposed on men…" [96]

As Gellner must have known quite well, this theory of how to control human beings was understood in pretty much this exact way many thousands of years ago. In the course of my reading, I once came across a passage translated from a Hittite tablet found at an archaeological dig where the king wrote that the priesthood needed the king to establish their religious authority and the king needed the priests to establish his right to rule. This control comes sharply into view in the falsification of history. History, itself, becomes part of the control. After all, control of daily information is just history in the making. As to how this process works on the individual level, a passage in Barbara Oakley's *Evil Genes* describes what 'dancing around the totem pole with ones social group' does to the human brain – including scientists and true believers, both of whom have very strong attachments to their belief systems:

A recent imaging study by psychologist Drew Westen and his colleagues at Emory University provides firm support for the existence of emotional reasoning. Just prior to the 2004 Bush-Kerry presidential elections, two groups of subjects were recruited – fifteen ardent Democrats and fifteen ardent Republicans. Each was presented with conflicting and seemingly damaging statements about their candidate, as well as about more neutral targets such as actor Tom Hanks (who, it appears, is a likable guy for people of all political persuasions). Unsurprisingly, when the participants were asked to draw a logical conclusion about a candidate from the other – 'wrong' – political party, the participants found a way to arrive at a conclusion that made the candidate look bad, even though logic should have mitigated the particular circumstances and allowed them to reach a different conclusion. Here's where it gets interesting.

When this 'emote control' began to occur, parts of the brain normally involved in reasoning were not activated. Instead, a constellation of activations occurred in the same areas of the brain where punishment, pain, and negative emotions are experienced (that is, in the left insula, lateral frontal cortex, and ventromedial prefrontal cortex). Once a way was found to ignore infor-

---

96. Gellner (1995), *Anthropology and Politics*.

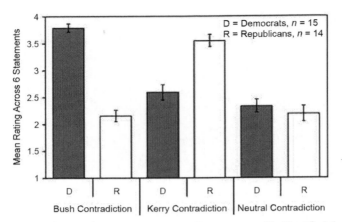

Ratings of perceived contradictions in statements. Democrats readily identified the contradictions in Bush's statements but not Kerry's, whereas Republicans readily identified the contradictions in Kerry's statements but not Bush's.

mation that could not be rationally discounted, the neural punishment areas turned off, and the participant received a blast of activation in the circuits involving rewards – akin to the high an addict receives when getting his fix.

In essence, the participants were not about to let facts get in the way of their hot-button decision making and quick buzz of reward. 'None of the circuits involved in conscious reasoning were particularly engaged,' says Westen. 'Essentially, it appears as if partisans twirl the cognitive kaleidoscope until they get the conclusions they want, and then they get massively reinforced for it, with the elimination of negative emotional states and activation of positive ones'...

Ultimately, Westen and his colleagues believe that 'emotionally biased reasoning leads to the "stamping in" or reinforcement of a defensive belief, associating the participant's "revisionist" account of the data with positive emotion or relief and elimination of distress. The result is that partisan beliefs are calcified, and the person can learn very little from new data,' Westen says. Westen's remarkable study showed that neural information processing related to what he terms 'motivated reasoning' ... appears to be qualitatively different from reasoning when a person has no strong emotional stake in the conclusions to be reached.

The study is thus the first to describe the neural processes that underlie political judgment and decision making, as well as to describe processes involving emote control, psychological defense, confirmatory bias, and some forms of cognitive dissonance. The significance of these findings ranges beyond the study of politics: 'Everyone from executives and judges to scientists and politicians may reason to emotionally biased judgments when they have a vested interest in how to interpret "the facts." [97]

The history of Judaism and Christianity has been an unquestioned premise upon which much that exists in our world today is founded. The very condition of our planet at the moment is based upon this Judeo-Christian history. In fact, when we observe the 'fruits' of these religions, we begin to see that our very lives may depend upon finding out what really did happen, to the best of our ability.

Jews, Christians and Moslems have a certain notion of the past that is conveyed to them in hagiography, Bible stories and the Koran, as well as in chronologies and historical accounts that are closely tied to the alleged history of the Bible. We tend to accept all of these as 'truth' – as chronological histories along with what else we know about history – and we often reject out-of-hand the idea that these may all be legends and myths that are meta-historical – special ways of speaking about events in a manner that rises above history; or just outright propaganda designed to gain control over masses of people.

If that is the case, then the chronologies – the way that we arrange dates and the antecedents that we assume for events – should be of some considerable concern to everyone. If we can come to some reasonable idea of the *real* events – the 'facts', the data that make up our view of the world in which we live and our own place within it – then perhaps such facts about our history can explain why our theologies and values tell us not what we believe, but *why* we believe what we do, and whether or not we ought really to discard those beliefs as 'historical'.

One could say, of course, that all history is a lie. Whenever we recount events or stories about people and times that are not immediately present to us, we are simply creating a *probable* picture of the past or a 'distant happening'. For most people, the horror and suffering of the Palestinians or the starving masses in India and Africa at the present moment in 'time' have no spatial meaning because it is 'over there'. It is quite easy for false images of such events to be created and maintained as 'history' by those who are not directly experiencing the events, particularly if they are not told the truth about them by those who *do* know. And so it has been throughout history.

It is true that 'the victors write the history', and it is also true that the peo-

---

97. Cited by Barbara Oakley in *Evil Genes* (2008). Study found here: http://www.uky.edu/ AS/PoliSci/Peffley/pdf/Westen%20The%20neural%20basis%20of%20motivated%20rea- soning.pdf

ple accept the new norm exactly as described above. In other words, the lie is more acceptable to the masses because it generally produces what they would *like* to believe rather than what is actually true because believing what you are told to believe, what the constituted authority wants you to believe, is safer and easier and allows your brain to have some ease.

The fact is, manipulation of the mass consciousness is 'standard operating procedure' for those in power. Nothing has changed since ancient times except that the methods and abilities to manipulate the minds of the masses with 'signs and wonders' has become high tech and global, while before the manipulators relied on natural signs and wonders and simply took advantage of them. There is a reason that we do not know our true history, and the truth is, we don't even have to look for extraordinary, evil forces to explain it; call it the Cosmic Murphy's law, if you like. But the implications of the normalizing bias in our world today, coupled with the downplaying of cosmic dangers that we are about to discuss, should be of some concern to us. Perhaps, in a sense, it is an evolutionary mechanism: only those who can correctly read the signs and act appropriately, when and if such action is called for, will survive. And obviously, those who normalize egregious political corruption – the Authoritarian types – have very little chance of stepping outside of the Normalcy bias.

CHAPTER THREE

COMET SWARMS
AND PLASMA COSMOLOGY

I have already briefly referred to the theory that cyclical, cosmic catastrophes have played a major role in the shaping of the history of our planet and its civilizations. Now it is time to explore the hard evidence for that idea.

Coincidentally enough, it was around the time when comet Shoemaker-Levy spectacularly collided with Jupiter in 1994 that the idea of companion stars sending swarms of comets into our solar system and periodically bombarding our planet came to the fore for me. So there I was, revisiting Velikovsky after something like 10 years, but with a lot more scientific data piling up, some of which confirmed *some* of his ideas and some which refuted conclusions he had drawn. That led to more research which revealed that this happens a lot more regularly than the known *mass* extinction cycle would indicate.[98]

Exodus to Arthur

First there was the work of dendrochronologist[99]/paleoecologist[100], Mike Baillie (now retired) of Queens University, Belfast, Ireland. Examining tree rings, Baillie found climate stress periods in 2354 BCE, 1628 BCE, 1159 BCE, 208 BCE, and CE 540. The evidence suggested that these were probably global events to one extent or the other. The CE 540 event coincides

---

98. This idea takes Velikovsky's theory of a cometary Venus a bit further and has considerable scientific support, based on the work of Bailey, Clube, Napier and others as we will see.

99. Dendrochronology is a scientific method of dating based on the analysis of tree rings. Every year trees form one extra ring. Its size is strongly correlated to the weather that occurred during the year.

100. Paleoecology aims to reconstruct the ecosystems of the past. Dendrochronology is particularly useful in this respect since it allows us to reconstruct weather of the past, a strong determinant of fauna and flora.

with the *second*-largest ammonium signal in the Greenland ice in the past two millennia, the *largest* signal showing in 1014 CE. Baillie explains the lack of historical references being due to the fact that the peoples of the time described what they saw in Biblical terms. Indeed, there were artistic representations of astonishing atmospheric events, but it was almost always explained as being a metaphor for a Biblical concept![101] There was also the problem that the Aristotelian view of the 'perfect heavens' held sway, and even if events were witnessed and reported, they were explained away or ignored in historical accounts, as we will see shortly.

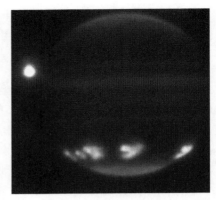

Fragments of Comet Shoemaker-Levy impacting Jupiter. (Near-infrared camera, University of Hawaii telescope).

Like Velikovsky, though with a pile of scientific data to hand, Dr. Baillie began to search through historical records and myth. He found that the environmental downturns *coincided with the collapse of civilizations*, such as the Roman Empire and the beginning of the Dark Ages in Europe. He wrote *Exodus to Arthur: Catastrophic Encounters with Comets*[102], which relates his tree-ring/ice-core data to a series of global traumas over the past 4,400 years, events that may relate to the biblical Exodus and dark ages in Egypt, China and Europe.

One of the more interesting things that Baillie writes in *Exodus to Arthur* is about his troubles getting evidence from ice-cores. I'm going to quote the passage more or less in full because this issue will be important further on when we come to deal with the records of the witnesses of the past.

> ... though the Irish trees did show a narrow ring in CE 536, the really narrow event – the *narrowest* rings – occurred in 540-541. Why was there a delay in the onset of the really extreme conditions? Questions like these raised the possibility of multiple eruptions: that is, was there one dust-veil in 536 and another a few years later? But the strangeness of the event was heightened con-

---

101. Not to mention the interpretations of these events as UFOs, which is not to exclude them, but to leave the identification open to where the evidence may ultimately lead.
102. Batsford (1999).

siderably when it was found that the date of the Greenland acidity layer in the Dye 3 core, which was given as 540+/-10 in 1980, had been changed to 516+/-4 by Claus Hammer in 1984. From the historical records, it was clear that there was a major dry-fog event in CE 536, with tree-ring effects afterwards; this movement of the ice acidity layer to CE 516 cast serious doubt on the ice-core chronology in the sixth century CE. In the wider ice-core record around this critical time, the original Crête core stopped at CE 553+/-3 and the Camp Century core turned out to be unusable down to the first century CE. This means that, until recently, the ice-core information for the sixth century CE relied solely on the Dye 3 core. Moving the 540+/-10 acid layer by 24 years meant that there was no good evidence for a layer of volcanic acide at CE 540; but surely there must have been a volcano at 540, the tree-rings events are volcanic, are they not?

With this situation in mind, the results of the early 1990s GISP2 (American) and GRIP (Danish) cores from Summit, Greenland, were awaited with interest. Unfortunately, preliminary results from the GISP2 core indicated no significantly enhanced acidity in the annual layers attributed to the years around CE 536-540. Then in 1983 something happened which served to colour my judgement still further on the nature of the CE 540 phenomenon. In the summer of 1983 I called on Greg Zielinski at the University of New Hampshire. Greg was heavily involved in the analysis of the GISP2 core and showed me many of the available results which were astounding, to say the least. As noted earlier, individual annual layers could be resolved back to beyond 40,000 years. While there I gave a talk for the postgraduate students on the tree-ring/volcano story, ending up with the CE 540 event as outlined so far. In particular I discussed why the ice-core evidence was critical to establish if more than one volcano was involved. After the talk one of the postgraduates called up the analysis data for the sixth century CE on his computer; another student, Greg and myself were also in the room. 'That's funny, we have 14 metres of missing record,' said the postgrad. 'No, we do not,' said Greg. 'Yes we do,' said the postgrad. 'There are no analyses between CE 614 and 545.'

Having just given a talk stressing why the sixth century was interesting and how the ice-core evidence was critical to understanding what had actually happened around CE 540, I was witnessing the revelation that most of the record of the sixth century was missing; 14 m (46 feet) of core equal to about seventy annual layers. Moreover, it was apparent that the extent of the missing core had not been fully appreciated even by the ice-core workers themselves. The GISP2 core is a full 3 km (2 miles) in length, made up of 1500 consecutive 2-metre (6.5 ft) lengths and the only significant bit that was lost was in the sixth century CE – 14 metres, just where the tree-rings indicated something interesting. As I was pondering this, the other student spoke up: 'Oh yes, I remember that, I was up on the ice at that time...

Elvis was up on the ice, all sorts of stuff was going down, the core was trashed, motors [the drill is a self-contained, motor-driven, 2-metre coring unit dropped on a hawser] were burning out ... there was carbon in the drill hole...'

There are times when real life out-does science fiction. It could be that just by ill luck the American team had run into problems at that point in the coring. It could be that the carbon had come from the burnt-out motor in the drill rig and that Elvis was indeed up on the ice-cap at that time. If it was not just coincidental ill luck then something might have affected the ice in the sixth century CE and the carbon in the drill hole might not be from the motor; what then? Greg and the students kindly checked the daily logs which confirmed that each of seven consecutive two-metre sections had come up 'trashed', that is, as shattered ice. The longest stretch of lost ice in more than 3000 metres (9842 ft) had indeed been lost in the sixth century CE. This missing 14-metre section ... introduces a slight imponderable into the dating of the core below the missing section and it is not beyond the bounds of possibility that the existing GISP2 core does not cover the CE 536-545 period at all.

The coincidence of 'problems' with no less than three ice-core records in the sixth century – Crête stops at CE 553+/−5; Dye 3 has the CE 540 to 516 'redating' and GISP2 has a 'lost' section – is hard to swallow. There simply must be something going on, especially as the significance of the period had been stressed in advance. I had even been to a conference in Hawaii in 1992 to tell the vulcanologists and ice-core workers of the possibilities of multiple eruptions around CE 540 and to ask that special attention be paid to this period. (Incidentally, I discount another possibility, which is that the CIA have been systematically trashing the cores around CE 540 to cover up the existence of debris from a crashed UFO.)

However, fortunately, a fallback situation exists. The Danish GRIP core (also 3 km (2 miles) long and from a site just 30 km (19 miles) from the GISP2 location) may provide the answers when the results of its detailed analysis become available. The Danes appear not to have lost any of their core, so a continuous record across the sixth century does exist. So far only an electrical conductivity survey (used to pick up strong acid, that is, volcanic signals) has been carried out on this section, but, interestingly, they see no large acid signal across the CE 536-545 period. It looks increasingly as if a volcano (still less volcanoes) was not the cause of the CE 540 environmental event. This raises a lot of questions, and Härke has picked up on this issue in the context of those anomalous eclipse records in the *Anglo-Saxon Chronicle* in CE 538 and 540. He posits that:

> ... the entire northern hemisphere was affected in the late 530s by a sudden climatic deterioration caused either by a major volcanic eruption (Baillie's suggestion) or by dust-veils from a cometary impact (Victor Clube's suggestion).

If the ice-core evidence is correct and there is no significant acidity layer in the Greenland ice around CE 540 then Clube's sug-

Nucleus and trail of Comet 2P/Encke.
(Spitzer space telescope.)

gestions will have to be taken seriously, and we would have to decide how one might separate ancient descriptions of the effects of volcanoes from those of cometary impacts. Bailey, Clube and Napier have already suggested that in their view the Earth was at increased risk of bombardment in the interval CE 400-600.

There can be no doubt that some momentous happening took place in the early-to mid-sixth century CE... the sixth century is as yesterday in geological time; something which could happen then could happen now.[103]

So, keep the above 'lost ice-cores' in mind, but mainly this: "something might have affected the ice in the 6th century CE and the carbon in the drill hole might not be from the motor."

A later book by Baillie, *The Celtic Gods: Comets in Irish Mythology*[104] focused on the CE 540 event which was recorded in the historical records and myths of Ireland. Baillie argues that the mythical imagery and the *periodicity* of the events are consistent with an earth-crossing comet that has fragmented such as 2P/Enke, as described by astronomers Victor Clube and Bill Napier (who we will get to shortly). Baillie's latest book, *New Light on the Black Death: The Cosmic Connection*[105], marshals the considerable evidence that the Black Death (1346-1350) was due to a series of comet related disasters.

---

103. Baillie (1999), pp. 86-88.
104. Baillie & McCafferty (2005).
105. Baillie (2006).

The Cycle of Cosmic Catastrophes

Next, along came the work of physicist, Richard Firestone[106] and geologists, Alan West and Simon Warwick-Smith, presented in a series of academic papers and a book for the general public: *The Cycle of Cosmic Catastrophes: How a Stone Age Comet Changed the Course of World Culture.*[107] They dealt with the – until then – inexplicable mass extinctions of mega-fauna that occurred simultaneously with the onset of the Younger Dryas mini-Ice Age (c. 13,000 years ago). I've covered this event in *Secret History of the World* but certainly not as well as Firestone and Co have done. Based on physical evidence, their theory was that a supernova 41,000 years ago was the cause of a mass extinction 28,000 years ago, and then again 13,000 years ago[108], the dates being based on the theorized timing of arrival of various waves of the supernova effects. The most damaging effects were, of course, the arrival of physical debris. As Firestone et al. point out, more species of large North American land mammals died out at the end of the last Ice Age than had gone extinct in the whole of the previous 3.5 million years! Some of the so-called experts advocate the 'over-hunting' theory, which is patently ridiculous since the extinctions occurred at nearly the same time across the whole Northern Hemisphere and parts of South America. These latter say that the extinctions 'finished' 12,900 years ago but Firestone and Co point out reasonably that this means that they could all have occurred at that time, simultaneously.

The dynamic description of what might happen, how it would appear to someone experiencing it, is not the usual way scientists write, but it is highly instructive. The scenario of exploding comets in the sky proceeds through several stages (as seen through the eyes of a Clovis-era tribe[109]) until they arrive at a solution to a problem that's been bugging me for years: how were mammoths flash-frozen in Siberia? Well, here's the explanation:

---

106. I had been following the work of Firestone after citing his paper about the re-setting of the atomic dating clocks he found evidence for all over North America, related to some kind of catastrophe. This is discussed at length in my book, *Secret History*.
107. Firestone, West & Warwick-Smith (2006).
108. I repeatedly referenced this event in *Secret History*, however Firestone et al's book had not then been published, so it was a great relief to know that I wasn't the only person asking questions about this period.
109. The Clovis culture is a prehistoric Paleo-Indian culture, named after stone tools that were found at sites near Clovis, New Mexico, in the 1920s and 1930s. The Clovis culture appears around 11,500 BCE at the end of the last glacial period, characterized by the manufacture of 'Clovis points' and distinctive bone and ivory tools. Archaeologists' most precise determinations at present suggest that this radiocarbon age is equal to roughly 13,500 to 13,000 calendar years ago.

... [A]n array of glowing blue-white comets stretched from horizon to horizon. Growing larger every second, they streaked into the atmosphere, each one lighting up brighter than the sun. One dustball comet was more than 300 miles wide; others were nearly as big. Shimmering fiercely, the largest fireball was too brilliant to watch. ...

Siberian baby mammoth frozen 10,000 years ago.

Heated to immense temperatures by its passage through the atmosphere, the lethal swarm exploded into thousands of mountain-sized chunks and clouds of streaming icey dust. The smaller pieces blew up high in the atmosphere, creating multiple detonations that turned the sky orange and red... the largest comet crashed into the ice sheet, instantly blasting a gigantic hole through the ice into Hudson Bay. Within moments, other comets exploded over Lake Michigan, northern Canada, Siberia, and Europe, as every northern continent took direct hits. ...

When the ground shock waves from the impacts arrived, the earth shook violently for a full ten minutes in great rolling waves and shudders. ... trees shook and swayed violently before toppling over. Short, narrow fissures opened and snaked across the rocky field...

Within seconds after the impact, the blast of superheated air expanded outward at more than 1,000 miles per hour, racing across the landscape, tearing trees from the ground and tossing them into the air, ripping rocks from mountainsides, and flash-scorching plants, animals, and the earth. ...

Across upper parts of North America and Europe, the immense energy from the multiple impacts blew a series of ever-widening giant overlapping bubbles that pushed aside the atmosphere to create a near vacuum inside...

Before long, the outward push of the shock wave slowed and stopped, and then the vaccum began to draw the air backward. As the expanded atmosphere rushed back toward the impact site, the bubbles collapsed sucking white-hot gases and dust inward at tornado speeds and then channeling them up and away from the ground.

Climbing high above the atmosphere, some of the rising debirs excaped Earth's gravity to shoot far out into space...

Some of the dust and debris lifted by the powerful updraft was too heavy for the atmosphere and began drifting and crashing back to earth. ...

The raging updraft through the hollow bubbles created an equally powerful downdraft of frigid high-altitude air, traveling at hundreds of miles per hour. With temperatures exceeding 150 degrees F below zero [110], the downward stream of air hit the ground and radiated out from the blast site in all directions, flash-freezing within seconds everything it touched. Some of the animals that had survived the initial fiery shock wave froze where they stood… and it was not over yet.[111]

Indeed, it was not over yet and the detailed description of the event continues, but you will have to read it yourself to learn about the effects on Earth's magnetic field, the massive number of atmospheric explosions that produced the Carolina Bays [112], the undersea landslides and tsunamis, the ice-sheet melt-water floods, the changing of the Gulf Stream

Geographic distribution of the Carolina Bays.

within days, massive rains followed by blizzards and a return to ice-age conditions. It's a veritable potpourri of catastrophes; enough to explain the many observations recorded by the ancients in myth and legend, depending on where they were and what effects impacted a given location.

In any event, as I mentioned, it was due to Firestone and Co that I became aware of the work of Bailey, Clube and Napier.

In 1990, Victor Clube, an astrophysicist, and Bill Napier, an astronomer, published *The Cosmic Winter*, a book in which they describe performing orbital analyses of several of the meteor showers that hit Earth every year. Using sophisticated computer software, they carefully looked backward for thousands of years, tracing the orbits of comets, asteroids, and meteor showers until they uncovered something astounding. Many meteor showers are related to one another, such as the Taurids, Perseids, Piscids, and Orionids. In addition, some very large cosmic objects are related: the comets Encke and Rudnicki, the asteroids Oljato, Hephaistos, and about 100 others. Every one of those 100-plus cosmic bodies is at least a half-mile in diameter and some are miles wide.

---

110. 101 degrees Celsius below zero.
111. Firestone et al. (2006), pp. 136-140, excerpts.
112. The Carolina Bays are a series of craters mostly located along the East coast of the USA. Estimates of the total number of craters range from 500,000 to 2.5 million.

And what do they have in common? According to those scientists, *every one is the offspring of the same massive comet that first entered our system less than 20,000 years ago*! Clube and Napier calculated that, to account for all the debris they found strewn throughout our solar system, the original comet had to have been enormous. ...

Clube and Napier also calculated that, because of subtle changes in the orbits of Earth and the remaining cosmic debris, *Earth crosses through the densest part of the giant comet clouds about every 2,000 to 4,000 years*. When we look at climate and ice-core records, we can see that pattern. For example, the iridium, helium-3, nitrate, ammonium, and other key measurements seem to rise and fall in tandem, producing noticeable peaks around 18,000, 16,000, 13,000, 9,000, 5,000, and 2,000 years ago. In that pattern of peaks every 2,000 to 4,000 years, we may be seeing the "calling cards" of the returning mega-comet.

Fortunately, the oldest peaks were the heaviest bombardments, and things have been getting quieter since then, as the remains of the comet break up into even smaller pieces. The danger is not past, however. Some of the *remaining miles-wide pieces* are big enough to do serious damage to our cities, climate, and global economy. Clube and Napier (1984) predicted that, in the year 2000 and continuing for 400 years, Earth would enter another dangerous time in which the planet's changing orbit would bring us into a potential collision course with the densest parts of the clouds containing some very large debris. Twenty years after their prediction, we have just now moved into the danger zone. It is a widely accepted fact that *some of those large objects are in Earth-crossing orbits at this very moment*, and the only uncertainty is whether they will miss us, as is most likely, or whether they will crash into some part of our planet. [Emphasis, mine] [113]

According to Bailey, Clube and Napier, et al., in the same way that Jupiter was struck repeatedly in 1994 by the million-megaton impacts of the comet Shoemaker-Levy, so Earth was bombarded 13,000 years ago by the fragments of a giant comet that broke up in the sky before the terrified eyes of humanity. The multiple impacts on the rotating planet caused tidal waves, raging fires, atomic bomb-like blasts, the mass extinction of many prehistoric species such as the mammoth and sabre-toothed tiger, most of humanity, and left the world in darkness for months if not years, pretty much as Firestone et al. describe so graphically. It was this event that left the hundreds of thousands of Carolina Bays, the millions of dead creatures – most of them megafauna –

---

113. Firestone et al. (2006), pp. 354-355.

piled up in jumbled masses around the globe, and would also have wiped the Earth almost clean of any existing human civilization. What Bailey, Clube and Napier propose, in addition to the scenario proposed by Firestone et al., is that our planet has been struck numerous times since then (and maybe even before that major event), and it isn't over.[114]

This 'new' type of natural disaster is beginning to be regarded by many scholars as the most probable single explanation for widespread and simultaneous cultural collapses at various times in our history. These ideas have been advanced largely by practitioners of hard science – astronomers and geologists, dendrochronologists, etc. – and remain almost completely unknown (or completely misunderstood) among practitioners of the soft sciences: archaeologists and historians. This fact significantly hampers the efforts of practitioners of the soft sciences to explain what they may be seeing in the historical record.

The new theory posits trains of cometary debris which the Earth repeatedly encounters at fairly regular intervals. We know most of these trains as meteor showers – tiny particles of cosmic material whose impact is insignificant. Occasionally, however, in these trains of debris, there are chunks measuring between one and several hundred meters in diameter. When these either strike the Earth or explode in the atmosphere, there can be catastrophic effects on our ecological system. Multi-megaton explosions of fireballs can destroy natural and man-made features on the surface of the Earth by means of tidal-wave floods (if the debris lands in the sea), fire blasts and seismic damage, leaving no crater as a trace, just scorched and blasted Earth. In the case of a significant bombardment, an entire small country could be wiped out, completely vaporized; or worse.

A recent example, known as the Tunguska Event, occurred over Siberia in 1908 when a bolide exploded about 5 km above ground and completely devastated an area of some 2,000 km² through fireball blasts. While it is still a matter of controversy among researchers, this cosmic body is thought to have measured some 60 m across (some say 190 m across) and had the impact energy of about 20 to 40 megatons (some say 3-5 megatons), equivalent to the explosion of about 2,000 (or at least several hundred) Hiroshima-size nuclear bombs, even though *there was no actual physical impact on the Earth*. In other words, if there were ancient, advanced civilizations destroyed by multiple Tunguska-like events (remember the hundreds of thousands of Carolina Bays?), it would be no wonder there is no trace, or very little, and

---

114. See: *The Cosmic Serpent* and *The Cosmic Winter* by Clube and Napier. See also: *The Origin of the Universe and the Origin of Religion*, by Fred Hoyle.

what evidence does exist, such as the bays, are usually ascribed to 'anomaly' or ignored altogether.

For years, the astronomical mainstream was highly critical of Bailey, Clube and Napier and their giant comet hypothesis. However, the impacts of comet Shoemaker-Levy 9 on Jupiter in 1994 led to a rather rapid turnaround in attitude, at least among the non-Authoritarian types. The comet, watched by the world's observatories, was seen to split into 20 pieces and slam into different parts of the planet over a period of several days.

The Tunguska overhead explosion knocked down an estimated 80 million trees over an area covering more than 2,000 km².

A similar event vis-à-vis our planet would have been devastating, to understate the matter. In recent times, the increasing numbers of fireballs and comets, the fact that Jupiter has been impacted yet again and again recently, suggests to us that Bailey, Clube and Napier are correct: we are in a very dangerous period.

Though there has been a lot of resistance to the idea (probably mostly by the Authoritarin follower-type scientists), just recently the *Proceedings of the National Academy of Science* published a study by an international team of scientists who now have reached general agreement that a meteorite or comet fragment storm hit the Earth more than 12,000 years ago and is likely to have been responsible for the extinction of megafauna and many prehistoric people that occurred at that time. It is also now being said that evidence for the extreme heat produced by the equivalent of thousands of overhead nuclear explosions has been found on two continents.[115] Thanks to authoritarian personalities seeking to please wealthy elite authorities, science changes its mind very, very slowly and the truly gifted and original researchers are either worn out from being attacked and defending themselves, or dead, by the time the consensus changes. This is very bad for science and very bad for humanity.

Bailey, Clube and Napier identified the progenitor of the Taurid complex as a giant comet that was thrown into a short-period (about 3.3 year) orbit, some time in the last twenty to thirty thousand years. The Taurid complex currently includes the Taurid meteor stream, comet Encke, 'asteroids' such

---

115. See: http://www.sott.net/articles/show/246657-Meteorite-storm-smashed-the-Earth-12-000-years-ago-and-killed-off-a-prehistoric-people-

as 2101 Adonis and 2201 Oljato, and enormous amounts of space dust sorted along the orbit in clumps that may include rather larger bodies. Asteroids in the Taurid complex appear to have associated meteor showers, which means that many asteroids are likely to be extinct comets. In other words, there can be more than just some dust and snow in a comet – there can be a significant rocky core and lots of poisonous gasses and chemicals as well. But, of course, having a 3.3 year orbit does not necessarily mean that every 3.3 years there will be disasters; there is rather more involved in bringing the Earth into the right position when the Earth-crossing bodies are present.

This view of the solar system gave me a whole different view of the ancient myths that I had been trying to sort out as historical actions of human beings that had been mythicized by the Greeks and then re-humanized by the Hebrews. You could say that it gave the 'Horns of Moses' a whole new face!

In *Secret History*, I proposed (and assembled evidence for the idea) that what was seen and reported by the Egyptians as 'Sothis' was not Sirius[116], but rather a cluster of comets. Since that volume was published, I've covered a lot more hard research ground and found that there is more than a little support for that idea, though I would now change it to a giant comet with satellite bodies formed from the natural breaking-up process that comets undergo, which is what Clube and Napier propose. In any event, Sothis is not Sirius, nor are the sightings of it, noted less than a handful of times in Egyptian records, in any way related to observations of 'the precession of the equinoxes'.[117]

Clube and Napier write:

> The ancient religions of prehistoric man were unmistakable polytheistic and astronomical in character. This raises questions concerning the basic nature of the gods that were worshipped. If comets were included among the principal deities, their erratic motion and changing appearance could well have inspired a ready acceptance of the fickle character of ancient gods. ... many Greek and Roman philosophers were, amongst other things, greatly concerned to explain comets in materialistic terms and rid them of any supernatural qualities. Inasmuch as the heads and tails of comets appeared often to take on a human form or that of animals, the aim seems to have been to

---

116. Sirius is the brightest star in the sky and it can be seen from almost every inhabited region in the world. Therefore, it has played a major role in calendars, astronomy, navigation, etc.

117. For a far more rational explanation of precession, see Walter Cruttenden's book *Lost Star of Myth and Time*, though take his conclusions about Sirius with some salt.

prove that these were illusions created by perfectly natural causes. ... In practice, however, belief in the gods was so entrenched that the arguments seem merely to have served to convince that the gods were invisible [in the sky]... the rise of materialism in classical times came with the passing away of some very important prehistoric gods which were comets in the sky. Many of the legends of mythology can thus be interpreted as highly embellished accounts of the evolution of one, or perhaps a few, very large comets during the last 2,000 years of prehistory.[118]

Giant Molecular Clouds

According to Bailey, Clube and Napier, in an ideal, unchanging cosmos, a planet orbiting a single sun would continue in an unchanging elliptical orbit forever. Indeed, planets disturb each other and these disturbances accumulate over long periods of time, but in that sense, the stability of the solar system is assured because those deviations are small. This is a good thing because the tolerances for life seem to be small, and if the Earth were 5% closer to the Sun, it would generate an unstoppable heating of the Earth, leading to boiling oceans; while a 10% movement away from the Sun would freeze our planet solid.

However, there are dark clouds of gas in our galaxy which actually constitute the most massive single bodies of the Milky Way. The typical giant molecular cloud is about 100 light years across and frequently contains dense concentrations of young stars and enormous numbers of newly formed comets. A few thousand of these monsters orbit the flat plane of our galaxy. Clube and Napier propose that our solar system has probably penetrated ten or twenty of these dangerous areas of space during its existence. During such passages through or near a molecular cloud, the outer shell of comets that travel with Sol and its planets, the Oort Cloud and the Kuiper belt, is subjected to extraordinary forces that can both strip away matter from comets, as well as send them careening into the solar system with devastating consequences. In other words, there are cosmic processes that are very, very dangerous to our planet.

At the same time that irregular danger is posed by galactic molecular clouds, there are more regular and periodic movements that can create similar stresses: the movement of the solar system in and out of spiral arms and up and down through the galactic plane. These motions are behind what is called the galactic tide, which ebbs and flows periodically. Periods of high

---

118. Clube and Napier (1982), p. 157.

or low stress on the cloud of comets surrounding our solar system lead to periods of high or low comet flux into the planetary system. The bottom line is, according to Clube and Napier, there are two main sources of disturbance, one erratic and the other periodic; the solar system's current position in relation to the galaxy is very relevant to whether or not we face cosmic hazards.

Most comets are only a few kilometers in diameter. Big ones are rarer in direct relation to size. However, giant comets can dominate an entire comet system. In a random sample of comets, half the total mass would be contained in the largest one or two. Clube and Napier point out that, in considering the mechanism of comets entering our solar system, it must be understood that the likelihood is higher that what comes in will be massive due to the fact that the more massive bodies are more susceptible to the influences of the tidal and gravitation forces.

Clube and Napier do not discuss a companion star, a brown or red dwarf, as is proposed in the Nemesis Hypothesis.[119] That has long been my favorite idea to explain the confirmed periodicity of extinction events but I'm perfectly willing to give it up if the evidence shows otherwise. In fact, for the moment, it is just an idea without proof, though there is some evidence to support it. The same evidence may actually point to a different mechanism.[120] An important thing to remember is that the same conditions that Clube and Napier describe would probably prevail whether the comet(s) knocked into our solar system were hurled by a molecular cloud, tidal forces of the galaxy, or a solar companion. So, whatever the risk period is, or the cause, the bottom line is that the astronomical surveys show that the Earth

---

119. Astronomers, Daniel P. Whitmire and Albert A. Jackson IV, and Marc Davis, Piet Hut, and Richard A. Muller, independently published similar hypotheses to explain Raup and Sepkoski's extinction periodicity. This hypothesis proposes that the Sun may have an undetected companion star in a highly elliptical orbit that periodically disturbs comets in the Oort cloud, causing a large increase of the number of comets visiting the inner Solar System with a consequential increase of impact events on Earth. This became known as the 'Nemesis' or 'Death Star' hypothesis. Muller suggests that the most likely object is a red dwarf while Daniel P. Whitmire and Albert A. Jackson argue for a brown dwarf. If a red dwarf, it would already exist in star catalogs, but it would only be confirmed by measuring its parallax; due to orbiting the Sun it would have a low proper motion and would escape detection by older proper motion surveys that have found stars like the 9th-magnitude Barnard's star. Muller expects Nemesis to be discovered by the time parallax surveys reach the 10th magnitude.

120. Melott & Bambach (2010), 'Nemesis Reconsidered'. In 2010, Melott & Bambach found strong evidence in the fossil record confirming the extinction event periodicity originally claimed by Raup & Sepkoski in 1984 (27 million years), but at a higher confidence level and over a time period nearly twice as long.

periodically encounters the debris spread in the inner solar system by a disintegrating giant comet.

An important thing to know about comets is that they do break up into pieces. Each fragment then leads an independent life until it, too, begins to split and disintegrate. Aside from reports of the ancient observers, there have been more recently observed disintegrations, such as that of Comet Biela and the famous Shoemaker-Levy 9. Then,

Fragments of the comet Schwassman-Wachmann. (Spitzer space telescope, 2006.)

there was Comet Schwassmann-Wachmann and the much more recent Comet Elenin which, it is said, can now be visually compared to Shoemaker-Levy.

In 1846, when Comet Biela split, under the very eyes of observers, into two parts, the companion was initially faint, but as the distance between them grew, it increased in brightness. The two comets were seen to be a million and a half miles apart on their return in 1852, but when they were due back, both appear to have vanished. They have not been seen since.[121]

On 27 November 1872, the Earth passed through a massive swarm of meteors with "shower after shower with blinding balls of light and noiseless explosions looking like cascades of fireworks."[122] It was estimated that over 160,000 'shooting stars' entered the Earth's atmosphere in a 6-hour period. This was the Andromedid shower[123], which is still encountered in the present time, though greatly reduced due to the meteors having been spread around its orbit as such things do.

But, lest you think that comets just split and turn to dust, think again! It now appears that there are comets that look like asteroids, plus there are so-called asteroids in comet-like orbits. It is as though these types of bodies have lost their gasses. The Plasma Theory of the Universe would say that comets

121. Comet Biela was a periodic Jupiter-family comet first recorded in 1772 by Montaigne and Messier and finally identified as periodic in 1826 by Wilhelm von Biela. It was subsequently observed to split in two and has not been seen since 1852. As a result it is currently considered to have been destroyed, although remnants appeared to have survived for some time as a meteor shower.
122. Clube & Napier (1990), p 138.
123. The Andromedids were formerly called the Bielids, after Biela's Comet disintegration which left a large cloud of cometary debris that the orbit of the Earth crosses every November.

are electrically charged bodies and those that turn into asteroids have simply been discharged to the point where their charge is not high enough for them to glow.

The topic of Plasma Cosmology is going to be important, so let's go ahead and look at it now and then come back to comets according to Bailey, Clube and Napier.

Plasma Cosmology

Plasmas are the most common phase of matter in the universe, both in terms of mass and volume. All the stars are made of plasma [124], and even interstellar space is filled with plasma.

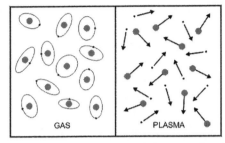

During ionization an energy input expels an electron from an existing atom. It results in one free electron and one positively charged ion.

This is widely acknowledged by astronomers and physicists. However, when anyone attempts to go further than that, the Authoritarians come out in force and invoke the god Einstein. So, let's take care of Einstein first.

Digression: How Einstein Ruined Physics

Roger Schlafly, Ph.D. (mathematics) has recently published a book entitled *How Einstein Ruined Physics*. According to Schlafly, most of Einstein's work was mistaken and has driven physics into areas that are totally without scientific foundation. Furthermore, Einstein was a plagiarist and publicity hound. He writes:

> Einstein's 1905 paper is the most overrated paper ever written. No other paper has been so thoroughly praised, and yet be so dishonestly unoriginal. [125]

The problem of Einstein has a larger context: the Einstein cult that has controlled physics for the past century, leading to "wasteful, un-falsifiable top-down theorizing" that leads nowhere.

---

124. Plasma is a gas where a specific portion of the particles have been ionized. An ionized particle has lost one or more electrons. So while a 'normal' gas is made of non-ionized particles, a plasma is made of dissociated positive particles and electrons.
125. Schlafly (2011), *How Einstein Ruined Physics*.

Einstein is the new Aristotle. Physicists love to ridicule Aristotle for his non-quantitative theory of physics, for his thought experiments, for his unsubstantiated realism, and for his (supposed) attempts to explain the world according to how he thought the world ought to be, instead of how it is. Most of all, they ridicule Aristotle followers for idolizing the master, and for blindly following what he had to say.

Aristotle was a great genius. [Aristotle's] reasoning was influential for well over a millennium. But Einstein's fame is based on the work of others, and his legacy is the pursuit of unscientific dreams. Now he is idolized more than Aristotle ever was, and his followers have created a subject more sterile than millennium-old Aristotelian physics.

Medieval monks are mocked for debating how many angels can dance on the head of a pin. They didn't really do that, but modern theoretical physicists write papers on topics nearly as silly. They write papers on alternate universes, black hole information loss, extra dimensions, and Boltzmann brains. Most of them are preoccupied with string theory, which has no connection to the real world. And they all say they are pursuing Einstein's dreams. [...]

$E = mc^2$ is not even needed for the atomic bomb. [It] does not give any clue on how to split an atom, or how to create a nuclear chain reaction, or any of the other necessary steps to making an atom bomb. Relativity is not even needed to understand the energy release in a uranium or plutonium bomb, as the release can largely be explained from electromagnetic considerations. ... Predictions about relativistic mass were being tested [by German physicist Walter Kaufmann] in 1901, before Einstein wrote anything about it.[126]

You could say that Einstein was to physics what Freud was to psychology, a purveyor of a top-down theoretical scheme that actually rejects the observation-hypothesis-experiment model of true science. Most modern psychologists today with access to laboratories and experimental data consider Freud to be little more than a perverted snake-oil salesman. Schlafly's comparison of Einstein to Aristotle in the excerpt above is very interesting, as we shall soon see when we deal with the Greek philosophers and their influence on, and contribution to, the 'official' historical record.

In any event, Schlafly knows his stuff and marshalls a pile of evidence to prove his points and, since I am married to a mathematical physicist who – along with many of his colleagues – has long considered Einstein to be a fraud for exactly the same reasons, I think we can go with Schlafly's views and dismiss anyone who claims that something cannot be true because it contradicts

---

126. Schlafly (2011), op. cit.

Einstein as an Authoritarian Follower who has drunk the snake oil.

Now, back to Plasma Cosmology. The central idea is that the dynamics of ionized gases (or plasmas) play the main role in the physics of the universe at the scale of planets, solar systems, galaxies and further. Many of the ideas of plasma cosmology came from 1970 Nobel laureate Hannes Alfvén. Alfvén proposed the use of plasma scaling [127] to extrapolate

Hannes Alfvén receiving the 1970 Nobel prize in physics.

the results of laboratory experiments and space plasma physics observations to scales orders-of-magnitude greater. The Einstein cultists certainly acknowledge that plasma physics plays a major role in many, if not most (they will admit), astrophysical phenomena, but they protest that many of the conclusions of plasma physics experiments performed in laboratories just *can't* be the explanation for the heavenly phenomena because they would 'contradict Einstein'! For mainstream science, gravity is the main force controlling celestial bodies behavior, despite the fact that electromagnetic forces are stronger than gravitational forces by a magnitude of 10^{39},[128] making electromagnetism the de facto driving force in our universe. Some plasma physicists even hypothesize that gravity is a by-product of electromagnetism [129]:

> The electrical model does not assume that a given quantity of matter will produce a given gravitational perturbation (i.e., "mass"). It sees gravity itself as an induced subatomic dipolar electric force, and when electric conditions change, mass changes with no change in the quantity of matter.[130]

Alfvén wrote a paper in 1939 supporting the theory of Kristian Birkeland, who had written in 1913 that what is now called the Solar wind generated currents in space that caused the aurora. Birkeland's theory was disputed at the time and Alfvén's work in turn was disputed for many years by the

---

127. Plasmas vary greatly in size from laboratory scale to the galactic one. However, there are strong similarities between plasmas of different magnitude. Similarity transformations allow us to apply laboratory observations to cosmic events.

128. "The ratio of the electromagnetic force to the gravitational force is 39 orders of magnitude." Peratt (1992), *Physics of the Plasma Universe*, p.48.

129. I would suggest that it is the other way around and that EM is some sort of gravity wave.

130. Thornhill & Talbott (2007), *The Electric Universe*, p. 77.

British geophysicist and mathematician Sydney Chapman, a senior figure in space physics, who argued the mainstream view that currents could not cross the vacuum of space and therefore the currents had to be generated by the Earth.

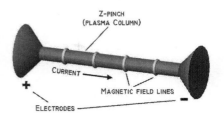

Magnetic field lines (light rings) 'pinch' the Birkeland current into long filaments (long cylinder).

However, in 1967 Birkeland's theory, referred to previously as 'fringe', was proved to be correct after a probe was sent into space (i.e. observation-hypothesis-experiment). These magnetic field-aligned currents are now named Birkeland currents in his honor.

Birkeland currents are possible because, contrary to a belief held by science for decades, space is not a perfect vacuum. There are particles in galactic space (about 1 per cubic centimeter), some of which are ionized. Plasma is a better conductor than copper or gold, however it is not a superconductor since its characteristic impedance[131] is about 30 ohms.[132]

A Birkeland current is simply an electron flow within plasma in the same way that an electric wire carries electrons. Birkeland currents have a filament shape because they are pinched by the magnetic force generated by the current itself. Like in a classic wire, Birkeland currents occur when an electric potential difference occurs between two regions of space. Then currents will form and tend to balance the potential of the two regions through electronic migration.

Mainstream science now also accepts that plasma effects are crucial to the slowing down of a star's spin as it is being formed. One proposal about how this happens is that magnetic braking helps to remove angular momentum. Alfvén hypothesized that Birkeland currents were responsible for initiating star formation.

This is interesting to me since it suggests that if our Sun had a solar companion and the two bodies approached one another at periodic intervals, they could conceivably interact during those close-approach periods in some sort of electrical dynamic which might significantly affect not only the stellar bodies, but any planetary bodies involved in the system.

To understand the electric interaction between the Sun and its planets,

---

131. Electrical impedance is the measure of the opposition that a circuit presents to the passage of a current when a voltage is applied.
132. Ibid, p. 39.

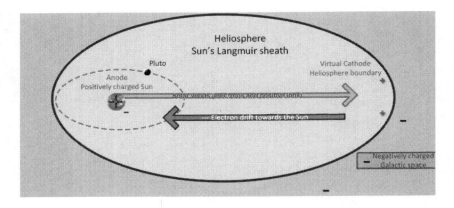

we must remember that one fundamental law of plasma theory is that in space, any electrically charged object generates an insulating bubble around it. This insulating sheath is called a 'Langmuir[133] Sheath'.

Like most celestial bodies, the Sun has its own Langmuir Sheath, which extends almost 100 AU (100 times the Sun-Earth distance) outwards. It's also called the 'heliosphere'. Electrically, the Sun-heliosphere couple acts like a giant condenser; the Sun being the positive electrode (anode) and the internal surface of the heliosphere being the negative electrode (cathode). Objects (comets, planets etc.) in the heliosphere can trigger electrical discharges from the Sun (solar flares, sunspots, CMEs[134]...).

One effect of this solar discharge might be to infinitesimally slow the rotation of the planets in our solar system in the same way an electric engine rotates slower when the electric field between its stator and its rotor decreases.

Another effect might even induce the Sun to contract slightly: an increase of the electric field within the Sun would lead to more negative charge on its surface and more positive charge in its core, which would increase its internal compression and cause it to contract.[135]

Both of these phenomena have been observed in process in the past dozen years or so. A second has been added to the world clock more than once during this time, and the Sun's quiescence during this latest solar maximum is puzzling. A possible reason for this effect is that there could be currents flowing between the Sun and its companion which would have an effect on the planets of our solar system.

---

133. Irving Langmuir (1881-1957), American chemist and physicist. Winner of the 1932 Nobel Prize in chemistry.
134. Coronal Mass Ejection.
135. Lefebvre & Kosovichev (2005), 'Changes in the subsurface stratification of the Sun with the 11-year activity cycle'.

Worlds, Antiworlds and the Big Bang

I would urge the reader to check out Alfvén's 1966 book *Worlds-Antiworlds*.[136] Alfvén postulated that the universe has always existed [137, 138] and he rejected models, such as the Big Bang, that were literally made up out of thin air, saying it was little more than a stealth form of creationism. I agree. While I am not a Creationist, and I do think evolution plays a significant role in life processes, I find it astonishing that evolutionists taunt creationists that their miracles of special creation can, by definition, be neither proved nor disproved. Yet the evolutionists arrive at similar propositions, especially when they exclude any possibility of something that guides and propels evolutionary processes which could be as simple as interactions between positive and negative charges, matter and anti-matter.

Karl Popper remarked in *Conjectures and Refutations* (1963) that "A theory which is not refutable by any conceivable event is non-scientific." The Big Bang is definitely one of those 'miracles of special creation' that can neither be proved nor disproved. In the final analysis, the Big Bang theory is a form of Creationism that was originally proposed by a catholic to support the Bible. Materialists – who generally tend to be Authoritarians and have worked on their theories ever since the church authorized the Big Bang – believe that matter sprang suddenly into existence with nothing prior. That primal atom was there, and they make no attempt to explain it. That's as crazy as saying 'God was just there' and decided to create the universe. Alfred Russell Wallace [139], the co-founder of the theory of evolution, came to the conclusion that natural selection could not account for human beings. He wrote that "nature never over-endows a species beyond the demands of everyday existence." This means that there is a major problem in accounting for many aspects of human beings – at least for some human beings – and thus, life itself. Stephen Jay Gould writes:

> The only honest alternative is to admit the strict continuity in kind between ourselves and chimpanzees. And what do we lose thereby? Only an antiquated concept of soul...

Here Gould is expressing the core of evolutionary materialism, the postu-

---

136. Alfvén (1966), *Worlds-antiworlds: Antimatter in Cosmology*.

137. Alfvén (1988), *Has the Universe an Origin?*

138. Peratt (1995), 'Introduction to Plasma Astrophysics and Cosmology'.

139. Alfred Russel Wallace (1823-1913), British naturalist, explorer, geographer, anthropologist and biologist.

late that matter is the stuff of all existence and that all mental and spiritual phenomena are its by-products. This is the pivot of the debate.

This reduction of all mental and spiritual phenomena to by-products of matter is no longer limited to biology and anthropology; it infects most of modern philosophy, the psychological and medical sciences, social systems, politics, and more. And this belief in evolution as the origin of life – being operative before anything at all came into being – works to limit research in such a way as to confirm their basic postulate. Essentially, it's right up there with Einstein and Freud in ruining science.

Back to our Plasma Cosmology, which is going to be important in relation to comets: Winston H. Bostick[140]

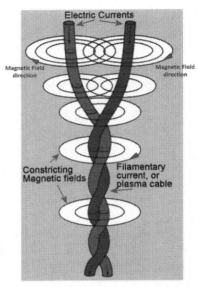

Electromagnetic interactions cause the two filaments to draw inwards and rotate around each other to form a helical filament pair, also known as a plasma vortex.

carried out laboratory experiments in the 1950s by vaporizing titanium wires with a 10,000 A current, which turned them into plasma. His experiments were "the first to record the formation of spiral structures in the laboratory from interacting plasmoids[141] and to note the striking similarity to their galactic analogs." Bostick was another who pointed out quite reasonably that plasma scaling applied to these laboratory experiments and demonstrated that galaxies had initially formed from plasma *under the influence of a magnetic field.*

Computer simulations of colliding plasma clouds by Anthony Peratt[142] in the 1980s also mimicked the shape of galaxies.[143] The simulation in the image above shows the cross-section of two plasma filaments joining in what is called a Z-pinch; the filaments start out at the equivalent of 300,000 light years

---

140. Winston H. Bostick (1916-1991), American physicist who discovered plasmoids, plasma focus, and plasma vortex phenomena.
141. Plasmoids are coherent cylindrical plasma structures elongated in the direction of the magnetic field.
142. Anthony L. Peratt is an American physicist specialized in plasma who has been working for the Los Alamos National Laboratory since 1981.
143. Peratt, Green & Nielson (1980), 'Evolution of Colliding Plasmas'.

apart and carry Birkeland currents of 1018 Amps.[144, 145] The simulations also showed emerging jets of material from the central buffer region, which resembles that observed from quasars and active galactic nuclei, which are attributed to 'black holes' according to Einsteinian physics. What was fascinating was that, letting the simulation continue to run revealed "the transition of double radio galaxies to radioquasars to radioquiet QSOs [146] to peculiar and Seyfert galaxies [147], finally ending in spiral galaxies." [148]

In short, many of the truly odd phenomena of the universe that are inexplicable – or explainable only with the most bizarre and contradictory ideas in an effort to support Einstein's relativity – turn out to be a natural evolution of electromagnetic phenomena.

The simulation accounted for flat galaxy rotation curves *without having to introduce exotic elements such as dark matter* in order to make the equations work. This is blasphemy since the discrepancy between observed galaxy rotation curves and those simulated based on Einsteinian gravity has had to be explained exactly that way: sheer invention of something to make the square peg fit the round hole. However, as Peratt's experiments demonstrated, a flat rotation curve emerges quite naturally in a galaxy governed by electromagnetic fields, the spiral arms of galaxies are like *rolling springs* that have the same rotational velocity along their length.[149] In other words, a galaxy is the physical and visible part of gigantic currents flowing through space.

In an electric universe, spinning galaxies, orbiting celestial bodies, spinning planets and stars, not to mention more mundane things like tornadoes and cyclones, are the logical consequences of Birkeland currents and the rotating electromagnetic fields they induce.

Plasma and Comets: a Short History

Plasma cosmology proposes that cometary comas [150] and tails are produced by an electrical exchange between the Sun and a comet. The coma is the Langmuir sheath of the comet. The intense electric field around the comet trig-

---

144. Peratt & Green (1983), 'On the Evolution of Interacting, Magnetized, Galactic Plasmas'.
145. Lerner (1991), *The Big Bang Never Happened*.
146. Quasi-Stellar Object or quasar.
147. Seyfert galaxies are characterized by extremely bright nuclei.
148. Peratt (1986), 'Evolution of the Plasma Universe: II. The Formation of Systems of Galaxies'.
149. Lerner (1991), op. cit.
150. The nebulous envelope around the nucleus of a comet.

gers massive discharges (hence the intense glow). These discharges also appear as jets which erode the surface of, and eject matter away from, the comet.

The tail is made of this ionized ejecta which remains cohesive because it forms electromagnetically guided Birkeland currents. Mainstream scientists are getting rather close to acknowledging this by calling the unexplained brightening of Comet Linear in 2000, a "charge exchange reaction." That is approaching heresy in the Einstein cult. The facts are that, before Einstein came along and ruined science, there were already speculations leading to an understanding of the *electrical nature of the universe.*

For example, in the late 19th century, *Scientific American*[151] published an article stating that Professor Zollner of Leipzig ascribes the "self-luminosity" of comets to "electrical excitement." Zollner proposed that "the nuclei of comets, as masses, are subject to gravitation, while the vapors developed from them, which consist of very small particles, yield to the action of the free electricity of the sun..." Then the 11th August 1882 issue of *English Mechanic and World of Science*[152] wrote regarding comet tails: "...There seems to be a rapidly growing feeling amongst physicists that both the self-light of comets and the phenomena of their tails belong to the order of electrical phenomena." In 1896, *Nature*[153] published an article stating that "It has long been imagined that the phenomenon of comet's tails are in some way due to a solar electrical repulsion, and additional light is thrown on this subject by recent physical researches."

But then, along came Einstein and science fell into a genuine black hole!

But all was not lost. Velikovsky proposed in *Worlds In Collison* that our ancestors had witnessed powerful electrical phenomena in the heavens, including electrical arcing between planets moving in erratic orbits. Well, as we will see, I think we can safely put that idea to rest and instead consider Clube and Napier's giant comet theory as being the more likely explanation for what the ancients were seeing.[154] So just hang on a minute, we are getting there.

In the 1960s, an engineer named Ralph Juergens, who had worked as a technical editor at McGraw-Hill publishing house, proposed that the Sun was a positively charged body at the center of an electrical system and that the Sun was itself the focus of a cosmic electric discharge which was the

---

151. 27 July 1872, p. 57.
152. pp. 516-7
153. No. 1370, Vol. 53, Jan 30, 1896, p. 306.
154. Comet activity and electrical activity are actually positively correlated. Because of their strong electric charge, comets can trigger all sorts of electric phenomena.

source of its energy – not the old $E = mc^2$ routine. Horror of horrors! Blasphemy!

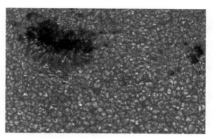

The granulated Sun's photosphere. 'Granules' are 'anode arcs' or anode 'tufts'. Because they have the same polarity, the current filaments arrange themselves so that they avoid each other.

In the Juergens hypothesis, a comet spends most of its time in the outermost regions of the solar system, where the electric field will be most negative. The comet nucleus, Juergens said, naturally acquires the negative charge of its environment. This leads to electrical stresses on the comet as it falls towards the sun. Juergens writes, "A space-charge sheath will begin to form to shield the interplanetary plasma from the comet's alien field. As the comet races toward the sun, its sheath takes the form of a long tail stretching away from the sun..."

Juergens' model of the electric Sun and of electrically discharging comets was immediately taken up by Earl Milton, professor of physics at Lethbridge University in Canada. Speaking at the annual meeting of the Society of Interdisciplinary Studies in April 1980, Milton offered a ringing endorsement of Juergens' hypothesis: "The cometary body takes on the [electric charge] of the space in which it has spent most of its time. On those infrequent apparitions when it comes into the space of the inner solar system, the body of the comet gets out of equilibrium because it now moving in an electrically different environment than the one it is adjusted to. An electrical flow then occurs to rectify the situation. The sheath which builds around the cometary body glows brightly and assumes the characteristic shape of the comet's head and tail." [155]

And, as comet experts know, that head and tail can take on dramatically different appearances, something that is inexplicable in terms of mainstream comet theories, but perfectly normal in electric comet dynamics. Professor Milton wrote about Juergens' ideas:

In August 1972 Ralph Juergens introduced the concept of the electrically powered Sun. ... Juergens, however, went farther than all of his preceptors in

155. Goodspeed (2011), 'The Electric Comet: The Elephant in NASA's Living Room?' http://www.thunderbolts.info/thunderblogs/goodspeed.htm

electrifying both the cosmic bodies and their interactions. He perceived the astronomical bodies as inherently charged objects immersed in a universe which could be described as an *electrified fabric*. The charges appearing locally on cosmic bodies, he posited, arose from the separation of positive ions and electrons on a galactic scale. Later, he discussed both the problems arising if the solar interior is truly the source of stellar energy and the nature of the phenomena observed as the solar photosphere.

In the first of his papers, Juergens related the Sun's ability to modulate the incoming flux of cosmic rays (which are protons impinging upon the solar system from all directions at relativistic velocities) to the Sun's driving potential, its cathode drop [156]...

Then, Juergens showed that the solar photosphere can be compared to a "tufted anode glow" in an electric discharge tube. The tufts form because the body of the Sun, *immersed in the interplanetary plasma*, which at its inner boundary is the weakly luminous outer solar region called the corona, cannot maintain an electrical discharge into the surrounding electrified galactic space. Juergens noted that the problem could arise from any one or more of the following conditions: (1) the solar body forms too small a surface to conduct the current required for the discharge, (2) the surrounding plasma is too "cool", and/or (3) the cathode drop is too large. The "anode tuft" detached from, and now lying above, the "surface" of the solar body increases the effective surface area over which the Sun can collect electrons. Within the "tuft", volatile material - vapourized from the Sun - increases the gas density and contributes large numbers of extra electrons because, now, many of the frequent collisions between the gas atoms result in ionization. [Emphasis, mine.] [157]

Juergens acknowledges:

Dr. Cook does not mention it, but it would seem that he has many years' priority over me in suggesting that the sun may be electrically powered. In his 1958 monograph, *The Science of High Explosives*, is an appendix in which he

---

156. A relatively rapid potential drop near the cathode occurs in an electrical discharge in a gas. In the case of the Sun, the cathode drop happens around the internal layer of the heliosphere. It is usually created by the protons carried away by the solar wind that slow down and bunch up when approaching the heliospheric sheath. However, in some forms of non-self-sustained electrical current in a gas where there is intense electron emission from the cathode, a cathode drop is developed by the negative space charge (an excess of electrons); such a cathode drop limits emission and inhibits further increase of the space charge.

157. Juergens, 'Electric Discharge as the Source of Solar Radiant Energy' (Part I), compiled by Earl R. Milton after the death of Juergens. http://www.velikovsky.info/Ralph_Juergens

points out that "the kinetic energy of accretion" of electric charge on the sun per unit time should be of the same order of magnitude as the sun's rate of radiating energy. He adds: "Apparently one thus has a likely explanation for the solar constant [rate of energy emission] that need not include, or is at least approximately of the same relative importance as, the [thermonuclear-energy generation] that is supposed to be taking place in the core of the sun.[158]

In short, the Sun is not a closed system that may run out of fuel one day. It appears that the Sun gets its energy from an electrical current that runs through the galaxy. As long as the current keeps flowing, the sun will keep going. However, when the sun goes quiet, that may mean that, somehow, it is discharging more efficiently. However we're not talking here about a usual intra heliosphere discharge like the ones that are triggered by comets and which increase Solar activity. Cometary activity seems to have increased over the last few years, which, according to electric comet dynamics, should increase the Sun's activity. How-ever, this is not the case. One scenario is that the Sun is being 'grounded', possibly by an oppositely charged object.

If a companion star is approaching our Solar system it could be responsible for both the increased meteor activity (because it propelled asteroid bodies from the Oort cloud towards our Solar system) and also for the decreased Solar ac-

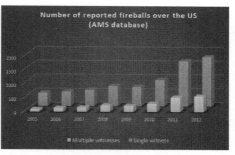

Number of fireballs observed over the USA (2005-2012). Note that the 2012 figure is underestimated since the data was collected in November 2012.

tivity ('grounding'). But Solar activity is one of the main phenomena that allows the destruction of incoming asteroid bodies by exerting intense electric fields upon them. In this way, such a companion star could pose a major threat to life on earth by both sending comets towards the earth and deactivating the 'protection system' (Solar activity) against the threat of cometary impact.

I've probably told you more about Plasma Cosmology than you wanted to know, but believe me, this basic background will help to understand the material that is coming further on.

Australian Plasma Cosmology researcher Wallace Thornhill writes:

---

158. Juergens (in reply to Melvin Cook), 'On Celestial Mechanics'.

As a comet accelerates toward the Sun and electrons are stripped from the comet's surface, it first develops a huge visible glow discharge, or coma, then the discharge switches to the arc mode. This results in a number of bright cathode 'spots' of high current density on the surface, etching circular craters and burning the surface black, giving the surface its extreme darkness. Each arc forms a 'cathode jet' that electrically accelerates the excavated and vaporized material into space.[159]

As already noted, Anthony L. Peratt and his colleagues at Los Alamos research laboratories conducted plasma experiments and discovered that powerful plasma discharges take on some amazing shapes, including humanoid figures, humans with bird heads, rings, donuts, writhing snakes and so forth. It just so happens that these kinds of shapes have been recorded by ancestral humans the world over, most particularly in rock carvings known as petroglyphs. He writes:

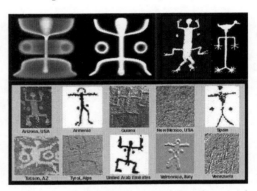

The discovery that objects from the Neolithic or Early Bronze Age carry patterns associated with high-current Z-pinches provides a possible insight into the origin and meaning of these ancient symbols produced by man. ...

Similarities between plasma shapes and ancient stone engravings.

A discovery that the basic petroglyph morphologies are the same as those recorded in extremely high-energy-density discharges has opened up a means to unravel the origin of these apparently crude, misdrawn, and jumbled figures found in uncounted numbers around the Earth.

Drawn in heteromac[160] style, these ancient patterns could mimic and replicate high-energy phenomena that would be recorded on a nonerasable plasma display screen. Many petroglyphs, apparently recorded several millennia ago, have a plasma discharge or instability counterpart, some on a one-to-one or overlay basis. More striking is that the images recorded on rock are the only

---

159. Thornhill (2007), *The Electric Universe*.
160. Heteromacs are self-similar plasmas, i.e. plasmas that retain their properties (including shape and forms) over several orders of magnitude.

images found in extreme energy density experiments; no other morphology types or patterns are observed.[161]

Plasma events can heat and fuse rock, incinerate things that would otherwise not burn, melt ice caps, induce earthquakes and volcanic eruptions, vaporize shallow bodies of water and create massive deluges of rain. Additionally, the radiation coming off the plasma can very likely affect genes in living creatures, including humans. In short, plasma interactions between the Earth and comets can create chaos. In the presence of such phenomena, humans would be terrorized and certainly think that they are in the presence of powerful and destructive living beings, i.e. 'gods'. During such periods, they might seek out caves, build underground shelters, build shelters of massive stone, and so forth. Evidence for all of these is present in the archaeological record.

Robert Schoch, the geophysicist at Boston University who created a controversy by pointing out that the Sphinx must be thousands of years older than mainstream archaeologists claim, due to the presence of extreme water-weathering on its surface, thinks that the plasma events recorded by the ancients in their rock art are due to extreme activity of the sun. But, as we are going to see from some of the actual written evidence further on, understanding comets as electrically charged bodies, and taking Clube's and Napier's giant comet hypothesis into account, makes a better fit. I'm not excluding the possibility that the sun may certainly have produced some frightening plasma phenomena at different points in history, but I think the most concise explanation that includes all of the data is that of the giant comet with a full electrical charge interacting with the electromagnetic field of the earth, including particularly terrifying displays from fragments entering the earth's atmosphere. A giant comet could also interact with the other planets in the solar system, doing such things as stripping the water and life off of Mars, exchanging electrical potentials and leaving horrific scars on that planet, interacting with Venus in such a way that Venus might strip charge from the giant comet, thus altering its own electro-chemical make-up, and so on.

The Giant Comet

Just *how* 'Giant' can a comet be?

There is no securely known upper limit to [the diameter of comets], but sev-

---

161. Peratt (2003), 'Characteristics for the Occurrence of a Hight-Current, Z-Pinch Aurora as Recorded in Antiquity'.

eral historical comets, such as the Great Comet of 1577 and Comet Sarabat of 1729, appear to have had diameters in the range 100-300 km. ... a giant long-period comet is ... expected to cross the Earth's orbit about once every 400 yrs. ...[162]

Clube and Napier suggest that it is inevitable, due to the nature of the galactic environment, that the occasional giant comet becomes trapped in our solar system and may even be precipitated into an Earth-crossing orbit of relatively short period. Due to the observed tendency of comets to gradually break up, which we now suspect is more due to electrodynamics than heat from the Sun on gases trapped in ice, such a giant comet can generate substantial swarms of bodies. Some of these 'children' become smaller periodic comets, some are flung out of the solar system, and some discharge and degauss, becoming asteroids.

The period Clube and Napier propose for the normal acquisition of a *giant* comet is approximately every 100,000 years. However, the inner solar system has to deal with the issues of a disintegrating giant comet for tens of thousands of years afterward.

> Because of the Sun's [current] position near to both the Orion spiral arm and the plane of the Galaxy, we expect that the Earth is even now in a period of enhanced risk. The risk is further enhanced by the fact that the Sun has recently passed through a complex of debris associated with Gould's Belt.[163] We should look therefore for *a currently disturbed comet cloud* and *a currently disturbed Earth*. ... *We expect the disturbances of the Earth and its biosphere to be profound*: ... the extinction rate, the incidence of mountain building, the rise and fall of oceans, reversals of the Earth's magnetic field, are all expected to be under the control of the galaxy. ...
>
> There is strong evidence, indeed, that the last giant comet entered an Earth-crossing orbit only a few tens of thousands of years ago, so its asteroidal debris (including its resultant zodiacal cloud) are in orbit even now. The comet should therefore indeed have made its mark on history, as well as on recent geology. Furthermore, a cometary body at least 250 kilometres in diameter, Chiron by name, has already been sighted in a chaotic orbit out beyond Saturn and there is good reason to believe it may be entering an Earth-crossing orbit... Chiron is obviously not of great urgency but the same cannot be said

---

162. Clube, Napier, Hoyle & Wickramasinghe (1996), 'Giant Comets, Evolution and Civilization'.
163. The Gould belt is a celestial ring containing some very bright stars and 'dark matter'.

of the asteroidal remnants of the most recent giant comet. Unfortunately most of *these Earth-crossing bodies are completely uncharted* and we have no means of knowing which of these will produce the next significant encounter with the Earth.[164] (Emphases mine.)

As noted above, Clube and Napier have backtracked orbits of comet streams and found that 9,500 years ago, two major streams were in identical orbits, i.e. they must have been a single body. That means that this was a time of major break-up. Comet Oljato, one of the bodies in question, is in an orbit which would have brought it into the Earth's orbital plane for several hundred years around 3000-3500 BCE, which means that there would have been quite a

The Taurids, a meteor shower occurring every year in the middle of November. Named after their radiant point in the constellation Taurus.

few close encounters of the disastrous kind at that period. At the same time, Comet Encke would have been a dramatic presence in the heavens as well. The present day northern Taurid meteors are calculated to have broken away from Comet Encke *about a thousand years ago*, consistent with Mike Baillie's tree ring and ice core evidence and recorded in the Chinese records. In short, backtracking orbits of meteor streams and asteroids reveals astronomically and scientifically what must have been going on in the skies at various periods *within the history of our current civilization*. Adding up the volume of the comets and asteroids in question, along with the estimates of the various connected dust clouds and streams, indicates that our most recent Giant visitor, which the ancients knew as Saturn [165], was indeed a monster. And it gave birth to a whole family of monsters. And some of the products of its initial splits went on to become monsters in their own rights, each with their own family of godlets.

Despite the fact that things going on in the skies have calmed down a great deal, the likelihood is that there are still hundreds of thousands of bodies capable of generating multi-megaton Tunguska-like explosions on the Earth, orbiting in the earth-crossing streams left by the Giant comet progenitor. The Moon encountered a storm of such between 22nd-26th June of 1975,

---

164. Clube & Napier (1990), pp. 145-146, excerpts.
165. Not necessarily modern planet Saturn, as we will see later.

as Lunar seismometers left by the Apollo astronauts recorded. The detectors revealed that as many ton-sized boulders hit during that five-day period as had struck over the previous entire five years.

In short, Clube and Napier have established a serious and secure astronomical frame-work, and a scientific rationale, for catastrophism that justifies an "urgent reappraisal of the ancient tales of celestial catastrophe." Of course, this deployment of true science leads to serious repercussions from a mainstream scientific community composed mostly of Authoritarian followers who willingly and gleefully attacked Velikovsky without mercy. As Clube and Napier write:

> Astronomers, indeed scientists generally, like to think of themselves as tolerant judges and very adaptable to fresh discoveries. The evidence in this instance is however mostly the other way. One may therefore expect that in some circles the data now emerging from the Taurid meteor stream will be ignored in the hope that something reassuring will turn up. While this is a time-honoured scholarly ploy for the handling of discordant new facts, there is a moral dimension in this instance: the swarm has teeth.[166]

As noted, the Tunguska event was very likely a member of the Beta Taurid stream [167] and the fact that an object of multi-megaton capacity impacted our planet should concern us. Of course, the fact that it exploded over a remote area of Siberia enables us to ignore it, but had it done so over a city, wiping out every single living soul, our perceptions would be significantly different, to say the least! Even so, the Tunguska body was a fairly trivial one in comparison to what is scientifically calculated to still be circulating in the Taurid streams! One of the more significant bodies apparently impacted the Moon in 1178 CE, recorded by Gervase of Canterbury, a medieval monk.

> In this year, on the Sunday before the Feast of St. John the Baptist, after sunset when the moon had first become visible a marvelous phenomenon was witnessed by some five or more men who were sitting there facing the moon. Now there was a bright new moon, and as usual in that phase its horns were

Impression of the 1178 lunar event (Peter Greco).

---

166. Clube and Napier (1990), p. 154.
167. Over time the Taurids meteor cloud has split into several streams. One of which is labeled 'Beta Taurids'. Earth crosses it annually in June/July.

tilted toward the east; and suddenly the upper horn split in two. From the midpoint of the division a flaming torch sprang up, spewing out, over a considerable distance, fire, hot coals, and sparks. Meanwhile the body of the moon which was below writhed, as it were, in anxiety, and, to put it in the words of those who reported it to me and saw it with their own eyes, the moon throbbed like a wounded snake. Afterwards it resumed its proper state. This phenomenon was *repeated a dozen times or more*, the flame assuming various twisting shapes at random and then returning to normal. Then after these transformations the moon from horn to horn, that is along its whole lengthe, took on a blackish appearance. The present writer was given this report by men who saw it with their own eyes, and are prepared to stake their honour on an oath that they have made no addition or falsification in the above narrative.[168] (Emphasis mine.)

The date of the event converts to 25 June in our modern Gregorian calendar. In short, a Beta Taurid. The description of the writhing, throbbing Moon is descriptive of electric discharge and/or arcing dynamics. Now, shall we believe the wild tale of this monk of a thousand years ago? As Clube and Napier point out, there is physical evidence left to support the story.

The meteorite expert Jack Hartung points out that the Giordano Bruno crater fits well with the description of Gervase as to location. Skeptics claim that such an impact would have caused a meteor storm on Earth and no such storm was recorded, but that is just Authoritarian-type damage control, in my opinion. The facts are that the 13-mile diameter crater and the system of rays that extend from it are noted for their brilliance as opposed to the visual effects of other craters. The significance of this is that the crater and its system are

The Giordano Bruno crater.

so recent that ongoing bombardment of the Moon by microscopic particles has not had time to dull the material ejected by the crater. Lunar astronomers Callame and Mulholland found that, since the crater was 15 degrees into the far side of the Moon, the ejecta would have been hurled in a direction that would not bring it into the atmosphere of the Earth. Additionally, they found that the blow of the object the size needed to produce the Giordano Bruno crater would

---

168. Quoted by Clube and Napier (1990).

have produced a particular wobble or vibration. Using lasers, thousands of observations were made and one of the results is that there is a 15 meter oscillation of the lunar surface about its axis with a period of three years. Such vibrations die out over time and the calculations were done with the result that this wobble can only be explained by a recent large impact, i.e. the one witnessed by Gervase of Canterbury.

The giant scarring of Mars is more than 3,000 km long.

How large an impact? Studies were done to figure that out, too. Turns out that the object was probably a mile across and struck the Moon with the energy of approximately 100,000 megatons.[169] Had it struck the Earth, it would probably have reduced human beings to a Stone Age existence – what few of them survived. And it is undoubtedly exactly this – and more – that caused the extinction of the megafauna 13,000 years ago and ended the ice age. Along with a large impactor, there were hundreds of thousands of bodies – products of disintegration – that caused the features we now know as the Carolina Bays.

Now, keep in mind that the Taurids are called that because they appear to come from the constellation Taurus, and at some point in the past what came from that constellation may have been far larger and more dramatic than the meteor streams that, in our modern times, seem so benign and decorative. Three or four thousand years ago, the objects emanating from Taurus were not so small and benign. Enormous, brilliant, celestial objects would have been seen traveling along the zodiac with attendant fragments, looking like a shepherd with his little fluffy sheep. Backtracking still further tells us that the giant comet came tens of thousands of years ago, and its initial appearance may have started the last ice age, which hit its peak around 20,000 years ago.

Thunderbolts of the Gods

In Neolithic and early historical times, there must have been a string of naked-eye comets moving along the zodiac much like the planets do. At any given time, there were probably only a few really large and dominant bodies, 'children' of the monstrous progenitor. Some of the 'children' came to earth and wreaked havoc or engaged in 'wars with one another', producing endless ter-

---

169. That energy amounts to about ten times the entire nuclear arsenals of man.

rifying spectacles. The comet nuclei would have been far brighter than Venus, even at a 'safe' distance. Fierce meteor storms must have been commonplace, with many fireballs exploding in the atmosphere during them: the veritable Thunderbolts of the Gods. And certainly the electrical displays must have been awesome, whether between the comets, or between them and the Earth, or between them and other planets in the solar system. As I noted already, the giant progenitor is probably responsible for the destruction and scarring of Mars and the loading of the atmosphere of Venus, though that was very early in its career.

In the figure on the right, we see various nodes of important intersections between the orbit of Comet Encke and the plane of the Earth's orbit. These approxi-

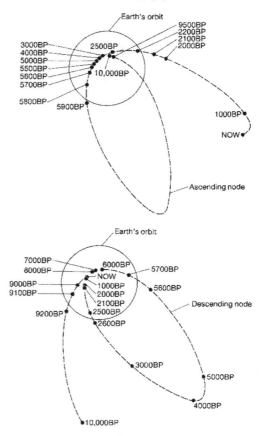

Intersection points of Comet Encke's orbit with the plane containing the Earth's orbit at various dates Before Present. After Clube and Napier.

mate dates match the scientific data obtained from the Earth itself. The ancient traditions of the 'End of the World', (yes, many 'worlds' have ended throughout history), the Egyptian intermediate periods, the collapse of the Bronze Age, the End of the Roman Empire, and more, all have to be re-examined with the inclusion of the scientific data based on astronomical observations and back-engineering of the data thus obtained.

As time passed, of course, the comets would begin to lose their charge and their gasses and their tails would have diminished and faded from view, leaving only the predictable, annual, meteor showers. The gods that once hurled celestial thunderbolts and periodically got angry at human beings and "destroyed the whole world" experienced their own immolation, the *Gotter-*

dammerung[170], though we suspect that their 'dead bodies' are still out there, blackened by the fire – invisible, so to say – but still lethal.

In the earliest times, the celestial catastrophes came from the constellation Aries, but due to the evolution of the orbits, they gradually shifted to Taurus. In the Pyramid Texts, the earlier celestial religion, even older than the pharaohs, was the worship of a god who was the giver of life, rain and 'celestial fire'. Worship of the sky god dominates both the Northern Indo-Europeans and the Southern Semitic peoples from the very earliest times. And even in the earliest times, the sky god did not exist alone: he gave birth and propagated a whole pantheon of lesser gods and demi-gods.

Quite a number of alternative researchers have gotten on the bandwagon of claiming that the actual planets of our solar system move out of their orbits and interact with one another in close and terrifying ways, including exchanging 'thunderbolts' and so forth. It seems that the reason for this interpretation is due to the confusion over the names of the gods later being given to the planets that were previously associated with a particular cometary event. I don't think that these people are really considering the mechanics of what they are proposing, which are actually improbable, if not impossible. We need to look for deeper understanding and that is where we find that the Clube and Napier theory of a giant comet – or more than one – and the research they have done into the ancient texts, completes the picture.

As we will discuss further on, it was in the 4th century BCE that cosmological thinking shifted in significant ways with the rise of the new, Greek rationalism. This could only have happened if the 'gods' that had been terrorizing the Earth for millennia were beginning to decline in size, number and frequency of appearance; to spread out and disperse in longer orbits. It is at this point that we discover that a study of planetary movement arose as an 'explanation' of what the former, ignorant, irrational peoples were actually talking about when they spoke of 'gods in the sky'. It was only *after* this time that the planets were given the names of well-known gods, names that had previously belonged to the giant comets and their offspring. At the same time, the *planets were assigned some cometary characteristics*, which makes no sense at all unless the names were originally attached to comets. As late as the 9th century, the Baghdad astrologer Kitab al-Mughni described Jupiter as 'bearded' and Mars as a 'lamp', Mercury as a 'spear' and Venus as a 'horseman'. These are terms that have always before, then and since, been used to

---

170. Literally 'Twilight of the Gods', a reference to the fourth and last opera of 'The Ring of the Nibelung' cycle by Wagner.

describe comets! (We are also reminded of the 'lamp' [171] that passed between the covenant offering of Abraham, not to mention burning bushes, pillars of fire and cloud, and so forth.)

The idea that the planets in their distant, placid orbits, were important in any way at all was due to the work of Plato and Eudoxus.[172] An explanation of orbits that were steady, circular, geometric and simple was elaborated by them, though Plato took some account of the ancient world-view and its events in the *Timaeus*. Then Plato's pupil, Aristotle, came along with his radical cosmology that banished anything that was not 'here and now' evident. Shades of Einstein and the modern scientific dogma, for sure. The cometary gods were reduced to distant folk memories of *earthly* heroes and the sense that 'there and then' things were very different was completely suppressed; there was undoubtedly a political motive behind this.

Aristotelian cosmology, with its focus on the perfect, planetary 'spheres', ascended and dominated religion and academia and this condition exists, more or less, right up to the present – Tunguska and all other evidence notwithstanding.

As the sky-gods faded, the myths about them became less and less comprehensible. The tales were obviously about celestial beings, but there was a problem with identifying them. The only apparent moving bodies in the solar system were the planets and the odd comet now and then, and it was clear that the planets were too few in number and too simple in movement to support the wild tales told in the celestial myths. Thus, along with the transfer of the names of some of the major comets to the planets, the names of many of the other gods came to be assigned to ancient heroes, founders of cities, and so forth.

The evidence seems to point to the idea that Aristotle (among others as we will see further on) was concerned with quieting the fears and stamping out the superstitions of the average man. He did the job well and we have suffered the consequences for a very long time, and may yet suffer even more.

The Comet Saturn/Chronos

Saturn, aka Chronos, appears to have played the most important role in ancient mythology. This is probably due to the fact that these were the names

---

171. "...when the sun went down, and it was dark, behold a smoking furnace, and a burning **lamp** that passed between those pieces" (Genesis 15:17).

172. Eudoxus of Cnidus (410 or 408 BCE – 355 or 347 BCE) was a Greek astronomer, mathematician, scholar and student of Plato.

given to the giant progenitor comet (first called Chronos by the Greeks and then later named Saturn by the Romans). It was so gigantic and so brilliant that it appeared in the ancient sky as a second sun on occasions. When we consider the ancient images of 'torches', 'bearded stars' and 'smoking stars', 'long-haired stars' or 'a great star scattering its flame in fire', and that there are also representations of Venus as a flaming serpent or dragon in the sky, and then realise that the names of the current planets became associated with these descriptions, it can all get a little confusing. Take a look at the following table:

Babylonian Divine name (very old, cannot be precisely dated)	Babylonian scientific name and late association with planets	Divine names used at the time of **Plato**, c. 430 BCE	Scientific names used in **Greece** after 200 BCE	Names of **Roman** gods attached to planets after 100 BCE
Ninib	Kaimanu	**Star of Chronos**	Chronos	Saturn
Marduk	Mulu-babbar	**Star of Zeus**	Zeus	Jupiter
Nergal	Sal-bat-a-ni	**Star of Ares**	Ares	Mars
Ishtar	Dili-pat	**Star of Aphrodite**	Aphrodite	Venus
Nabu	Bu-utu	**Star of Hermes**	Hermes	Mercury

Notice that at the time of Plato, the name 'Star of _____' was still being used. This 'Star of...' designation was a direct reference to the brilliant nature of the comets that had evoked these names. But by 200 BCE, the term 'Star of' had been dropped, and by 100 BCE, probably no one even remembered that the names had once belonged to comets. (In the next few chapters, we will be looking at the evidence that the names of these Babylonian 'gods' were originally names of comets/comet fragments.)

The point I am making here is that it is not necessary to invoke absurd planetary interactions that violate the most elementary – and certainly correct – laws of celestial mechanics. There is an abundance of scientific paleoclimatological evidence of repeating environmental disasters during the Pleistocene and Holocene epochs.[173] Archaeological evidence reveals strong signals of these periods of stress as well. The comparisons between plasma shapes and ancient rock art are compelling. Mythology and ancient religious practices indicate the overwhelming preoccupation with appeasing the gods – gods that could destroy cities in an instant. And here, in the work of Victor Clube and Bill Napier is the scientifically provable, traceable, confirmable,

---

173. Geological epochs spanning from 2.5 million years ago to today. Those two epochs have been punctuated by numerous ice ages.

checkable data of exactly what was *actually happening* throughout all that time, based on the calculated volumes and orbits of comet streams. There is no need to invoke the planets playing impossible games of musical chairs, dragging their gargantuan tidal forces near the Earth and trying to figure out why the planet didn't just explode into bits at the approach. There is no need to invoke solar storms so severe that they create astonishing aurorae that fry areas of the planet in conjunction with a few possible fireballs to explain other features of the events. All you need is one giant electric comet!

Just to be clear, Clube and Napier et al. have not gone in the direction of their giant comet being an electrical phenomenon; that is my idea on the theory. But truly, it makes everything else fit together, like finding the last piece of the puzzle.

The bottom line is this: the 'hard' sciences must have the last word on what exactly transpired in astronomical terms and that is what Clube, Napier, Bailey, Hoyle and a few others have provided.

CHAPTER FOUR

LEGENDS OF THE FALL AND GENETIC MUTATIONS

Our civilization has known about the flood legends of the Bible for about two thousand years; it was only in the 19th century that we became aware that this story was derived from a more ancient source; the Sumerians. It was then, in the late 19th and early 20th century, that ethnologists and other experts began to collect the flood legends of

The Deluge by Nicolas Poussin (c. 1664).

the North Eurasian peoples and to compare them with similar stories of other peoples. What they found was that the North Eurasian peoples spoke not only of a water-flood, but also bombardments of fire and numerous evil suns in the sky, described as 'burning mountains'. There were also fire-breathing serpents in the sky and earthquakes that lasted for days, violent storms, torrents of water falling for days and boiling waves as 'high as a tent' or mixed with stones. There were descriptions of *roaring from the skies* and other horrifying noises, followed by grey darkness in the day and nights as black as pitch. Snow storms that lasted for months rounded off the scenarios. Obviously, these stories did not exactly match the relatively benign – even if world-covering – Flood of Noah that resulted from a rain lasting 40 days and nights and "fountains of the deep." [174]

---

174. "…When he established the clouds above: when he strengthened the fountains of the deep…" (Proverbs 8:28).

The appalling cosmic catastrophe had long-term consequences for all life on our planet, and was, obviously, a world-wide event in one respect or another.

Spirals and Cosmic Divers

A selection of the stories of the Northern Eurasians – mainly those living between the Black Sea and the Caspian Sea[175] – have been collected together, along with some of the geological and archaeological evidence, by Heinrich Koch in a book entitled *The Diluvian Impact.*[176] It is highly recommended, with a small caveat: he seems to have conflated a number of events. Nevertheless, I found there the origin of certain stories that are said by Yuri Stoyanov[177] to be the oldest forms of dualism:

> The Palaeo-Siberians have created remarkable rock drawings, so-called petroglyphs, which not only represent a peculiar early artistic style, but also reveal incredibly precious traditions from hoary antiquity. One motif, which is repeatedly outlined, is the *Mudur*, the divine sky-dragon… The Mudur is connected to coiled and crooked-line ornaments, the *Amur*-spiral, and the Amur-network, symbolizing the divine serpent, another figure that represents the comet. …
>
> It is the primeval myth of the three suns which is permanently repeated among almost all Palaeo-Siberian peoples, and it says this:
>
> *In former times, three evil suns were standing in the sky which brought death and devastation over Earth in a violent fire-storm and an everything-destroying forest fire. The heat, as it is reported, even softened stones, so that birds left marks of their claws on them when stepped upon. The legendary hero Boa-Enduri destroyed two of the suns by arrowshots, however, he missed the third one. The splinters and fragments of the evil suns got spread as stars over the whole firmament. Earth and water boiled in the ardour. Finally, the whole globe was covered with water. Thereafter, the sky or water-dragon disappeared from the firmament, and since that time it lives hidden in the swamp or under water. Also the diver's motif re-appears here: Three swans fetch earth from the bottom of the water which covered the whole country for seven days. After this, the ground solidified again.…Recent newborns died from the ardour, later on from the cold… On Earth, the corpses piled up, however, it was impossible to bury them… (p. 51)*

---

175. Today's Azerbajian, Armenia and Georgia.
176. Koch (2000).
177. Stoyanov (2000), *The Other God.*

The pattern of concentric circles and spirals is not only the basic motif of the Neolithic engravings, it is also the basic repertoire of the complete Far Eastern ornamentation, and also a characteristic element of the contemporary popular art in whole Eastern Siberia. Even the Ainu preserve the volute, the spiral and the wavy line in their ornamental art.

Beside the primeval myth of the three evil suns in the Far Eastern cycle of legends, we can also find the wide-spread myth of the creation of the world by diving water-birds bringing up soil from the ground, and also the legend of the world-tree which we already know from the Ural-Altaians. (p. 54)

In the Old Persian Zend-Avesta, the approach of the comet which is there called Gurcher and Musper, and its appearance is decribed as follows: *From the South, an ardent dragon was rising and everything was devastated by it. The day turned into night, the stars disappeared, and the zodiac was covered by its monstrous tail. The struggle of the dragon or demon, the horrible scream of which could be heard everywhere. It lasted 90 days, then it sank down into the depth of the earth. ...*

It is significant that here almost the same word is used ... for the celestial body as in the Old Norse Edda, which talks about the Fire-As *Muspel* who is accompanied by a crowd of red-hot *Muspelsons*. *Muspel* and the fire-giant *Surtur* pull behind them a glowing sheet of fire like a sword. The same motif is also well-known in the South Germanic legends... for instance in the ancient Saxon *Muspilli*, the poem of the Last Judgment. *Muspilli* means "end of the world caused by fire." (p. 65)

Clearly, it is in these cometary experiences described as struggles between various evil and noble forces that we find the origin of the Aryan [178] dualistic principle that was at the foundation of gnostic religious formations such as that of Mani, the Bogomils and Cathars. Koch suggests that dualism is an infallible sign of the cataclysmic experience. Apparently, after such, no one in their right mind continues to believe only in a good and loving god who is master of the universe.

Werewolves, Vampires and Cannibals, Oh My!

In addition to the tales collected by Koch, a related book (already mentioned earlier) is a collection of the accounts from *Native Americans: Man and Impact in the Americas* by E. P. Grondine. One very interesting thing about both of these volumes is that the issue of genetic mutation is described in

---

178. Indo-European.

the myths. In both the Americas and Eurasia, the stories of the impacts and floods include related legends of *giants, dwarfs* and *cannibals* which are not the instigators of the cataclysms as one might infer regarding the Nephilim in the Bible, but rather the consequence of it.

Indian cemetery, Santa Rosa Island, containing abalone shells radiocarbon dated at 7,070 years. Tops of skulls were painted red, several skeletons measured over seven feet tall. Photo courtesy of Santa Barbara Museum of Natural History, 1959.

Generally, these stories are about very aggressive, warlike, humanoid monsters. The ancient Native American myths of the Windigo [179] can be traced back to comet catastrophes. Nowadays, of course, the Windigo is thought of as a malevolent, cannabilistic spirit that can possess the bodies of humans and cause them to transform, rather like the legends of werewolves, but what if it is not possession but rather mutation? They were strongly associated with cold and famine which can be the results of comet events and it is known from medical research that a ketogenic [180] diet and cold adaptation can induce genetic upregulation or downregulation. Generally, these effects are extremely beneficial and neuroprotective, but perhaps it depends on the individual genetic make-up? Windigos and their Eurasian counterparts were also described as greedy and never satisfied with killing; they were always on the march looking for new victims. [181] Koch writes:

> Hungarian folklore knows the myth of the world-wide conflagration with a variety of features. However, all the legends are spoiled by later additions under Christian influence. Anyway, there is a genuine element from North Asia in the mythical cycle, and this is distributed among all Uralians and Mongols in quite the same manner. It says that Earth received new inhabitants after the extinction of the earlier human race by a flood of water and

179. The name is *wiindigoo* in the Ojibwe language (Brightman 1988:344), *widjigò* in the Algonquin language, and *wihtikow* in the Cree language; the Proto-Algonquian term was *wi·nteko·wa*, which probably originally meant 'owl' (Goddard 1969, cited in Brightman 1988:340).
180. A ketogenic diet is very low in carbohydrates, low in proteins and high in animal fat. It is believed to have been the diet of our hunter ancestors for hundreds of thousands of years.
181. Brightman (1988), 'The Windigo in the Material World'.

fire. It is reported that the novel individuals were partly giants and partly dwarfs (i.e. mis-shaped beings...)

The Turkish Tatars in the Altai Mountains have a song about the end of the world reporting the enormous damages in the inanimate and living world. Apart from the usual description of the catastrophe, there are things of particular interest, pointing at the genetic damages in the human population:

As soon as the end of the world will have come, the sky will be of iron... solid stone will crumble away, solid wood will crash... the water-wells will flow with blood, the land will roar, the mountains will turn upside down, the slopes will collapse, the sky will tremble, and the sea will rise in waves, so that the bottom will be visible; Sun and Moon will not be shining anymore; the trees will be torn out with their roots, the moss will turn into ashes, all the plants will be destroyed, their seeds will be extinct; and the humans will grow just one span high... the child will not know its father [because of the shortness of human life]... (p. 47)

According to Olrik, the Mongols were also aware of the phenomenon of human malformations, due to the world-wide cataclysm. It is said there: *"The horses will not grow larger than rabbits, and people will hardly be one yard tall. The outmost possible age that humans will reach will hardly extend over ten years... No fruits will grow on Earth for seven years. Hunger and diseases will be the consequences among the dwarfs..."*[182]

Obviously, vegetarians will have a much harder time in a cataclysmic environment. Or perhaps it is vegetarians who turn into cannibals under the influence of genetic changes?

The Electrophonic Cosmic Logos

In respect of the idea of genetic mutations accompanying cometary cataclysms; as it happens, a reader sent me an interesting paper back in 2008 discussing the possibility that the Tunguska event caused genetic changes. The abstract tells us:

One of the great mysteries of the Tunguska event is its genetic impact. Some genetic anomalies were reported in the plants, insects and people of the Tunguska region. Remarkably, the increased rate of biological mutations was found not only within the epicenter area, but *also along the trajectory* of the Tunguska Space Body (TSB). At that no traces of radioactivity were found,

---

182. Koch (1998), p. 41-49.

which could be reliably associated with the Tunguska event. The main hypotheses about the nature of the TSB, a stony asteroid, a comet nucleus or a carbonaceous chondrite [183], readily explain the absence of radioactivity but give no clues how to deal with the genetic anomaly. A choice between these hypotheses, as far as the genetic anomaly is concerned, is like to the choice between "blue devil, green devil and speckled devil", to

A dramatic tree ring enlargement is noticeable after year 1908.

quote late Academician N. V. Vasilyev. However, if another mysterious phenomenon, electrophonic meteors, is evoked, the origin of the Tunguska genetic anomaly becomes less obscure.[184]

The author proposes the idea that electrophonic effects produced by comets/meteors can induce genetic changes in biological organisms. What is curious is that the observed growth anomalies in the trees measured by tree ring width is not strongly correlated to the blast area itself, but rather to the land under the aerial path of the body.

Ecological consequences of the Tunguska event have been comprehensively discussed by Vasilyev (1999, 2000). They constitute another conundrum of this intricate phenomenon. There were two main types of effects observed. The first type includes accelerated growth of young and survived trees on a vast territory, as well as quick revival of the taiga after the explosion. The second type of effects is related to the genetic impact of the Tunguska explosion. ...

The first systematic pilot study of growth of the tree vegetation in the catastrophe region was performed during 1958 expedition (Vasilyev 1999). Anomalously large tree ring widths up to 9 mm were found in young specimens which were germinated after the catastrophe, while the average width of the growth rings before the catastrophe was only 0.2-1.0 mm. Besides the young trees, the accelerated growth was observed also for the survived old trees.

---

183. Carbonaceous chondrites are a class of meteorites.
184. Silagadze (2003), 'Tunguska genetic anomaly and electrophonic meteors', found here: http://arxiv.org/PS_cache/astro-ph/pdf/0311/0311337v2.pdf

Stimulated by these first findings, a large scale study of the forest recovery in the Tunguska area was performed in a series of following expeditions after 1960. In the 1968 expedition, for example, morphometric data for more than six thousand pine specimens were collected. This vast material establishes the reality of the accelerated growth without any doubt (Vasilyev 1999). More recent study of Longo & Serra (1995) confirms this spectacular phenomenon and indicates that the growth has weakened only recently for trees of the respectable age of more than 150 years...

The paper next mentions something that piqued my interest:

An interesting fact is that the Tunguska epicenter almost exactly coincides with the muzzle of a Triassic volcano.

This is discussed in terms of whether the volcanically enriched soil was involved with the accelerated tree growth. That's interesting in itself, but I wondered if there was something about a volcano that could actually *attract* a body from space? Volcanoes are the location of very frequent plasma discharges between the ionosphere and the surface of the planet (in the form of lightning) and comets are highly electrical bodies. Is there a link between volcanoes and comets of an electrical nature? Obviously, that's a wild question, but still, one wonders! Anyway, regarding the trees:

What is surprising was found by observing later generation trees. It turned out that the younger the trees, the higher the concentration of the accelerated growth effect towards the projection of the TSB trajectory (Vasilyev & Batishcheva 1979, Vasilyev 1999). Therefore there should be one more factor, directly related to the TSB and possibly of mutagenic nature.

For the old survived trees the effect of the accelerated growth is more scattered and patchy character. One can find such trees in the forest fall area, as well as outside of it. Again, *the effect is more prominent in regions nearby to the TSB [Tunguska Space Body] trajectory*. Besides, the contours of the areas, where the effect is observed to have *oval shapes stretched along the direction of the TSB trajectory* (Emelyanov et al. 1979, Vasilyev 1999).

The stretched oval shapes certainly remind us of the Carolina Bays.

One has an impression that the flight of the TSB was accompanied by some unknown agent capable to induce remote ecological and maybe even genetic changes.

The paper goes on for a bit talking about trees and then mentions a possible effect on a human being:

> A very interesting genetic mutation, possibly related to the Tunguska event, was discovered by Rychkov (2000). Rhesus negative persons among the Mongoloid inhabitants of Siberia are exceptionally rare. During 1959 field studies, Rychkov discovered an Evenk woman lacking the Rh-D antigen. Genetic examinations of her family enabled to conclude that a very rare mutation of the Rh-D gene happened in 1912. This mutation may have affected the woman's parents, who in 1908 lived at some 100 km distance from the epicenter and were eyewitnesses of the Tunguska explosion. The woman remembered her parents' impressions of the event: a very bright flash, a clap of thunder, a droning sound, and a burning wind (Rychkov 2000).
>
> ...
>
> A recurrent appearance of the TSB trajectory and some special points related to it in the above given stories suggests nevertheless that the flight and explosion of the TSB was accompanied by some unknown stress factor. A great challenge for the conventional Tunguska theories is where to find and explain the nature of this factor. We think that such a factor might be electromagnetic radiation. Interestingly, a powerful electromagnetic radiation is suspected to accompany electrophonic meteors - an interesting class of enigmatic meteoritic events.[185]

Let's stop here and talk about electrophonics and meteors. Reports of noisy meteors date back to at least the year 817, when a Chinese observer documented a meteor with a sound "like a flock of cranes in flight." In 1676, Italian astronomer Geminiano Montanari observed one that sounded like "the rattling of a great Cart running over Stones." Montanari's calculations put the meteor thirty-eight miles up in the sky, which was – as he well knew – too far away for its sound to reach him instantly so he doubted that he had actually heard it, though – thankfully – he recorded the data anyway. Later, in 1833, an intense Leonid meteor storm resulted in more reports of meteors that swished, whooshed, or "resembled the noise of a child's popgun." Once again, it was deemed impossible for the sound to have traveled that fast, so the reports were discounted.

These odd reports were unexplained until Colin Keay[186], of the University

---

185. Silagadze (2008), op. cit.
186. Keay (1980) 'Audible Sounds Excited by Aurorae and Meteor Fireballs', found here: http://home.pacific.net.au/~ddcsk1/

of Newcastle in Australia suggested in 1980 that as meteors fall through the Earth's magnetic field, they generate radio signals audible to the human ear.

Keay knew that, ordinarily, radio waves are electromagnetic, not acoustic, and thus are not something that one ordinarily 'hears'. In order for something to be heard, acoustic waves – vibrations of molecules of air – have to be present. These waves impinge on the eardrum and vibrate the inner ear, which then converts the vibrations into sound. Electromagnetic waves such as radio signals and visible light don't need a medium to propagate, don't make waves in the air, and thus don't vibrate the human eardrum. Even radio waves of 20 Hz to 20,000 Hz – low frequencies, corresponding to the range of acoustic frequencies that humans can register as sound – are, by themselves, inaudible.

To make radio waves audible, humans invented the transducer, a device that efficiently translates electromagnetic waves into air-moving waves which can then be heard as sound. What Keay discovered was that even ordinary objects can act as such transducers. When slips of paper, aluminum foil and even eyeglasses were exposed by Keay to rapidly shifting electromagnetic fields (that is, radio waves of very low frequency), the objects oscillated ever so slightly, creating weak – and faintly audible – acoustic waves.

Keay postulated that falling meteors generate very low-frequency radio signals that travel at the speed of light to the ground, where they cause any number of things in the environment to vibrate, from your eyeglasses to your hair! That means that, at the exact time that you see the meteor, you may also hear crackling, whistling or swishing sounds; sounds like a jet airplane or whatever. That is to say, you are not actually hearing sound from the fireball but rather hearing sound from local objects vibrating in response to the intense VLF[187] emission of the fireball. That is also why the phenomenon may be heard by one person and not another.

If you need a bit more on why and how this can happen, the idea is that the turbulent plasma trail behind the fireball interacts with the Earth's magnetic field, twisting and distorting it, and then, as the field relaxes within milliseconds, it emits the VLF waves. Obviously, details such as entry angles and turbulence are probably involved which may be why all meteorites don't produce sounds, though many do.[188] ELF[189] and VLF electromagnetic fields can also be generated by comet or meteor explosions the same way an EMP[190] can be generated by a nuclear explosion.

---

187. Very Low Frequency.
188. Colin Keay's list of publications on the topic of Electrophonic Meteors can be found here: http://home.pacific.net.au/~ddcsk1/bibliog.htm
189. Extremely Low Frequency.
190. Electro Magnetic Pulse.

Getting back to our Tunguska comet/meteor: are there any accounts of anyone hearing it?

> ... at 8-9 in the morning, not later, the sky was completely clear, without any clouds. I entered the bath (in the yard) and had just taken my shirt off when suddenly I heard sounds resembling a cannonade. At once I ran to where I could see toward the south-west and west. The sounds still continued at that time, and I saw in the south-west direction, at an altitude about half way between the zenith and the horizon, a flying red sphere with rainbow stripes at its sides and behind it. The sphere remained flying for some 3-4 seconds and then disappeared in the north-east direction. The sounds were heard all the time the sphere flew, but they ceased at once as the sphere disappeared behind the forest.

And:

> I was a leather master. In summer at about 8 AM tanners and I washed wool on the bank of the Kana river when suddenly a noise as from wings of a frightened bird, emerged from the direction south to east. ... and a wave went up the river like ripples. After this a piercing strike followed and the other duller strikes, as if from underground thunder. The strike was so powerful that one of the workers... fell into the water. With the emergence of the noise, a radiance appeared in the air, of spherical shape, the size of half Moon and with a bluish tinge, quickly flying in the direction from Filimonov to Irkutsk. Behind the radiance a trail was being left in the form of sky-bluish stripes, stretching along almost all the track and gradually decaying from the end point. The radiance disappeared behind the mountain without any explosion. ... the weather was absolutely clear and there was stillness all around...

Two witnesses recall that the sound was heard *before* the appearance of the object. One said it sounded like low thunder, another said it was "cavernous" and of a low tone. The scientist who took down these accounts, E. L. Krinov[191], thought that they were likely psychological in nature, that the witnesses changed the order of seeing and hearing, or thought they heard something when they didn't. With the information about the potentials for actually hearing these things via electrophonics, let's assume they were giving an accurate report.

What we notice is that the Tunguska sounds appear to have been very

---

191. Krinov (1949), 'The Tunguska meteorite', cited and quoted by Silagadze.

powerful. A similar terrible roar was said to have been heard by eye-witnesses to the South American event in 1935.[192] The more recent 2002 Vitim [193] meteorite, which fell on 25th September of that year, was reported to have been accompanied by St. Elmo's fire [194]:

Artificial St Elmo's fire triggered by a tethered rocket.

It was night and there was no electricity because the settlement was disconnected. I woke up and saw a flash in the street. The filament lamps of the chandelier lighted dimly to half their normal intensity. After 15-20 seconds, an underground boom was heard. Next morning I went to the dispatcher office of the airport. Security guards... told me that they had seen balls of light burning on the wooden poles of the fence surrounding the airport's meteorological station. They were very frightened. Fires glowed on the perimeter of the protection fence for 1-2 seconds.

The settlement described above where all these electrical phenomena occurred was *30 or 40 kilometers distant* from the bolide's flight path. The Tunguska event was about 3 orders of magnitude greater than the 2002 event, so one suspects that it may have caused even greater electric anomalies had there been anybody but reindeer to take note of it, or any lightbulbs around to react to the charged atmosphere.

The question is; could this electrical phenomenon be related to genetic mutations?

Even relatively brief exposures to high intensity ELF electric fields were shown to be fatal to mice, Drosophila and bees. For example, above 500 v/cm, *bees sting each other to death*. And 30-500 v/cm at 50 Hz is sufficient to change metabolic rate and motor activity.

ELF electric field exposure affects the central nervous system. For exam-

192. Iron/nickel meteorite Maria Elena (Chile).
193. River in Eastern Siberia, Russia.
194. St. Elmo's fire is a weather phenomenon in which luminous plasma is created by a coronal discharge from a sharp or pointed object in a strong electric field in the atmosphere (such as those generated by thunderstorms or created by a volcanic eruption).

ple, a significant increase in hypothalamic activity was recorded from the microelectrodes implanted in anesthetized rats during the 1 h exposure period to the inhomogeneous electric field of 0.4 v/cm maximum at 640 Hz. Some in vitro studies indicate effects on the calcium release and biochemical function. For example, 1.55 v/cm electric field at 60 Hz caused *complete loss of biochemical function in brain mitochondria* after 40 min exposure.

Exposure to the ELF electric or magnetic field *produces a physiological stress response*. For example, rats exhibited depressed body weights, decreased levels of brain choline acetyltransferase activity, and elevated levels of liver tryptophan pyrrolase after 30-40 days exposure to 0.005-1.0 v/cm electric field at 45 Hz.

It was found that an asymmetrically pulsed magnetic field repeating at 65 Hz with a peak value of several G accelerates the healing of a bone fracture in dogs. Some studies indicated a slight enhancement of growth in plants near high-voltage transmission lines. The growth rate of beans was significantly (about 40%) effected by 64 days exposure to 0.1 v/cm electric field at 45 Hz, when the bean seeds were planted in soil. But no significant effect was observed when the soil was replaced with a nutrient solution. ...

Some studies suggest that exposure to power frequency electromagnetic fields may lead to increased risks of cancer, especially for leukemia and brain cancer. ... For example, eight of the eleven studies conducted in 1991-1995 found statistically significant elevation of risk for leukemia. And four of the eight investigations that studied brain cancer also found some increase in risk (Heath 1996). Nevertheless Heath considers the overall evidence as "weak, inconsistent, and inconclusive".

For energetic reasons, VLF/ELF radiation of not thermal intensity can not damage DNA or other cellular macromolecules directly. On this basis, the possibility that such weak electromagnetic fields can induce any biological effects was even denied for a long time (Binhi & Savin 2001), until a plethora of experimental evidence proved that "Nature's imagination is richer than ours" (Dyson 1996). Let us mention one such recent experiment of Tokalov et al. (2003).

Cells have very effective emergency programs to cope with adverse environmental conditions. Remarkably, cellular stress response is rather uniform irrespective to the stress factor nature. Some cellular functions that are not essential for survival, for example cell division, are temporarily suspended. Besides special kind of genes, the so called heat shock proteins (HSP), will be activated. Their major function is the proper refolding of the damaged proteins. Heat shock proteins, notably the HSP70, were first discovered while investigating cellular responses to a heat shock, hence the name. Tokalov et al.

(2003) studied effects of three different stressors on the induction of several heat shock proteins and on the cell division dynamics. The stress was produced by 200 keV X-ray irradiation, by exposure to a weak ELF electromagnetic field (50 Hz, 60 ± 0.2 µT), or by a thermal shock (41°C for 30 min)....

The fact that weak electromagnetic fields can induce the stress proteins indicates that cells consider electromagnetic fields as potentially hazardous (Goodman & Blank 2002). This is surprising enough, because the magnitude of an effective magnetic stimulus is very small. Electromagnetic fields can induce the synthesis of HSP70 at an energy density fourteen orders of magnitude lower than heat shock (Goodman & Blank 2002).

Such extra sensitivity to the magnetic field must have good evolutionary grounds. The interesting thermo-protective effect of the ELF electromagnetic field exposure mentioned above, and the absence of any effects of weak electromagnetic fields on the cell proliferation, may indicate that cells are not really expecting any damage from the weak electromagnetic impulse, but instead they are using this impulse as some kind of early warning system to prepare for the really hazardous other stress factors which often follow the electromagnetic impulse. There is another aspect of this problem also: some recent findings in evolutionary biology suggest that heat shock proteins play an important role in evolution. HSP90 guides the folding process of signal transduction proteins which play a key role in developmental pathways. When HSP70 functions normally, a large amount of genetic variation, usually present in genotype, is masked and does not reveal itself in phenotype. However, under the stress HSP70 is recruited to help chaperone a large number of other cellular proteins. Its normal role is impaired and it can no longer buffer variation.

Therefore some mutations will become unmasked and individuals with abnormal phenotype will appear in the population. If a mutation proves to be beneficial in the new environmental conditions, the related traits will be preserved even after the HSP70 resumes its normal function.

Therefore *HSP70 acts as a capacitor of evolution.* If environmental conditions are stable, the buffering role of HSP70 ensures the stability of phenotype despite increased accumulation of hidden mutations in genotype. When the environmental conditions suddenly change, as for example after the asteroid impact, which is believed to cause the dinosaur extinction 65 million years ago, this great potential of genetic variation is released in phenotype and the natural selection quickly finds the new forms of life with greater fitness. The Drosophila experiments of Rutherford and Lindquist (1998) demonstrated this beautiful mechanism, which may constitute the molecular basis of evolution....

Further studies have shown that the HSP70 and HSP60 protein families also buffer phenotypic variation (Rutherford 2003). As was mentioned above, experiments demonstrated that ELF electromagnetic fields can induce various heat shock proteins and in particular HSP70. Therefore we can speculate that ecological and genetic consequences of the Tunguska event are possibly *not related to mutations which happened during the event, but are manifestations of the latent mutations, already present in the Tunguska biota*, which were unmasked due to the stress response. ELF/VLF radiation from the Tunguska bolide might act as a stressor thereby explaining why the effect is concentrated towards the trajectory projection. ...

We do not know whether the TSB flight was also accompanied by ionizing radiation. This is not excluded as well because the strong electric fields associated with the alleged space charge separation could produce energetic enough runaway electrons. Even if present, this radiation maybe will be too attenuated before reaching the ground to produce significant biological effects. However, it seems very plausible that at least the explosion was accompanied by intense bursts of ionizing radiation from lightnings with possible biological consequences...

Cometary bombardments are now considered as the cause for the dinosaurs' extinction.

Interestingly, if the above given explanation is correct, the Tunguska genetic anomaly represents in miniature the action of the molecular basis of evolution. On a much greater scale, global catastrophic events, like the asteroid crash 65 million years ago which ended the dinosaur era, boost[ed] the evolution by the same mechanism. We are left to admire the Grand Design of Nature and try to survive its next evolutionary turn. [Emphasis, mine.] [195]

However, as we notice, the genetic changes that might be induced by these electromagnetic phenomena can be positive or negative and it gives an all-new meaning to creation having taken place by the 'Word of God'! [196]

---

195. Silagadze (2008), op. cit.
196. One also wonders, in passing, about the possible relationship between electrophonic sounds and the many reports of strange and mysterious sounds coming from the earth and sky in the past few years. Is there a relationship between them and the increasing reports of cannibalism around the planet?

Legends in the Making

There is something else of interest to us here from the above paper that isn't directly related to physical effects. The author reports that a Siberian tribe in the region of the Tunguska event had already derived a spiritual significance from the impact.

> It starts with the battle between two Tunguska Evenki clans. Over the years, their feud escalated, both clans using their powerful shamans to curse to the other, with evil spirits, misfortune and disease. The hostility between them grew until one shaman called upon the Agdy to destroy the hated enemy forever. These fearsome iron birds fly above the earth in huge clouds, flapping their terrible wings to cause thunder, flashing lightening from their fiery eyes. On that sunny morning in June, the sky became black as a never ending legion of the fearsome birds swooped low over the unfortunate Shanyagir clan. Their devastating blasts of fire blew the Shanyagir's tents up into the air over the tree tops. The clan's belongings were destroyed, two hundred and fifty of their reindeer vanished without a trace, the ancient forest was flattened in every direction, and those who still could, fled in panic. To this day, the Evenk believe that *only the Agdy can live in the area where the explosion took place.* Only a few will risk visiting. And none will live there." (Gordon & Monkman 1997)

Although the cultures are different, this Evenk myth has some resemblance with the Sodom and Gomorrah Biblical story of miraculous destruction of these cities by the raining down of fire from heaven. One can even think that this ancient myth was also born due to real cosmic event (Clube & Napier 1982). In the Koran, the holy book of Islam, one finds a similar story (Wynn & Shoemaker 1998) "about an idolatrous king named Aad who scoffed at a prophet of God. For his impiety, the city of Ubar and all its inhabitants were destroyed by a "dark cloud brought on the wings of a great wind."

This last story has an unexpected and adventurous continuation. In 1932 an eccentric British explorer John Philby (Monroe 1998), obsessed by the idea to find Ubar, made an arduous trip into the Empty Quarter of southern Saudi Arabia, which is one of the most inaccessible and formidable deserts of our planet (Wynn & Shoemaker 1997). He really found something interesting, the place he dubbed Wabar – fortunate misspelling because it was not the Lost City of Koran, but the place of a fierce meteorite impact (Wynn & Shoemaker 1997, 1998). The real Ubar city was allegedly found much later and this is another breathtaking adventure (Clapp 1999). Radar images from the Landsat and SPOT remote sensing satellites, which uncovered old caravan routes, played the crucial role in this discovery (El-Baz 1997). Evidence indicates that Ubar was not destroyed from heaven, instead it *fell into a sink-hole* created by the underground limestone cavern collapse. But the Wabar meteorite was certainly capable of destroying Ubar or any other ancient city, because the 12 kilotons blast was comparable to the Hiroshima bomb (Wynn & Shoemaker 1998). The Tunguska explosion was a thousand times more powerful, capable of destroying any modern city. Therefore we come to the conclusion that the unconscious fears of modern man about hazards from the outer space are not completely groundless, although not aliens but minor space bodies cause the peril. [Emphasis, mine.] [197]

One wonders, of course, if the increasing number of sinkholes in recent years [198] can be related in any way to cosmic phenomena? For example, if the Earth were to move into a dust stream left by some ancient disintegrated comet, would it create infinitesimal drag on the rotation of the planet, thereby causing a slowing of the lithosphere in relation to the mantle?

Guatemala City, February 2007. A near-perfect circle of earth dropped some 30 stories almost instantly.

Another possibility is the previously mentioned grounding of the Sun by its approaching companion star. Such grounding would reduce the Sun's activity and the subsequent solar winds received by Earth. The positive ionosphere would become less positive and therefore attract less of the Earth electrons to its surface. The result would be a reduced electric field within our planet, i.e. a decrease in the attraction between the surface electrons and the positive ions in the core, leading to a literal 'opening up' of the planet.

In concluding this section, I'd like to remind the reader that hair was one of the elements that Colin Keay of the University of Newcastle in Australia proposed could 'transduce' electrophonic radiation. One then thinks of 'long-haired Franks' and Nazarites and Samson and his strength 'in his hair' and so on.

Comets and Earthquakes

We noticed in the description of cometary events given by Firestone and Co that it was said the impacts would stimulate earthquakes and volcanic eruptions. Apparently, it doesn't have to be a global cataclysm to do this. In *Rain*

---

197. Silagadze (2008).
198. See my website Sott.net for regular updates on sinkholes and other phenomena.

of Iron and Ice[199] by John Lewis, we learn that the Earth is regularly hit by extraterrestrial objects and many of the impacting bodies explode in the atmosphere, as happened in Tunguska, leaving no craters or long-lasting visible evidence of a body from space. These impacts or atmospheric explosions *may produce earthquakes or tsunamis without any witnesses being aware of the cause.* After all, the Earth is 75% water, and lots of things can – and do – happen without any eye-witnesses, so we really have no way of knowing if all the earthquakes on our planet are caused by normal movement or not.[200] So, the main thing that Lewis brings to the table is the idea that some well-known historical earthquakes could very well have been impact events.

According to Lewis, our Earth actually experiences these types of events rather often, even if somewhat irregularly. He reiterates the point that has been made by our previous experts: that *the ablative effects of an overhead cometary explosion can be such that literally nothing survives.* Explosions in the sky – some of them enormous – have profoundly affected the history of humanity. Strangely, as already mentioned, historians, as a group, don't speak about such things. That is one of the things that are making this research so difficult. It's not just a matter of going and reading a history book and noting the author saying something like: 'Well, in 325 CE Constantine was terrified by an overhead cometary explosion, decided to adopt Christianity as a consequence and to make it the state religion. The people were ripe for it since they were scared by the many "signs in the heavens."'

The dates that the various researchers have given to large events that can be discerned in the scientific records are 12800, 8200, 7000, 5200, 4200, 3000, 2354, 1628, 1150, 500, 208 BCE, and 550, 850 and 1300 CE.[201] (These can be adjusted as more precise dating methods are developed or applied.)

> All of these peaks coincide with climatic, and many of them with known cultural, downturns. It is suggested that most of the rapid climate shifts during the Holocene[202] could be attributed to cosmic activity. It is also believed that the cosmic events, in one way or the other, are responsible for the Dark Ages in our history.[203]

---

199. Lewis (1997), *Rain of Iron and Ice*.
200. About the Tunguska event, Innokentiy Mikhaylovich Suslov (1926) writes that the seismograph of Irkutsk recorded a really extraordinary type of earthquake.
201. Ice core, peat bog, tree ring dates combined.
202. 10000 BCE to today.
203. Franzen (2007), 'The peatland/ice age hypothesis revised, adding a possible glacial pulse trigger'.

If you do the math with the above numbers, you will notice the time distance between them as follows: 4,600, 1,200, 1,800, 1,000, 1,200, 646, 726, 478, 650, 292, 758, 300, 450 years. I don't think this means that the time periods between events are getting shorter, but rather that the evidence from the older periods is just much harder to detect (not to mention that the dates themselves may be somewhat inexact). Plus, a lot really depends on the potentials for the elements within the comet stream orbit to cross the Earth orbit at the exact point where there are large clusters of larger-than-dust objects, boulders and such. But do consider that the events of the distant past were probably as close together as the ones of the more recent past; we just can't detect it yet. Some events may have been milder than others. That means that we may have had a mild event some 4 or 5 hundred years ago, and are overdue for the next one at present. On the other hand, it could be that the time between events *is* getting shorter!

The 12800 BCE[204] event is the one of most interest because that is the one which, apparently, nearly destroyed all life on Earth. At the very least, it destroyed the mega-fauna on all continents. Plato wrote about the catastrophic destruction of Atlantis[205] that occurred in a day and a night about 11,600 years ago, which is pretty darn close in time and gives one pause. Again, this event is the topic Firestone, West and Warwick-Smith cover exhaustively in their book *The Cycle of Cosmic Catastrophes*, discussed above. I understand that they have modified their ideas now, and fall more in line with what Baillie, Bailey, Clube and Napier and others propose regarding a giant comet. It almost overwhelms the mind to consider the *hundreds of thousands* of Carolina Bays and the enormity of the mass death dated to that time that is in evidence around the planet.

Fear of Comets

The question that Baillie asks, but never really answers is: What was it that so successfully stopped people asking why there is a traditional and deeply ingrained fear of comets in the psyche of humanity? He points out that, yes,

---

204. You will note variations on the 13,000 years ago events that is due to the dating variations of the different sources.
205. "But at a later time there occurred portentous earthquakes and floods, and one grievous day and night befell them, when the whole body of your warriors was swallowed up by the earth, and the island of Atlantis in like manner was swallowed up by the sea and vanished; wherefore also the ocean at that spot has now become impassable and unsearchable, being blocked up by the shoal mud which the island created as it settled down." *Timaeus* 25c-d, Bury translation.

there are people outside of mainstream academia who ask these questions. But why, against all good common sense, is this subject so widely and systematically ignored, marginalized and ridiculed? The odd thing is that, even though Baillie points out that many high-level scientists and government agencies are taking these things seriously (John Lewis, referenced above, for example), it is still *ignored, marginalized and ridiculed to the general public via the mainstream media*! Baillie writes:

> Impacts from space are not fiction, and it seems highly likely that quite a number have taken place in the last few millennia (over and above the small crater-forming examples already mentioned). It is just that, for some reason, most people who study the past have chosen to avoid, or ignore, the issue.[206]

For many years I have struggled with the dichotomy between mainstream archaeology and alternative archaeology, which included reports of 'out of place artifacts' that are collected into books and marketed for their curiosity and shock value. When you read the mainstream works, you begin to doubt the sanity of the alternative views: that there were ancient civilizations from which all the numerous oddities derive. The mainstream archaeologists never, ever mention certain things. An example: Ian Tattersall wrote a nice little book with the ambitious title: *The World From Beginnings to 4000 BCE*, which is only 143 pages long, including its index! It's a pretty good overview of the current mainstream perspective, but the margins of my copy are full of notes that refer to items that totally contradict many things that Tattersall writes, not to mention pointing out his own self-contradictions – sometimes he does it on the same page! What really baked my noodle was Tattersall's short section on the Natufian[207] culture. He discusses their primitive way of life, mentions their stone toolkit, and completely ignores certain stone vases that I examined in the Louvre that are labeled 'Natufian' and which could not possibly have been made without some sort of advanced technology[208]; they actually have signs of machining on them which, having been raised by an engineer, are obvious to me! I can't believe that any scholar with two firing neurons can accept that these objects were produced by a stone-age culture that gave no other evidence of such mechanical sophistication.

So, how to reconcile these OOPARTs with the fact that large scale archae-

---

206. Baillie (2006), op. cit.
207. Epipaleolithic culture located in the Levant (today's Lebanon). 12500-9500 BCE.
208. See: Petrie (1883), *Pyramids and Temples of Gizeh*. Also: Dunn (1998) *The Giza Power Plant*.

ology does not seem to turn up any evidence of prior great and advanced civilizations? A simple answer might be that archaeologists are not trained in engineering so it is unlikely that they would even recognize the marks made by machine type tools on the materials they uncover.[209] But I think it is more than that.

One gets the feeling from reading Tattersall's little book that there was so much more that he wanted to say about some things and that he didn't even believe all he was writing himself. There was no conviction in his tone and once in awhile he would write something that just hinted that he knew much more than he felt he could say; he knew which side his bread was buttered on and was sorry for it. He came across as a thoroughly nice guy. That is what makes it so hard. I am married to a mainstream scientist who has gone a bit maverick. We know many scientists who would very much like to work in a system that was less controlled by financial concerns and less dominated by politics. But, as is the case in almost any unhappy line of work, they sigh, look up at the ceiling and say 'what can you do?' They have to make a living too, and they want to make enough so that they can work on what really interests them in their spare time.

On the other side, authors of revisionist/alternative history usually write very popular, sensationalist books, make plenty of money and, because of their lack of scientific rigor, earn the enmity of many mainstream scientists. (Not always, though. I know of several very good mainstream experts who have written acknowledgements to some of the alternative writers for bringing anomalies to their attention!) These authors do, however, make certain of the mainstream scholars – the authoritarian types – angry because they bring to light many excellent points and valid evidence that is often ignored, dismissed, or ridiculed within the academic community.

As Edward Malkowski writes in his book, *Before the Pharaohs*, archaeological remains:

> ...can be compared to a crime scene that has gone unnoticed for years... Since moving objects around can mask clues as to what happened, when police investigators arrive at a crime scene, they prefer that everything remain as it was when the offense occurred. ... If enough facts can be established through deduction, an explanation of all the evidence leads the sleuth to a theoretical conclusion as to 'whodunit'. It serves as the basis for further investigation and, hopefully, apprehension of the person who committed the crime.

---

209. I think that archaeologists should also be required to study engineering before they are turned loose.

Investigating prehistory is not all that different from investigating a crime scene, but it takes place on a much broader scale. The greater the evidence, the greater the possibility that researchers can ascertain what happened when, and who was involved. As do police investigators, archaeologists and other historical researchers prefer that the evidence discovered remain in situ – in its original place when discovered – and untouched by human hands. This reveals irrefutable facts that are essential for the formation of a viable theory.

However, in the formulation of theory, the interpretation of evidence may be problematic. Physical evidence and historical facts are often viewed with a certain bias. This bias is a set of assumptions an individual brings to the evaluation of evidence. For example, researchers who believe civilization has only recently achieved technical sophistication will tend to disregard any evidence to the contrary, sometimes no matter how strong. One way to work around this bias is to consider expert analysis from other disciplines.[210]

I couldn't agree more. Archaeologists should be trained in engineering and physics to some extent; they should have a good grasp of astronomy and climatology, geology and, most of all, good psychology, especially in reference to understanding how their own minds work and how easy it is to be either deceived or delusional. It's basically the difference between Sherlock Holmes and Dr. Watson; nowadays, most science – particularly archaeology and history – is of the Dr. Watson variety.

There certainly appears to be 500,000 years of Neanderthal remains to be found, all static and of the same level of primitivity for most of that time. Then, suddenly, comes the 'arrival' of Cro-Magnon[211], the cave painters of Europe. This is a huge problem because they just showed up in Europe with mental capacities that were, apparently, equal to our own, with nary a sign of slow and gradual 'evolution'. Archaeologist Marc Azéma of the University of Toulouse – Le Mirail – in France and independent French artist Florent Rivère have done a study[212] showing that Paleolithic artists *used animation effects* in their cave paintings that utilized the visual property of retinal persistence to create 'moving pictures' in flickering light. They deconstructed some of the images that have multiple layers in slightly different positions, put them on videos and ran the video sequentially, and darned if it wasn't an exact depiction of the creature in action! And yet, there have been found

---

210. Malkowski (2005), *Before the Pharaohs: Egypt's Mysterious Prehistory*.
211. First known Homo sapiens sapiens (modern humans). The earliest remains of Cro-Magnon-like humans are radiocarbon dated to 43,000 years before present.
212. June 2012 issue of *Antiquity*.

remains of 'primitive lamps' in the caves. They painted using a wick in a dish of fat. How can that be reconciled with the sophistication of their art? Remains of their lunches have been found, showing what they were eating – usually red deer – while they were painting bison and horses (so it wasn't 'hunting magic' they were aiming for with the images). Campsites and places where feasts were held have been found with all the more-or-less primitive accoutrements that one would expect to find lying about (though they usually have to dig pretty deep to get to those layers). It's as if a high civilization was destroyed and the survivors included animation artists from the Walt Disney studios who sought to re-create experiences that they were familiar with in their 'pre-cataclysm life'.[213]

But if such a high civilization existed and was brought low by comet impacts and explosions, wiping the planet fairly clean or re-setting the radiometric dating clock, how do we explain those 500,000 years of Neanderthal activity on a planet where we are proposing that there were also advanced cultures? How do we reconcile mainstream archaeological finds, some of them dating back hundreds of thousands of years, with ideas of an ancient, high civilization that was wiped out in a shattering cataclysm 13,000 years ago?

The eight-legged bison at Chauvet cave. In flickering light, the superimposing of two images of the creature in different stances create the appearance of running.

I could go on and on.[214] Do you see my problem here? I have spent years reading both sides of this argument and something is drastically wrong with the picture. How can mainstream archaeologists spend years and years on this, conducting massive, excruciatingly meticulous digs and site surveys, and not find things from an ancient civilization? I think they do find such things often enough to be significant. And when they do find something, it is automatically interpreted as an OOPART, an intrusion, and excluded from the studies entirely, or reinterpreted in ways that would make a child laugh at the stupidity of the explanation. Lord knows, I've seen that often enough! And the only thing that can explain how a generally intelli-

213. See: http://www.sott.net/articles/show/246506-Stoneage-Artists-Created-Prehistoric-Movies
214. See: *Cataclysm* by Allan and Delair for one of the most impressive lists of evidence I've ever encountered, though their cosmology leaves a lot to be desired.

gent human being can say some of the stupid things that get said by some academics and other experts (not to mention the true believer types) is the Authoritarian Follower theory. Anything that doesn't fit the pre-conceived assumptions imposed by the constituted authorities is treated this way. I have even read of cases where such finds were actually destroyed deliberately so as not to harm the reputation of the researcher!

As to why more widespread smaller artifacts are not found everywhere, I think the answer is in the evidence of the Carolina Bays: overhead cometary explosions and the resulting ablation and radiometric re-set.[215] Added to that, the obviously incredible floods that accompanied the rapid melting of the ice sheets on the planet, not to mention tsunamis caused by impacts, earthquakes, underwater landslides and more. All of these things, taken together, could easily have wiped out the traces of any ancient high civilization, leaving only bits and pieces here and there, and some few megalithic and monumental structures that do, in fact, survive, though they are dated much later based on pure assumption and Darwin. Meanwhile, the stone artifacts have a much longer shelf-life, so they are found in great quantity almost everywhere.

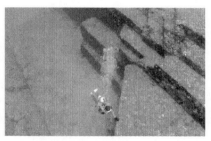

A stepped pyramid-like structure measuring 180 m long and 27 m wide was discovered off the coast of Japan. The monument has been dated to at least 8000 BCE.

I do think that we have plenty of evidence of prior high civilizations all over the planet in ancient monuments that have been misdated. The fact that mainstream geologists, archaeologists, paleontologists and historians reject it as such is one of the consequences of Judeo-Christian norms, one of the 'Horns of the dilemma' created by the Mosaic doctrine, as we will see soon enough.

Clube et al. point out that modern observations of comets show that they break-up and fragment into dust and bolides over time, which is why we no longer see a terrifying spectacle in our night skies as the ancient peoples did. But, as his calculations show, the giant comet, which must have been the progenitor of numerous meteor showers that our planet experiences every year in the present day, was undoubtedly huge. Its initial fragmentation events would not only have been stupefyingly frightening, but the records suggest that rains of cometary debris did, in fact, *repeatedly* bring ruin and de-

---

215. Discussed at length in *Secret History*.

struction on Earth. Most of these rains consisted of overhead explosions of the fragments which left no craters but were certainly capable of ablating the landscape for many miles in all directions under the blast zone. Further, the fact that what we have today are regular meteor showers of generally small particles suggests that in times past, these showers would not have consisted of such small bits, but rather larger bodies capable of destroying a kingdom in an instant.

In a paper addressed to the European Office of Aerospace Research and Development, dated June 4th, 1996 and entitled, 'The Hazard to Civilization from Fireballs and Comets', Clube writes:

> Asteroids which pass close to the Earth have been fully recognized by mankind for only about 20 years. Previously, the idea that substantial unobserved objects might be close enough to be a potential hazard to the Earth was treated with as much derision as the unobserved aether. Scientists of course are in business to establish broad principles (e.g. relativity) and the Earth's supposedly uneventful, uniformitarian environment was already very much in place. The result was that scientists who paid more than lip service to objects close enough to encounter the Earth did so in an atmosphere of barely disguised contempt. Even now, it is difficult for laymen to appreciate the enormity of the intellectual blow[216] with which most of the Body Scientific has recently been struck and from which it is now seeking to recover.
>
> The present report, then, is concerned with those other celestial bodies recorded by mankind since the dawn of civilization which either miss or impinge upon the Earth and which have also been despised. Now known respectively as comets (>1 kilometre in size) and meteoroids (<10m).
>
> Confronted on many occasions in the past by the prospect of world-end, *national elites have often found themselves having to suppress public panic* – only to discover, too late, that the usual means of control commonly fail. Thus an institutionalized science is expected to withhold knowledge of the threat; a self-regulated press is expected to make light of any disaster; while an institutionalized religion is expected to oppose predestination and to secure such general belief in a fundamentally benevolent deity as can be mustered. [...]
>
> There are fundamental paradoxes to be assimilated as a result of this unexpected situation. Thus the perceived culture of enterprise and enlighten-

---

216. Here Clube is talking about the Comet Shoemaker-Levy fragment impacts on Jupiter which produced a huge amount of excitement at the time and which occurred just two years before the date of this letter. Clube was probably commissioned to make this report as a consequence of Shoemaker-Levy.

ment which underpins the two centuries culminating with the Space Age and which led mankind to spurn comets and fireballs may now be seen as the prelude to a profound paradigm shift: the restoration of an environmental outlook more in keeping with that which preceded American Independence and which paid serious heed to comets and fireballs. [Emphasis mine] [217]

That is the answer to Mike Baillie's question in a nutshell. The thing is, it sounds surprisingly like our own era, does it not? In fact, Clube draws the direct connection:

...the Christian, Islamic and Judaic cultures have all moved since the European Renaissance to *adopt an unreasoning anti-apocalyptic stance*, apparently unaware of the burgeoning science of catastrophes. History, it now seems, is repeating itself: it has taken the Space Age to revive the Platonist voice of reason but it emerges this time within a modern anti-fundamentalist, anti-apocalyptic tradition over which governments may, as before, be unable to exercise control. ... **Cynics (or modern sophists), in other words, would say that we do not need the celestial threat to disguise Cold War intentions; rather we need the Cold War to disguise celestial intentions!** [Emphasis in the original] [218]

There are differences in detail and in scale, but the dynamics of a world gone mad, incredible cruelty running rampant, and global climate fluctuations are the same as we see before us now. How our monumental blindness came about is worth examining in some detail so that we can have some models that may help us evaluate the evidence regarding Moses that will come soon enough; be patient.

---

217. Clube (1996), op. cit.
218. Clube (1996), op. cit.

CHAPTER FIVE

COMET HUNTING –
THE ORIGIN OF ASTROLOGY

I have here before me on my desk a stack of books about Mesopotamian myths. One is called *Myths from Mesopotamia: Creation, The Flood, Gilgamesh and Others.*[219] Next: *Sumerian Mythology: A Study of Spiritual and Literary Achievement in the Third Millennium BCE.*[220] Next: *Myths of Babylonia and Assyria.*[221] Next: *The Storm God in the Ancient Near East.*[222] Next: *The Epic of Gilgamesh: Translated, with an Introduction and Notes.*[223] Next: *Gods, Demons and Symbols of Ancient Mesopotamia: An Illustrated Dictionary.*[224] I think that you can well imagine the content of these books from their titles.

I also have a slim little monograph entitled *A Sumerian Observation of the Köfels' Impact Event.*[225] The description of this item is as follows:

> Around 700 BCE an Assyrian scribe in the Royal Palace at Nineveh[226] made a copy of one of the most important documents in the royal collection. Two and a half thousand years later it was found by Henry Layard in the remains of the palace library. It ended up in the British Museum's cuneiform clay tablet collection as catalogue No. K8538 (informally called 'the Planisphere'), where it has puzzled scholars for over a hundred and fifty years. In this monograph Bond and Hempsell provide the first comprehensive translation of the tablet, showing it to be a contemporary Sumerian observation of an Aten asteroid over

---

219. Dally (2009), *Myths from Mesopotamia: Creation, the Flood, Gilgamesh, and Others.*
220. Kramer (1944), *Sumerian Mythology: A Study of Spiritual and Literary Achievement in the Third Millennium BCE.*
221. MacKenzie (2010), *Myths of Babylonia and Assyria.*
222. Green (2003), *The Storm God in the Ancient Near East.*
223. Kovacs (1989), *The Epic of Gilgamesh.*
224. Black & Green (1992), *Gods, Demons and Symbols of Ancient Mesopotamia.*
225. Bond & Hempsell (2008), *A Sumerian Observation of the Köfels' Impact Event.*
226. Today's Mosul, Northern Iraq.

a kilometer in diameter that impacted Köfels in Austria in the early morning of 29th June 3123 BCE. Alan Bond is a mechanical engineer specializing in trajectory analysis of launch vehicles and missiles and Mark Hempsell has degrees in physics, astronomy and astronautics. He is Senior Lecturer in Astronautics at the University of Bristol.

The Sumerian clay tablet called the 'Planisphere' (No. K8538, British Museum).

The Köfels geological structure is 5 km in diameter and was originally discussed as a volcanic feature but this was questioned by other scientists who proposed that it was the site of a meteorite impact. There is no clear crater at Köfels which implies a mid-air explosion. It clipped a ridge before doing so and cut out a 2km piece with a 6 degree slope. Other impact sites are associated with this object, secondary impacts of fragments that broke off during its flight through the atmosphere. These secondary impacts form an elliptical pattern with the primary impact at the furthest point. Fission track dating suggests a Bronze Age date consistent with the Sumerian observation.

What do these books – the mythology on the one side and the translation and analysis of the Planisphere on the other – have in common?

They are all about the same thing(s). If you read the books about the myths while keeping the scientific information compiled by Bond and Hempsell [227] in mind, you can dispense with all the woo-woo nonsense that experts in myths babble on about because literally everything begins to make sense. Unfortunately, the authors of all those books on Mesopotamian mythology, gods and demons didn't have the advantage of this information and so it seems that their entire careers were focused on illusions that they have propagated to others. Remember our 'Dark Interlude'? [228] Well, we are told lies for history and the myths that tell the truth about history are pronounced to be superstitious lies.

In their more technical and comprehensive book entitled *The Origin of*

---

227. Bond & Hempsell (2008).
228. Second chapter of the present book. Sub-sections are: 'What is Reality?' and 'The Authoritarians'.

Comets[229], astronomers Bailey, Clube and Napier recount the history of astronomy and astrology – and the related myths – as it developed among the Babylonians:

> In particular, the Babylonians combined their astronomy with the idea that history repeats itself, and with a very strong belief that celestial events exercised control over terrestrial ones. Why the latter assumption should have arisen amongst the ancient cultures of Mesopotamia has always been something of a mystery to historians, conditioned, as one now is, to the idea of the rotating celestial sphere serving merely as a passive backdrop against which to register celestial events.
>
> Indeed, it is clear that astronomy in the ancient Near East assumed an urgency in public affairs quite unlike the remote and detached business it has now become. The importance attached by these early civilizations to astronomical observations is reflected, for example, in the fact that watchtowers or ziggurats were provided for the use of astronomer-priests in almost every city of the land, rather like the churches and municipal buildings of modern times. Indeed, the amount of time and energy apparently devoted to such activities seems to have been quite out of proportion to anything which might reasonably be justified or explained on the grounds of idle curiosity, suggesting that the primary motivation for making the observations was once perhaps as compelling and as powerful as the defence of the realm. [...]
>
> [S]tudies of other civilizations at about this time also hint at a strong degree of astronomical involvement in everyday activities, suggesting that these cultures too were similarly obsessed by celestial affairs. Indeed, even the scattered communities of Western Europe developed strong cultural ties with the heavens, constructing stone circles and astronomically aligned megaliths at almost every conceivable opportunity. ...it is tempting to speculate that certain extremely precise megalithic alignments, which surprisingly have no obvious lunar, solar or even stellar connexion might now be interpreted as indicating the radiants of previously recognized intense meteor showers such as the Taurids. [...]

The ziggurat of Ur after its restoration.

---

229. Bailey, Clube & Napier (1990).

It is still customary to suppose that astronomy would inevitably have originated in an agricultural community of the kind known to have been present
in Mesopotamia through its calendrical ... requirements, never to have become an urgent occupation of the state. ... The dilemma facing modern scholars who confront this situation is well expressed by Neugebauer (1946, p. 38),
who admits: 'Mesopotamian "astrology" can be much better compared with
weather prediction from phenomena observed in the skies than with astrology in the modern sense of the word.' [...]

Indeed, the use of the meteorological analogy is particularly apt, since the
Chaldeans not only *expected periodic astronomical phenomena to affect the
earth but the same weather to recur in cycles of twelve solar years*, along with
good crops, famines, and pestilences. The ancient Mesopotamian attitude to
astronomy is thus generally recognized as being very strange, the more so since
it appears also to have involved a considerable element of fear and trepida-
tion: the overriding impression to emerge from the cuneiform literature as a
whole is of an astronomical phenomenon with a potential vastly more op-
pressive than the weather![230] [Emphases, mine.]

As noted, the main purpose of astrology seems to have been to provide a
sort of almanac of the relations between celestial events and how they affected the Earth. Obviously, if there were impacts (overhead explosions),
kings might die, lands might be laid waste, but it was undoubtedly difficult
to determine if a particular sighting was going to lead to an impact or not.
Obviously, many did not. Or they impacted somewhere else and that may
have proven to be beneficial to the Chaldeans[231] (or other astronomers in
question). The interpretation might then have been that the comet or fire-
ball(s) were the gods' way of saluting their king or smiting their enemy.

The research strongly suggests that ancient civilizations had very different experiences with the objects in the heavens than we think of as normal
today; for them it was normal, however, to have destructive, noisy, gods flying overhead at periodic intervals, smiting the land with thunderbolts or explosive catastrophes, or, at the very least, accompanying a period of dense
dust-loading of the atmosphere that led to crop failure and famine. Obviously,
this astronomical research has important implications for the interpretation
of ancient cosmologies and traditions, not to mention history.

Historians of all kinds who work in ignorance of modern astronomical

---

230. Bailey, Clube & Napier, op. cit.
231. Chaldea was a part of the Babylonian empire located around the estuaries of the Tigris
    and Euphrates, in modern-day Iraq.

(and geological) research are at a severe disadvantage. Many of them completely dismiss the physical reality of what the ancients experienced and thus not only do not understand their subjects, they mislead future generations.

Clube et al. propose that an extra-luminous, giant – I mean really giant! – comet in an earth crossing orbit underwent violent fragmentation, producing at least two, but likely more, conspicuous bodies – children – that were then explained by the Babylonian elites as gods, a pantheon of celestial beings.

Modern astronomers think of ancient astrology as irrational as opposed to modern astronomy, which is of course rational. The Babylonian astrologers were certainly committed to the idea of a physical association between celestial and terrestrial events, an idea that has been completely abandoned by modern astronomy in the post-Newtonian era. This was due to the perceived need to oppose the magical and miraculous from natural philosophy in order to oppose the counter-reformation theologians[232] of the 16th and 17th centuries: direct celestial interference in terrestrial affairs had to be denied in all contexts.

There were four phases in the evolution of astronomy: 1) judicial astrology; 2) zodiacal astrology; 3) horoscopic astrology; 4) scientific astronomy.

Judicial Astrology

Judicial Astrology assumed a very strong connection between purposeful celestial bodies and disasters on Earth. It was clearly so evident a fact to the ancients that much of the energy and financial resources of whole empires was devoted to observing the skies, developing a way to predict what was going to happen based on observation, and developing prophylactic measures that included appeals to the gods, sacrifices, and so forth. The idea was that a supreme deity was capable of imposing order and control on the activities in the skies; it just needed the proper rites and behavior of the king and his people to engage the care of that god. It is clear from ancient writings that human actions could bring on the wrath of the gods, or that the gods could and would use their smiting capabilities to punish bad behavior and 'pass over' without destruction if they knew that right conduct was being observed. This concept persists to this very day in the sense that religion means to bind oneself to a god who is supposed to protect one from harmful influences or events.

---

232. Period of reformation of the Catholic Church that lasted from 1545 to 1648. Its most influential theologians included Ignatius of Loyola, Teresa of Ávila and John of the Cross.

It also appears that some kings assumed their right to rule or conquer other states based on whether or not the god(s) cooperated by either sending a harmless comet or fireball to salute the king, or conveniently laying waste the land of the enemy. The birth of this idea, the Divine Right to Rule, has been a potent, persistent and pernicious force down through history.

This is, then, the broad outline of Judicial Astrology as understood by the Sumerians and their successors, the Babylonians. Real celestial things were impacting earth and affecting their lives, and their science and religion was devoted to trying to figure out how to survive.

Zodiacal Astrology

Over time, it appears that the chaos in the skies began to calm down. By the early part of the 1st millennium BCE, it's clear that astrology had taken on a new role in a different environmental context. The region of the sky once dominated by Anu, Enlil, Ninurta, Ishtar and others – essentially, the zodiacal belt – had been divided into sections, each of which was held to wield some kind of influence. It may have been that comets first sighted in any one of those segments had been known to behave in certain characteristic ways vis- à-vis the Earth. It does not appear that astrology, at this phase of its development, even considered any influences of the Sun, Moon and planets at all. The signs of the zodiac appear to have been markers of previous great events in the sky and were dated by the positions of the Sun, Moon and planets. This interpretation is supported by recent studies of astronomical iconography which denote that planets were observed purely for calendrical purposes.

For example, the previously-mentioned monograph written by astrophysicist Mark Hempsell and engineer Alan Bond about the clay tablet recovered from the Royal Palace archives in Ninevah demonstrates these assertions thoroughly and convincingly. The tablet was analyzed and shown to be a contemporary Sumerian observation of an Aten asteroid over a kilometer in diameter that impacted Köfels, Austria, in the early morning of 29th June, 3123 BCE. They were able to date it exactly because of the notation of the positions of the planets. They were able to estimate its size, trajectory and other elements, thanks to the Sumerian exactitude of observation. And yes, indeed, there is evidence of the event at the site in question.

My point here is that noting the position of planets in reference to the zodiac was merely a dating method and not part of the 'prediction' process of ancient astrology! Short-period comets in Earth-crossing orbits that were generated by the break-up of a giant comet would have been recognized by their meteor streams appearing from different 'signs of the zodiac', as they do today. In those times, when these streams were still very heavy and potent, it was undoubtedly recognized that they exerted an influence on Earth, even if serious impacts (overhead explosions) were in decline. Many formerly bright cometary bodies had become asteroidal and dark in appearance, though still possibly deadly, and thus arose the understanding of hidden or 'occult' influences.

Köfels' landslide. The concave escarpment lowered the mountain by about 200m. Displaced rockslide masses are circled with stippled dark lines.

The conclusion is that Babylonian zodiacal astronomy was developed due to the attempts to understand and predict the flux of fireballs and comets. At the same time, the Chaldeans used the zodiac for time-keeping and developed a very sophisticated lunar calendar. The Babylonians also developed a basic theory about the perturbation of the Moon to help them in calculating ephemerides. It was their arithmetic and algebra that the Greeks took over to form the geometric model of the cosmos.[233] Unfortunately, the Greeks were so enamored of the geometric model of epicycles and planetary motions that they imposed a physical scheme on the model, a series of nested crystalline spheres. The presence of these spheres, which were supposed to support the movements of the Sun, Moon and planets, meant that no celestial bodies could pass from one sphere to another. This ruled out completely the idea of any celestial body influencing the Earth and relegated comets to being earth-based atmospheric phenomena. Most people of the time still understood and accepted that comets were celestial bodies and that they did, indeed, affect the Earth, so it is interesting that the Greek world view so completely obviated this understanding.

---

233. See Neugebauer (1948, 1967).

Horoscopic Astrology

The geometric view of the cosmos advocated among Greek intellectuals was advanced beginning around 300 BCE. This is what led to 'horoscopic astrology', including a number of famous Egyptian tomb horoscopes which do *not* date earlier than this. The Greeks clearly had to explain things that were commonly known among the masses, that there were 'influences in the skies', and thus it was proposed that the planets exerted a distant influence on terrestrial affairs. Importantly, this was a *remote* influence.

A direct result of this 'geometric view' of the solar system was that planetary conjunctions and alignments were now seen to be important modifiers of influence. Here we detect a hint of ancient understanding transformed: clusters – or conjunctions – of comets that generally indicated bad fortune due to extended swarms of fireballs affecting the planet were now transformed into conjunctions of distant planets having positive or baleful influences on Earth.

Because it was geometric and mathematical, horoscopic astrology was intensely attractive to the puzzle-solving tendencies of the human mind among the educated and elite, and – as a result – it became very influential. It didn't hurt that the Greeks had also imposed a rather far-reaching hegemony on the Near East. This ultimately meant that horoscopic astrology completely replaced zodiacal astrology in the last few centuries BCE.

End of the Early Bronze Age

Getting back to the Middle East from whence our civilization supposedly originated; for almost 500 years the Hittites were the dominant power in Anatolia, the area that is mostly modern day Turkey, though they were completely forgotten for a very long time, remembered only in completely inaccurate renderings in the Bible. Modern studies reveal that the Hittites themselves were not a highly creative or innovative people, but that they drew most of the inspiration for their social, religious, literary and artistic renderings from the cultural traditions of both earlier and contemporary Near Eastern civilizations. Their greatest legacy is that, by absorbing the elements of their neighbors, they preserved them. This is typical of a regime that is 'new' or different within a given population: to seek to validate their legitimacy by connecting themselves in some way to the traditions of the native population.

We should note here that the arrival and rise of the Hittites in Anatolia follows a period of historical discontinuity, i.e. probably as a result of cometary destruction.

Scientists have found the first evidence that a devastating meteor impact in the Middle East might have triggered the mysterious collapse of civilisations more than 4,000 years ago. Studies of satellite images of southern Iraq have revealed a two-mile-wide circular depression which scientists say bears all the hallmarks of an impact crater. If confirmed, it would point to the Middle East being struck by a meteor with the violence equivalent to hundreds of nuclear bombs. Today's crater lies on what would have been shallow sea 4,000 years ago, and any impact would have caused devastating fires and flooding. The catastrophic effect of these could explain the mystery of why so many early cultures went into sudden decline around 2300 BCE. ...

The crater's faint outline was found by Dr Sharad Master, a geologist at the University of Witwatersrand, Johannesburg, on satellite images of the Al 'Amarah region, about 10 miles north-west of the confluence of the Tigris and Euphrates and home of the Marsh Arabs. ... Dr Benny Peiser, who lectures on the effects of meteor impacts at John Moores University, Liverpool, said [if confirmed, it would be] one of the most significant discoveries in recent years and would corroborate research he and others have

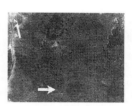

Satellite image of the crater discovered by Dr Sharad Master.

done. He said that craters recently found in Argentina date from around the same period – suggesting that the Earth may have been hit by a shower of large meteors at about the same time.[234]

Hundreds of years after the event, a cuneiform collection of 'prodigies', omen predictions of the collapse of Akkad, preserved the record that "many stars were falling from the sky" (Bjorkman 1973:106). Closer to the event, perhaps as early as 2100 BCE, the author of the *Curse of Akkad* alluded to "flaming potsherds raining from the sky" (Attinger 1984). Davis (1996) has reminded us of Clube and Napier's impact theory, and asked "Where is the archaeological and geological evidence for the role of their 'Taurid Demons' in human history?" The abrupt climate change at 2200 BCE, regardless of an improbable impact explanation, situates hemispheric and social collapse in a global, but ultimately cosmic, context.[235]

234. Matthews, 'Meteor clue to end of Middle East civilisations', *The Sunday Telegraph*, 4 November 2001. Retrieved here: http://www.telegraph.co.uk/news/worldnews/ 1361474/Meteor-clue-to-end-of-Middle-East-civilisations.html
235. Weiss (1997), *Late Third Millennium Abrupt Climate Change and Social Collapse in West Asia and Egypt*, p. 720.

It is not a surprise that, of all the various factors and data examined for clues that could explain the environmental and social upheavals at the end of the Early Bronze Age, catastrophe is the subject matter *most avoided by archaeologists and historians.* Yet most archaeologists are certainly aware of Claude Schaeffer's [236] enormous work, *Stratigraphie Comparée et Chronologie de l'Asie Occidentale* [237], which is an incredible collection of archaeological evidence demonstrating extensive earthquake and other catastrophic damage detected in Bronze Age settlements throughout the Near and Middle East.

Claude Schaeffer, the 20th century's most eminent French archaeologist, was the first researcher to present evidence for widespread seismic catastrophes in large parts of Asia Minor and the Levant at around 2300 BCE. Based on a comparative study of destruction layers in more than 40 sites, he ordered and classified earthquake horizons as synchronous and interrelated benchmarks in archaeological stratigraphy and chronology. Evidence for major earthquake damage in Early Bronze Age strata had been detected in many Anatolian and Near Eastern settlements, such as Troy, Alaca Hüyük, Boghazköy, Alishar, Tarsos, Ugarit, Byblos, Qalaat, Hama, Megiddo, Tell Hesi, Beit Mirsim, Beth Shan, Tell Brak and Chagar Bazar (Gammon 1980; 1982).

Most scholars, however, have refrained from taking Schaeffer's main research-findings into consideration. The recent and most comprehensive textbook on 3rd millennium BCE civilisation collapse *fails to mention his research altogether* (Dalfes et al. 1997). One looks in vain for any reference to his theory of Early Bronze Age collapse. This reticence is even more remarkable in view of the fact that Schaeffer was also, to my knowledge, the first archaeologist to claim that a distinct shift in climate was synchronous with civilisation collapse… « Au Caucase et dans certains régions de l'Europe protohistorique, des changements de climat semblent, à cette période, avoir amené des transformations dans l'occupation et l'économie du pays ». (Translation: "In the Caucasus and in some parts of protohistoric Europe, climate changes seem, at this time, to have brought changes in the occupation and economy of the country." [Emphasis, mine.] [238]

---

236. Schaeffer (1898-1982) was a French archeologist. His work led to the uncovering of the Ugaritic religious texts. Ugarit was a port city in Northern Syria.
237. Schaeffer (1948), *Stratigraphie Comparée et Chronologie de l'Asie Occidentale.*
238. Schaeffer (1948: 555/556), quoted by Peiser (1998), 'Comparative Analysis of Late Holocene Environmental and Social Upheaval: Evidence for a global disaster around 4000 BP', in *Natural Catastrophes During Bronze Age Civilizations: Archaeological, Geological, Astronomical, and Cultural Perspectives*, Peiser et al. (Eds.), pp. 117-139.

Gilgamesh, Odysseus and the Hittites

Hittite and Luwian texts have been found in large numbers; they are the earliest complete texts in any Indo-European language. The Hittites played an important role in transmitting the customs, traditions and institutions first attested in the earliest societies of Mesopotamia. The Hittite religion was a composite of rituals and beliefs of the native Hattians, the Indo-Europeans, Hurrian and other early Mesopotamian elements. Hittite literature was also composite, consisting of stories that were Hattian, Sumerian, Akkadian, Babylonian and Hurrian. So why is the Hittite version of the *Epic of Gilgamesh* so similar to *The Odyssey*, aside from the fact that we suspect that both are tales told around cometary events?

The fact is, some of the similarities cannot be explained by simply creating similar stories at widely separated locations based on observing similar events.

One of the as-yet-unanswered questions about the Hittites is: Where did they come from? And the related question is: Why did they come? The fact that there was clearly a cometary event in the couple of centuries before their rise to power suggests that they came from the same place that all the 'barbarian hordes' came from time and again throughout history: the Central Asian steppes. David W. Anthony writes:

> [A]rchaeologists generally do not understand migration very well, and migration is an important vector of language change ... Migration disappeared entirely from the explanatory toolkit of Western archaeologists in the 1970s and 1980s. But migration is a hugely important human behavior...
>
> Scholars noticed more than a hundred years ago that the oldest well-documented Indo-European languages – Imperial Hittite, Mycenaean Greek, and the most ancient form of Sanskrit, or Old Indic – were spoken by militaristic societies that seemed to erupt into the ancient world driving chariots pulled by swift horses. ...
>
> If Indo-European speakers were the first to have chariots, this could explain their early expansion; if they were the first to domesticate horses, then this could explain the central role horses played as symbols of strength and power in the rituals of the Old Indic Aryans, Greeks, Hittites, and other Indo-European speakers.
>
> The oldest written Indo-European languages belonged to the Anatolian branch. The Anatolian branch had three early stems: Hittite, Luwian, and Palaic. All three languages are extinct but once were spoken over large parts of ancient Anatolia, modern Turkey. Hittite is by far the best known of the

three, as it was the palace and administrative language of the Hittite Empire. Inscriptions place Hittite speakers in Anatolia as early as 1900 BCE. ...

The Hittites called themselves Neshites after the Anatolian city, Kanesh, where they rose to power. But Kanesh had earlier been a Hattic city, its name was Hattic. ... Hattic was a non-Indo-European language, probably linked distantly to the Caucasian languages. ... Hattic seems to have been spoken across all of central Anatolia before Hittite or Palaic was spoken there. The early speakers of Hittite and Palaic were intruders in a non-Indo-European central Anatolian landscape dominated by Hattic speakers who had already founded cities, acquired literate bureaucracies, and established kingdoms and palace cults. ...

The Hittite capital city, Hattusas, was burned in a general calamity that brought down the Hittite kings, their army, and their cities about 1180 BCE. The Hittite language then quickly disappeared; apparently only the ruling elite ever spoke it. ...

Proto-Anatolian is the language that was immediately ancestral to the three known daughter languages in the Anatolian branch. Proto-Anatolian can be described fairly accurately on the basis of the shared traits of Hittite, Luwian, and Palaic. ...

The Anatolian languages are quite different phonologically and grammatically from all the other known Indo-European daughter languages. They are so peculiar that many specialists think they do not really belong with the other daughters.

Many of the peculiar features of Anatolian look like archaisms, characteristics thought to have existed in an extremely early stage of Proto-Indo-European. ...

The best explanation for [the peculiarities of the Anatolian languages] is that Pre-Anatolian speakers became separated from the Proto-Indo-European language community at a very early date... [Other experts] suggest that Anatolian is an Indo-European language only in the broadest sense, as it did not develop from Proto-Indo-European. But it did preserve, uniquely, features of an earlier language community from which they both evolved. ...

[A] separation date of about 4000 BCE between Pre-Anatolian and the archaic Proto-Indo-European language community seems reasonable.[239]

Naturally, many experts think that Homer was influenced from the East, and that the reason the Homeric and Hesiodic pictures of the gods and life in general has so much in common with the picture presented in Babylonian and

---

239. Anthony (2010), *The Horse, The Wheel and Language.*

Ugaritic[240] poetry is that it must have been formed under Eastern influence because, of course, civilization began in Mesopotamia with the advent of agriculture, cities, writing (to keep accounts), and so on. The idea that agriculture, the wheel and writing may not necessarily be the bedrock of truly civilizing systems generally doesn't enter the discussion. It is taken as a given that control over vast numbers

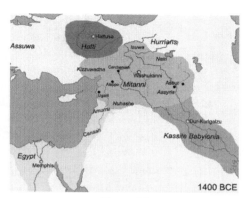

1400 BCE

The Middle East in 1400 BCE.

of people, the ability to mobilize them into armies to kill vast numbers of other people, and to thus have the means of establishing vast empires, is 'civilization'. It is possible that there was contact between the Hittites and the Mycenaeans, and it is through this channel that the stories were transmitted.

The Mycenaean civilization also appeared rather suddenly at about the same time as the rise of the Hittite empire. What is clear is that they didn't come from the same place because the languages were so different. Greek – as recorded in the Linear B tablets[241] – was the language of the warrior kings who ruled at Mycenaea and – surprise, surprise – were destroyed during the same period as the Hittite empire. There are numerous indications that Mycenaean Greek was an intrusive language in a land where non-Greek languages had been spoken. The Greek speakers who showed up in Greece, which wasn't Greece until they got there, obviously came from somewhere else.

While I'm on the subject, I should mention that Old Indic, the precursor of Sanskrit, the language of the *Rig Veda*[242], was recorded earliest in, of all places, *northern Syria*. The deities, moral concepts, and the language itself, first appeared in written documents far from India. The Mitanni dynasty, who we are going to encounter again later (along with the Hittites, which is why I'm writing about this at some length now), ruled over what is now northern Syria and they spoke a non-Indo-European language – Hurrian[243] – which was a dominant language of the region, including Eastern Turkey. Hurrian was native to the Anatolian uplands and is related to the Caucasian languages.

---

240. See note 234.

241. Clay tablets in Mycenean recovered from Knossos, Crete.

242. One of the oldest extant texts in any Indo-European language, conventionally thought to be of Indian origin.

243. Ancient people living during the Bronze Age in today's Southeastern Turkey (Anatolia).

However, all of the Mitanni kings – without exception – took *Old Indic throne names*, even if they had Hurrian names before they became king.[244]

The Mitanni had a military aristocracy called *maryanna*, which derives from an Old Indic word *márya* meaning 'young man'. The same word was used in the *Rig Veda* to refer to the heavenly war-band assembled around Indra. The Mitanni texts indicate that not only did the Old Indic language exist at that time, but that the religious pantheon and moral instructions of the *Rig Veda* did as well. The possible explanation for how this made its way to northern Syria is that charioteers from the East were hired by a Hurrian king at some point, and they later usurped his throne and power, founding a dynasty that continued to recite the hymns and prayers that were already being collected into the *Rig Veda*.

The Köfels event mentioned above was only one of a number of cataclysmic disruptions in recorded history. We are going to talk about later ones soon enough, but for the moment, let's skip from 3123 BCE to around 1200 BCE, the end of the Bronze Age. As the experts note, the archaeological evidence shows a widespread collapse of Bronze Age civilization in the Eastern Mediterranean world at the outset of the period, as the great palaces and cities of the Mycenaeans [245] were destroyed or abandoned. Around this time, the Hittite civilization [246] suffered serious disruption and cities up and down the Levant were destroyed. Following the collapse, fewer and smaller settlements suggest famine and massive depopulation. This is the signal of cometary influence, either by direct destruction or by distant bombardment with related climate stress.

After the collapse of Early Bronze Age societies in the 3rd millennium BCE, which led to mass migrations of peoples and the emergence of new empires such as the Hittites and Mycenaean, the Late Bronze Age was also destroyed in 1200 BCE, provoking more mass migrations and another Dark Age that lasted from at least 1100 to 800 BCE, some three hundred years.

End of the Late Bronze Age

Referring back to Claude Schaeffer, who we discussed above, we note that he found that Bronze Age sites over a huge area of the Near and Middle East showed *evidence of four destructive episodes*, the three most prominent being at 2300 BCE, 1650 BCE and 1200 BCE.

---

244. See: Anthony, *The Horse, The Wheel, and Language* for more information and citations.
245. Mycenaean civilization spanned from c. 1900 BCE to c. 1100 BCE. It was located where modern Greece now is.
246. Located where modern Turkey is. The Hittite Empire lasted from c. 1750 BCE to c. 1180 BCE.

It was the 1200 BCE event that finished off the Bronze Age. The Shang dynasty[247] in China and the Mycenaean civilization in Greece disappeared at the same time.

The problem is that even the biggest earthquakes have only local effects, which is one of the reasons his analysis was put aside and is ignored, for the most part, today. The alternative explanation, that during the Bronze Age the Earth was hit not once but several times by debris from space, most likely from a comet broken into pieces, fits the evidence exactly. As we have noted, meteors or asteroids do not have to hit the earth to destroy large areas; remember Tunguska.

> Here's our dilemma: All archaeologists agree that around the end of the 13th century B.C.E., the great Bronze Age civilizations of the Aegean and Eastern Mediterranean collapsed within 50 to 100 years of one another. But, alas, there is no consensus as to what actually brought about this devastation. Whatever the cause, one of the most glittering eras in human history came to an end.[248]

The archaeology reveals widespread collapse of the Eastern Mediterranean world at the beginning of this period, with cities being abandoned and/or destroyed. Many explanations attribute the fall of the Mycenaean civilization and the Bronze Age collapse to climatic or environmental catastrophe, combined with an invasion by Dorians or by the Sea Peoples or the widespread availability of new iron weapons.

In the period immediately prior to the full-bore onset of the disasters, there is evidence of large-scale revolts and attempts to overthrow existing kingdoms. This suggests economic and political instability. This appears to have been exacerbated due to the influx of surrounding peoples who were experiencing famine and hardship due to climate changes that appear to be associated with increased comet flux.

I will note here that, for the past hundred years or so, we have been experiencing similar things, with the intensity increasing dramatically since 2001, though it is much harder to see when you are in the middle of it than when you look back on it with the 20/20 vision of hindsight. And certainly, most of what is happening in our environment is disregarded in favor of focus on political and social issues.

---

247. The Shang started ruling in 1766 BCE. Their five centuries' reign left tens of thousands of bronze, jade, stone, bone and ceramic artifacts, which attest to a high level of civilization.
248. Stiebing (2001), 'When Civilization Collapsed: Death of the Bronze Age'.

In respect of the Greek Dark Age, with the collapse of the palatial centres of Mycenaea, no more monumental stone buildings were built and the practice of wall painting ceased; writing in the Linear B script ceased, pottery became simple in style and minimal in quantity, vital trade links were lost, and towns and villages were abandoned. The population of Greece was massively reduced, and the world of organized state armies, kings, officials and redistributive systems disappeared.

Some areas recovered more quickly than others; there was still farming, weaving, metalworking and pottery-making during these centuries, but it was on a staggeringly reduced level in both volume and technique. It appears that necessity was the mother of invention and hard times led to the survival of pockets of smarter, more creative and more socially engaged individuals. At the same time, such periods also encourage the survival of Machiavellian cheater types – Authoritarian leaders looking for followers. It could be said that disaster purifies both the best and the worst of humanity. And so it was that, during this period – the Greek Dark Age – the smelting of iron was learned, exploited and improved, ultimately to replace weapons and armor previously cast and hammered from weaker bronze, and the Machiavellian types took over – as seems to be the case again and again throughout history.

CHAPTER SIX

COMETS IN MYTHOLOGY

Ancient Greece is supposed to be the seminal culture of modern Western civilization. This is because classical Greek culture was adopted, to some extent, by the Roman Empire, which then spread its hegemony over the ancient world, including the philosophical ideology of Greece, which morphed into Christianity with a bit of Orientalizing influence from Judaism.

Classical Greece is generally said to have begun about the 8th century BCE when an 'oriental influence' was imported, including writing, which enabled the beginning of Greek literature, e.g. Homer and Hesiod and, later, Herodotus and others. These beginnings of Greek civilization began after a 'Dark Age' that we may justifiably think was a period following global stress and disruption due to cometary bombardment. Supposedly, this Dark Age followed the collapse of the Mycenaean civilization (which had its own script, as mentioned above), and which came with the general, overall collapse – more or less in its entirety – of the Bronze Age civilization.

Homer was supposed to be Greek and the Homeric stories were supposed to be the bedrock of Greek culture and civilization. Yet the Greeks and Trojans depicted by Homer were nothing at all like the Greeks that later accepted these stories as part of their heritage. In the *Iliad* and *Odyssey*, Homer calls the various groups Achaeans, Argives, and Danaans; they did not refer to themselves as Greeks.

The Sacrifice of Iphigenia at Aulis.
Roman painting. Notice the predominance
of sky elements.

Homeric Greece (though it obviously wasn't Greece as we know Greece) was more like a tribal society linked by language; it was far more like Central Asian nomadic society, or even Norse society, than what we know of today as the Orientalized Greek society with its city-states. In Homer's world, there was a ruling class called *basileis*, and their responsibilities included providing the individual who would be king, war leader, judge, (and with religious duties included), with advice and counsel. The king's power was based on the principle of 'first among equals' and was restricted by the *aristoi*, or nobility, who comprised an advisory council. There was also the *agora*, an assembly of the warrior class who had the power of voting on issues. Women enjoyed high status, despite the fact that the society was patriarchal and acknowledged a common ancestor and a common king. The main pursuits of life seem to have been fighting, hunting, herding, rudimentary agriculture and the pursuit and enjoyment of 'manly activities'. Hospitality was the chief virtue, and *bards were highly valued*. In short, there was a significant lack of any formal government or any kind of economic system. Most transactions of goods appear to have been based on reciprocity. In short, it is definitely not the 'city-states' of Greece.

The events depicted in the *Iliad* and *Odyssey* are supposed to date to around 1190 BCE, which would put it right in the middle of a serious cosmic onslaught and climate downturn; the *composition* by Homer dates to around 800 BCE (though some date him to the time of the Trojan War). The war supposedly originated in a quarrel between goddesses: Athena, Hera and Aphrodite.

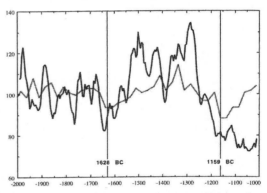

Graph from Mike Baillie's book *Exodus to Arthur* showing the Bristlecone pine chronology from Campito Mountain and temperature variations (dashed line).

Right away, we detect the comet element and wonder if the Trojan War was a real war between human beings at all. Of course, the mythologists, historians and archaeologists are sure that something like the Trojan War happened and they spend a lot of time trying to figure it out and make square pegs fit round holes. In any event, the dating of the *Iliad* and *Odyssey* to 1190 BCE is due to this being the estimated time of said 'war', which we now strongly suspect to have been a battle in the heavens. I will note here that Baillie's tree rings show the time of greatest stress to be in 1159 BCE.

The tree-ring record points to global environmental traumas between 2354 and 2345 BCE, 1628 and 1623 BCE, 1159 and 1141 BCE, 208 and 204 BCE and CE 536 and 545. Baillie argues that the tree rings are recording first the biblical flood, then the disasters that befell Egypt at the Exodus, famines at the end of King David's reign, a famine in China that ended the Ch'in (sic) dynasty, and finally, the death of King Arthur and Merlin and the onset of the Dark Ages across the whole of what is now Britain.

His conclusion comes as a shock. Not only did the five episodes coincide with the onset of 'dark ages' for society, but they were triggered by cometary impacts. If Baillie is right, *history has overlooked probably the single most important explanation for the intermittent progress of civilisation.* Worse, our modern confidence in benign skies is foolhardy, and our failure to appreciate the constant danger of comet 'swarms' is the result of a myopic trust in a mere 200 years of 'scientific' records. Our excuse is that Christianity probably suppressed the dire warnings of earlier sages in an effort to downplay their influence, as Baillie points out.

The biblical account of the Exodus and contemporary annals from China speak of cometary activity preceding calamity. Previous writers have wondered if the hail or red-hot stones that befell the Egyptians were due to the eruption of Santorini, the Aegean volcano that destroyed Minoan civilisation. The pillar of smoke that guided the Israelites may have been the plume. But a single volcano is an unlikely cause of a global downturn.

So Baillie goes a step further, arguing that a series of cometary impacts around the size of the 20-megaton explosion at Tunguska in Siberia might be enough to trigger earthquakes, tidal waves, volcanic eruptions and ocean floor outgassing. This would explain why comets are seen as portents, along with the occurrence of flooding and poisonous fogs – all reported at the time of Exodus and during others of Baillie's five catastrophes. [Emphasis, mine][249]

We've noted that Homer's world does not describe the world of the Greek city-states. It also does not describe the world of the Hittite Empire nor the other Mesopotamian empires that shared the story of Gilgamesh. The earliest versions are Sumerian, dating to at least 2150 to 2000 BCE and were a collection of stories rather than one long epic. It was only around the 17th or 18th centuries BCE when it was fashioned into a single tale of many adventures; this was the time of the arising of the Hittite Empire which lasted about 500 years as a great power. After about 1180 BCE, the empire disintegrated, though several independent 'Neo-Hittite' city-states survived until the 8th century

---

249. Rudder (1999), 'Fire, Flood and Comet', *New Scientist Book Review*, p. 42.

BCE. The Old Babylonian version of the Gilgamesh epic dates to the 18th century BCE. The Standard Babylonian version dates from the 13th to the 10th centuries. Some of the best copies were discovered in the library of the 7th century BCE Assyrian king, Ashurbanipal. So the difference in time between the *earliest* complete Epic version of the combined, originally separate, stories and the Homeric version is around a thousand years.

'Odysseus suffering Neptune's wrath'. Theodore Van Thulden, 1633.

Nevertheless, noting the extraordinary comparisons between the compositions, as Trevor Bryce does in *Life and Society in the Hittite World*[250], highlights exceptional faithfulness to, at the very least, particular mythic topos. The experts think that this is remarkable considering the fact that the empires of Mesopotamia had been in the dust for some time before Homer wrote the story down and it wasn't until Berossus, writing in the 3rd century BCE, that texts from Babylon were translated, possibly commissioned by Antiochus I.[251] So they are certain that Homer couldn't have copied anything from the later composite Gilgamesh Epic. It is certainly a puzzle that deserves research.

What emerged from this Dark Age was the early Greek civilization: city-states similar to the city-states of the ancient Sumerians a few thousand years earlier.

Speaking of Greek civilization, that naturally leads us to think of Greek myths. At the time the Greeks emerged as a power in the ancient world, the natural world was perceived as a purpose-driven, overwhelming and overpowering system of larger-than-life forces which could, in the blink of an eye, act negatively toward human beings. This is the view of the world that comes through loud and clear in the works of Homer. The people of the time did not question this view of reality, and thus issues of morality were not debatable. You behaved according to the precepts outlined in the *Odyssey* and exemplified by Odysseus, or you suffered the fate of the suitors. These ideas and the related myths had apparently taken shape during the Dark Age.

As described above, the Babylonians appear to have considered comets

---

250. Bryce (2002).
251. Antiochus I Soter or Antiochus the Savior, king of the Hellenistic Seleucid Empire. He reigned from 281 to 261 BCE.

to be astronomical: wanderers in the sky. First comets and then fixed stars were associated with events and thus omens were developed. These omens, however, were not personal, not something that applied to an individual, but rather were concerned with the survival and prosperity of the state and the king. Comets were associated with bad weather which could bring on famine, or war which could disrupt the peace. For example, an omen of the Dynasty of Akkad states:

> If Ishtar appears in the East in the month of Airu and the Great and Small Twins surround her, all four of them, and she is dark, then will the king of Elam fall sick and not remain alive.[252]

It was the Egyptians who first used the description 'hairy star' which then became, in Greek, *kometes* or 'hairy one'. An unidentified hieroglyph which, for many years, was interpreted as 'woman with disheveled hair' may, in fact, directly refer to a comet since this hieroglyph is almost identical to that of the Sky goddess Nut, except for the addition of the flowing hair.[253]

Cúchulainn: The Comet of a Thousand Faces

In Mesopotamian, Greek, Egyptian, Celtic and Native American mythology (and others), we are able to see the characteristics of comets, their celestial 'Olympus', and come to some reasonable understanding of their adventures. The representations of gods taking the form of animals and animal-headed gods can be seen in the many forms and configurations taken by comet heads and tails, not to mention their electrical activities. And obviously, there were some of the comets in the ancient sky that were regular, recognizable visitors that became the principal gods. Fragmenting comets acquired partners, children and extended families. Comets could have 'virgin births' or parents could devour their children or vice versa. The name of the principal comet can be traced in the various cultures and the time described when the founder of the dynasty of the gods was single and alone in the sky: the giant comet that entered the solar system perhaps 70,000 years ago. As years passed, the stories mixed and mingled in confusing ways. But still, the primary features remain clear as long as the 'supernatural' elements are not stripped out, which is what I was doing myself in the early days of research. Mike Baillie gives an example using the Celtic god, Cúchulainn:

---

252. Schaumberger, cited by Clube and Napier (1982), p. 163.
253. Clube and Napier (1982), p. 167.

Cúchulainn became … a monstrous thing, hideous and shapeless, unheard of. His shanks and joints, every knuckle and angle and organ from head to foot, shook like a tree in the flood or a reed in the stream. His body made a furious twist inside his skin, so that his feet and shins and knees switched to the rear and his heels and calves switched to the front. The balled sinews of his calves switched to the front of his shins, each big knot the size of a warrior's bunched fist. On his head, the temple-sinews stretched to the nape of his neck, each mighty, immense, measureless knob as big as the head of a month-old child. His face and features became a red bowl: he sucked one eye so deep into his head that a wild crane couldn't probe it onto his cheek out of the depths of his skull; the other eye fell out along his cheek. His jaw weirdly distorted: his cheek peeled back from his jaws until the gullet appeared, his lungs and liver flapped in his mouth and throat, his lower jaw struck the upper a lion-killing blow. His heart boomed loud in his breast like the baying of a watch-dog at its feed or the sound of a lion among bears. Malignant mists and spurts of fire – the torches of the goddess Badb – flickered red in the vaporous clouds that rose boiling above his head, so fierce was his fury. The hair of his head twisted like the tangle of a red thorn bush stuck in a gap; if a royal apple tree with all its kingly fruit were shaken above him, scarce an apple would reach the ground but each would be spiked on a bristle of his hair as it stood up on his scalp with rage. The hero-halo rose out of his brow, long and broad as a warrior's whetstone, long as a snout, and he went mad rattling his shield, urging on his charioteer and harassing the hosts. Then, tall and thick, steady and strong, high as the mast of a noble ship, rose up from the dead center of his skull a straight spout of black blood darkly and magically smoking…[254]

This description of Cúchulainn is not what most people read in their edited children's versions of the myths. This one describes Cúchulainn's *'ri-astradh'* or frenzy, which Baillie calls a "warp-spasm." The point is that Cúchulainn is being described shaking violently, covered with lumps and bumps, making terrifying sounds, his *hair* twisted and standing up with "vaporous clouds boiling above his head" and with "a spout of dark blood jetting from his skull". That pretty much describes a very, very close comet interacting electrically with the atmosphere and magnetic field of the Earth.

Cúchulainn next climbs into his "thunder chariot" that was *bristling with all kinds of spikes* and bits of metal that are there to rip the enemy to shreds,

---

254. Kenny (1986), 'A Celtic Destruction Myth: Togail Bruidne Da Derga', quoted by Baillie in his Introduction to *The Celtic Gods* (2005).

then the chariot is "speedy as the wind ... over the level plain" pulled by two horses with *flowing manes*. Cúchulainn starts killing people first a hundred at a blow, then two-hundred, then three-hundred, and so on. His chariot wheels sink so deeply into the earth that they tear up boulders, rocks, flag-stones, gravel, creating a dyke high enough to be a fortress wall. He mowed more people down, leaving the bodies six deep. He made this "circuit of Ireland" *7 times* according to this particular story and "This slaughter ... is one of the three uncountable slaughters on the Táin[255] ... only the chiefs have been counted. ... In this great carnage on Muirtheimne Plain, Cúchulainn slew one hundred and thirty kings. Not one man in three escaped" without some injury.

Most people don't know about this aspect of Cúchulainn since the woman who translated the tales from Irish into English (Lady Augusta Gregory), thought that "the grotesque accounts of Cúchulainn's distortion" only meant that in time of great strain or danger he had more than human strength, so she changed all that to "the appearance of a god." Baillie reacts to this:

> Reading these comments carefully, the idea that the full description of Cúchu-lainn's frenzy reduces to 'more than human strength' does seem like an un-derstatement. That he 'took on the appearance of a god' likewise does not do full justice to the awfulness. ... But it appears that, in studying and trying to make sense of the myths, it is the supernatural elements – that seem to make no sense – that are regarded as gilding. They are seen as exaggerations, or padding, or the product of over-fertile imaginations. Thus they are often the bits that are ignored, or left out of the tales ... the result of this is that the tales tend to be left with only the natural elements. King Arthur, a Celtic god, ends up described only as a king; Cúchulainn becomes a heroic Irish youth. Thus readers are pressurized towards regarding these heroes as real flesh and blood people, when in reality they were always supernatural or, if you like, gods.[256]

King Arthur

This was also the time assigned to the legendary King Arthur, the loss of the Grail, and the manifestation of the Wasteland. Although scholars place the historical King Arthur in the 5th century, the date of his death is given as CE 539. According to Mike Baillie, the imagery from the Arthurian legend is in accordance with the appearance of a comet and subsequent famine and

---

255. The Táin is one of Ireland's greatest legendary epics.
256. Baillie & McCafferty (2005), *The Celtic Gods: Comets in Irish Mythology*, p. 15.

plague: the 'Waste Land' of legend. Ireland's St. Patrick stories feature a wasteland as well. And although St. Patrick is credited with ridding Ireland of snakes, we might consider that there never were snakes in Ireland, and that snakes and dragons are images associated with comets.

The Red Dragon was officially recognized as the Welsh national flag in 1959. Henry VII used it as early as 1485 during the Battle of Bosworth Field.

Until that point in time, the Britons had held control of post-Roman Britain, keeping the Anglo-Saxons isolated and suppressed. After the Romans were gone, the Britons maintained the status quo, living in towns with elected officials and carrying on trade with the empire. After 536 CE, the year reported as the 'death of Arthur', the Britons, of the ancient Cymric empire that at one time had stretched from Cornwall in the south to Strathclyde in the north, all but disappeared and were replaced by Anglo-Saxons. There is much debate among scholars as to whether the Anglo-Saxons killed all of the Britons, or assimilated them. Here we must consider that they were victims of possibly many overhead cometary explosions which wiped out most of the population of Europe, plunging it into the Dark Ages, which were – apparently – really dark, atmospherically speaking.

The mystery of the origins of the red dragon symbol, now on the flag of Wales, has perplexed many historians, writers and romanticists… In the ancient Welsh language it is known as 'Draig Goch' – 'red dragon', and in *Y Geiriadur Cymraeg Prifysgol Cymru, the University of Wales Welsh Dictionary* (Cardiff, University of Wales Press, 1967, p. 1082), there are translations for the various uses of the Welsh word 'draig'. Amongst them are common uses of the word, which is today taken just to mean a 'dragon', but in times past it has also been used to refer to 'Mellt Distaw' - (sheet lightning), and also 'Mellt Didaranau' - (lightning unaccompanied by thunder).

But the most interesting common usage of the word in earlier times, according to this authoritative dictionary, is 'Maen Mellt' the word used to refer to a 'meteorite'. And this makes sense, as the Welsh word 'maen' translates as 'stone', while the Welsh word 'mellt' translates as 'lightning' - so literally a 'lightning-stone'. That the ancient language of the Welsh druids has words still in use today which have in the past been used to describe both a dragon and also a meteorite, is something that greatly helps us to follow the destructive 'trail of the dragon' as it was described in early Welsh 'riddle-poems'. […]

In recent years certain astronomers have increasingly come to appreciate that encoded in the folklore and mythologies of many cultures are the accurate observations of ancient skywatchers. Almost all tell of times when death and mass destruction came from the skies, events that are often portrayed as 'celestial battles' between what they variously depicted as 'the Gods'. And curiously the imagery in these 'myths' have many common features, even between the mythologies of cultures widely spaced in time and location.[257]

So it is that the Arthurian cycle of legends and myths fits rather well into the comet scenario. There are links between the characters of the Irish stories of Cúchulainn, who is the rebirth of Lugh, "the bright god who comes up from the West", and then there is Arthur as Lugh.

The Holy Grail

The Grail legends are the context in which the story of Arthur was set and the esotericists and nutzoids of the world have been arguing for ages over whether it was a cup, a platter, or the womb of Mary Magdalene.[258] R. S. Loomis, author of *Celtic Myth and Arthurian Romance* (1927) and *The Grail* (1963) points out that "Wolfram von Eschenbach[259], author of 'Parzival', declared flatly that the Grail was a stone, much to the bewilderment of scholars." The Grail is described as something that gives off a brilliant light and floats through the air covered with a veil. Then, there is a lance (read: comet ion tail) from which blood flows down, and we are reminded of Cúchulainn who spurted blood from

Titurel Receives the Grail and Spear. Oil painting by Franz Stassen.

his head while going through his 'warp-spasm'. In connecting the Irish tale of Conn's visit[260] to the palace of Lug with Perceval's visit to the Grail castle, Loomis writes:

---

257. The Morien Institute, 'The European 'Dark Age' And Welsh Oral Tradition on the trail of The Dragon', retrieved here: http://www.morien-institute.org/darkages.html

258. In *Holy Blood, Holy Grail*, Baigent, Leigh and Lincoln concluded that the legendary Holy Grail is simultaneously the womb of Saint Mary Magdalene and Jesus' bloodline.

259. German knight and poet (c. 1170 – c. 1220).

260. Conn Cétchathach ('Conn of the hundred battles'), high king of Tara and therefore of all Ireland.

Lug's spear was one of the four chief treasures of the Tuatha De Danaan, the Irish gods… one might expect to see it in Lug's mansion. What better explanation is there for the functionless lance in the Fisher King's castle? Later Chretien informs us that it will destroy the whole realm of Logres (England) – a prophecy which accords with the origin of the lance in the spear of Lug, noted for its destructiveness.[261]

Thus, when the grail 'floats' through the castle, which is the 'otherworldly fortress', we can derive that it is a comet passing in the sky. It is associated with the spear that delivers the 'dolorous stroke' and when that happens, there is mist, earthquakes and the earth becomes a wasteland. Loomis again:

> His (Lug's) approach is thus described: "They saw a great mist all round, so that they knew not where they went because of the greatness of the darkness; and they heard the noise of a horseman approaching. The horseman (Lug) let fly three throws of a spear at them." [262]

As Baillie notes, all you need to add in now is Cúchulainn's auroral display when the comet approaches and engages with the atmosphere and magnetic field of the Earth, and you have the origin of the Holy Grail, which is "a stone."

Taliesin

Taliesin is said to have been an early British poet of the immediate post-Roman period, i.e. the Dark Ages, some of whose work has survived in a Welsh manuscript.

The legend tells us that Taliesin was a companion of Bran the Blessed [263] and King Arthur. Mike Baillie points out that, given who Taliesin was (his name means 'shining brow'), the list of places he had traveled and the things he did all suggested the description of a comet.

In the poem, 'The Battle of the Trees', Taliesin tells us, among other things, that "I have been in many shapes", i.e. he is a shapeshifting god; "I have been a shining star", i.e. he has been something bright in the heavens; and "There shall be black darkness, there shall be a shaking of the mountain, there shall be a purifying furnace, there shall first be a great wave." In other

---

261. Loomis (1963), *The Grail: From Celtic Myth to Christian Symbol.*
262. Loomis (1927).
263. Giant and king of Britain in Welsh mythology.

words, everything associated with him just happen to be the symptoms of environmental disruption of the rather severe sort. Lastly, Taliesin comes right out and says: "I have been an evil star formerly." Traditionally, for millennia, the term 'Evil Star' has referred to a comet. "Everywhere on Earth, with only a few exceptions, comets were harbingers of unwanted change, ill-fortune and evil."[264]

So, we have a radiant browed bard who dates back to the mid-6th century writing the following lines, which Mike Baillie rearranged 'for maximum effect':

> My original country is the region of the summer stars;
> I was in the court of Dön[265] before the birth of Gwydion.
> I have been in Asia with Noah in the ark,
> I have seen the destruction of Sodom and Gomorrah.
> I strengthened Moses through the waters of Jordan;
> I am now come here to the remnant of Troia.[266]
> I was in Canaan when Absalom was slain
> I was with my Lord in the highest sphere,
> On the fall of Lucifer into the depth of hell;
> I shall be until the day of doom on the face of the earth...[267]

What is astonishing here is that a supposed 6th century bard wrote a poem that connects cometary activity to the Flood, the destruction of Sodom and Gomorrah, the Exodus, the times of David and Goliath (a comet story if ever there was one!), and the future doomsday: Armageddon.

Let's go back even further and take a look at these older Comet Gods.

Gilgamesh

The name was originally Bilgamesh, but that was changed early on, so 'Gilgamesh' it is. Exactly as Baillie has described, the experts studying the epic and myths have come to the conclusion that Gilgamesh is *likely to have been a real person*, a king who ruled the Sumerian city of Uruk[268] in the era from 2700 BCE to 2500 BCE. However, there are no known inscriptions that es-

---

264. Sagan & Druyan (1985), *Comet*.
265. Dön is the Irish mother-goddess Dana whose son Gwydion is equivalent to Arthur.
266. A reference to the claimed origin of the Britons: Troy, but may actually have a deeper meaning, as revealed in Iman Wilkens' book *Where Troy Once Stood* (1990).
267. Quoted and arranged by Baillie (1999), pp. 247-248.
268. Today's Warka, Southern Iraq.

tablish this. There is only one person he is associated with in a story that is actually attested by inscriptional evidence, a king Enmebaragessi. But that's as close as it gets. Gilgamesh was associated with the expansion of the Ziggurat at Uruk, but the inscription that claims this dates only to 1800 BCE.

It is assumed that the stories about Gilgamesh were circulating in his own time and were later written down, but actually the earliest written stories about him date to the reign of King Shulgi around 2000 BCE, i.e. at least 500 years later. These stories were written in Sumerian and King Shulgi made the claim that the gods and ancient kings of Uruk (including Gilgamesh) were his ancestors and thus legitimized his kingship. One hymn produced at the time is a back-and-forth paean to each other, put in the mouths of Gilgamesh and Shulgi. In short, we can think that the stories produced at this time were little more than political propaganda based on some already existing myth about a very powerful being such as Cúchulainn, i.e. a comet. So, at that time, offerings were made to Gilgamesh as a divinized ancestor, but after the end of Shulgi's dynasty, official support for the cult of Gilgamesh faded.

It is likely that it was Shulgi who commissioned the writing of the earliest Gilgamesh stories (though the epic as we now know it did not exist at that time) and authentic traditions were thereby *consciously composed with a view to furthering the agenda of this ambitious king*[269]. No tablets dating back to this period actually exist, only later copies, some of which are more elaborate than others, and some have contradictory details. Obviously, we can't be sure of having all the stories, but thus far, the separate epics consist of the following:

Gilgamesh and Agga – This short story describes a strange confrontation between Agga of Kish (son of the aforementioned Enmebaragessi) and King Gilgamesh of Uruk, after a meeting of Elders and Young Men. Gilgamesh has a "terrifying aura" that basically smites the army of King Agga, though Gilgamesh spares Agga. The "terrifying aura" that smites an army naturally inclines one to think of a cometary event *à la* Cúchulainn, not to mention Moses and his "Ark." The echoes of this story that are retained in the later Epic are the consultations with the Elders and the Young Men, and Gilgamesh sparing Humbaba (Agga).

Gilgamesh and Huwawa (Humbaba) – This story is known in two versions, a long one and a short one, with variations from city to city where it is found. Gilgamesh sees a dead body floating in the river and this excites his fear of death. He proposes to his servant, Enkidu, to embark on a heroic quest to ensure his fame, thus achieving a kind of immortality. The task chosen is to go to the Cedar Forest and kill its monstrous guardian, Huwawa. The Sun

---

269. Keep this in mind; you are going to be seeing a lot of it soon!

god provides some helpful demons, and a crew of fifty men is selected for the voyage. (This is already starting to sound like Perseus against Medusa meets the Argonauts.) This story, too, includes some strange auras, only this time they belong to Huwawa. The effect of the auras on Gilgamesh is that he is overcome, stunned, and experiences terrifying visions. In one version, he describes the visions and Enkidu encourages him to go on and complete the quest. In an-

Reproduction of a Babylonian seal depicting Gilgamesh and Enkidu slaying the Bull of Heaven.

other, it is Enkidu who has the visions and then tries to dissuade Gilgamesh from continuing. Gilgamesh tricks Huwawa (variations exist on the types of trickery), and *Huwawa gives up his auras and Gilgamesh shackles him.* Then Gilgamesh feels sorry for Huwawa and wants to release him, but Enkidu doesn't like that idea; he kills Huwawa and puts his head in a sack to give to the god Enlil (shades of Medusa and Goliath). However, Enlil curses both of the adventurers for killing the divinely appointed Guardian of the Cedar Forest and distributes the seven auras to Nature. Most of this makes it into the later Epic of Gilgamesh.

Nevertheless, for our purposes here, Humbaba/Huwawa is an interesting comparison to Cúchulainn. His face was "as that of a lion. When he looks at someone, it is the look of death." His roar was as that of a flood, his "mouth is death and his breath is fire!" His face is described as like coiled entrails, which harkens back to the 'warp-spasm' of Cúchulainn.

Gilgamesh and the Bull of Heaven – This story is not well preserved in any version, missing the beginning, most of the middle, and the very end. The text begins with the goddess Inanna refusing to allow Gilgamesh to administer justice in her sanctuary. She demands the Bull of Heaven from her father, Anu. At first he refuses, but she threatens to cry out to all the other gods which scares Anu into complying. He gives her the Bull and Inana sends it to Uruk. Probably Gilgamesh and Enkidu kill the bull. This story is included in the later Epic by the Middle Babylonian period, though it was probably not part of the earliest version of the whole Epic. Obviously, the Bull of Heaven is a comet story. The Bull of heaven is also familiar from Egyptian mythology. The Irish saga where Cúchulainn goes into his 'warp-spasm' is called the 'Táin Bó Cúailnge' (The Cattle Raid of Cooley) and involves great battles (including Cúchulainn's 'warp-spasm') over a magnificent brown bull.

Gilgamesh in the Netherworld – Early texts are fragmentary and what comes across is that it is a death lament. One passage states: "The great mountain Enlil, the father of the gods, ... decreed kingship as Gilgamesh's destiny, but did not decree for him eternal life." Then, later: "He lay on the bed of destined fate, unable to get up." That could be a description of a comet that fragmented and the fragments exploded or dissipated in the atmosphere, or were swept along into a trail of comet debris circling through space.

In addition to this small selection of specific Gilgamesh stories, the later formulated Gilgamesh Epic incorporated other traditional Sumerian literary productions that were not originally connected to Gilgamesh. The early life of Enkidu, as it is told in the Gilgamesh Epic, seems to be based on a portrayal of primitive man as described in a text entitled 'Lahar and Asnan', where we read: "Mankind of that time knew not the eating of bread, knew not the wearing of garments. The people went around with skins on their bodies, drank water from ditches." The creation of Enkidu by the Mother Goddess, as described in the first tablet of the Gilgamesh Epic, may be another tale that has not yet been discovered elsewhere.

The Flood of Utanapishtim – In the standard version of the Epic, Gilgamesh asks Utanapishtim how he attained eternal life like the gods even though he was obviously a mere mortal. Utanapishtim then tells him "a hidden thing, a secret of the god", which is how he survived the Great Flood. This account of Utanapishtim is taken from the Akkadian 'Myth of Atrahasis' which was composed about 1600 BCE. The story talks about the creation of mankind, how mankind became noisy, corrupt, too numerous, etc., so the gods plot to exterminate all humanity. There is a Great Flood which only Atrahasis and his family survive. What Utanapishtim tells Gilgamesh is just a short version of the Atrahasis Myth because the longer version, unrelated to Gilgamesh, includes a lengthy justification for the destruction of mankind. Utanapishtim presents the events as just a whim of the gods. What is curious is that the Flood Myth in no way advances the action of the Gilgamesh story and is, in fact, just a lengthy digression. The original Old Babylonian version of the Gilgamesh Epic only had an allusion to the Flood Myth. However, we are fortunate that the Myth of Atrahasis was included in the Epic of Gilgamesh since it is not well-preserved in texts on its own.

It is clear that the Gilgamesh Epic was created by assembling parts from basic stories about Gilgamesh, similar to the many stories about Cúchulainn, and other parts from unrelated myths and stories. This took place, it seems, over a period of a thousand years! The Standard Version was based on an earlier Epic of Gilgamesh that was first composed in the Old Babylonian period – 1800-1600 BCE – which came in several variants. There are other fragments from later periods that were found in Anatolia, Syria and Canaan. In

Anatolia, the Epic was also adapted or translated into Hurrian and Hittite during the Middle Babylonian period.

In conclusion, it seems that the original epic was a creative assembling of already existing mythic literature about earlier comet interactions, none of which was focused on the theme that apparently occupied the thoughts of the author/editor of the final epic. The Epic of Gilgamesh is full of adventures and encounters with creatures, interesting people, and even gods and goddesses, with the unifying topic being human relationships and emotions. There is loneliness contrasted with friendship, love contrasted with loss, revenge and regret, and, most of all, *the fear of oblivion in death*. It appears that the philosophical slant of the Epic confined it to mainly literary circles for much, if not all, of its existence. It was obviously known in Mesopotamian scribal circles for some 1,500 years, and in Anatolia and Syria-Palestine during the 2nd millennium BCE. Until the Hittites translated it, it was only known to those who read and wrote cuneiform. However, the epic does not seem to have been something that was widely known to the masses of people; it was never a byword nor did it generate any colloquial expressions. No king ever claimed to be as strong or as wise as Gilgamesh. No writings invoke Gilgamesh and Enkidu as paragons of friendship as they do David and Jonathan from the Bible. In all the productions of writings from the culture of Mesopotamia, the few allusions to Gilgamesh occur only in scholarly writings. There are almost no artistic depictions of any element of the story except for the killing of Humbaba. This act appears on a few dozen cylinder seals and a few decorative objects and reliefs from the 15th to 5th centuries BCE. The killing of the Bull of Heaven also appears on a few cylinder seals from the mid-second millennium to the 7th century BCE.

The latest fragment of the epic dates to the 1st century BCE. It seems that, with the decline and ultimate disappearance of cuneiform writing, the Epic of Gilgamesh was doomed to oblivion, even in literary circles. With the exception of the translations into Hittite, virtually none of the Mesopotamian literature was translated into other languages. There is a complete lack of references to Gilgamesh in the Syro-Phoenician cultures of the first millennium, which is puzzling since cuneiform literature was otherwise widely known in this area during the second millennium BCE (because Akkadian was the language of international diplomacy). The Hebrew Bible has allusions to other persons or themes derived from Mesopotamian sources, including the flood story, but nary a mention of Gilgamesh or anybody like him.

However, in one of the oldest stories that talks about the Greek 'gods' – *The Odyssey* – we find an epic that is, in many ways, extraordinarily similar to the Epic of Gilgamesh.

The Hellenistic Greeks were interested in the ancient history of Mesopotamia, but not in the native Mesopotamian form. Berossus[270] wrote in Greek of "the histories of heaven and earth and sea and the first birth and the kings and their deeds" between 280-261 BCE. He extracted his information from cuneiform documents and Gilgamesh probably only received a citation for being on a king list: name and length of reign.

The Tale of the Vanishing God

In recent years, some scholars have been applying themselves to this problem, coming to the idea that the Near East had a pervasive influence on early Greek literature, particularly Homer and Hesiod.[271] The story of the Vanishing God is a case in point. This is one of a group of Old Anatolian myths, *not* a Sumerian or Hurrian story (as far as is known to date).

Telepinu, the son of the Storm God, has flown into a rage, leaves the land and goes into hiding. Due to his absence, the crops die, livestock become barren, people die everywhere and even the gods starve. The Storm God becomes alarmed and sends out an eagle to search for his son, but the eagle fails. Various gods, including the father Storm God himself, search in vain. Becoming desperate, the Storm

Telepinu, the Hittite god of farming and prosperity.

God sends a bee to look for Telepinu and the bee finds him and stings him to bring him to awareness. Not surprisingly, the god is still in a rage, exacerbated by being stung by the bee! He commences an orgy of destruction, unleashing thunder, lightning, great floods, and so on. The goddess of magic is sent to pacify him by conducting cleansing rituals. Finally, Telepinu returns home and resumes caring for his land; fruitfulness and prosperity return.

Based on the study of tablets in the Hittite archives, it seems that the Vanishing God myth was actually a script for a dramatic performance. It is written with words spoken by a narrator interspersed with short speeches by various characters. There are even stage set and props directions in-

270. Hellenistic-era Babylonian writer, a priest and astronomer, who was active at the beginning of the 3rd century BCE.
271. Greek oral poet, active between 750 and 650 BCE, around the same time as Homer.

cluded. While it was a grand and glorious show, with wonderful sights and sound and fury, the performance was obviously more than that: it was a ritual that it was hoped would sooth a raging god via analogic magic; it was a purification ritual with the leading practitioner being Kamrusepa, the goddess of magic speaking through wise old women in the performance.

What this tells us is that the civilizations of Mesopotamia – and elsewhere – had fallen victim to repeating disasters, probably brought on by the break-up of a giant comet in the sky that regularly rained down death and destruction. It seems that the only way they could understand this was to reduce it to human terms: gods are like humans with likes, dislikes, emotions, etc., and they then sought a practical method of controlling it by setting things to rights so that the god would return with a benevolent face. It has been suggested elsewhere that sacrifice of living creatures, including humans (including infants), was instituted for this very purpose, i.e. it was obvious the god(s) were after destruction, someone was 'unclean', so 'let's offer some really clean victims and maybe the god will pass over us this time!'

I'm sure that you can easily recognize the Vanishing God traditions of other cultures. These myths concern the disappearance of fertility deities and the resulting withering of the land and loss of fertility. In Mesopotamia, there was the abduction of the shepherd god, Dumuzi, to the Underworld. The Greeks told the story of Persephone's abduction to Hades. These stories are interpreted nowadays as the ancient means of explaining the recurring cycles of seasons: in some cases, the Persephone story divides the year into 4 and 8 months, in others it is 6 and 6. But is the modern explanation for why these stories developed the correct one? If we consider what we have already covered regarding repeating cometary bombardment, the story begins to make a lot more sense. Also, with the recovery of the texts of these dramatic extravaganzas, we may be justified in thinking that this is what was going on in the 'Mystery Religion' initiatory performances.

Illuyanka

The Illuyanka Myth is about a serpent that comes up out of the earth to engage in combat with the Storm God. The Storm God has to call in reinforcements – divine and human – and must use trickery to win the battle. Two versions of this myth were written on a single tablet by a scribe who took dictation from a priest named Kella.

The theme of the human hero who helps the god fight the cosmic monster is familiar to the mythology of many cultures. Greek myths, in particular, include abundant examples: Zeus and Typhon, Apollo and Python,

Bellerophon and Chimaera, Perseus and Medusa, Herakles and the hydra; and in a more modern version, St. George and the Dragon. In the Greek myths, it was only through the services of a human – Herakles – that Zeus and his troop of gods were able to triumph over the Giants that had been spawned from the blood of the mutilated Ouranos.

The Sky God kills the dragon Illuyanka.

In the two versions of the Illuyanka Myth, the human is called upon to rescue the god from utter defeat. In the first version, where the hero's name is Hupasiya, the Storm God's daughter asks him to help her, which he agrees to if she will sleep with him. She does and then they put their plan into action:

> Inara led Hupasiya away and hid him. She dressed herself up and called the serpent up from its hole (saying, 'I'm preparing a feast. Come eat and drink'). So up came the serpent and his children, and they ate and drank. They drained every vessel and became drunk. Now they do not want to go back down into their hole again. Hupasiya came and bound the serpent with a rope. Then the Storm God came and slew the serpent, and the gods that were with him.[272]

Hittitologist Trevor Bryce discusses the elements of subterfuge and trickery that set these stories apart from most of the monster-slaying myths. He points out that the hero – the Storm God – is obviously not 'covering himself with glory', which is an understatement. In both versions he is defeated, and in the second, his victory only comes after his daughter has essentially prostituted herself to a mortal; that is to say, deception, trickery and fraud are used when the god's prowess has failed. This is similar to the Homeric code of conduct, so that is not the outstanding issue; the issue that stands out is the one of violating the code of hospitality (which we will come to soon). According to the ancient codes of hospitality, if a man gives food and shelter to another, he is bound to ensure that his guest is protected from harm. However, in both these stories, that code is blatantly and grossly violated. It seems that the human is the one who pays for this violation; in the first story, we don't know the fate of Hupayasa because the tablet is broken off, but in the second version, the human faces this moral dilemma and, overwhelmed with guilt, he begs the Storm God to take his life, which is done.

---

272. Hoffner (1990), *Hittite Myths*, quoted by Bryce (2002), *Life and Society in the Hittite World*.

The question that modern scholars ask is: why, in such a clear-cut conflict between good and evil, is the Storm God portrayed in such a pusillanimous way? I think that the answer to that could very well be in the nature of the cosmic conflict witnessed by ancient peoples, where different pieces of a once single, giant comet were assigned parts and names in the conflict, none of them being originally perceived as benevolent. More than anything, the story depicts the gods' indifference to humankind. Certainly, comets do not play favorites.

These stories owe their survival to the fact that they were incorporated into grand, public rituals, and that stories relating to them were later collected by scribes and written down. Many of these stories are similar to Greek tales, including a story about the Sun God's lust for a cow, similar to the story of Zeus and Europa, Zeus and Io, Pasiphae and the Bull. Bryce notes that, in the Hittite context, these tales are surprising because they depict the gods committing sexual acts that were strictly forbidden in the Hittite law code.

In the sequel to the tale of the Sun God and the cow, the cow is horrified at giving birth to a two-legged child that is only saved by the intervention of the god who carries the child away and leads a childless fisherman to where the child has been placed. The fisherman takes the child home, persuades his wife to enter the deception and pretend she has given birth, which indicates that the story is one of the earliest versions of the story of the origins of certain great heroes, including Sargon the Akkadian king, Moses, the Persian Darius, the Greek hero Perseus, Romulus and Remus, founders of Rome, and so on. In one sense, it could be conjectured that these stories would have been about individuals who survived cometary cataclysms.

Myths Merged with History

A similar story is that of a Queen of Kanesh who gave birth to 30 sons in one year. She was so horrified by this that she put all of them in reed baskets and set them in the river which carried them to the Black Sea. They grew up and returned to Kanesh/Nesa, where they found that the Queen (whom they did not know was their mother), had given birth to 30 daughters. The brothers were about to marry their sisters when the youngest discovered the truth and called for a halt to the proceedings. Though we don't know how the story ended, we see here another example of the Hittite aversion to sexual perversion, including incest. The story is intended to provide the reason for historical hostilities between Hattusa and Zalpa, which ended with Hattusili I destroying the latter. This is similar to Virgil's use of the story of Dido and Aeneas to provide a context for the historical conflict between

Rome and Carthage. Thus, the Zalpa story is a hybrid; it begins as a myth and ends as genuine history. However, some scholars see a seed of truth in the mythical part which might record an incursion of peoples from the north; that is, it may record the arrival of the Indo-Europeans at the end of the 3rd millennium BCE.

Blind Isaac blessing Jacob who pretends to be Esau. Govert Flinck, 1628.

Another Hittite story of interest to us here is about the two sons of a wealthy man named Appu. The sons are called 'Evil' and 'Just' and – as you might guess – they live up to their names. Evil attempts to cheat his brother in the division of their father's estate. This is a repeating theme in biblical and Egyptian literature, where an evil brother attempts to cheat a good brother and gets his comeuppance from a god. However, in the Bible, it is the Evil son, Jacob [273], who triumphs.

There are other myths, apparently *not native to the Hittites*, that were preserved in the Hittite archives. These texts were literary because they were written down for their own sake and were not part of the ritual performance tradition. The most important of these imported myths was the Hurrian cycle which starred Kumarbi, the 'father of the gods'. This *Theogony* is about the struggle between successive generations of gods: Alalu is overcome by Anu; Anu is overcome by Alalu's son, Kumarbi, who bites off and swallows Anu's genitals, thereby becoming impregnated with the Storm God Teshub, the Tigris river and Tasmisu. The text is fragmentary, so not much more is known about the outcome, but we can guess because it is strikingly similar to the Greek poet Hesiod's *Theogony*.[274] The gods of three successive generations in the Kumarbi myth correspond exactly to Ouranos, Kronos and Zeus. And, in each case, this marks the beginning of a new era. The main difference between the Near Eastern and the Greek traditions is that the former begin one generation earlier in respect of the *male* gods: Alalu has no counterpart in Hesiod's *Theogony*, which begins with Ouranos.[275] Hesiod's version says that all the gods belong to one family: Gaea, the mother and

---

273. Reference to Israel (Jacob) and his brother Esau. Jacob stole Esau's birthright by deceiving their blind father Isaac.
274. Poem describing the origins and genealogies of Greek gods (c. 700 BCE).
275. The primal Greek god personifying the sky.

wife of Ouranos. In the Near Eastern version, the warring gods come from two different families and appear in alternate generations. To me, this suggests that the Greek version is the older since it actually does include the 'first generation', only it is Gaea, the *mother* of Ouranos, who later becomes his wife as well. If we consider the theory of the giant comet breaking up into many pieces, or gods, then it makes perfect sense for them to have been conceived of as being all of one family. Moreover, the element of Gaea – Earth – and Ouranos – heaven – being engaged together in the production of the elements of the conflict would reflect the dynamic interactions between a comet and the Earth. This is exactly what is reflected in Hesiod's poem, which has nothing to do with ritual; it tells a story and establishes a genealogical frame for the comet-gods. Herodotus [276] tells us about Hesiod [277]:

> [2:53] … it was only yesterday or the day before, so to speak, that the Greeks came to know the provenance of each of the gods, and whether they have all existed for ever, and what they each look like. After all, I think that Hesiod and Homer lived no more than four hundred years before my time, and they were the ones who created the gods' family trees for the Greek world, gave them their names, assigned them their honours and areas of expertise, and told us what they looked like. Any poets who are supposed to have lived before Homer and Hesiod actually came after them, in my opinion.
>
> [4:32] … Hesiod, however, has mentioned the Hyperboreans [278], and so has Homer in the Epigoni. [279]

This last remark is quite interesting because it suggests a much more ancient Greek tradition that may have included *written* epics. That the Hyperboreans were said to have been mentioned by Hesiod and Homer is more than passingly curious, as we will see.

Bryce notes that a common feature of these ancient myth cycles of the

---

276. Greek historian (c. 484 – 425 BCE), author of *The Histories*.
277. Waterfield (1998), *The Histories*, translation.
278. People who, according to Greek mythology, lived in an unspecified region in Northern Europe.
279. Epigoni ('The Progeny') was an early Greek epic, a sequel to the Thebaid and therefore grouped in the Theban cycle. The epic was sometimes ascribed to Homer, but Herodotus doubted this attribution. The Theban Cycle is a collection of four lost epics of ancient Greek literature which related the mythical history of the Boeotian city of Thebes (not in modern Egypt). They were composed in dactylic hexameter verse and were probably written down between 750 and 500 BCE. The stories in the Theban Cycle were traditional ones: the two Homeric epics, the Iliad and Odyssey, display knowledge of many of them. The story of the Epigoni was afterwards retold by Sophocles.

Hittites is that no matter how decisively the evil is defeated, even to the point of being totally fragmented and scattered all over the place, like the villain in *Terminator II*, he manages to reassemble himself and come back. That is to say, the Storm God's triumph is only temporary. In one story, the enemy Kumarbi *mates with a mountain peak* to produce a diorite [280] monster to be a champion:[281]

> Henceforth let Ullikummi be his name. Let him go up to heaven to kingship. Let him suppress the fine city of Kummiya (Storm God's home town). Let him strike Teshub. Let him chop him up fine like chaff. Let him grind him under foot like an ant. Let him snap off Tasmisu like a brittle reed. Let him scatter all the gods down from the sky like flour. Let him smash them like empty pottery bowls. Let him grow higher each month, each day.[282]

The cometary imagery is quite clear. Bryce writes:

> When he has grown so large that the sea comes only to his middle, the Sun God sees him and is greatly alarmed. He reports the news to Teshub, who resolves to do battle with the monster. But when he sees him he is filled with dismay: 'Who can any longer behold the struggle of such a one? Who go on fighting? Who can behold the terrors of such a one any longer?'
>
> Teshub is powerless against such an opponent. His sister Shaushka volunteers to approach Ullikummi and attempt to win him over by her songs and her charms. To no avail. 'For whose benefit are you singing?' A great sea-wave asks of her. 'For whose benefit are you filling your mouth with wind? Ullikummi is deaf; he cannot hear. He is blind in his eyes; he cannot see. He has no compassion. So go away, Shaushka, and find your brother before Ullikummi becomes really valiant, *before the skull of his head becomes really terrifying.*[283] (Emphasis, mine.)

Again, we observe the cometary nature of the god, a god whose head can become terrifying in the same way Cúchulainn was described.

Parallels to Hesiod's story of Typhoeus rising up against Zeus can be included here, certainly. Typhon, like Ullikummi, grows higher and higher in

---

280. Very hard volcanic rock.
281. Which immediately suggests that a comet impacted a mountain top and also indicates the rocky nature of the evil god.
282. Hoffner (1990), op. cit., quoted by Bryce (2002).
283. Bryce (2002), op. cit., pp. 226-227.

the heavens and, significantly, in both traditions, the conflict is located at Mt Hazzi/Kasios [284] on the coast of northern Syria.

The obvious question asked by scholars about these myths is: Why were they preserved at all? They certainly do not provide any sort of spiritual or moral teachings. And the answer is, of course, that *they were recording things that actually happened*: a giant comet entered the solar system, broke up into numerous still-large pieces, as comets are wont to do, and, being on an Earth-crossing orbit, periodically interacted with our planet with cataclysmic results.

Typhon by Nazari (1589).

The multiplicity of gods and the possibility that one might be destroyed by any one of them is reflected in the subtext of religious beliefs exposed by the study of the Hittite and other Near Eastern archives. In a world where there are many gods (comets with the potential to bring destruction), supplicants had to be careful to not inadvertently leave out one or two who might then take offense and go on a smiting rampage. The Near Eastern religious landscape did not incorporate any sort of divine omnipresence; one had to make sure that the god was on hand to listen and that meant performing rituals to entice the god from his presently unknown location to where he was needed. For the Near Eastern worshipper, the entire cosmos was vibrating with 'godly life' and they were not abstract entities; they were vital and living.

At the beginning of their empire, the Hattian deities predominated, but as the Hittites expanded their political influence, they also expanded their

---

284. Also known as Mount Aqraa or Zaphon in the Bible, Mt. Casius to the Greeks. According to Ugaritic texts, it was the sacred mountain of the storm god Baal (Baal-Hadad in ancient Canaanite mythology), where his palace was erected of blue lapis and silver and where his lightning overcame the nearby sea (Yam) and Death (Mot) himself. The thunderstorm-gathering mountain was an object of cult itself, and on it dwelt also the goddess Anat. On its bare limestone peak the cult-site is represented by a huge mound of ashes and debris, 180 feet wide and 26 feet deep, of which only the first 6 feet have been excavated. The excavators reached only as far as Hellenistic strata before closing down. The earliest Hellenic foothold in the Levant, at Al Mina, lies at the beach on its northern flank, dating from the early 8th century BCE onwards. The Hittite name persisted in neo-Hittite culture into the 9th century BCE and so when Greeks settled on the north side of Mount Hazzi they continued to call its main peak 'Mount Kasios'. Greek theophoric names Kassiodora and Kassiodorus, meaning a 'gift of Kasios', signify a vow parents made to ensure fertile conception.

pantheon of gods. When they would capture a city, they would physically remove the statues of the local gods to their own temples, thereby declaring their adoption of the new deity and, hopefully, the new deity would adopt them as well. It could be said that the Hittites went far beyond the relatively systematic godly pantheons of their neighbors, and boasted that Hatti was 'the land of a thousand gods'. The end result was that their divine assemblies were a majority of foreign gods. This was not without its advantages, of course. It was a dimension of the tolerance that the Hittite kings worked to cultivate among their subjected peoples; it was "conscious politically conditioned religious tolerance".[285] The absence of any official religion or dogma may have been one of the reasons that the Hittites survived as long as they did and achieved the power they did. It was during the final period of the empire that attempts were made, at the highest levels, to impose political order on the religious beliefs of the populace. Perhaps that was one of the things that contributed to the downfall of the empire?

As noted, the Near Eastern gods, and the gods of Greece, as well, offered nothing to their supplicants in terms that were morally or spiritually uplifting; they were just human beings on a grand scale. The gods experienced love, anger, jealousy, fear, and could be liars and cheaters. They enjoyed sex, dancing, music and horse races; they were pacified by comedy, plays and athletic contests. However, unlike human beings, they were endowed with immortality and great powers. They could represent either natural forces or social institutions. Moreover, because of their natures, they could not possibly be ordered into a rigid hierarchy because you never knew when one or the other would break out of the mold and wreak havoc on the rest!

The gods' interests in justice, morality and right conduct were not for the sake of those virtues, but because it was in their own best interests that human society should order their conduct. A human being who lived his life in obedience to certain values was better able to serve the gods. If one made an oath in the name of the god and then later violated it, was a shame on that god, so best not violate the oath! Oaths and contracts were the basis of social order, and thus the gods were interested that they should be upheld. It was understood that the god's wrath would fall on everyone in contact with the 'sinner', too. In King Mursili II's[286] prayer, we read:

> It is indeed true that man is sinful. My father sinned and offended against the word of the Storm God, My Lord. Though I myself have in no way sinned, it

---

285. Akurgal (1962), *The Art of the Hittites*, p.76.
286. King of the Hittite Empire (New kingdom), c. 1321 – 1295 BCE.

is indeed true that the father's sin falls upon his son, and my father's sin has fallen upon me. ...[287]

When someone arouses a god's anger, is it only on him that the god takes revenge? Does he not also take vengeance on his wife, his children, his descendants, his family, his male and female slaves, his cattle and sheep together with his crop? Will he not destroy him utterly? Be sure to show special reverence for the word of a god! [288]

Again we discern the cometary nature of the gods. The recorded Hittite prayers exhibit the character of a legal defense presented in a court of law. In the first lines of the Hittite Appu Myth [289], we read of a deity "who always vindicates just men but chops down evil men like trees." Bryce states that the unnamed deity is undoubtedly the Sun God, the supreme lord of justice whose counterpart in Babylon was Shamash. He invariably appeared first in the lists of deities who witnessed treaties. Of all the surviving Hittite royal prayers, more than half are addressed to the Solar deities. There are two possible reasons for this: 1) blazing comets and Earth-impacting fireballs perceived to be sun-like, or possibly sons of the Sun; 2) the absence of sunlight due to cometary dust loading and consequent crop failure. Another point to be noted is that it appears that a supreme lord of justice, an all-seeing Sun God, was a deity acknowledged everywhere in the ancient world as omnipresent in some sense. Despite this, the notion of an omnipresent god simply does not appear in the religious tradition which, again, suggests that this was not a 'god' in any sense of the word that we understand today.

There were, of course, as might be expected, multiple versions of the Sun God; and here we find something curious. The concept of the sun deity adopted from the indigenous Hattian culture was that of a Sun Goddess! She was not only Goddess of Heaven, but also of the Underworld. She was 'Queen of Heaven' and the 'Torch of the Hatti-Land' (a cometary reference if ever there was one). These epithets existed side-by-side with the chthonic ones: 'Mother Earth'

Teshub holding a triple thunderbolt and an axe. The sacred bull, represented by his horned crown, was his signature animal.

---

287. Weidner (1922), *Keilschrifturkunden aus Boghazkoi* (KUB), and Laroche (1971), *Catalogue des Textes Hittites* (CTH), cited by Bryce (2002).

288. From the instructions to temple officials, KUB XIII 4 and CTH 264.

289. Mythological Hittite text about Appu, a rich man who is unhappy because he has no son.

and 'Queen of the Earth'. It seems obvious that this duality arose as an attempt to explain destructive comets that disappeared below one horizon, only to reappear on the other. What happened to the Queen and Torch of Heaven? She must have passed some time within the Earth and was, therefore, also Queen of the Earth. Interestingly, this connects us back to Velikovsky's cometary Venus, Queen of Heaven.

The question here is: why a female deity and then a male deity? Is this because of two conflicting traditions? Was the central Anatolian Earth goddess transformed by the Indo-European intruders into a Sky Goddess and then to a deity that had both male and female aspects according to whatever role was needed? The Sun Goddess was identified as the Hattic goddess Lelwani who was 'Queen of the Gods of the Infernal Regions'.[290] Also belonging to the circle of sun goddesses was the great Sun Goddess of Arinna who was the consort of the mighty Storm God. It was to her, in fact, that most of the prayers to solar deities were addressed. I think that the relationship between a Sun Goddess and a Storm God, in the context of cometary disaster, is obvious.

The Storm God

As might be expected, the Storm God, depicted in art with an axe and a lightning bolt, was preeminent all over the ancient Near East. It was his wrath that devastated the lands, destroyed empires, cities, crops and human beings. He was Taru, Tarhung, Teshub, Adad/Hadad, Ba'lu, and certainly, the much later Yahweh of the Jews had much in common with him; his chief powers and functions were those of the Greek Zeus. What is curious about this Storm God is that he was never thought of as a universal god of all peoples; in each individual region, he was a god specific to the people of that region alone, their god, and they were his people that he would 'pass over' in his raging furies and certainly would inflict his anger on anybody they asked him to destroy if they could just get the right prayers, do the right rituals and behave in the right way to invoke his protection. Again, we see the reaction to arbitrary cosmic destruction.

In conclusion, the Hittite religion – and religions of the Near East in general – were not very much concerned with theology or contemplation, they

---

290. This cult had been established in Hattusa during the Old kingdom. It was in the last century of the reign of King Hattusili II that she came to prominence. This will become important later on, so keep it in mind.

were purely and simply attempts to understand an environment that was plagued with repeated brutal and arbitrary destruction from the sky.

Here, I would like to say something about the problem of transmission of information. We are talking here about a main event 13,000 or more years ago, and then numerous subsequent events that either included actual physical bombardment of the planet, or events that consisted of dust loading and related climate stress with probable frequent meteor storms. Obviously, the transmission of information over a period of 13,000 years is problematical. It is only for the past 3-4 thousand years that we have had written accounts and, for the most part, they have been badly mangled by modern interpretations. This means that for about two thirds of that time, oral systems played the major part in the transmission of legends of destruction. Is it possible that the correspondences between the works of Homer and the Epic of Gilgamesh are simply two examples of the extraordinary fidelity of this method of passing on the knowledge of historical events? Or is it that one of them is the original and the other a copy and variation?

Zeus

Considering other Greek myths, the earliest literary references to Zeus are found in Homer. However, the god is of much greater antiquity. Of special note are the myths of the many bestial transformations of Zeus, which must have originally been similar to the warp-spasm of Cúchulainn. He had a lot of children and a large pantheon of lesser gods hanging around and doing battle with one another, all of which is typical of gods that appear and disappear over the horizon, crash into the ocean, cause floods and fire and whatnot. A reading of Greek mythology will reveal that the underlying themes are all pretty much the same, though the names and events may change. This could be due to different eyewitness accounts or the combining of different tribal versions. In any event, Apollo, at some point, supplanted Zeus in becoming the major new figure and this may actually represent the dominance of a new tribal group with the name that they had given the same god known to others as Zeus.

Hesiod's *Theogony* is well worth reading for an account of the evolving, multiplying, warring gods where one can envisage a giant, disintegrating comet coming about every three years, producing progeny prolifically and disastrously. A passage from Hesiod actually depicts the group of gods at some early stage, sailing through the heavens with Mount Olympus itself in motion. Olympus, the home of the gods, has assembled around itself the nine daughters of Zeus:

And at their birth *they went with Olympus*, exulting in their beautiful voice, in their immortal song, and around them, as they sang, dark earth was re-echoing, and a winsome sound arose from their feet as they went.

The muses, the nine daughters of Zeus.

But then, things turned ugly.

On that day all of them, male and female, the Titan gods and all who were born of Cronus and those terrible mighty ones with their insolent strength whom Zeus brought up to the light from beneath the ground from Erebus, stirred up the sad battle. A hundred hands shot from the shoulders of all of them alike and fifty heads on stout limbs grew on the shoulders of each one of them. Then with high rocks in their stout hands they fought against the Titans in a mournful battle. ... The boundless sea rang terribly around, the earth crashed loudly, broad heaven quaked and groaned, and high Olympus shook from its base. ... The heavy shaking, the noise on high of feet in ceaseless pursuit and of mighty blows reached murky Tartarus; so then they threw at each other their grievous bolts.

It seems that the giant body was disintegrating and causing all sorts of electromagnetic phenomena on the Earth, including terrifying clanging sounds and violent electrical storms. Apparently, the stream of hundreds of thousands of comet debris became known as 'Ocean' in some contexts, different from the oceans on the planet.

Then Zeus no longer held back his ferocity but now immediately his mind was filled with fury and he showed forth all his strength; at the same time, continually hurling his lightning, he came from heaven and Olympus. Thick and fast the thunderbolts, with thunder and lightning, flew from his stout hand and they made a holy flame roll

The war of the Titans or 'Titanomachy'. Notice the prevalence of flying Titans equipped with spears.

188

along, as they came in quick succession.

The life-giving earth blazed and crashed all around, and all around immense woods crackled loudly in the fire. The whole land, Ocean's streams, and the unfruitful sea seethed; the hot blast surrounding the earthborn Titans and an immense flame reached the shining upper air.

The gleaming brilliance of the thunderbolt and lightning blinded their eyes, strong though they were.

An awful heat seized Chaos; to look at it straight on with the eyes or hear the sound of it with the ears, it seemed just as if earth and broad heaven threatened to meet above us; and so great was the din

Ancient Egyptian wall painting from the Temple at Abydos, c. 1300 BCE. Assisted by Isis, Pharoah Seti I is raising the Djed Column.

which arose from the former collapsing in ruins and from the latter dashing her down from above; so great was the din when the gods met in conflict.

Together with this the winds stirred up earthquakes, dust, thunder, lightning and smoky thunderbolts, the arrows of great Zeus, and carried shouts and war-cries into the midst of both sides...

Notice the distinction between "thunderbolts" and "thunder and lightning". That, of course, was not the end of the story. Years passed, Zeus defeated the Titans, and Earth gave birth to Typhoeus which we can visualize as Zeus rising over the horizon with an enormous tail! The bottom line here is that it seems that Hesiod's account is a quite literal description.

Raising the Djed

Turning to Egyptian mythology, Clube and Napier note that they tended to simplify and unify things in accordance with the 'unification of the state'. Local gods and stories were combined into single, though multi-purpose, gods. However, the primeval figure behind it all was the Djed Column which was both a lotus (many-petalled) tree and a cosmic serpent, the symbol of light and motion. It had the quality of both brightening under the influence of the sun as well as shadowing the sun. The Memphis tradition had Ptah spewing Nunet and Nun from his mouth. The Hermopolitan story had Atum producing Shu and Tefenet. Nun was also the progenitor of Atum. A variation had Shu producing Nut and Geb and later Nut gave birth to Isis and Osiris. Osiris, of course, we recognize as Zeus-like and having been cut to pieces by Set, a classic comet 'battle' with fragmentation. Isis was the 'sister-wife' who, after the murder of Osiris, gave birth to Horus, the counterpart of Apollo. Meanwhile, Osiris descended to the underworld to be the judge of the dead, i.e. went below the horizon, fragmented, and smaller pieces re-emerged later.

The whole of the Egyptian religion seems to have been geared toward trying to keep Maat – the guiding principle of harmony in the heavens – operative. Their religion consisted almost entirely of rituals and prayers that had to be performed at the right time, round the clock, in order to effect the magic that would combat the threats from the skies that were obviously very, very real.

Important to the Egyptians was the presence of the god's representative on Earth: the king. This belief was common to other societies of the time, though it took on a particular flavor and intensity in Egypt. The idea was so ingrained in the Egyptians, and persisted for so long, that we can take it as a given that it was accepted as a certainty by all, probably due to propaganda. The Egyptians would not have been the least inclined to try to define and understand the gods as 'natural phenomena' as the Greeks sought to do. To the Greeks, the panoply of the Gods was like a heavenly show and their mythology of 'entertainment' has become an integral part of Western civilization. On the other hand, the Egyptians seem to have been so deadly serious about the matter that one suspects their lands and people must have suffered severe trauma time and time, again as the 'Intermediate Periods'[291] strongly suggest.

Yggdrasil

Similar to the Egyptians, the dominant image of Norse mythology is the World Tree, Yggdrasil, which spread its limbs over every land and was a sort

---

291. The history of ancient Egypt is punctuated with three intermediate periods, which are similar to the Dark Ages that Europe experienced at the end of the first millennium CE. The 1st Intermediate Period lasted about one century and occurred c. 2000 BCE between the Old Kingdom and the Middle Kingdom. The 2nd Intermediate Period lasted about one century and occurred around 1600 BCE between the Middle Kingdom and the New Kingdom. The 3rd Intermediate Period started around 1050 BCE and lasted for four centuries. It occurred between the New Kingdom and the Late Period.

of ladder reaching up to heaven and down to the underworld. The tree was the realm of the gods just as Mount Olympus was to the Greeks. Clube and Napier note that:

Comet-Hale-Bopp passing in front of M-35. It had two tails, a white dust tail and a blue ion tail.

> No such analogy has previously been drawn but it is not at all unreasonable to see Yggdrasil as a giant comet, the dragon of other mythologies, to which the rest of the world is subordinate. In several myths the dragon of chaos is also represented by or associated with a World Tree or Tree of Life: this is seen for instance in Genesis 1 where serpent and dragon are identical. This dragon/Tree equation is rather strange on its own but makes sense if both were descriptions, ultimately merged, of a comet. In classical times Seneca used the term cyparissia (Cyprus tree) to describe comets.

So huge was the Norse World Tree that its branches stretched out over heaven and earth. It apparently had three main roots and daily reappeared with all the other gods, galloping over the Bifrost that some have identified as the Milky Way, a rainbow bridge that glowed with fire. We wonder whether it was really a meteor stream in the ecliptic. As it grew and flourished, the tree was continually threatened by the living creatures that preyed upon it. On the topmost branch sat an eagle of whom it is said the flapping of its wings caused the winds in the world of men. At the root of the tree lay a great serpent with many scores of lesser snakes and these gnawed continuously at Yggdrasil. The serpent was at war with the eagle... the celestial aspects, e.g. the diurnal reappearance, is clear, and the vision of a vast ever-changing complex of cometary bodies hurtling together around the sky seems to emerge without much difficulty. Once again, we detect a hierarchy of genealogy among the gods: first the Tree of Life gives birth to Loki ... Loki seems in due course to be the progenitor of Surt, who may also be Balder due one day to return from the dead. Surt is thus the Apollo of Greek mythology and Thoth (later Osiris) of Egyptian mythology.[292]

Something to note about comets here in reference to Clube and Napier identifying the World Tree of Norse mythology and the Djed column of Egyptian myths as originally being a giant comet, from Mike Baillie:

---

292. Clube & Napier (1982), p. 187.

... Comets have a dust tail and an ion tail. The dust tail is generally curved following the elliptical path of the comet and can be interpreted as hair, or a beard or column. The ion tail is made of gas that has been excited by the solar wind to emit light; we could think of this as an extremely long fluorescent tube in the sky. The ion tails stream away in a straight shaft of fluorescent light from the comet, in contrast to the curved tail of ejected dust and gas. Comets can have one or more ion tails.[293]

A comet that is passing very, very close to the Earth might very well have a humongous ion tail that stands straight up in the sky. In any event, the text from the northern myths is so stunning, I'm going to include a bit of it here:

There Loki must lie until Ragnarok, the time of the destruction of the gods. This fearful time will be ushered in by many portents. First there will be great wars through the world, and a time of strife and hatred between men. The bonds of kinship will hold them no longer, and they will commit appalling deeds of murder and incest. There will also be a period of bitter cold, when a terrible pursuing wolf catches the sun and devours her; the moon too is swallowed up, and the stars will fall from the sky. The mountains will crash into fragments as the whole earth shakes and trembles, and the World Tree quivers in the tumult. Not all fettered monsters break loose, the wolf Fenrir advances, his great gaping jaws filling the gap between earth and sky, while the serpent emerges from the sea, blowing out poison. The sea rises to engulf the land, and on the flood the ship Naglfar is launched, a vessel made from the nails of dead men. It carries a crew of giants, with Loki as their steersman. From the fiery realm of Muspell [the South?], Surt and his following ride out with shining swords, and the bridge Bifrost is shattered beneath their weight. His forces join the frost-giants on the plain of Vigrid, and there the last battle will be fought between this mighty host and the gods.

... Thor meets the World Serpent, and Freyr fights against Surt ... All the gods must fall, and the monsters be destroyed with them. Thor kills the serpent, and then falls dead overcome by its venom... Only Surt remains to the last, to fling fire over the whole world, so that the race of men perishes with the gods, and all are finally engulfed in the overwhelming sea:

The sun becomes dark, Earth sinks in the sea

---

293. Baillie (2005), p. 75.

The shining stars slip out of the sky
Vapour and fire rage fiercely together,
Till the leaping flame licks heaven itself.

Yet this is not the end. Earth will rise again from the waves, fertile, green, and fair as never before, cleansed of all its sufferings and evil. The sons of the great gods still remain alive, and Balder will return from the dead to reign with them. They will rule a new universe, cleansed and regenerated, while two living creatures who have sheltered from destruction in the World Tree will come out to re-people the world with men and women. A new sun, outshining her mother in beauty, will journey across the heavens.[294]

It would take several entire books to lay out and comment on all the myths of the world systematically, but I did want to bring a tiny bit of exposure to very similar stories from the Americas. E. P. Grondine writes in *Man and Impact in the Americas*:

The northern peoples' cosmological theories were widely held, with variants. In these astronomical systems asteroids and comets are viewed as "horned snakes", which were known by various names: by the Cherokee as Unktena and on the plains as Unkteni or Uncegila, for example. ... Sometimes the horned snakes are grouped together with "spitting snakes", which are comets, and sometimes not. As in Middle Eastern societies, there is no differentiation between asteroid and cometary impact and lightning, which is simply seen as a smaller snake.

One of the key facts which generally eludes modern mythologists is that Native Americans often saw space as a cold dark lake, and the "water" aspect of these "snake" myths is a complete bafflement to them ...

Either the "thunders" or the "thunderbirds", the second known as Tlanuwa to the Cherokee, were man's protectors against the cosmic snakes, the comets and asteroids. Naturally, when either the "thunders" or the "thunderbirds" defeated a "horned snake", lightning and the sound of thunder would be heard, coming from where the asteroid or comet hit the Earth. Similarly, thunder was heard after lightning, strikes, and this was viewed as a sign of the thunders' or thunderbirds' defeat of the lightening "serpent" or "snake".[295]

The following account is just a sampling of the material Grondine has

---

294. Quoted by Clube and Napier, p. 187-188.
295. Grondine (2005).

collected and is from Tuscarora Chief Elias Johnson's history of Hiawatha.[296]

> While Hiawatha was thus living in domestic life quietly among the people of the hills, and administering their simple government with wisdom, they became alarmed by the sudden news of the approach of a furious and powerful enemy from north of the great lakes.
>
> As the enemy advanced, they made an indiscriminate slaughter of men, women and children. The people fled from their villages a short time before them, and there was no heart in the people to make a stand against such powerful and ruthless invaders.
>
> In this emergency, they fled to Hiawatha for his advice. He counseled them to call a general council of all the tribes from the east and west ... He appointed a place on the banks of Onondaga Lake for the meeting... All but the wise man had been there for three days, anxiously awaiting the arrival of Hiawatha ...
>
> The day was calm and serene. No wind ruffled the lake, and scarcely a cloud floated in the sky above. But while the wise man was measuring his steps towards the place designated for the council, and while ascending from the water's edge, a rumbling and low sound was heard, as if it were caused by the approach of a violent, rushing wind. Instantly all the eyes were turned upwards, where a small and compact mass of cloudy darkness appeared. It gathered in size and velocity as it approached, and appeared to be directed inevitably to fall in the midst of the assembly ...
>
> ... But the force of the descending body was that of a sudden storm. They had hardly taken the resolution to halt when an immense bird, with long, extended wings, came down with a swoop. This gigantic agent of the sky came with such force that the assembly felt the shock..
>
> ... Hiawatha was inconsolable for his loss ...[297]

We notice in the above account that there were tribes on the move from the North and an impact event which Cusick, the compiler of the legends, dated to about 600 CE.

Grondine's book covers legends of cyclical events going back to the 13,000 years ago event and coming forward to the arrival of Europeans. The book

---

296. Cusick (1828), *Sketches of Ancient History of the Six Nations.* This is an early (if not the first) account of Native American history and myth, written and published in English by a Native American.

297. Quoted by Grondine (2005), op. cit., excerpts.

includes the full text of Cusick's history as well as the Ancient History of the Shawnee [298] and the Lenape [299], and more.

Reflecting on the fact that the Native Americans saw the sky as 'a cold, dark lake' reminds one of the Chinese stories that tell of dragons *wrestling in ponds*. In the West, the legend of Beowulf has him wrestling Grendel's mother *in a pond*. The Chinese stories are dated to 503 and 524 CE and the context of the Beowulf stories suggest dates between 495 and 533. What is fascinating is that these stories give evidence of the same concepts, and in the case of the Chinese legends and Beowulf, they appear at almost exactly the same times. The Chinese help us out by coming right out and saying that their dragons were associated with fireballs and that where the dragons passed "all the trees were broken" *à la* Tunguska. Baillie points out that, in Beowulf, as Grendel's mother takes off across the moors, "The forest paths were marked all over with the monster's tracks ..." And, of course, there is the 'Castle of the Fisher King', the heavens where the shining Holy Grail floats, hidden in mists.

Quetzalcóatl

The *Annals of Cuauhtitlan* were compiled by anonymous authors around 1570 CE and consisted of a number of local histories collected together and arranged chronologically, year by year. The dates were correlated to the European dating system so that the native date, such as '1 Reed' was related to 1519 CE, the year Cortez arrived.

In these annals, we learn that Quetzalcóatl, after having been driven from Tollan, immolated himself on the shores of the Eastern sea, and from his ashes rose *birds with shining feathers* while his 'heart' became the Morning Star, wandering for eight days in the underworld before it ascended in splendor. In several of the legends, we again see the 'battling comets' theme where Quetzalcóatl's adversary is Tezcatlipoca. In one story, Tezcatlipoca defeated Quetzalcóatl in a ball game and "cast him out of the land into the east, where he encountered the sun and was burned." [300]

A strong tradition of 'Sun Ages' existed among the peoples of South and Central America and one certainly wonders just what kind of 'sun' they were actually talking about?

---

298. Algonquian-speaking people, native to the East coast of North America.
299. Native American people also called Delaware Indians after their historic territory along the Delaware River.
300. Alexander (1964), *The Mythology of All Races*, Vol. 11, p. 68.

..."The Sun of Air," Ehcatonatiuh, closed with a furious wind, which destroyed edifices, uprooted trees, and even moved the rocks ... Quetzalcóatl appeared in this third Sun, teaching the way of virtue and the arts of life; but his doctrines failed to take root, so he departed toward the east, promising to return another day.

With his departure "the Sun of Air" came to its end, and Tlatonatiuh, "the Sun of Fire," began, so called because it was expected that the next destruction would be by fire.[301]

Quetzalcóatl in the Codex Borbonicus.

Obviously, their experiences with comets as 'suns' was quite different to what we, in modern times, are accustomed. What is more, the myths seem to be saying that Quetzalcóatl was associated with a period of cosmic destruction, the sudden onset of famine conditions and extreme hardship.

The Origin of the Mâgên Dâwîd

Among the many symbols that come down to us from the Sumerians via the Hittites via the Babylonians, there are stars with varying numbers of rays and crescent moons. My thought is that these 'stars' are actually 'guest stars' in the sense the Chinese described them: comets. Further, when they are associated with the Moon, it may suggest that they were comets that passed in sub-lunar orbits, quite close and terrifying and certainly having terrifying physical effects on the Earth due to plasma and/or electrophonic interactions. Such events could definitely be perceived by humans as the 'speech' of the gods, and a dramatic electrical exchange at that scale would likely produce equally dramatic sound effects, including roaring that might sound like a cosmic bull.

Assyriologist Hildegard Lewy addressed the problem of the origins of the Mâgên Dâwîd in a paper published in 1950[302] which draws on material generally little known to the wider public, and which makes fascinating com-

---

301. Ibid, p. 91.
302. Hildegard (1950), 'Origin and Significance of the Magen Dawld'. Parts of my discussion are based on some elements from her research though, certainly, my interpretations are widely at variance with hers! I will indicate the relevant sources, but for full citations the paper itself ought to be accessed.

parisons between Judaism and Islam in terms of their origins which, it seems clear, were due to cometary cataclysms.

In modern times, we find that Muslim mosques are topped by a crescent moon while Jewish synagogues are topped by the six-pointed star that is usually referred to as the Mâgên Dâwîd (Mogen David) or 'the shield of David' aka the 'Seal of Solomon'. Both stars and the symbol for the Moon are found in Mithraism [303] and other ancient cults. Lewy notes that the same symbol of the Mâgên Dâwîd is found on two Old Assyrian seal impressions on cuneiform tablets now residing in the Louvre. On the first of the tablets, the Mâgên Dâwîd is in front of a god who is *carrying in two hands something that looks like a Menora, or seven-branched candlestick*. There is no evidence for the practice of the Jewish religion in the Old Assyrian period so we might speculate that both objects represent a comet [304] and its effects, possibly one with 7 tails or one that broke into seven pieces.

On the second tablet, the Mâgên Dâwîd is placed with the lunar crescent and the solar disc. So, we have a star, a sun, and the Moon which, again, suggests to me that the 'star' is a comet since stars, *per se*, would not ordinarily be presented as equivalent luminaries with the Moon and Sun, nor would planets. There would really have been no reason for the ancient astronomers to have singled out any of the fixed stars that blanket the sky unless there was something truly unusual about its behavior. Even the slow-traveling planets would not have excited much attention. But rapidly traveling comets with a dramatic appearance would definitely have been something that excited both attention and the necessity for recording same. Otherwise, a 'star' symbol on a tablet or monument or seal would have been just one of 'billions and billions' with nothing in particular to identify it or set it apart. The ancient astronomers were recording things they saw and a star that was as big and bright as the Sun and/or the Moon would be represented in this way. Again, these same elements are present in the Mithraic iconography which will be explored in the next volume.

We already know from the research of Bailey, Clube and Napier, presented in previous chapters, that star images were originally used to represent comets, and what we now know as the names of planets were first assigned to these 'star comets' and only later transferred to planets. For example, the behaviors of the goddess Innana/Ishtar in the old Mesopotamian

---

303. Mithraism will become important as we move on.
304. A reproduction of the seal impression is found in Lewy, *Tablettes Cappadociennes*, 3rd series, 3rd part (Louvre Museum, Department of Oriental Antiquities, Cuneiform Texts, vol. XXI) Paris, 1937, Plate CCXXXV, no. 74.

epics are the actions of a comet, not a star or a planet, yet later the eight-pointed star of Ishtar was assigned to the planet Venus. Another eight-pointed star represented Mercury in both its cometary and later planetary incarnation, and, interestingly, both of them are morning and evening 'stars'.

The point Mme. Lewy is making is that specific symbols were established early on to represent specific celestial bodies and the Mâgên Dâwîd is just such a specific symbol that it can only represent one of the three remaining bodies known to the ancients: Jupiter, Mars and Saturn.[305] Lewy is speaking strictly of planets, of course, but if we expand the search to include threatening comets of the past, 'Jupiter', 'Mars', and 'Saturn' could all have been names applied to a single, reappearing comet that rapidly changed form due to disintegration. The same could have originally been true of Mercury and Venus.

The Mâgên Dâwîd is also incised on the wall of a sanctuary of the Megiddo cult dating to the 9th or 8th centuries BCE, a time that we recognize as the period when the peoples of the Mediterranean began to emerge from the so-called Greek Dark Age.[306]

Tradition connects the six-pointed star with David as well as with Solomon, so the question Lewy asks is: which of these three planets played a role in the religion of these two kings? Here, I will interject again that it was very likely not a planet, but rather a comet and the religions in question obviously emerged during those periods that Bailey, Clube and Napier describe, when the skies of our planet were populated by the 'gods' in their cometary incarnations. Nevertheless, Lewy's collection of data and arguments are important (with that caveat) because, even if it does not lead us to a planet, it will certainly lead us to a comet!

Lewy, writing in 1950, assumed that the kings David and Solomon were historical characters as described in the Bible, so one of the points she makes is that there are many indications that Yahweh was not the *only* god associated with David and Solomon. However, since the archaeology reveals that the alleged 'kingdom of Israel' ruled over by David and Solomon never existed[307], nor did the famous temple[308], we can assume that the stories of them as ancient historical kings of a historical Israel were fabricated, though certainly based on some model from elsewhere. In any event, it appears that whoever these kings might have been, assuming they were ever real kings

---

305. For a reproduction of this seal impression see Lewy, op. cit., plate CCXXXIII, no. 48.

306. See May (1935), *Material Remains of the Megiddo Cult*, p. 6 and fig. 1 on p. 7.

307. Finkelstein & Silberman (2007), *David and Solomon: In Search of the Bible's Sacred Kings and the Roots of the Western Tradition*.

308. Finkelstein & Silberman (2002), *The Bible Unearthed: Archaeology's New Vision of Ancient Israel and the Origin of its Sacred Texts*.

at all and not just historicized comet legends, and wherever they may actually have reigned (probably somewhere other than Palestine, under different names), Yahweh was unknown to them and his worship was only retroactively applied to them in later historiography. More importantly, the authors of that history must have been utilizing not only the histories of other peoples in composing their work, but possible histories or oral legends from Palestine which, considering the bits and pieces of a more ancient religion that were preserved therein, makes Lewy's point valid in any case.

One of the clues to this earlier layer of tradition is that Solomon was engaged in the practice of offering sacrifices on 'high places', which was the normal practice of celestial religions: the top of a mountain or hill (or Ziggurat) was the place to worship or confer with such gods. Of course, with the understanding that these gods were actually comets and not planets, the 'worship' on mountains and hills could have originated as astronomical observation points utilized as a sort of 'early warning' system. Even today, observatories are usually located on elevated points for optimal viewing of the night sky. As it happens, great wisdom (about comets?) was bestowed on Solomon while he was said to have been sleeping on the top of Mt. Gibeon. This type of event was also generally connected with princes who were worshippers of heavenly bodies. Perhaps their 'great wisdom' included not just astronomical observations that taught them about the heavens and impending cometary disasters, but also preparations for potential destruction such as 'Comet is coming, get in the cave!'; or even the building of massive stone-walled enclosures designed to protect people from such cosmic encounters, including tsunamis. The building of monumental fortified enclosures – cyclopean walls, as they are called – is characteristic of the Mycenaean civilization that flourished between 1550-1060 BCE, approximately. It appears to be a certainty that such structures were not needed to protect people from one another when the only weapons of the time were bronze swords and daggers, minimalist bows and arrows, and spears, either bronze-tipped or hardened in a fire. In short, the ancient monumental architecture seems to be more suited to bunker-buster bombs of the modern era than the weaponry of ancient times. Maybe that should suggest something to us? Finally, the Mycenaeans apparently revered the bull.

It was in that period of time that Mesopotamian divine pictography changed to what is called 'boundary-stone' pictographs, dated 1350 to 1000 BCE (close enough to the Mycenaean dates for horseshoes). These were royal charters carved on boundary stones that called on the gods to witness and protect the ownership of land. The boundary stone charters included lengthy and detailed divine curses and symbols of gods, most of which corresponded to 'planets' and constellations. My suggestion would be, of course, that the gods were comets and the constellations represented their usual locus of appearance, and the prayers and curses and protection invoked were directed at the cosmic intruders, not necessarily land-based trespassers![309] The gods had long been associated with places – witness the different gods of the Mesopotamian city-states – but this activity suggests that there was a

The Lion Gate at Mycenaea.

new phase of cometary activity that was causing some anxiety and need for protection.

In respect of boundary stones, curses, gods, and so forth, recall the activity of Romulus; how he built a wall and the big issue was that Remus 'jumped over it'. Perhaps what we are seeing here is something similar to what happened in Siberia after the Tunguska event, as discussed in chapter four, where the author reported that a Siberian tribe in the region of the Tunguska event had already derived a spiritual significance from the impact.

> It starts "with the battle between two Tunguska Evenki clans. Over the years, their feud escalated, both clans using their powerful shamans to curse to the other, with evil spirits, misfortune and disease. The hostility between them grew until one shaman called upon the Agdy to destroy the hated enemy forever. These *fearsome iron birds* fly above the earth in huge clouds, flapping their terrible wings to cause thunder, flashing lightening from their fiery eyes. On that sunny morning in June, the sky became black as a never ending legion of the fearsome birds swooped low over the unfortunate Shanyagir clan. Their *devastating blasts of fire* blew the Shanyagir's tents up into the air over the tree tops. The clan's belongings were destroyed, two hundred and fifty of their reindeer vanished without a trace, the ancient forest was flattened in every direction, and those who still could, fled in panic. *To this day, the Evenk believe that only the Agdy can live in the area where explosion took place. Only a few will risk visiting. And none will live there.*" [Emphasis, mine.][310]

Apparently, localized Tunguska-type events could demarcate regions and des-

---

309. King (1912), *Babylonian Boundary-stones and Memorial-tablets in the British Museum.*
310. Silagadze (2008), 'Tunguska Genetic Anomaly and Electrophonic Meteors'.

ignate some as holy and not to be entered, and others as belonging to a particular group. It would all depend on the *boundaries* of the event!

In the ancient Near East, gods were associated with places sometimes in a general way, as in a tribal god, and other times in a specific way, as 'the spot whereon you stand is holy ground' sort of thing. And so, if a prince wanted to conquer a city, he had to gain the favor of its patron god or goddess. Obviously, you couldn't fight the gods if you were a mere mortal, so getting the god on your side was the first order of business and could include dedicating a child to a god and naming them after said god and certainly sacrificing to that god. (This belief was abandoned when the conception of a universal god was generally accepted, though that 'universal god' happens to have been the tribal god of later Jews who, apparently, continues to favor them and be tied to Israel somehow, in the pagan conception of god and place; most confusing.)

According to Lewy, in preparation for the conquest of Israel (never mind that it was already supposed to have been conquered by Joshua after the Exodus), David did exactly that, naming his first son 'Amnon' or 'he who belongs to the stable one', i.e. Saturn. Of course, the stories of David and his 'conquest' could be tales of a real, local tribal chieftain who did worship Saturn conflated with grandiose tales of the great conquest of an important city (which Jerusalem never was) and the founding of a great kingdom, (again, which never happened in Palestine *vis-à-vis* Israel), since such tales are common founding stories of the real, historical, great empires of Mesopotamia. Again, we see the 'borrowing' of the history of others and assimilating it to one's own uses; in this case, someone in the early 3rd century BCE was making use of the library at Alexandria to create a great and expansive history for the followers of a local tribal god in Palestine that had attracted a certain number and type of followers. (I'll leave the psychoanalysis of *that* to Freud, who seemed to be quite in touch with his own twisted, primal nature and busy projecting it on the rest of the world.)

In respect of Jerusalem, the alleged city of the Jews, it is recorded in the Old Testament that this land was 'given' to the Jews by Yahweh. One would then assume that he was the tutelary deity who had Palestine in his gift. But that actually turns out not to be the case, unless, of course, Yahweh was just another name for Saturn because the god who apparently 'owned' Jerusalem can be inferred from the name of the city as *Ur-sa-li-im-mu*[311], which means

---

311. Neo-Assyrian. See col. III, 1.8, of Sennacherib's Taylor Prism, dated to 691 BCE, in Ling-Israel, (1990), The Sennacherib Prism in the Israel Museum, Jerusalem, pp. 213-47. The Taylor Prism and Sennacherib Prism are clay prisms inscribed with the same text, the

that a god named Šalim was considered to be the creator and protector of Jerusalem. The city is even mentioned in one of the Amarna letters[312] as *Bît Šulmâni*, or 'city of the temple of the god Šulmânu'. That is, the god Šalim or Šulmânu was the principal deity of Jerusalem, which was edited out of the ancient texts used during the writing of the Old Testament, as Russell Gmirkin proposes. The Assyrians identified him with their god, Ninurta who was, effectively, Saturn (though in comet form, certainly, not planetary). One bit of evidence that it was a comet is that the Assyrian astronomers and astrologers referred to Saturn as 'the nocturnal sun', or an object shining as bright as the sun in the night sky, a characteristic of a Giant Comet, for sure!

The name of the god Šalim, or Šulmânu, was honored again in the name of David's son, Ab-salom, and, of course, the name Solomon, itself. Lewy thinks that this is evidence that David honored Šulmânu in preparation to conquer the city; I would suggest that it is even stronger evidence for the fact that this was the god worshiped in that city right down to the last few centuries BCE. It was only after the Assyrians imposed their imperialistic domination on the region that 'the poorer, more remote, and more religiously conservative individuals' – followers of a strange tribal god, Yahweh – formed a cultic center at Jerusalem. It was members of this cult that later utilized many ancient texts to literally create the false history of Israel and it was in those stories that the names were forever inscribed in the minds of the people and could not be erased, nor changed, leaving testimony to the truth.[313]

---

annals of the Assyrian king Sennacherib, notable for describing his siege of Jerusalem during the reign of king Hezekiah. This event is recorded in Isaiah, chapters 33 and 36; 2 Kings 18:17; 2 Chronicles 32:9; also recorded by Herodotus. The Sennacherib Prism is in the Oriental Institute of Chicago; the Taylor Prism is in the British Museum. Another Sennacherib Prism is in the Israel Museum in Jerusalem. The Bible recounts a successful Assyrian attack on Samaria, as a result of which the population was deported, and later recounts that an attack on Lachish was ended by Hezekiah suing for peace, with Sennacherib demanding 300 talents of silver and 30 talents of gold, and Hezekiah giving him all the silver from his palace and from the Temple in Jerusalem, and the gold from doors and doorposts of the temple. Compared to this, the Taylor Prism proclaims that 46 walled cities and innumerable smaller settlements were conquered by the Assyrians, with 200,150 people, and livestock, being deported, and the conquered territory being dispersed among the three kings of the Philistines instead of being given back. Additionally, the Prism says that Sennacherib's siege resulted in Hezekiah being shut up in Jerusalem "like a caged bird", Hezekiah's mercenaries and 'Arabs' deserted him, and Hezekiah eventually bribed Sennacherib, having to give him antimony, jewels, ivory-inlaid furniture, his own daughters, harem, and musicians. It states that Hezekiah became a tributary ruler.

312. VAT 1646, Berlin Amarna Collection reference.
313. See Finkelstein and Silberman (2002), *The Bible Unearthed.*

Akkadian Cylinder Seal c. 2250 BCE depicting Ninurta, Ishtar, Shamas and Ea. Note that Ninurta holds a bow and arrow, there is a lion and bird and a river of fish in the sky. Also note that the tree resembles certain plasma shapes or even a comet itself breaking up with multiple ion tails.

A very ancient temple in the environs of Jerusalem is known to have been built by the Hyksos [314], but it was never a temple of Yahweh until extremely late, if it was ever a temple of Yahweh at all. It may very well be that the first temple of Yahweh was actually the one built by the small number of individuals who were sent to Palestine from Babylonian 'captivity' by Cyrus. The archaeological record shows that no more than 25% of the population was actually deported, and when descendants of this select group were sent back to establish an outpost of the Persian empire to guard the trade routes, they refused to integrate with the people of the land – the descendants of *the 75% of people that had not been deported.* That suggests strongly that the Yahweh cult had actually grown up and refined itself in Babylon and was not, actually, the religion of the ancient Hebrews resident in Palestine. However, even now it is uncertain what god was actually worshipped in the new temple, considering some later evidence that we will get to shortly. It is entirely possible that Herod's alleged temple was the first, truly *Jewish* – as in, exclusive worship of Yahweh-Jehovah – temple ever built, and it was built based on myth and legend that a former temple of Yahweh had existed since the time of Solomon. We are told by Josephus that Herod completely rebuilt the Temple, even *replacing the foundation stones,* which suggests strongly that whatever temple was rebuilt by the returned exiles wasn't much of a temple. On the other hand, contradictions to that story exist. Tra-

---

314. Ibid. p. 55.

ditional rabbinic sources state that the Second Temple stood for 420 years and, based on the 2nd century work, *Seder Olam Rabbah*, placed the construction in 350 BCE, *166 years* later than usual estimates, which leaves out not only Herod's rebuilding from the foundations up, but also the temple being rebuilt by the returned exiles.[315] Something very fishy is going on there, but we don't have time to sort through it right now; we have other fish to fry.

Saturn aka Ninurta

In any event, it seems that the temple that did actually exist in Jerusalem at some time or another was dedicated to Šalim, or Saturn, because by its very name *Jerusalem was the 'city of the temple of the god Šulmânu'*. As it happens, Saturn as 'Ningirsu' was also the protector of the Babylonian city of Lagaš.[316] Ningirsu, aka Ninurta, was revered together with 'his beloved consort', the goddess Bau, the daughter of the sky god, Anu. Ningirsu was a mighty warrior who had powerful weapons and was often designated as 'he who restrains the raging water', which compares to Moses and his water miracles, as we will see. The legend that preserves this role of Ningirsu reports that there was a time when a terrible flood threatened all living beings with death and destruction. Ninurta then decided to come to the assistance of his creatures and so, in a boat (keeping in mind that the heavens were often perceived as 'waters above' by the ancients), he met the enemy. He found that 'the stones had sided with the rising waters', which reflects the idea that the raging flood was caused by a rain of stones. Some of the 'stones' then apparently changed sides and dammed the raging waters. What occurs to me is that this describes a tsunami-type flood during a period of cometary bombardment, following which the waters receded and this was later attributed to the 'help' given by one or more of the still reigning comets designated as the 'good guys'. In any event, the cometary Saturn as Ninurta/ Ningursu was hailed as 'he who restrains the raging water' and was credited with having ended the flood by *building a wall of stones*.[317]

However, all was not well after this emergency mop-up operation. The result of confining the flood-waters to the 'enemy country' was that there was a lack of water in the land, bringing on famine. (Indeed, all the elements

---

315. Goldwurm (1982), *History of the Jewish people: the Second Temple era*, Appendix: 'Year of the Destruction', p. 213.
316. Jastrow (1910), *Review d'Assyria*, VII, p. 173.
317. The ritual for the New Year's festival celebrated in Nippur in honor of its patron-god, Marduk, included the recitation of Enûma Eliš, the story of Marduk's victory over Tiamat and the subsequent creation of the world, which is virtually the same story.

that go with cometary encounters are coming together nicely here.) Ninurta solved this problem by building a city and draining the flood waters into the Tigris river, which then rose and filled a network of irrigation canals that he had also constructed. Well, obviously, people either relocated following a catastrophe and built a city and dug canals, or emerged from the crisis and simply dealt with the new conditions that they found themselves in at their original location. After a time, the leaders who had spearheaded the restoration activities were conflated with the gods who had originally been the cause of the destruction.

In Arabic literature, Ninurta's father is forewarned by a dream that the son who would be born to him would kill him and inherit his throne. He then ordered the child to be killed immediately after his birth, but his mother saved him. Ninurta grew up without knowing his parents and eventually defeated and killed his father, seized the throne and brought the whole Earth under his rule. This version of the story was not told in Nippur because Ninurta and his cult did not supplant the older cult of his father, Enlil, who remained the city's chief deity. Yet, it is possible that the Sumerian version was adapted to local conditions from a legend in which Ninurta's enemy was his own father, the parent Giant Comet. From the *Babylonian Deluge Story*, we know that it was Enlil who was said to have sent the flood to annihilate all life on Earth. Therefore, the flood against which Ninurta fought in the Nippurian epic may, in the original version, have been caused by Enlil. The fact is, the Ninurta Epic repeatedly refers to him as Enlil's son, but also as 'he who did not sit with a nurse' and 'my father I do not know', etc.[318] One is reminded of the Nimrod Legend in which Ninurta-Nimrod was nursed by a tigress and grew up without knowing his mother or father; the same general background applies to Perseus, Moses, Lugh and even Romulus and Remus.

The Phoenician historian Sanchuniathos is said to have written three books in the Phoenician language that are lost to us. (You are going to get very, very tired of hearing what is lost to us in terms of our history. Thank the Christian monks in cahoots with the Carolingians for that.) The only things we know about Sanchuniathos comes from Eusebius's *Praeparatio Evangelica*[319], which includes a paraphrase and summary that Eusebius extracted from the work of Philo of Byblos, i.e. second-hand.[320]

In addition to quoting the extracts from Philo, Eusebius quoted the pagan

---

318. Weiss (1913), *Kissat Ibrahim*, pp. 1-8.
319. *Praeparatio Evangelica*, I. chs. ix-x.
320. Philo of Byblos, aka Herennius Philon (c. 64-141 CE), was an antiquarian writer of grammatical, lexical and historical works in Greek. He is chiefly known for his Phoenician history, assembled from the writings of Sanchuniathon.

Porphyry, who said that Sanchuniathon of Berytus (Beirut) wrote *the truest history about the Jews* because he obtained records from 'Hierombalus' ('Hiram'baal'), priest of the god Ieuo (Yahweh); that Sanchuniathon dedicated his history to Abibalus king of Berytus, and that it was approved by this king and other investigators – the date of this writing being before the Trojan war (!); that is, about the

A relief showing Ninurta chasing a monster. From A. H. Layard, *Monuments of Nineveh*, vol. II (1853). Notice the plasmoid thunderbolts in his hands and the curved knife hanging from his back in front of the wing on the right.

time of Moses, 'when Semiramis was queen of the Assyrians'. Thus Sanchuniathon was projected by Porphyry backward into the pre-Homeric heroic age, an antiquity from which no other Greek or Phoenician writings are known to have survived to the time of Philo. We also find that Sanchuniathon was said to refer disparagingly to Hesiod at one point, who lived in Greece ca. 700 BCE!

Nevertheless, this sort of historiography wasn't entirely created out of whole cloth because usually older available histories were utilized as skeletons, at the very least. One wonders if Sanchuniathos was one of the important sources for the authors of the Old Testament? Perhaps the story of the Great Temple of Solomon was derived therefrom since, as we will see further on, the Great Temple of Baalbek was known to the ancients as the 'Temple of Solomon'.[321]

In any event, Sanchuniathos claimed that the gods were originally human beings who came to be worshipped after their deaths and that the Phoenicians had taken what were originally names of their kings and applied them to elements of the cosmos, as well as also worshipping forces of nature and the Sun, Moon and stars. That is, as we have seen, exactly opposite to what really must have happened. What is so ironic is that Eusebius' intention in citing Sanchuniathos is to discredit pagan religions in favor of an even more corrupted version of a pagan religion: Christianity! Some have suggested that Sanchuniathos' whole work was a fraud created by Philo of Byblos or as-

---

321. Attridge & Oden (1981), *Philo of Byblos: Phoenician History, Introduction, Critical Text, Translation, Notes.*

sembled by him from various materials and claimed to be "collections of se-cret writings of the *Ammouneis*"; that is, discovered in the shrines and de-ciphered from mystic inscriptions on the pillars of Phoenician temples, etc.

The Phoenicians are said by Herodotus to have formerly dwelt on the east-ern side of the Arabian peninsula. However, there is no archeological evi-dence of them there and there does not appear to be any disruption of Phoe-nician societies in Lebanon between 3200 and 1200 BCE. Further, the male populations of Lebanon, Syria, Malta, Sicily, Spain and other areas settled by the Phoenicians, share a common Y chromosome type – m89 – that arose about 40,000 years ago. That is, "the Phoenicians were the Canaanites – and the ancestors of today's Lebanese." [322, 323] And Jews and Arabs; well, at least the original ones, not the Ashkenazi.

Be that as it may, despite his euhemeristic tendencies [324], it seems that what has been preserved of the writings of Sanchuniathos actually turns out to be supported by Ugaritic mythological texts excavated at Ras Shamra since 1929! Thus, it now seems that what must have happened was that Philo gave the texts the Euhemeristic treatment. Sanchuniathos' history of the 'gods' goes more or less as follows, following Greek and Hittite theogonies closely:

> Elus-Cronus overthrows his father Sky or Uranus and castrates him. However Zeus Demarûs, that is Hadad Ramman, purported son of Dagon but actually son of Uranus, eventually joins with Uranus and wages war against Cronus. *To El-Cronus is attributed the practice of circumcision.* Twice we are told that El-Cronus sacrificed his own son. At some point peace is made and Zeus Adados (Hadad) and Astarte reign over the land with Cronus' permission.

His passage about serpents is interesting if we recall the nature of electri-cally charged comets:

---

322. *National Geographic Magazine*, October 2004. Available online here: http://ngm. na-tionalgeographic.com/features/world/asia/lebanon/phoenicians-text/1
And: http://www.pbs.org/previews/phoenicians/
Ancient DNA was included in this study, as extracted from the tooth of a 2500 year-old Phoenician mummy.
323. Phoenician is a Semitic language of the Canaanite subgroup; its closest living relative is Hebrew, to which it is very similar; then Aramaic, then Arabic.
324. Euhemerism is a rationalizing method of interpretation which treats mythological ac-counts as a reflection of historical events, that is, human activity, and mythological characters as historical personages but which were later mythologized by retelling. In more recent literature of myth, such as in Bulfinch's *Mythology*, Euhemerism is called the "historical interpretation" of mythology. Euhemerism is defined in modern aca-demic literature as the theory that myths are distorted accounts of real historical events.

The nature then of the dragon and of serpents Tauthus himself regarded as divine, and so again after him did the Phoenicians and Egyptians: for this animal was declared by him to be of all reptiles most *full of breath, and fiery*. In consequence of which it also exerts *an unsurpassable swiftness by means of its breath*, without feet and hands or any other of the external members by which the other animals make their movements. It also *exhibits forms of various shapes, and in its progress makes spiral leaps as swift as it chooses*. It is also most long-lived, and its nature is to put off its old skin, and so not only to grow young again, but also to assume a larger growth; and after it has fulfilled its appointed measure of age, it is *self-consumed*, in like manner as Tauthus himself has set down in his sacred books: for which reason this animal has also been adopted in temples and in mystic rites.[325]

If that was originally an account of cometary behavior, it's fascinating! According to Sanchuniathos, at third-hand at least, the same legends and traditions as are contained in the Sumerian Ninurta Epic are to be found in the *history of the Phoenicians*, and a particular god is named as the main player: *Kronos-Elos*, who was revered as the 'star of Kronos'. Well, we recognize that as a comet designation! Lewy notes that:

... the extant text represents *Elos-Kronos* as a human king who was deified after his death. We meet here with *the well-known tendency of Greek writers to depict the ancient gods as human beings* to whom divine honors were accorded after their death. *A similar tendency is traceable in the Bible.* ... Laban, the brother-in law of Isaac and father-in-law of Jacob was none other than the Moon-god, the divine lord of Harran, who, in the region of Mt. Lebanon, was revered under the name Laban. Mohammedan writers, in turn, frequently represent the pre-Islamic Arabian gods as deified human beings. ... In all these cases men who, while not, or no longer, believing in the existence of these ancient gods, *had to reckon with the persistence of the mythological legends* in the popular memory, *transformed the former deities into human beings* and thus retained the old stories and legends as part of the national folklore.[326]

Indeed, we've already examined this tendency, as well as the fact that the Greeks transformed the 'star of Kronos' into the planet Saturn. So it seems that the high god of the Phoenicians, El, was actually a comet god – Saturn, aka Kronos – later morphed into a planet. El, like his Babylonian counter-

---

325. Attridge & Oden, ibid.
326. Lewy (1950), op. cit.

part, was involved in a terrible fight in the heavens against his own father, Uranos, and after his victory, '*surrounded his abode by a wall* and founded as the first city Byblos in Phoenicia'. What we can infer from this is that a sanctuary to Saturn was built, surrounded by a defensive wall, and a city grew up around it. The new city was given by Saturn to a goddess, Baaltis, or 'Lady of Byblos'. Sanchuniathon's account, transcribed by Eusebius, adds an extra bit of information that is not extant in other sources about the doings of those times, which Lewy summarizes as follows:

> If, in consequence of a war, pestilence, or other public calamity, Saturn's congregation was threatened with catastrophe, *it was customary that the ruler of the respective community sacrificed his most beloved child to that planet*. This custom, in turn, is explained by the legend that *Saturn himself sacrificed his son on an altar* when pestilence threatened his congregation. In fact, child-sacrifices appear to have been so typical a trait of the cult of the planet Saturn that still in the Middle Ages this star was known as the "children-devouring planet".[327]

As I pointed out in Volume I of *Secret History*, there is certainly evidence in the story of Jepthah's daughter that Yahweh (or, as we are now considering, the original god of the peoples of Palestine, including early Hebrews) was originally a God who may have demanded human sacrifice. I would also note that the story of Jepthah's daughter is just a variation of the almost-sacrifice of Isaac by Abraham. The Abraham-Isaac story is also almost identical to a Vedic story of Manu. These acts were based on what was called *sraddha*, which is related to the words *fides, credo*, 'faith', 'believe' and so on. The word *sraddha* was, according to Dumezil and Levi, too hastily understood as 'faith' in the Christian sense. Correctly understood, it means something like the trust a workman has in his tools and techniques as acts of magic! It is, therefore, part of a 'covenant', wherein the sacrificer knows how to perform a prescribed sacrifice correctly, and who also knows that if he performs the sacrifice correctly, it must produce its effect. In short, it is an act that is designed to gain control over the forces of life that reside in the god with whom one has made the covenant. Such gods as make covenants have a tendency to get out of control if the sacrifices are not performed correctly, which can certainly describe our 'comet gods'.

Mediaeval Arabic sources include legendary memories of the pre-Islamic Arabian religions, as practiced in the Near East before the Turks extinguished

---

327. Lewy (1950), op. cit., p. 339.

the last remnants of the ancient Semitic religions. Ad-Dimisqui[328] devotes a full chapter of his *Cosmography* to this star – or comet, as we should say – worship. He notes that a temple of Saturn 'was built in the form of a *hexagon*, black [was] the color of the stone work and the curtains'. In the cuneiform sources, Saturn is known as the 'black' or 'dark' star. Al-Masudi[329] suggests that, in the opinion of the worshippers of the stars, the Kaaba at Mecca used to be a shrine of Saturn, referring to the presence of the sacred black stone within the sanctuary. The name of the stone-idol was *Hagar al-aswad*.[330] It appears that the Black Stone was worshipped in the Kaaba in pre-Mohammedan times. It was called *Hubal* then, a name that has the meaning of 'He who violently deprives the mother of her children'.

There is a well-known legend about Mohammed's grandfather, Abd al-Muttalib, who was reported to have vowed to sacrifice one of his sons to Hubal if he would be blessed with ten sons.[331] In short, the god worshipped in the Kaaba accepted or even demanded, child sacrifice and such sacrifices were a trait of the worship of Saturn; thus, the Kaaba is also a sanctuary of Saturn.

Coming back now to the cult norms in Jerusalem and the so-called Solomonic Temple, we note that the Holy of Holies measured 20 cubits in length, width and height. It was, therefore, a cube. And, since the name Kaaba means 'cube', it must originally have had a similar shape. In the Song of Solomon, there is the exclamation, "I am black, but comely, oh ye daughters of Jerusalem; as the tents of Kedar, *as the curtains of Solomon*."[332] So the Temple of Solomon had black curtains, characteristic of the worship of Saturn.

Of more importance to us here is the relationship between wells and courses of water to the worship of Saturn, because that relates back to Moses and other Biblical figures and their "women at the Wells". There is a legend in the Jerusalem Talmud that Lewy recounts and explains as follows:

> When David was digging the canals for the sanctuary, he dug fifteen-hundred cubits deep[333] but did not reach the nether waters. Finally he hit a rock wich he wanted to remove, even though the rock warned him not to do so because it was covering up the abyss. When, in spite of this warning, David

328. Al-Dimashqi (1866), *Kitab al-nukhbat al-dahr fi 'ajaib al-barr w'al-bahr*, in Mehren (Ed.), p. 40.
329. Arabic historian, born c. 896, Baghdad; died September 956, Cairo, Egypt.
330. 'Al-Hajar al-Aswad' in modern Arabic, meaning 'Black Stone'.
331. See Tabari's *Annals*, Leiden edition, vol. I, 3, 1881-1882, p. 1074.
332. Song of Solomon 1:5.
333. A cubit is 18 inches or 44 cm, so that's over 2,000 feet!

lifted the rock, the great primordial waters rose and threatened to flood the earth. Thereupon it was decided to *inscribe the Name of the Lord upon the stone* and to throw it into the flood waters. Immediately the flood subsided, but the waters sank to so great a depth that the earth was now menaced by a drought.

The beginning of this legend vividly recalls a passage in Assurnasirapli's Annals where, describing the preparations for the construction of the Ninurta-temple... the Assyrian king expresses himself as follows: "I dug down to the level of the water, to a depth of one hundred and twenty layers of brick I penetrated. The temple of Ninurta, my Lord, I founded in its midst."

The reason why both David and Assurnasirapli dug down to the level of the nether water is somewhat illuminated by the fact that in the interior of the Kaaba at Mecca, there is a well across the opening of which was placed, in the pre-Islamic period, the statue of the god Hubal. ... This peculiarity suggests that *a special relation was assumed to have existed between the deity inhabititing the shrine and the subsoil waters.* ... The nature of this relation is elucidated by the ... fact that the statue of Hubal was placed upon the opening of the well; for this indicates that the deity's own body was thought to prevent the nether waters from rising and flooding the earth. ... this same belief had once been current in Jerusalem.[334]

In the Talmudic legend Lewy recites above about David digging down and releasing the flood waters, the stone that the name of the lord was inscribed on and thrown back into the well was called Eben Šetîjâ (*eben shetiya*) or 'fire stone'. In other passages from extra-biblical sources, the Eben Šetîjâ was in the center of the Holy of Holies in Solomon's Temple and the Ark of the Covenant supposedly stood on top of it, being the 'earthly throne' of Yahweh. It appears that, already, ideas of being able to invoke the god – and protection – by the use of his name had already entered the consciousness of the people.

The Seal of Solomon

This situation explains the Arabic legends that have passed into occult-type literature about the 'seal of Solomon'. The six-pointed star, or hexagram, was believed by the Arabs to have given Solomon command over the whole Earth and over spirits, good and evil. There is a story in the *Arabian Nights* about a ghost who, having rebelled against King Solomon, was imprisoned in a bottle. The container was eventually found by a fisherman, and was sealed by a

---

334. Lewy (1950), pp. 344-345.

lead plug bearing 'the seal of our lord, Solomon'. Exactly as Ninurta-Šulmânu confined the hostile spirits of the flood in the shaft of a well which was sealed by a stone, so Solomon by means of the *six-pointed star emblem* of Saturn, could confine a rebellious spirt to a bottle. Another tale is that the great god, by entrusting to Solomon the ring bearing his emblem, delegated part of his power to the king he had chosen to rule in his name over the inhabited Earth. Interestingly, the name Solomon is a diminutive of Šalmân, 'little Šalmân', implying that 'great Šalmân' was the god who chose Solomon.

So, just as the image of the god Hubal stood over the well in the Kaaba, connecting the sanctuary with the nether waters, so was Yahweh enthroned above the opening to the nether waters in the temple at Jerusalem. However, before Yahweh had the job of holding back the flood, the Eben Šetîjâ apparently held the position with the weighty sigil[335] of Saturn inscribed thereon. Both stony gods were wont to receive offerings of sacrificial blood and incense and, apparently, this was still going on in Jerusalem as late as 333 CE, as reported by the *Itinerarium Burdigalense*, which is the oldest known Christian itinerary that tells of the writer's journey to the Holy Land.[336] What is so interesting about it all is the fact that this central element of Israelite worship was considered by the writers of the Old Testament to be objectionable and so it was redacted completely from the Old Testament, even if it was not removed from the customs and beliefs of the people.

The Woman at the Well

Another important item about the theme of the well and the water miracles is that the pre-Islamic cult of Mecca was one of the astral religions practiced by the Semites throughout the ancient Near East. Hubal, the chief deity, was not the only god worshipped in the Kaaba. Besides several daughters of his, the sources mention a divine couple, Naila and Isaf, who may be assumed to be Hubal's next of kin. In Nippur, Saturn was revered along with his parents and the mothers of these gods played important roles. In cuneiform literature, Ninurta's spouse, Gula or Bau, is frequently referred to as the Great Physician. Since the Muslims ascribe healing properties to the bitter-tasting water of the well *Zemzem*, located in the court-yard of the Kaaba, we are justified in thinking that this well represents the healing goddess consort of Saturn in his embodiment there.

---

335. A seal, signet, sign or image that is considered magical.
336. Bowman (1998), 'Mapping History's Redemption: Eschatology and Topography in the Itinerarium Burdigalense'.

By the same token, in Jerusalem, Šulmânu appears to have also been worshipped together with his divine consort. We can note that below the western boundary of the temple area there is a well today known as *Hammâm aš šifâ*, the 'Healing Bath'. The water is as bitter and undrinkable as the water from the Meccan Zemzem well, but it is said to have the power of healing. Thus in the cult of Jerusalem there must have also been a healing goddess who played the same role as in Mecca and the other holy sites of Saturn.

Stones as Gods

It is among the same peoples that worshipped celestial bodies that we most often find the concomitant worship of stones. The connection is explained by Sanchuniathon (via Eusebius, who was, of course, citing the passage to disparage it), who said that it was believed by the Phoenicians that meteorites were 'stars fallen from the air'. The meteorite that Sanchuniathon was speaking about in particular was one that was worshipped at Tyre. The name of that meteorite-god has been deduced by Lewy to have been *Ba-a-a-ti-ilani*, related to the West Semitic *Bêt-êl* (house of El), which is well known from the Bible as the place where Jacob fell asleep with his head on a stone and dreamed of a ladder between Heaven and Earth, thronged with angels going up and down. (Hold onto that item, it's coming up again soon!) The Tyrian stone-god is described as an 'inspirited stone' because it was part of the body of the god, and therefore some of the god's essence was there, rather like relics of saints are believed to retain some of their holiness.

The *Hağar al-aswad*, the black stone in the Kaaba in Mecca, is quite possibly a meteorite that was revered in a sanctuary dedicated to the 'Black Planet', Saturn.[337] Therefore, we may suppose that the stone was thought to be a piece of the 'Black Planet', a part of the body of the great god, which therefore deserved the same veneration as the great Comet Saturn itself. This connects us back to the issue of the sealing of the nether waters in the well – waters that were undoubtedly released during some cometary cataclysm in the past – and, after the danger had passed, it was thought that one or another of the parts of the body of the god that may have fallen to Earth, could be assumed to be capable of stopping floods or bringing rain or preventing famine, and so on.

The fact that the ancient worshippers of celestial objects, comets, had to deal with gods that had shorter or longer periods of visibility and activity, led them to create images and statues of their gods that they could worship

---

337. Burke (1991), *Cosmic Debris: Meteorites in History*, pp. 221–223.

or pray to at any given moment. Obviously, if they had an actual piece of the god in the form of a meteorite, that was the best thing; such an item might be set up in the sanctuary to be visible to all the people all the time, or might be housed in its temple and cared for and only taken out for processions. Obviously, if a piece of the god was available, one would not need a 'graven image'. So, why was the image of Hubal placed over the well inside the Kaaba?

Islamic histories say that during the years of Mohammed's early manhood, the Kaaba was rebuilt.[338] It is reported that Abd al-Muttalib, Mohammed's grandfather, had a dream in which the long-forgotten location of the well Zemzem was revealed to him.[339] The story further relates that Abd al-Muttalib went through the same routine that David and Assurnasirapli had done, digging at a spot he had seen in his dream and found there the well and the black stone which was subsequently placed by Mohammed in its present place. This suggests that the holy stone had been placed in a well at some time in the past in an effort to deal with a flood and, during a later period of catastrophe, the well and stone were lost, which necessitated the statue to take the place of the visible symbol of the god. Then, when the stone was recovered, the statue was removed. In short, it really wasn't a break in the old religion when Mohammed disposed of the idol and replaced it with a stone; it was just a continuation of the worship of Saturn under a new regime which was the old regime! The sources make it clear that the *Eben Šetîjâ* in the temple at Jerusalem was also regarded as being of cosmic origin and played there the same role as was played by the *Hağar al-aswad* in Mecca.

In the Ninurta epic, the god threw a piece of his own body into the raging flood waters and thereby forced them to recede. However, this act resulted in a period of drought which is exactly paralleled in the David story mentioned above. All of this demonstrates that the legends surrounding the temple in Jerusalem and its divine founder are identical to the stories told about other centers of the Saturn cult. The tradition that the temple was built to house the body of the Comet-God Saturn, represented by the *Eben Šetîjâ*, and that there was a tradition that this same site was where the almost-sacrifice of Isaac had taken place, confirms for Lewy that there was a tradition of human sacrifice at the site; thus, Saturn-worship. Furthermore, the tem-

---

338. Guillaume (1955), *The Life of Muhammad.*
339. According to Islamic belief, it is a miraculously-generated source of water from God, which began thousands of years ago when Abraham's son Ishmael was thirsty and kept crying for water.

ple exhibited the features of temples of Saturn including the *cubic* Holy of Holies and *black curtains.*

And so it seems, the temple of Solomon story was originally created to propagate the worship of the comet-god Saturn, and the six-pointed shield of David or Seal of Solomon is, in fact, a representation of their favored deity: Saturn in his comet incarnation and later, in the astral version of the religion connected to the planet then named Saturn, a dark lord indeed.

What About Yahweh?

Where does Yahweh come in here? How did the Jews assimilate the ancient comet and astral religion so completely to their Yahwistic doctrines that there do not appear to be any differences between the two? It seems that it was when the Jews and their tribal god conquered Jerusalem that the idea took hold that Yahweh was just a certain part of the body of the cosmic Saturn who had come to represent the whole universe.

The idea that minor deities are part of the supreme god's body, and thus executors of his will, implicitly suggests a universal supreme god. It is taken for granted in the *Septuagint* that El Elion, the Most High, assigned different peoples to different gods, and Yahweh was one of the lower deities assigned to the Jews.[340] It was assumed that when a nation gained ascendency over other nations, its national god also assumed rule over the other gods of those people and places. Conversely, it might also be thought that a people wishing to gain control over the whole world might claim that their god is the sole universal god, as the authors of the Septuagint actually did. In their view, since the Jews had conquered Jerusalem in their re-writing of history, their god Yawheh was now conceived of as the supreme deity and other gods were just supposed to carry out his wishes, including the now demoted Šalim.

Curiously, this replacement did not deprive Šalim of any of his characteristics; the name of the city was never changed. Extra-biblical evidence shows that such things as the *Eben Šetîjâ* and the related cycle of legends were still going as late as medieval times and must have featured as well-known ritual in the temple at Jerusalem throughout its existence. In spite of the Jews' aversion to representations of the deity, they used a stone with the six-pointed star graven into it – the symbol of the Black Comet, Saturn – as an image of their faith. Throughout the Middle Ages, the Jews were known as 'the people of Saturn' to astrologically-minded people who thought in terms of 'planetary influences' on the lives of individuals and peoples; they

---

340. Deuteronomy 32:8 f.

just didn't know how accurate the appellation actually was, nor was it exclusive to the Jews.

In the book of Genesis we are told that Abraham's almost-sacrifice of his son (which he was ordered to do by Yahweh and apparently took it as a normal request from the god) took place in 'the land of Moriah … upon one of the mountains…' The book of Chronicles tells us that there was a threshing floor belonging to a Jebusite named Araunah "in mount Moriah" and that the Temple of Solomon was built over it.[341] Some have assumed this to be the same spot. Yet, Genesis also tells us that Jerusalem was already a city during the time of Abraham with a temple and a priest, Melchizedek, so either Abraham went into the wilderness of the area around Mt. Moriah, or (assuming that any of the story is even remotely historical) he actually went to the temple there to make the sacrifice of his son and the setting was changed later to avoid the connection.[342]

What concerns us here is the threshing floor. The narrative in question can be found at both 2 Samuel 24 and 1 Chronicles 21. In the Samuel narrative, God incites David to punish the Israelites by imposing a census upon them. In the Chronicles version, it is Satan, not God, who incites David to make the census. Strangely, taking a census was regarded by Yahweh – who may or may not have suggested it – as a sin deserving of punishment! So, Yahweh sent a prophet named Gad to offer David his choice of smiting. David had three options:

> Samuel version: seven years of famine. Chronicles version: three years of famine; three months of fleeing from an invader: three days of *pestilence from the Angel of the Lord*. Chronicles specifies: "three days of the sword of the Lord and pestilence in the land, and the angel of the Lord destroying throughout all the borders of Israel." (I Chr. 21:12)

In both versions, David chose the three days of plague. An angel was duly sent to smite the people (remember, it was David alone who allegedly sinned at the instigation of either Yahweh or Satan) with a pestilence. Now here we want to pause to consider something important. Jaume d'Agramunt, a doctor writing at the time of the Black Death in Europe in the 14th century:

> … said nothing concerning the term epidemia, but he extensively developed what he meant by 'pestilencia'. He gave this latter term a very peculiar etymology, in accordance with a form of knowledge established by Isidore of Se-

---

341. 2 Chronicles 3:1.
342. Genesis 14:18-20.

ville (570-636) in his *Etymologiae*, which came to be *widely accepted throughout Europe during the Middle Ages*. He split the term pestilencia up into three syllables, each having a particular meaning: pes = tempesta: 'storm, tempest'; te = 'temps, time', lencia = clardat: 'brightness, light'; hence, he concluded, the pestilencia was 'the time of tempest caused by light from the stars.'[343]

With that bit of information, we can better understand what happened next in II Samuel 24:

> So the Lord sent a pestilence upon Israel from the morning even to the time appointed; and there died of the people from Dan even to Beersheba 70,000 men. And when the angel stretched out his hand upon Jerusalem to destroy it, the Lord relented of the evil and reversed His judgment and said to the destroying angel, It is enough; now stay your hand. And the angel of the Lord was by the threshing floor of Araunah the Jebusite. (vs. 15-16)

I Chronicles has additional information:

> God sent an angel to Jerusalem to destroy it, and as he was destroying ... And the angel of the Lord stood by the threshing floor of Ornan the Jebusite. David lifted up his eyes and saw the angel of the Lord standing between earth and the heavens, having a drawn sword in his hand stretched out over Jerusalem. ... Now Ornan was threshing wheat, and he turned back and saw the angel; and his four sons hid themselves. (21:15, 16, 20)

Given the etymology of the word 'pestilence', we suspect we are not dealing with an epidemic here. But we have more than that; we have an angel of the lord standing between heaven and Earth with a drawn sword. Plus, this angel is destroying, not just spreading germs, and that destruction obviously can raze a city.

The detail that a harvest was underway is interesting considering the fact that Ninurta and others are depicted with curved knives; the one Ninurta is carrying is specifically a harvesting knife.

Since the destruction stopped at the threshing floor, David was instructed to build an altar there and make a sacrifice (70,000 men wasn't enough?!). He bought the land from Araunah/Ornan and that, supposedly, is how the lot for the building of the temple was acquired. Another interesting con-

---

343. From Arrizabalaga, Garcia-Ballester, French & Cunningham (Eds.) (2010), *Practical Medicine from Salerno to the Black Death*.

nection is that Araunah/Ornan is identified as a Jebusite which most scholars believe refers to Hittites. In the Hittite language, *araunah* means 'the lord' and is a title, not a name. So it is thought that he was the Jebusite king of Jerusalem. The land purchase associated with the event connects us back to the boundary-stone gods of the Babylonians.

Thus Lewy concludes that David and Solomon – who she considered to be historical characters – built a temple to honor Saturn and it was the worship of this god that they sought to impose on their subjects, the early Hebrews. If that is the case, then I would suggest that it occurred back in Hyksos times after they made their Exodus from the Nile Delta at the time of the eruption of Thera (1645-1600) and established themselves in Palestine.

Allah, the Star

In the *Koran*, Sura 106.3, Mohammed urges his kinsmen to worship 'the Lord of this house', which means simply the god of the Kaaba. At this point, we realize that this was not to encourage a new religion. Then in Sura 24.35 Allah is characterized as a *star* and as 'the light of heaven and earth' – terms familiar to us in descriptions of comets though, of course, we realize that all has been 'astralized' by the Greeks. Rather often, puzzled Christians will ask how it is that Mohammed could have identified his god, Allah, with Yahweh, the god of the Jews. Therein lies a tale.

It seems that the recovery of the stone that was the visible symbol of the cometary god to whom the Kaaba was dedicated confronted Mohammed with the problem of restoring the proper rituals. Failing to perform the ritual correctly in the presence of the actual body of the god could bring on disaster ('dis'-'aster'!). The Cuneiform literature that I have recounted above in this text, provide examples of this problem. In an inscription of a Babylonian king, we read how he is commanded by the Moon God to restore the office of a priestess, and the sanctuary in which this priestess must perform a certain rite, as had been done in days of old. But the ritual had become obsolete and forgotten. The king ordered a search to be made for the ancient documents that would reveal how the project was to be realized. Apparently, the search took eight years. In the meantime, the king traveled to other centers of Moon worship to interview the local priests about the traditions. It was ultimately discovered that the tablets containing the instructions had been carried off as war booty many years earlier, so a priest was sent to copy them and succeeded in the end.[344] We read rather similar sto-

---

344. Clay (1915), *Babylonian Texts*.

ries in the Bible about the recovery of an old Torah that had been forgotten, and a king of Judah tearing his hair and so on in the realization that nobody has been following the rules for a long time! The story is told in the context of repairs being done on the temple, which is similar to the recovery and restoration that Mohammed was doing. I covered that in the first volume of *Secret History*, so I won't belabor it here.

Apparently Mohammed's search for documents in the deserts of Arabia didn't produce the needed results, so the only obvious place to go for advice as to what to do and how, was to consult the priesthood of the Jews.[345] The Mohammedans well knew that there was a close relationship between the cults of Mecca and Jerusalem. This is expressed in their belief that, at the last day, the Black Stone of Mecca will come to Jerusalem as a bride to join the Ṣahra, the rock of Jerusalem, and then the Most High God will be seated. This brings up the question as to whether or not the genuine Eben Šetîjâ was still in place when the Muslims conquered Jerusalem.

The location of the Dome of the Rock was established by Caliph Omar ibn' al Khattab, who was advised by his associate, Ka'ab al-Ahbar, a former Jewish rabbi who had converted to Islam, that the Night Journey, which is mentioned in the Quran and specified by the hadiths of being located in Jerusalem, took place at the site of the former Jewish Temple. We are told that, not long after this, the Muslims 'recognized the Ṣahra', which was, in reality, part of the surrounding 90 million year old Late Cretaceous limestone. In short, it seems that after the rubble had been cleared away, they thought that the Eben Šetîjâ had been found.

A passage from the Mishna[346] describes the Eben Šetîjâ as a stone slab only about 3 fingers above the floor level and smaller than the Ark of the Covenant which was 1.25 by 0.75 meters. The stone is referred to by Ibn Abdrabbihi, writing about 913 CE:

> Now when thou enterest the Ṣahra (Dome of the Rock), make thy prayer in the three corners thereof; and also pray on the slab which rivals the Rock itself in glory, for it lies over a gate of the Gates of Paradise.

The measurement of the rock within the Dome of the Rock is 10 to 12 feet. Lewy says that the real Eben Šetîjâ is (or was) about 12 meters North of the

345. Apparently some documents and pictorial records were uncovered in the Kaaba when the old structure was demolished. See Masaudi (1877), *Les prairies d'or*, IV, p. 126; Dozy (1864), *Die Israeliten zu Mekka*, pp. 155.
346. See: *The Mishna, Treatise Yoma*, chapter V.2, and cf. Tosifta III. 6.

northern end of the Dome and was only recovered after the original erroneous identification of the Eben Šetîjâ with the Şahra had already been sanctioned to such an extent that it was impossible to correct the error. Thus, the genuine Eben became part of the sacred inventory as another sacred stone that was made holy by the assumption that Suleiman was buried under it. There are enough medieval references to this stone cited by Lewy, to be convinced that it was still there in very late antiquity. Another point that supports this is that the Muslims, being fully aware of the identity and functions of the sacred stones of Mecca and Jerusalem, before designating the Kaaba as the *qibla* (direction to face while praying) for all the Muslims, Mohammed ordered his followers to turn their faces in prayer toward the sacred rock of Jerusalem. Keep in mind that the qibla is rooted in the belief of comet-star worshippers that a man must address his prayers only to a being visible to his eyes. When such worshippers prayed, they either turned their faces to the being in the sky, or its 'part' or image. In the case of distance from the sanctuary, the individual turned his gaze in the direction of the sanctuary and was expected to have, at least once in his life, visited the sanctuary and seen the body (or part) of the god with his own eyes, i.e. made direct contact with his sensorium. At one point Mohammed's 9th successor, Abd al-Malik, ordered his subjects to replace the pilgrimage to Mecca by a pilgrimage to Jerusalem because he held the knowledge that the sacred stone of Jerusalem represented (was a part of the body of) the same god as the Black Stone of Mecca. Thus, we can see that the way Mohammed restored the cult of Mecca to its orginal form was to take over from Jewish tradition those things that pertained to the old, genuine religion of Jerusalem which he knew to be identical with that of Mecca: the worship of Saturn.

It appears that Mohammed was fully justified in that belief. And so the Muslims, too, attached great importance to Abraham, David and Solomon, who they consider to have been perfect Muslims since a Muslim is a person who professes his complete submission to the god of Mecca and of Jerusalem by whatever name he is called: Salim, El or Allah.

When the Mohammedans adopted the theory that the Kaaba had been built and dedicated by Abraham and his son Ishmael, it became necessary to find an explanation for the fact that, prior to Mohammed, the cult of the idol Hubal and not the worship of the aniconic god of Abraham was practiced in the famous old sanctuary. And so, it was said that Hubal and other Arabian idols were 'un-Arabian' and imported from Syria. However, from cuneiform inscriptions found in the 20th century, it is learned that Hubal and other Arabian deities are genuinely Arabian.

CHAPTER SEVEN

THE GREEK PHILOSOPHERS – WHAT DID THEY KNOW?

The recovery of Greece was percolating along by the beginning of the 8th century BCE. Communities had developed that were ruled by an elite group of aristocrats rather than by a single god-like king as had been the case in earlier periods. The Greek language combined with the Phoenician alphabet gave birth to our alphabetic writing system which spread throughout the region and the Greeks began to colonize the Mediterranean. Who the Greeks were, and where they came from, is an interesting question. Certainly there must have been a few survivors in the areas of Greece itself but there was also a sudden upsurge of population and material goods that occurred c. 750 BCE, so somebody came from somewhere! And this brings us to something extraordinary about the area of the collapsed Hittite Empire colonized by settlers during the Greek Dark Age: it seems to have given birth to Greek philosophy, which then gave birth to Greek culture, which led to the Greek Empire.

Now, even though it does not seem to be all that important, trust me, covering the lives of some of the early philosophers and their ideas will help to make sense of things. It is here that we notice the most peculiar fact that civilization needed to be re-created, re-thought, re-organized, which bears witness to the incredible destruction that must have preceded the Dark Age. All the ideas and discussions that went on amongst these groups are about creating laws, constitutions, social norms, and so on, when those things had been completely settled and well-known hundreds of years previously. But the Greek philosophers talk as though human society was just arising out of the slime of the primordial ocean and the memories of what existed and prevailed before was dim and partial.

The lives and doings of various Greek philosophers is one area where you can do some reading and research on your own, and I don't think it will be painful at all! My pop-culture imbued offspring have read Diogenes Laërtius'

Lives of Eminent Philosophers with a great deal of amusement, often breaking out into uproarious laughter. They have pointed out that it's like reading *Bill and Ted's Excellent Adventure*, and they imagine Keanu Reaves and George Carlin speaking the lines. I'll be quoting or paraphrasing a bit here and there from Diogenes, but not so much on the philosophical ideas as the scientific ones, mostly assembling the facts and data following the ideas of Bailey, Clube and Napier, with a longer section in respect of the Stoic philosophers, who I suspect preserved some of the ancient knowledge of the reality of cometary bombardment and periodic destruction. But do avail yourself of the Loeb Classical Library series of ancient texts for hours of entertainment and amusement! You may also learn some very interesting things along the way!

Homer and Hesiod

The 19th century discovery of the Mycenaean civilization by the amateur archaeologist Heinrich Schliemann, and then the discovery of the Minoan civilization by Sir Arthur Evans in the early 20th century, provided hard evidence for many of the mythological details about the gods and heroes of Homer and Hesiod. Unfortunately, the evidence is primarily monumental, not written, since the Linear B script form of ancient Greek found there was used mainly to record practical concerns of daily life such as inventories of goods. Additionally, there are visual representations that are not known in any literary source, so obviously a great deal was lost between the collapse and the re-emergence of human societies.

Archaeology reveals that the earlier inhabitants of the Balkan peninsula were agricultural settlers that appear to have practiced a form of Animism that assigned a spirit to every aspect of nature. At the time of the collapse, with the inrush of tribes from the North, probably driven by widespread, catastrophic destruction, a new pantheon of gods appeared, probably reflecting the experiences of the northern peoples. These were gods of violence, conquest, force and destruction, obvious evidence of the trials and tribulations endured by the northern peoples of Europe and central Asia at the time of the collapse and destruction of the Bronze Age.

The earliest literary survivals we have of the foundations of Western civilization are Homer's two epic poems, the *Iliad* and the *Odyssey* (8th century BCE). Hesiod is a possible near-contemporary of Homer (750-650 BCE) and gives us the Origin of the Gods in his *Theogony*. Hesiod's *Works and Days* is a teaching poem about farming life and offers advice on how to survive in a world made dangerous by the gods. In this latter work, Hesiod makes use of a scheme of Four Ages of Man: Golden, Silver, Bronze and Iron, a clear exposition of repeating cataclysmic destructions. These ages are separate 'creations', or time periods of the reign of the gods, signifying the gradual break-up of the Giant Comet and the disasters brought by the various 'offspring'. The Golden Age belonged to the reign of Cronos; the subsequent ages were dominated by Zeus. Hesiod regarded this last period as the worst since it was overrun with evil. He explained the presence of evil by the myth of Pandora, when all of the best of human capabilities, save hope, had been spilled out of her overturned jar. This reminds us of the possibility of genetic mutation due to comets, as we covered earlier, and periods of utter horror where cannibalism and human sacrifice were rampant practices devised by pathological deviants who had taken control, supported by terrified authoritarian followers.

> All who came forth from Gaia and Ouranos, the most dire of children, from the beginning were hated by their own begetter; and just as soon as any of them came into being he hid them all away and did not let them into the light, in the inward places of Gaia; and Ouranos rejoiced over the evil deed. And she, prodigious Gaia, groaned within for she was crowded out; and she contrived a crafty, evil device... she sent him [Kronos] into a hidden place of ambush, placed in his hands a jagged-toothed sickle, and enjoined on him the whole deceit. Great Ouranos came bringing Night with him, and over Gaia, desiring love, he stretched himself, and spread all over her; and he, his son, from his place of ambush stretched out with his left hand, and with his right he grasped the monstrous sickle, long and jagged-toothed, and swiftly sheared off the genitals of his dear father, and flung them behind him to be carried away...[347]

Parts of Hesiod's account reveal parallelisms with the Hurrian account of the succession of the oldest gods preserved in the Hittite Kumarbi-tablet dating, in its extant form, to around the beginning of the Greek Dark Age. In the Hittite version, the first king in heaven is Alalu, who is driven out by Anu and then Anu is deposed by the father of Kumarbi. As Anu tries to escape into the sky, Kumarbi bites off and swallows his genitals. After being told that he has become impregnated with the Storm God and two other 'terrible gods', he spits it out but it is too late: he's pregnant! He eventually gives birth to the equivalent of Zeus, who deposes Kumarbi and becomes king of heaven. However, the Greek version incorporates non-Mesopotamian ele-

---

347. Hesiod, *Theogony* 154.

ments. Perhaps we see in the cutting off of the genitals, a physical interaction with plasma components, discharging a comet and thereby dissolving its tail. What is evident in the above account is that much of this activity occurred in daylight and brought deep darkness to the Earth.

Hesiod's *Theogony* is not only the fullest surviving account of the gods, but also the fullest surviving account of the archaic bardic function, with its long preliminary invocation to the Muses. *Theogony* became the subject of many poems, including those attributed to Orpheus, Musaeus, Epimenides, Abaris, and other legendary seers, which are now lost to us. It seems that these were written accompaniments to ritual purifications and mystery-rites designed to appease the gods, some of which must have included sacrifice, but not necessarily all. Obviously, many groups in many places were trying desperately to find the right formula that would bring the chaos and destruction to an end. In fact, it can be said that Hesiod's work not only deals with the 'genealogical' relationships between the gods (the parent comet and its ongoing disintegration), but also to demonstrate how, finally, something seems to have worked and Zeus became the ultimate authority and established order by 'defeating' (destruction via impact?) the Titans. Zeus hurls thunderbolts at them and...

> The whole earth boiled, and the streams of Okeanos, and the unharvested sea; and them, the earth-born Titans, did a warm blast surround, and flame unquenchable reached the holy aither, and the darting gleam of thunderbolt and lightning blinded the eyes even of strong men. A marvelous burning took hold of Chaos; and it was the same to behold with the eyes or to hear the noise with the ears as if earth and broad heaven above drew together; for just such a great din would have risen up...[348]

The heroic age presented in the *Iliad* and *Odyssey* was more entertaining than the divine-focus of the *Theogony* and therefore is better known. Homer's tales were clearly set in a world that was under the constant threat of bombardment and the relations between gods and humans were rather clearly defined, though later interpreters have completely misread and misinterpreted these things. Homer appears to be presenting a clear formula of how to be in right relations with the gods, and the main focus was Theoxeny[349] and hospitality. One needed to behave decently, even to strangers and foreign-

---

348. Hesiod, *Theogony* 695.
349. 'Theoxeny, the belief that strangers had magical powers or were deities themselves. From 'theo' meaning 'god' and 'xeno' meaning 'alien', 'strange', 'guest'.

ers, because they might be gods in disguise, and bad hospitality could bring the fires of heaven down on one's head, literally. One of the attributes of Zeus was 'Xenios', or the stranger. This relates back to the evils of mankind decried by Hesiod. Theoxeny could demonstrate the character of a man and thus determine whether or not he would be spared from destruction. A good man will treat the aged and humble well; a bad man will abuse the helpless and down-trodden. In the Odyssey, this point is made abundantly clear with Odysseus taking the role of the god and the story being mainly about the different forms of hospitality that are shown to Odysseus and then, finally, how Odysseus, in the role of the god, brought absolute and total destruction on the suitors who abused his hospitality. This view is rather more interesting than one might suppose as it appears that xenophobia, increasing economic disparity, abandonment and abuse of the poor, etc., are among the primary characteristics of a society on the verge of collapse; and such collapse can ultimately include cosmic disaster.

As time passed, and things began to quiet down in the skies, these tales gave rise to cults of heroes who were strictly human, though associated with the gods as either offspring or close affiliation. After a bit more time had passed, it appears that these works were considered to be impossibly wild tales born from primitive imaginings, and subsequent works on these themes became less narrative and more allusive visions, leading to the vision of the world presented by the later emerging philosophers. Certainly, there may have been heroic individuals during those times; as I've already mentioned, such times refine both the best and the worst in human beings. But reducing real, cosmic activity to the level of exaggerated human doings amounted to a cover-up, whether it was intentional or not.

And so, we find a group of people – obviously a minority – in the area of the ancient Hittite Empire, emerging from the darkness, building societies and trying to bring order out of chaos. They read the myths and knew the stories of their immediate forebears, but they did not see anything going on in the skies, or the world at large, that would explain these things, so they assumed, disastrously, that the language describing the doings of gods was really about forces of nature that had been misunderstood. They didn't have precise scientific terminology as we do today, and they weren't precisely scientific in the beginning, so they utilized the only language they had to do this with: the language of myth. They were concerned with the early history of the Earth, with its creation, its structure, how it worked, and, of course, man's place within it.

The sky was seen as a solid hemisphere, similar to a bowl. It was solid and bright, even metallic. It covered the flat earth and the lower part of the space between earth and sky, up to and including clouds, contained mist (aer); beyond that, from clouds up to the starry sky, was aither, the 'shining upper air' which, interestingly enough, was often conceived of as fiery. In the *Iliad*, Homer writes, in obvious comet imagery, "the fir-tree reached through the aer to the aither." [350] Below the surface of the earth, its mass continued far down, with roots in Tartaros.

> Or seizing him I will hurl him into misty Tartaros, very far, where is the deepest gulf below earth; there are iron gates and brazen threshold, as far beneath Hades as sky is from earth. [351]
>
> Around it [Tartaros] a brazen fence is drawn; and all about it Night in three rows is poured, around the throat; and above are the roots of earth and unharvested sea. [352]

So we see something like a big globe surrounding the Earth, though the part that surrounds the world underneath the flat surface, embraces a big mass of Earth's foundations, as well as the underworld, and is either brass or iron. (This will be important further on, so hang on to it!) Some conceived of the Earth's foundations as continuing on indefinitely, but that was a later idea of Xenophanes.

Around the edges of the flat Earth ran the vast river, Okeanos. However, in the Odyssey, a broad outer sea was described. So the idea of Okeanos being a river of fresh water may be Mesopotamian. The encircling river meant that the Sun, after finishing his transit of the sky, sailed in a golden boat around the Earth in the stream of Okeanos and returned to the place of arising the next morning. This may be derived from Egypt where the Sun was depicted as traveling from West to East across subterranean waters.

Okeanos – along with Tethys or the earth itself – was perceived as the 'begetter of gods' and the place where the gods went to sleep. That is, it was over the horizon that the comets arose and then subsequently set. Obviously, they could also go below the horizon to Tartaros or could even be born from Tartaros.

> There of murky earth and misty Tartaros and unharvested sea and starry sky, of all of them, are the *springs in a row* and the grievous, dank limits which even the gods detest; a great gulf, nor would one reach the floor for the whole

---

350. *Iliad*, XIV 288.
351. *Iliad*, VIII, 13, Zeus speaking.
352. Hesiod, *Theogony* 726.

length of a fulfilling year, if one were once *within the gates*. But hither and thither storm on grievous storm would carry one on; dreadful is this portent even for immortal gods; and the dreadful halls of gloomy Night stand covered with blue-black clouds.[353]

There are *gleaming gates*, and brazen threshold unshaken, fixed with continuous roots, self-grown; and in front, far from all the gods, dwell the Titans, across murky Chaos.[354]

We see that this may be an attempt to describe the regions beyond and below the horizon, which are said to be surrounded by night, and above it are the roots of the Earth and the sea.

Alcman

Around 600 BCE, or not long after Hesiod, there was a Spartan poet named Alcman who apparently wrote a theogonical cosmogony. We only have a 2nd century CE papyrus commentary with limited extracts of the work. It obviously puzzled the commentator who wrote a load of Aristotelian nonsense about it. Too bad more of the poem and less of the commentary is not preserved.[355] What is important about it is that the fragment preserves a couple of unusual terms: *poros*, as 'paths in the primeval sea', and *tekmor*, as 'signs of direction through it', or through the stars. This appears to us to be a description of a physical path or passage through the heavens, described in terms of the background stars though, as yet, there were no constellations. The new terms are neither oriental nor Hesiodic, so where did they come from in 7th century BCE Greece? At the very least, it demonstrates that cosmogonical ideas were existent in Greece, proper, prior to the exportation of the Anatolian, Ionian ideas.

Pherecydes

Pherecydes flourished in the 6th century BCE. According to one ancient authority, he was contemporary with the Lydian king Alyattes, i.e. 605-560 BCE. He was born on the Greek island of Syros[356], and is said by many scholars to have been the bridge between the ancient myths and pre-Socratic Greek

---

353. Hesiod, *Theogony* 736.
354. Hesiod, *Theogony* 811.
355. Kirk, Raven & Schofield (1983), *The Presocratic Philosophers*, pp. 46-49.
356. Greek island in the Cyclades, in the Aegean Sea, located about 144 km south-east of Athens.

philosophy. According to Diogenes, Pherecydes' work survived into his own time, the 3rd century CE. Diogenes recites miracle stories about Pherecydes, such as prediction of an earthquake, a shipwreck, the outcome of a battle, and so forth. What is problematical is that the same miracles were also attributed to Pythagoras. Associations between the two were assumed only *after* the 5th century BCE, probably due to a passing comment made by Ion of Chios[357] and recorded by Diogenes:

> Thus did [Pherecydes] excel in manhood and honor, and now that he is dead he has a delightful existence for his soul – if Pythagoras was truly wise, who above all others knew and learned thoroughly the opinions of men.[358]

The confused association between Pherecydes and Pythagoras suggests that there were few reliable details about either and people could just make stuff up at will. Thus, it is probably best to be skeptical of a connection.

In addition to Diogenes, there is a reference to Pherecydes in the *Suda*[359], which says:

> There is a story that Pythagoras was taught by him [Pherecydes]; but that he himself had no instructor, but trained himself after obtaining *the secret books of the Phoenicians*.[360]

Well, we've encountered these secret books of the Phoenicians already, haven't we? Remember Sanchuniathos who was reported by Philo of Byblos to have obtained his knowledge from "collections of secret writings... discovered in the shrines and deciphered from mystic inscriptions on the pillars of Phoenician temples"? This is a very doubtful claim we find in the *Suda*, probably influenced by the later creation of the legend of Pythagoras, as we will discover soon.

From another direction, there is something most interesting that Diogenes has reported about Pherecydes:

> There is preserved of the man of Syros the book ... and there is preserved also *a solstice-marker in the island of Syros.*

---

357. Ion of Chios (c. 490/480 – c. 420 BCE) was a Greek writer, dramatist, lyric poet and philosopher.
358. Diogenes, I, 120.
359. A massive 10th century Byzantine encyclopedia of the ancient Mediterranean world, formerly attributed to an author called Suidas.
360. Suda, s.v. Pherecydes.

This may possibly be related to a few lines from the Odyssey:

> There is an island called Syrie – perhaps you have heard of it – above Ortygie, where are *the turnings of the sun.*

The "turnings of the sun" would refer to the summer and winter solstices when the Sun reaches its highest and lowest points and appears to 'turn back' due to the angle of the Earth's axis *vis-à-vis* the Sun through the annual orbit. Kirk, Raven and Schofield add in a footnote:

> ... the only other place in Homer where Ortygie is mentioned is Odyssey V, 123, where Orion, having been carried off by Eos, is slain in Ortygie by Artemis. The implication is that Ortygie was the dwelling-place of Eos, the dawn, and therefore that it lies in the east. ... since solstices would normally be observed at sunrise and in summer, and so in the north-east-by-east direction, that is what the phrase might suggest. Thus the intention may be to indicate the general direction of this probably mythical Ortygie. In fact the dwelling-place of Eos was often conceived as being *Aia*, commonly identified with Colchis; and Colchis does lie roughly north-east-by-east from the centre of the Ionian coastline.[361]

Obviously, if these people would just wake up and think about comets and astronomy in general, they would have much better results with their interpretations. Kirk et al. also include comments, aka scholia, on the couplet from Homer written by later scholars:

> Aristarchus comment: They say there is a cave of the sun there, through which they mark the sun's turnings.
> Herodian: As it were toward the turnings of the sun, which is in the westward direction, above Delos.[362]

The comments (scholia) show that two interpretations (at least) of this couplet from Homer were being discussed in Alexandria. One of them suggests that it was thought there was a solstice-marker that had been used by Pherecydes. Well, since I do think that Pherecydes was making astronomical observations, that suggestion is going in the right direction. But what is more interesting is that it appears that the existence of this marker was known by Homer. One wonders if Pherecydes discovered it by following

---

361. Kirk et al., p. 55.
362. Kirk et al., p. 54.

clues in Homer? But of course, this whole thing needs to be taken with a grain of salt or two since, according to the scholars, there is no other evidence that Pherecydes was a practical scientist, although, to me, the evidence is obvious. Further, the fact that many cave-like megalithic structures of northern Europe have been shown to be designed to mark the solstices and/or equinoxes is very intriguing, and suggests to me that Pherecydes had a northern source for his information.

Pherecydes is said to have been the first to write about the gods in *prose* as opposed to poetry. That is, poetic works appear to have had ritual purposes, while Pherecydes broke with this tradition, which suggests to me that he was attempting to write about these things in a pragmatic way. His major work was entitled *Heptamychos*, or 'the seven sanctuaries' or recesses. Some sources say it was *Pentemychos*, which is translated as meaning 'five recesses' and the later Pythagoreans were said to have developed their pentagram and 'spiritual purification' system based on the 'five recesses', so I'm inclined to think it was actually *Pentemychos*. It is assumed that he was teaching esoteric things via the medium of mythic representation, i.e. allegorically. One ancient commentator wrote:

> Also, Pherecydes, the man of Syros, talks of *recesses* and *pits* and *caves* and *doors* and *gates*, and through these speaks in riddles of becomings and deceases of souls.[363]

Well, sure, we could interpret this in view of the many astronomically oriented megalithic structures and conclude that there was some metaphysical or spiritual purpose to them, as well as a connection between them and Pherecydes' 'recesses'. However, as we have seen from our brief review above starting with Homer and Hesiod, particularly discussions of gates and doors and so forth, this is undoubtedly incorrect; Pherecydes was talking about regions of the sky exactly as did Homer and Hesiod.

Pherecydes described a cosmogony based on three 'principles': Zas (Zeus), Chthonie (earth) and Chronos which I will interpret to be three main bodies of a formerly single giant comet. *Pentemychos* was about a cosmic battle taking place, with Chronos as the head of one side and Ophioneus – the serpent – as the leader of the other. As we know, the same story is elsewhere enacted with Zeus and Typhon/ Typhoeus, Marduk vs. Tiamat, and parallels we've covered above. The semen (seeds) of Chronos was placed in the 'recesses' and *numerous other gods and their offspring were the result*. This

---

363. Kirk et al.

is described in a fragment preserved in Damascius' *On First Principles*[364] and we've read almost exactly the same thing in Hesiod, quoted above in the story of the castration of Chronos.

With the understanding of giant comets, and that they were perceived to arrive from certain areas of the sky with regularity, as explained by the science we have reviewed above, we can better interpret the 'recesses' as being particular areas of the sky that were later defined as constellations, created and named in accordance with the cometary activity.

This point can be understood by reviewing the development of the history of astrological signs. John H. Rogers, in *Origins of the ancient constellations*[365] (in 2 parts), explains that the division of the zodiac into 12 equal parts was not done by even the Babylonians until between 600 and 475 BCE, around the time that zodiacal horoscopes were introduced. The 48 constellations of the classical world were first described by Eudoxus and Aratus (see Chapter Eight), and the definitive list was not made until the time of Ptolemy (90-c.168 CE). Only a subset of the classical constellations came from Babylonia – the zodiac and four associated animals: serpent, crow, eagle and fish.

An idea of how the sky was divided for the purpose of recording astronomical events can be gained by a review of Stanislaus Lubienietzki's (1623-1675) *Theatrum Cometicum*[366], published in 1668 in Amsterdam, which contains 80 fabulous illustrations that accompany over 400 comet sightings. The book records the observations of such scholars as Athanasius Kircher, Christian Huygens and Johannes Hevelius (plus others), and each of them provided their own *constellation charts* which reflect different sky-mapping traditions. Let's look at a few of them here.

The first image (overleaf) is a comet observation by R. P. A. Curtio. Notice how particular stars are designated in the grid he has drawn so as to accurately place his comet in relation to those stars. Notice the triangulation from Cygnus and Polaris to the head of the comet. In this chart, we also see the oblique line of the zodiac crossed by the horizontal line of the celestial equator. (Keep all this in mind; it is going to solve a great, ancient mystery further on!)

---

364. Ahbel-Rappe (2010), *Damascius' Problems and Solutions Concerning First Principles*. Damascius was head of the Neoplatonist academy in Athens when the Emperor Justinian shut its doors forever in 529. His work, *Problems and Solutions Concerning First Principles*, is the last surviving independent philosophical treatise from the Late Academy.

365. Rogers (1998), *Origins of the ancient constellations, Part I: The Mesopotamian Tradition* and *Part II: The Mediterranean Tradition*.

366. http://www.polona.pl/dlibra/doccontent2?id=643

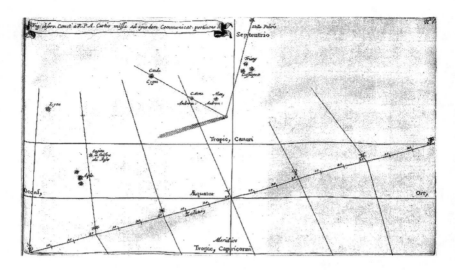

The image below is a more horoscopic type of map which shows the symbols of the zodiac and designates which sign the Sun is in. The little circle at the bottom probably designates the Earth from where the comet is viewed and notice how the tail of the comet changed over the duration of the observation (this is like time-lapse engraving!) in relation to the Sun. One can easily imagine how the segments of the zodiac, before they were named constellations, could have been thought of as 'caves' or 'recesses', especially if the sky was alive with comet activity!

The top image on the next page is another way to record the sighting. Again, it is 'time-lapse', showing the position of the comet over a series of days,

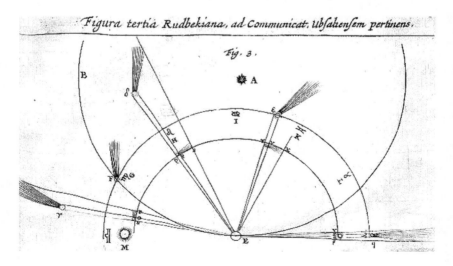

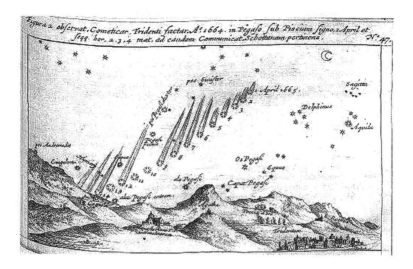

beginning April 1st, 1665. Notice how, on the 14th, the comet reaches the horizon, after which all that is seen is the tail for several days longer. Also notice how specific star clusters are included so as to convey to others where in the sky the comet was located.

Some of the observers from that time utilized fancy drawings of the constellations to spice up their observation records (see the illustration below).

But even with the graphics, they still included the grid. Later on, some of them dispensed with the grid and just drew in the constellation figures (the image overleaf).

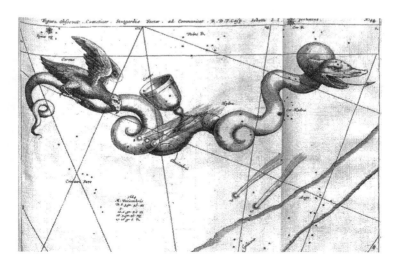

Well, they did include some triangulation lines from major stars, so the map was still accurate.

That's just a small selection from the *Theatrum Cometicum* that I have selected to make my point that I think Pherecydes was either making direct comet observations, or was studying the myths and legends and knew what they were and was endeavoring to standardize locations in the sky where those terrifying events took place. It is worth noting that a significant number of the comet maps in the *Theatrum Cometicum* depict comets in the area of the sky between Taurus and Scorpio, though along the celestial equator rather than the zodiac. It isn't difficult to imagine Pherecydes including just such charts as illustrations to his idea about the 'recesses', 'pits', 'gates', 'caves', and so on.

A relationship appears to exist between these recesses and Chthonie, which is another of the three first-existing things. Chthonie has to do with the origin of the word 'chthonic'; her name means 'underlying the earth'. That can be explained by the fact that the comets either appear from, or pass below, the horizon, seeming to be either born from the Earth, or to go 'inside the earth' or into the ocean from the constellation 'recesses'. (See the land-based image above.)

Ophioneus and its brood of serpents are depicted as ruling the birthing cosmos for some time, before finally falling from power thanks to the arrival of the cavalry in the form of Zeus who 'orders and distributes' things, i.e. kicks most of the comets out of play like a massive bowling strike. The story describing this has Zas making a cloth which he decorates with earth and sea and presents as a wedding gift to Chthonie, wrapping it around her as a wedding garment. In another fragment it is not Chthonie, but *a winged oak* that is wrapped in the cloth. The winged oak in this cosmology has no prece-dent in Greek tradition but, thanks to Ballie, Clube and Napier, we certainly know of trees of life as comets, with their attendant ion tails and other elec-trical activity, and the World Tree is *typical of northern cosmogonies*. Nevertheless, we perceived something of the decorated cloth wrapped around the earth in the quote above from Hesiod: "Great Ouranos came bringing Night with him, and over Gaia, desiring love, *he stretched himself, and spread all over her...*" And, since the topic is on the table at the moment, I should mention here that many of these sexual images that were used to describe the activities of the comet gods, were later used to justify such things as in-cest and pederasty. After all, if the gods do it, why can't we? That's due, of course, to the 'astralizing' influence taken to a sick and revolting extreme.

Back to Pherecydes story; apparently, the chaotic forces – or comets, as we know them – are eternal and cannot be destroyed, so Zeus takes pos-session of the sky, space and time, and throws Ophioneus and the gang out from the ordered world and locks them away in Tartaros. As noted, Hesiod described Tartaros as being "in a recess (*mychos*) of broad-wayed earth", i.e. they disappeared below the horizon.

The locks to Tartaros are fashioned in iron by Zeus, and in bronze by Poseidon, which could mean that some of the comet fragments came to Earth and others plunged into the ocean. Judging from some ancient frag-ments, Ophioneus is thrown into Okeanos, but not into Tartaros. In one ver-sion, it is Kronos who orders the offspring – the comet fragments – out from the cosmos to Tartaros. In short, they were flung off into space, i.e. were prob-ably moved into different orbits, passing from view below the horizon or, more intriguingly, passing out of the plane of the ecliptic into other regions of the sky. The question is: do they still exist in these orbits?

We are told about chaotic beings put into the *Pentemychos*, and we are told that the Darkness has an offspring that is cast into the *recesses* of Tartaros. No surviving fragment makes the connection, but it is possible that *the prison-house in Tartaros and the* Pentemychos *are ways of referring to es-sentially the same thing.*[367] Was Pherecydes dividing the sky into 10 seg-ments with five of them always being below the horizon? Notice that the image drawn by Hevelius (overleaf) does exactly that, though with six 're-cesses' based on the 12-sign zodiac and the sexagesimal circle later obtained via the Babylonians, as we will read further on.

A comparatively large number of sources say Pherecydes was the first to teach the eternity and transmigration of human souls, i.e. reincarnation.[368]

---

367. Kirk et al. (1983).

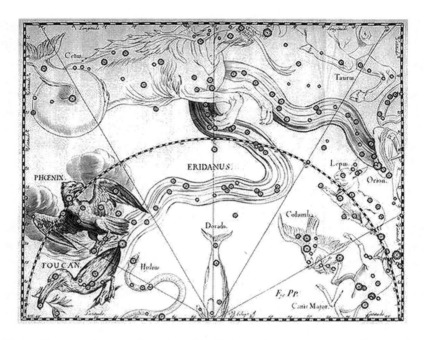

Both Cicero and Augustine thought of him as having given the first teaching of the 'immortality of the soul'[369] and Hellenic scholar Hermann S. Schibli writes that Pherecydes "included in his book [*Pentemychos*] at least a rudimentary treatment of the immortality of the soul, its wanderings in the underworld, and the reasons for the soul's incarnations."[370] One gets the impression that this 'astralizing' of the behavior of perfectly astronomical comets was the origin of the idea of reincarnation itself, derived from the reappearance, at regular intervals, of the Comet Gods from their 'wanderings in the underworld' beyond the horizon of the Earth! And that isn't to say that reincarnation isn't an idea worth exploring; I'm just pointing out that there is a far more rational explanation for what Pherecydes was talking about than reincarnation.

Finally, the material that comes to us from Pherecydes is dotted with original terms and imagery that strikes me as 1) possibly derived from northern sources, and 2) a quasi-scientific attempt to depict real events, not myth. The flying oak with the marriage cloth that covers Earth is just fascinating!

Pherecydes was said by Diogenes to have been the student of Pittacus (640-

---

368. Schibli (1990), *Pherekydes of Syros*.
369. *Encyclopedia Britannica*, 9th edition, Volume 18: Pherecydes of Syros.
370. Schibli, ibid., p. 108.

568 BCE) who was a Mytilenaean[371] general who defeated the Athenians and was named as one of the 'Seven Sages'. According to the story, when the Athenians were preparing to attack, Pittacus challenged their General to single combat to decide the war and avoid senseless bloodshed. He won and was chosen ruler of his city. In *Protagoras*, Plato has his character, Prodicus, refer to Pittacus as a barbarian because he spoke Aeolic Greek derived from Boeotia, one of the earliest inhabited regions of Greece, the home of Oedipus, Kadmus, Ogyges, the legend of the Deluge, etc. So, that may be one of the sources of information available to Pherecydes. Hesiod was also born in Boeotia.

The Agenda of the Milesian School

In 1997, William Mullen, Professor of Classical Studies at Bard College, gave a conference talk entitled: *Natural Catastrophes during Bronze Age Civilisation* in which he outlined what he saw as the Agenda of the Milesian School.

Topics held in common by the first three pre-Socratic philosophers from Miletos in the Sixth Century B.C.E., Thales, Anaximander, and Anaximenes, and by Xenophanes[372] from neighbouring Colophon, taken together may be viewed as constituting the agenda of a "Milesian School".

> The agenda included a survey of the known kosmos (the orderly arrangement of the inhabited world surrounded by regularly moving heavenly bodies); *re-definitions of divinity*; and theories of the natural processes, constantly in operation, by which both kosmos and divinity are to be understood. It also included *explanations of phenomena most men deemed terrifying*: thunder, lightning, earthquakes, eclipses, and periodic destruction of the kosmos itself. It set about to explain these phenomena in terms of the same elemental processes (transformations of water, rarefaction and condensation of air, separating out of fire, air, water and earth, periodic reabsorption of these elements into a state of dynamic equilibrium) as it invoked to explain the orderly arrangement of the earth and the heavenly bodies. In so doing, *it implied the baselessness of the traditional Olympian religion* which attributed lightning and earthquakes to whims of Zeus and Poseidon and world-destructions to battles of the sky-gods.

---

371. Mytilene is a town on the Greek island of Lesbos.
372. (c. 570 – c. 475 BCE), Greek philosopher, theologian, poet, and social and religious critic. He satirized traditional religious views of his time as human projections. Xenophanes wrote about two extremes predominating the world: wet and dry (water and earth). These two extreme states would alternate between one another and with the alteration human life would become extinct, then regenerate. He was one of the first philosophers to distinguish between true belief and knowledge.

The ultimate Milesian agenda may therefore have been to liberate people from paralysing fear of the immediate recurrence of celestial disturbances in the recent past. By insisting that world-destructions occurred only in vast cycles of time (such as a "great year" whose winter solstice was Deluge and summer solstice Conflagration) the Milesian School was schematically distorting memories of recent disturbances, and its activity may be seen as part of a general pattern of oblivion and psychological distancing common to all cultures after the end of the Bronze Age catastrophes. But by insisting that these world-destructions occurred only as the result of unalterable elemental processes, it was also erecting a proto-scientific bulwark against apocalyptic thinking and behavior.[373]

So, indeed, it may have been a conscious program to quell the disorder that inevitably arose when comets appeared, which suggests that comets were, indeed, appearing with some regularity, though they were no longer as threatening as they had been in the previous era of mass destruction. Nevertheless, the philosophers of the Milesian school lived in very interesting times. The period of time during which they philosophized dated (roughly) from 630-475 BCE. During that time period our catalogue of historical comet sightings[374] include:

> 633 BCE, China: A broom star comet appeared in Auriga with its tail pointing toward Shhu State. (Ho, 4)
>
> 613 BCE, Autumn, China: A broom star comet entered the constellation of the Great Bear. (Ho, 5)
>
> 532 BCE, Spring, China: A new star was seen in Aquarius. (Ho, 6)
>
> 525 BCE, Winter, China: A bushy star comet appeared in the winter near Antares. (Ho, 7)
>
> 516 BCE, China: A broom star comet appeared. (Ho, 8)
>
> 500 BCE, China: A broom star comet was seen. (Ho, 9)
>
> 482 BCE, Winter, China: A bushy star comet appeared in the east. (Ho, 10)
>
> 481 BCE, Winter, China: A bushy star comet was seen. (Ho, 11)
>
> 480 BCE, Greece: At the time of the Greek battle of Salamis, Pliny noted that a comet, shaped like a horn (ceratias type), was seen. (Barrett, 1)

So keep that in mind as you consider the details of these philosophers' lives.

---

373. From a talk given by William Mullen, Professor of Classical Studies at Bard College, SIS Conference: Natural Catastrophes during Bronze Age Civilisations, 11th-13th July, 1997.
374. Most comet references from Yeomans (1991), *Comets: A Chronological History of Observation, Science, Myth, and Folklore.*

Thales 624 – 548 BCE

The earliest blossoming of Greek *science* following the Dark Age that prevailed after the collapse of the Bronze Age is associated with the Ionian or Milesian school located at Miletus, *on the Western coast of Anatolia*, in what is modern day Turkey. During the 6th century BCE, it was considered to be the greatest and wealthiest Greek city. This city, formerly occupied by speakers of an Indo-European language, Luwian (closely related to Hittite), who disappeared in the collapse of the Bronze Age, was said to have been resettled by Ionian Greeks around 1000

Thales of Miletus.

BCE. Please notice that Ionia really isn't Greece. So it looks like 'Greek Civilization' as we know it actually belongs to Anatolia, and only later did they colonize Greece, proper. That, of course, doesn't mean that there weren't connections between the Mycenaean Greeks and the Ionians; perhaps some of them fled Greece to Anatolia during the disruptions. It might even be thought that the Thracians were the remnant of the Mycenaean Greeks. We do know that there was intellectual discourse taking place in Greece, proper, i.e. Homer, Hesiod, Alcman and Pherecydes, and that it was somewhat different from what was going on in Anatolia.

In any event, Thales founded a school at Miletus (Diogenes tells us that his parents were Phoenician) around 600 BCE, that was destined to be the root of 'Greek art and philosophy'. Thales taught that the Earth was a flat disc or short cylinder floating on a vast primordial ocean of sorts. His main agenda seemed to be to explain natural phenomena without involving mythology. As we will see, almost all of the pre-Socratic philosophers followed this trend.

Thales is hailed as the first true mathematician because he used geometry to calculate such things as the height of pyramids and the distance of ships from the shore. According to Herodotus, Thales predicted a solar eclipse which has been determined to have occurred on May 28th, 595 BCE. He supposedly wrote works concerning the solstices and equinoxes, but nothing has survived. Diogenes apparently had some texts to hand because he quotes letters of Thales to Pherecydes and Solon. In these letters, he states that the Milesians were actually Athenians, which suggests that they were, in fact, refugees from Greece.

Thales was apparently into making weather predictions based on his studies and utilizing his accuracy in this respect to make the point that philosophy wasn't a waste of time. *He also engaged in political life.* It was in the context of the military defense of the region against the Persians that he made his solar eclipse prediction. Apparently, it was so impressive that the two peoples laid down their arms and made peace sworn with a blood oath!

Thales was counted among the 'Seven Sages of Greece', a list made up (obviously) sometime after all of them were dead. According to Demetrius Phalereus, the list of honorees was made up about 582/1 BCE. Dicaearchus of Messina [375] (350-285 BCE) commented that *none of them were either sages or philosophers, but merely shrewd men with a turn for legislation.* That suggests even more strongly that their ideas were driven by a need for political stability and to change the way the public perceived the relationship between the leaders and the cosmos. A parallel (and complementary) perspective is that Thales and his colleagues represented a new kind of community: one that inquires into the nature of things without recourse to the 'old ways and explanations'. They were possessed by the ideal of Truth, so to say, and it strikes me as being similar to a modern Christian who loses his faith because he perceives that the Bible cannot possibly be 'truth', only he doesn't understand that the Bible was composed of re-written stories of ancient, real, cataclysmic events!

Thales profoundly influenced later philosophy, and we are told that his student was Anaximander, who was alleged to be one of the teachers of Pythagoras. As we will see, not all of these philosophers thought the same things. This age is often referred to as the 'Axial Age' and it is notable for the fact that revolutionary thinking arose in widely separated places at the same time: China, India, Iran, the Near East, and so on. One really gets the idea that something about the environment had changed dramatically since the cosmic and environmental cataclysms at the end of the Bronze Age.

---

375. Greek philosopher, cartographer, geographer, mathematician and author. Also Aristotle's student. Very little of his work remains extant. He wrote on the history and geography of Greece, of which his most important work was his *Life of Greece*. He was among the first to use geographical coordinates in cartography.

Anaximander 610 – 545 BCE

Thales was followed by Anaximander, who is thought to have introduced the sundial to the Greeks, which *he got from the Babylonians*. He also drew a map of the inhabited world. He claimed that nature, like human societies, is ruled by laws and anything that breaks natural laws suffers repercussions. Right there we have a hint of his interest in power politics and social control.

This is the only existing Roman relief of Anaximander from the ancient world.

Anaximander thought that everything was derived from some undifferentiated living mass (as opposed to the primordial ocean). Things just grew out of this 'cosmic egg', the first four things being fire, air, water and earth. This cosmology partly resembles modern cosmological theories such as the Big Bang.

Anaximander proposed that air or denser vapors would have burst out of fiery surrounding membranes, and then enveloped the remaining flames, producing *wheels of fire enclosed in mist*. These enveloped wheels of fire then encircled the Earth. Planets and stars were circular wheels of fire which became visible due to holes in the enclosing hoops (globes?) that permitted the fire to 'leak out'. That is, Anaximander's cosmic bodies were rather like lighted jets of gas shooting through a punctured sheet of metal.

Anaximander taught that the world was transitory and would eventually dissolve back into infinite space (the 'Big Crunch'). He also said that there were many worlds, which he identified with the gods who were also transitory and renewable. He associated this dissolution and renewal with *definite cycles* and this strongly suggests influence from Iranian cosmology and, possibly, *study of comets*.

An important point about Anaximander's cosmology was his insistence that the hoops-with-holes, that were supposed to be 'stars', all lay *beneath* the Sun and Moon. This idea has puzzled many commentators, but it might be understood if Anaximander was actually talking about comets or even fireballs in the Earth's atmosphere. Intense meteor showers associated with a bright comet would easily give the impression that the stars lay below the Sun and Moon.

We can, of course, ask the question: was the Greek word for 'star' used to describe a single class of objects? The fact that some stars were described as *disappearing due to their increasing distance* from the viewer on Earth suggests that some of these 'stars' were actually comets.

Important to our study is the fact that the 3rd century Roman rhetorician Aelian claims that Anaximander was *the leader of the Milesian colony to Apollonia* on the Black Sea coast. Aelian's *Various History*[376] tells us that *philosophers often dealt with political matters*. Most scholars suppose that leaders of Miletus sent him there as a legislator to create a constitution or simply to maintain the colony's allegiance. But we are reminded of the comment of Dicaearchus cited above: that these really weren't philosophers, but shrewd men with political agendas and I will make note (as I have already) of those who appear to have had political connections.

If they were, truly, philosophers and, by some miracle, the powers of the time saw wise men as useful in government, one is still compelled by the idea that there was a political agenda to giving philosophers of this orientation such roles so as to establish and maintain certain ideas in respect of the cosmos for political reasons, as Ballie, Clube and Napier suggest. Is it even possible that leaders of those times could sit down and consciously decide that 'this business about comets being gods needs to be dealt with since it threatens the control of the rulers'? It would probably have been clear that it did, in fact, threaten them because the 'old way' had been to sacrifice the leaders if it was perceived that the gods were angry or hungry.

Pythagoras – The Italian School

Pythagoras of Samos (570-495 BCE) was the founder of the religious movement called Pythagoreanism. Let me first tell you the briefest outline of the story about him before we get to the actual facts, as far as we can find them out.

Pythagoras was born on the Greek island Samos and traveled widely seeking knowledge. He had himself initiated into all of the mystery schools in Greece and foreign countries. He learned the Egyptian language and journeyed to the lands of the Chaldeans and Magi. Then, in Crete, he went into the cave of Ida with Epimenides where the baby Zeus was said to have been hidden from his father, Chronos. After all that, he returned to Samos and found his country under the rule of a tyrant, Polycrates, so he sailed to Croton (about 530 BCE) and there, became a leader who created a constitution for the Italian Greeks. He and his 300 followers thereby instituted a 'true aristocracy' or government by the best qualified (as Diogenes puts it). According to other sources, when Polycrates effected his coup at Samos, members of the old aristocracy were either sent into exile or voluntarily

---

376. Aelian, *Varia Historia*, III, 17.

left. Otherwise, Polycrates was said to have been a very popular ruler who worked hard to improve the quality of life of the people of Samos. He was an ally of the Egyptian king Amasis who paid the Samians well to maintain naval defense in the region.

Getting back to Pythagoras, at this point, Diogenes quotes Heraclitus in refutation of the idea that Pythagoras left no writings:

> Pythagoras, son of Mnesarchus, practiced inquiry beyond all other men, and in this selection of his writings made himself a wisdom of his own, showing much learning but poor workmanship.[377]

He then goes on to say that Pythagoras wrote three books: *On Education*, *On Statesmanship*, and *On Nature*. Then he mentions that Aristoxenus said that Pythagoras derived his moral doctrines from the Delphic priestess, Themistoclea. In short, at least one of his teachers was a woman. Diogenes then enumerates the teachings of Pythagoras from the three books as follows:

> He forbids us to pray for ourselves, because we do not know what will help us. Drinking he calls, in a word, a snare, and he discountenances all excess, saying that no one should go beyond due proportion either in drinking or in eating. Of sexual indulgence, too, he says, "Keep to the winter for sexual pleasures, in summer abstain; they are less harmful in autumn and spring, but they are always harmful and not conducive to health." Asked once when a man should consort with a woman, he replied, "when you want to lose what strength you have ..."

The following are excerpts from Diogenes' life of Pythagoras.

> According to Timaeus[378], he was first to say "Friends have all things in common"... indeed, his disciples did put all their possessions into one common stock ...
>
> Indeed, and his disciples held the opinion about him that he was Apollo come down from the far north ...

This is interesting considering other clues that Pythagoras' (and Pherecydes) ideas had a more northern origin.

---

377. Diogenes Laërtius, VIII, 4-6.
378. Greek historian (345-250 BCE), born at Tauromenium in Sicily. He was a student of Isocrates and wrote some 40 books of history.

> We are told by Apollodorus the calculator that he offered a sacrifice of oxen on finding that in a right-angled triangle the square on the hypotenuse is equal to the squares on the sides containing the right angle. ...

Apollodorus, surnamed Logisticus (the Calculator), may have been Apollodorus of Seleucis, a Stoic philosopher and pupil of Diogenes of Babylon. He wrote on ethics and physics and is otherwise frequently cited by Diogenes Laërtius. Cicero (who I consider to have been an insufferable prig) comments on this statement, saying that he does not question the discovery, but doubts the story of the sacrifice of the ox.

> He is also said to have been the first to diet athletes on meat, trying first with Eurymenes – so we learn from Favorinus [379] in the third book of his *Memorabilia* – whereas in former times they had trained on dried figs, on butter (cheese), and even on wheat-meal... some say it was a certain trainer named Pythagoras who instituted this diet, and not our Pythagoras, who forbade even the killing, let alone the eating, of animals... as we are told by Aristotle...

Here we have a little difference of opinion on the dietary matter. I would suggest that, if it is true that Pythagoras was strongly influenced by northern teachings, he most certainly advocated the eating of meat strongly and it was only later mythmakers who created the vegetarian fraud. In fact, it is most likely that the life and doings of Empedocles, a philosopher cum religious prophet born in Sicily about 490 BCE, was conflated with Pythagoras.

Empedocles was reputed to have miraculous powers such as the ability to cure disease, avert epidemics, control storms, etc. He wrote in verse and one of his poems is entitled *Purifications* and seems to have promised miraculous powers, rejuvenation, destruction of evil, etc. He was associated with various Pythagoreans, and his abstinence from meat was widely known. He also claimed to be a god incarnate. His doctrine of the four elements remained fundamental for the theory of matter for more than twenty centuries. In this we see that the dual role of a religious prophet and a mathematical philosopher that the tradition assigns to Pythagoras is certainly possible – even a common topos of the time – but not necessarily historical.

---

379. A Gaulish Roman sophist and philosopher (80-160 CE) during the reign of Hadrian. He was described as a congenital hermaphrodite. He was once silenced in an argument with the emperor when he could easily have won, but later explained that it was foolish to criticize the logic of the master of 30 legions. See: Holford-Strevens (1997), *Favorinos: The Man of Paradoxes*, in J. Barnes et M. Griffin (eds.), *Philosophia togata*, vol. II.

Down to the time of Philolaus it was not possible to acquire knowledge of any Pythagorean doctrine and Philolaus alone brought out those three celebrated books which Plato sent a hundred minas to purchase. Not less than six hundred persons went to his evening lectures; and those who were privileged to see him wrote to their friends congratulating themselves on a great piece of good fortune ...

Here we discover something crucially interesting: that the alleged books of Pythagoras were placed into the hands of none other than Plato!

The rest of the Pythagoreans used to say that not all his doctrines were for all men to hear, our authority for this being Aristoxenus in the tenth book of his *Rules of Pedagogy...*

This next excerpt is particularly interesting in light of the diet issue:

Above all, he forbade as food red mullet and blacktail, and he enjoined abstinence from the hearts of animals and from beans and sometimes, according to Aristotle, even from paunch and gurnard (two types of fish) ...

Obviously, if his students are warned not to eat the hearts of animals, that is an explicit acknowledgement that they were eating the rest of the animal.

He used to practice divination by sounds or voices and by auguries, never by burnt-offerings, beyond frankincense ... some say that he would offer cocks, sucking goats and porkers... but lambs, never. However, Aristoxenus has it that he consented to the eating of all other animals, and only abstained from ploughing oxen and rams ...

Diogenes cites Aristotle:

Aristotle says, in his work *On the Pythagoreans*, that Pythagoras enjoined abstention from beans either because they are like the privy parts, or because they are like the gates of Hades (for this is the only plant that has no joints), or because they are destructive, or because they are like the nature of the universe, or because they are oligarchical (being used in the choice of rulers by lot). Things that fall from the table they were told not to pick up – to accustom them to eating with moderation, or because such things marked the death of someone. And Aristophanes, too, says that the things that fall belong to the heroes, when in his *Heroes* he urges: 'Do not taste what falls inside the table.' They must not touch a white cock, because this animal is sacred to the Month and is a suppliant, and supplication is a good thing. The cock was sacred to the Month because it announces the hours; also, white is of the nature of the good, black of the nature of the bad. They were not to touch any fish that was sacred, since it was not right that the same dishes should be served to gods and to men, any more than they should to freemen and to slaves. They must not break the loaf (because in old times friends met over a single loaf, as barbarians do to this day), nor must they divide the loaf which brings them together. Others explain the rule by reference to the judgment in Hades; others say that dividing the loaf would produce cowardice in war; others explain that it is from the loaf that the universe starts.[380]

The first thing to point out is that none of these rules enjoin vegetarianism. There is, in fact, no 5th century evidence whatsoever that the Pythagoreans renounced animal sacrifice and the subsequent eating of the sacrifice. In fact, since the focal point of the Greek polis, in which Pythagoras and his followers played such a leading role for several generations, was the regular public sacrifice and feasting, is a powerful implication that they were not, at all, in any way, vegetarians. The evidence for Pythagoras being a meat eater are more numerous, and older, than the evidence for vegetarianism which seems to be both a conflation with Empedocles and a consequence of the later Platonic myths.

> Hieronymus ... says that, when he had descended into Hades, he saw the soul of Hesiod bound fast to a brazen pillar and gibbering, and the soul of Homer hung on a tree with serpents writhing about it, this being their punishment for what they had said about the gods; he also saw under torture those who would not remain faithful to their wives.

According to Diogenes, this is what Aristotle said about Pythagoras at one point:

> But Pythagoras' great dignity not even Timon overlooked, who, although he digs at him in his *Silli*, speaks of: *Pythagoras, inclined to witching works and ways, Man-snarer, fond of noble periphrase. ...*
>
> Further, we are told that he was the first to call the heaven the universe and the earth spherical (according to Favorinus), though Theophrastus says it was Parmenides, and Zeno that it was Hesiod. [Emphasis, mine.] [381]

---

380. Diogenes Laërtius, VIII, 34-5, trans. W. D. Ross, cited by Kirk, op. cit.
381. Diogenes Laërtius, VIII, excerpts in order.

The spherical Earth was actually first asserted in the work of Parmenides and Empedocles while the Ionian school continued with their flat-earth theories for a rather long time.

Allegedly, Pythagoras' followers practiced rites developed by him based on what he had learned and developed via his travels and studies. What is more, the Pythagoreans took an *active role in the politics* of Croton and this is what led to their downfall, apparently. The Pythagorean meeting places were burned and Pythagoras and his followers were forced to flee and he is said to have ended his days in Metapontum, not far from Tarentum, which will figure in our tale shortly.

As we see from this very quick review of a few of the things Diogenes collected together, Pythagoras is presented in a vast body of literature as the genius of marvels, the inventor of mathematics, music theory, heliocentric astronomy, and metaphysical philosophy. The 20th century philosopher, Alfred North Whitehead sang paeans of praise about Pythagoras. But the sources closest in time to the man (who certainly existed) are satirical, mildly insulting, or completely ambiguous. So why did the figure of Pythagoras accumulate so much baggage so that, even down to the time of the Renaissance, there were people claiming to be 'followers of Pythagoras'? The Pythagoreans are said to have taught that a release from the wheel of reincarnation was possible but only via a process of purification of the soul including a vegetarian diet. Aristoxenus said that they also used music to purify the soul just like medicine was used to purge the body; another Orphic connection. Pythagoras was said to have proclaimed that the highest purification of a life is in pure contemplation. It is the philosopher who *contemplates about science and mathematics* who is released from the 'cycle of birth'. The pure mathematician's life is, according to the tradition created for Pythagoras, the life at the highest plane of existence.[384, 385]

Thus the root of mathematics and scientific pursuits in Pythagoreanism is also based on a spiritual desire to free oneself from the cycle of birth and death.

It's a great story, isn't it? I didn't even include all the miracle parts, including the one telling how Pythagoras had a golden thigh, could bi-locate, and so forth. So what is true? Well, let's look at the evidence, starting with a rather surprising remark made by Heraclitus (we'll come to him shortly) and preserved by Diogenes:

382. Burnet (1892), *Early Greek Philosophy*.
383. Russell (1967), *History of Western Philosophy*.

The learning of many things does not teach understanding; if it did, it would have taught Hesiod and Pythagoras, and again Xenophanes and Hecataeus.[384]

Empedocles wrote, preserved in Porphyry's *Life of Pythagoras*, as follows:

And there was among them a man of surpassing knowledge, master especially of *all kinds of wise works*, who had acquired the utmost wealth of understanding: for whenever he *reached out with all his understanding*, easily he saw each of all the things that are, in ten and even twenty generations of men.[385]

The impression that Empedocles gives is that Pythagoras' methods were most definitely not mathematical or scientific! But that he was widely perceived as a seeker and having a great range of knowledge and extraordinary influence over people appears to be a secure fact.

Diogenes Laërtius reports that Xenophanes (we'll also meet him soon) had this to say about Pythagoras:

Now I will turn to another tale and show the way... Once they say that he [Pythagoras] was passing by when a puppy was being whipped, and he took pity and said: "Stop, do not beat it; for it is the soul of a friend that I recognized when I heard it giving tongue." [386]

Obviously, this is a joke made by Xenophanes with Pythagoras as the butt of it. In any event, that the teaching of reincarnation by Pythagoras was widely enough known to be the topic of ordinary conversation – and even jokes – makes that something that we can securely attach to him.

Additional evidence provides a weak connection between Pythagoras and the Orphic Mysteries. Orphism appears to have been mainly a system of purification that was practiced privately at that time, while the Pythagoreans definitely formed a very secretive sect. The Orphics taught that the body was a prison, a tomb, in which the soul is buried until it finds or earns its way out. Their methods were designed to purify and release men *and cities* from their errors. They neither ate nor sacrificed animals and taught complete avoidance of bloodshed.

The later Orphic poems seem to imply that certain behaviors could forestall, avoid, or end cosmic punishment. But were Orphic practices and con-

---

384. Diogenes Laërtius, IX, 1.
385. Porphyrius, *Life of Pythagoras*, 30.
386. Diogenes Laërtius, VIII, 36.

cepts part of the original Pythagorean ideas, or were they simply connected thanks to Plato?

Next we have a quote from Porphyry, the 3rd century CE Neoplatonic philosopher of Phoenician extraction:

> What he said to his associates, nobody can say for certain, for silence with them was of no ordinary kind. Nonetheless the following became universally known: first, that he maintains that the soul is immortal; next, that it changes into other kinds of living things; also that events recur in certain cycles, and that nothing is ever absolutely new; and finally, that all living things should be regarded as akin. Pythagoras seems to have been the first to bring these beliefs into Greece.[387]

It could be said that a lot of historically worthless literature about him began, mainly, with Plato. It seems that he, and his followers, radically altered not only accounts of the life of Pythagoras, but actually invented doctrines and assigned them to him. One expert suggests that "all the discoveries attributed to Pythagoras himself, or to his disciples by later writers were really the achievement of certain South Italian mathematicians of Plato's time."[388] What is more, it wasn't until after Plato spent time with Archytas at Tarentum that his formerly rather cool view of Pythagoras warmed up, and this can be definitely noted in his dialogues, as analyzed by Charles Kahn in *Pythagoras and the Pythagoreans*.[389] There are surviving fragments from the work of Archytas that strongly suggest that it was he, not Pythagoras, who formulated many of the *scientific and mathematical ideas* attributed to Pythagoras by Plato. Perhaps Plato was jealous of Archytas, stole his ideas, and attributed them to Pythagoras with the idea that, of course, everyone would know that it was all him, only he was so modest! Or he sought to attach his ideas to someone who everyone else held in awe.

The main players in the *Phaedo* are represented by Plato as a sort of link between the Pythagoreans and Socrates.[390] The implication is that Plato set a fashion of presenting *his* newest theories as age-old wisdom. While he may have done it more or less playfully, as some suggest, assuming that everyone would naturally understand that he was being modest, but that in reality he, of course, thought all this stuff up, it appears that his students and

---

387. Porphyrius, *Life of Pythagoras*, p.19.
388. Frank (1923), *Plato und die sogenannten Pythagoreer*, vi.
389. Kahn (2001).
390. Phaedo, 61 d.

followers took him literally. Two of his students in particular, Speusippus and Xenocrates, took him very seriously and treated the cosmology of the *Timaeus* as the teaching of Pythagoras, which may have been partly true.[391] Walter Burkert, in a massive monograph on the subject published in 1962 (translated into English in 1972), says that the evidence shows only that Pythagoras was a shamanistic figure, a charismatic spiritual leader *rather like Moses*, who was very influential in the *politics* of his day but contributed nothing whatsoever to mathematics or philosophy.[392] All that we know of 'Pythagoreanism' was created later by Plato and others. (But we don't want to toss the baby out with the bathwater.)

Thus it was right there, in Plato's Academy, that the twisting and distortion of the work of Pythagoras was formulated. Aristotle, Plato's student, vigorously resisted this development and spent some time carefully studying Philolaus and the pre-Plato Pythagorean system. Aristotle became the last author to draw a distinction between the two schools.

At the beginning of the 4th century there was another refugee from the conflict in Southern Italy who came to Thebes: Lysis of Tarentum. He became the teacher of the general Epaminondas. So there were respectable Pythagorean communities from which Plato could both extract ideas as well as influence with his possession of the inside scoop on what Pythagoras actually said, since he had possession of the three books.

There is another type of Pythagorean represented by Diodorus of Aspendus in Asia Minor, a 4th century ascetic vegetarian who was described as having long hair, long beard, worn cloak, a beggar's wallet and staff.[393] Also, in Athens at the same time, there were barefoot vegetarians who were mocked in comedy skits as 'Pythagorists'. In other words, the barefoot vegetarian Pythagorean is a much later appearance of half-crazed mendicant philosophers that were little more than comic figures of the time and were used to attack Pythagoras. This lifestyle was actually taken over later by the Cynics, and after their appearance there are no further references to Pythagoreans in this light; the Cynics are the comic relief! It appears to be a fairly typical response of social and political power structures to ridicule and defame their critics. Thus, we should pay attention to whether a particular philosopher was on the side of the power elite, or a critic thereof. Such an observation won't necessarily say anything about their philosophies or cosmologies, but it could, especially when we notice whose work has been 'lost' and whose has been preserved.

---

391. Kahn (2001), ibid.
392. Burkert (1972), *Lore and Science in Ancient Pythagoreanism*.
393. Kahn, op. cit. p. 49.

As mentioned, after Plato got hold of a few ideas, and stole many others from wherever he could get them, the two central ideas of Pythagoreanism become 1) the destiny of the immortal soul as expounded by Plato; and 2) mathematics as the key to unlock the secrets of the universe. This last was, I believe, his own spin and a red herring put out there to keep generations of seekers spinning in circles trying to work out the right formula. It was in Plato's imagination that mathematics enabled a soul to become free and only in his mind do these ideas reach their culmination.

Of this massive mess, only three sources seem to have anything of value to offer us: Diogenes Laërtius, Porphyry and Iamblichus, in that order, with each one giving an account that is more fantastic than the previous one. Eduard Zeller, in his 19th century history of Greek philosophy, noted that the further a document is from Pythagoras' own time, the fuller the account becomes! [394]

These histories amount mainly to cut and paste compilations from the Christianizing era which followed Plato, and contain a lot of nonsense, but they also include summaries of fairly early traditions about Pythagoras to which they still had access.

The invented tradition of Plato tells us that the school of Pythagoras split at some point and one group followed the more mathematical line, extending the scientific work of Pythagoras. The other group focused on the more religious aspects, declaring that the 'scientific' breakaway group was not really following Pythagoras, but rather the renegade Hippasus, about whom pretty much nothing is known.

The more scientific ideas appear to be those of Philolaus, who developed the work of Anaximander of the Milesian school who – along with Pherecydes – was also *said* to be one of the teachers of Pythagoras. Why are we not surprised?

The idea most central to Pythagorean mystical teachings was the transmigration of souls which was an idea that was actually native to India *and* to the Celts and related Germanic tribes (all three of which had their origins in the steppes of central Asia). Much of the Pythagorean mysticism concerning the soul seems similar to the Orphic tradition. The Orphics included various purification rites and practices as well as incubatory rites of descent into the underworld, which bring to mind Central Asian Shamanism. Orphism was said to have originated in Thrace which brings us to the following story from Herodotus:

---

394. Zeller (1892), *Die Philosophie der Greichen in ihrer geschichtlichen Entwicklung.*

> As I have heard from the *Greeks who live on the Hellespont and the Black Sea*, this Salmoxis was a man, who was a slave in Samos, the slave in fact of Pythagoras son of Mnesarchus… The Thracians lived a miserable life and were not very intelligent, whereas this Salmoxis knew the Ionian way of life and minds deeper than the Thracians', since he had associated with Greeks and among Greeks with Pythagoras, not the weakest of their wise men. So he [Salmoxis] built a hall in which he received and entertained the leading citizens, and taught them that neither he nor his guests nor any of their descendants would die, but that they would go to a place where they would survive forever and possess every good thing.[395]

This story of Herodotus' is quite intriguing since Salmoxis, or Zalmoxis, is a divinity of the Getae mentioned by Jordanes (who we will meet in a subsequent volume when we encounter the Goths). He is saying that he heard from Greeks in Western Anatolia that a certain Salmoxis, who was a former slave of Pythagoras, was hoodwinking the poor, ignorant Thracians. Now, the Getae were not Thracians but rather a Gothic tribe, so I'm wondering if this is a hint of the source of Pythagoras' ideas about reincarnation: that he gathered them from Gothic tribes to the north or even along the Black Sea coast? (Because, as we will see further on, they were certainly north of the Black Sea for some time before they intruded into the Roman Empire.)

The archaism of the Salmoxis doctrine (which I omit here) points to an Indo-European heritage.[396] Diogenes reports in an epitome of Aristotle's *Magicus* that Aristotle compared Zalmoxis with the Phoenician Okhon and the Libyan Atlas. Anthropologist Andrei Anamenski suggests that Zalmoxis was another name of Sabazius, the Thracian Dionysus, or Zeus. Sabazius appears in Jordanes as Gebelezis. Without the suffixes -*zius*/-*zis*, the root *Saba-* is equivalent to *Gebele-*, suggesting a relationship to the name of the goddess Cybele, as in 'Cybele's Zeus'. Mnaseas of Patrae identified him with Chronos. Plato mentions Zalmoxis as *skilled in the arts of incantation*. Zalmoxis also gave his name to a particular type of singing and dancing, i.e. 'Hesych', which is a word meaning 'to be still or quiet' and is used to describe a mystical sect of the Greek Orthodox Church of the 14th century. (One naturally wonders how a person can sing and dance being still and quiet?!) A curious connection indeed. Salmoxis' realm as a god is not very clear, as some considered him to be a sky-god, a god of the dead or a god of the Mysteries.[397]

---

395. Herodotus IV, 95.
396. Paliga (1997), 'La divinité suprême des Thraco-Daces'.
397. Znamenski (2007), *The Beauty of the Primitive: Shamanism and Western Imagination*.

All of this merely suggests a northern version of the same old comet bombardment stories and myths but possibly with a cleaner transmission.

Lactantius (240-320 CE, we'll meet him formally soon), referring to the beliefs of the Getae, quoted the emperor Julian the Apostate, who was quoting the emperor Trajan (in other words, three removes in the chain of evidence):

> We have conquered even these Getai (Dacians), the most warlike of all people that have ever existed, not only because of the strength in their bodies, but, also due to the teachings of Zalmoxis who is among their most hailed. He has told them that in their hearts they do not die, but change their location and, due to this, they go to their deaths happier than on any other journey.

Another item from Herodotus:

> Moreover, the Egyptians are the first to have maintained the doctrine that the soul of man is immortal, and that, when the body perishes, it enters into another animal that is being born at the time, and when it has been the complete round of the creatures of the dry land and of the sea and of the air it enters again into the body of a man at birth; and its cycle is completed in 3,000 years. There are some Greeks who have adopted this doctrine, some in former times, and some in later, as if it were their own invention; their names I know but refrain from writing down.[398]

Herodotus erroneously gives the Egyptians credit for the idea of reincarnation. Nothing of the kind is attested in anything Egyptian. In fact, they believed that the body had to be preserved in order for the dead person to have any afterlife at all; when the body was destroyed, so was the afterlife 'life', which could only be experienced through a well-preserved physical body. Curiously, Herodotus often ascribes thoroughly Greek ideas and practices to Egyptian origins. One wonders if he was even talking about the Egypt we know as Egypt! (It wasn't even named 'Egypt' until after Alexander the Great.)

Ion of Chios, who we met earlier in the account of Pherecydes, seems to have expressed doubt about Pythagoras' ideas of reincarnation, though he didn't seem to doubt that he was a learned man. He was writing in the middle of the 5th century, as was Herodotus, who presented the former slave of Pythagoras as a rogue selling salvation. These stories strike me as pejorative but interesting nonetheless for what they convey in an offhand way. Nevertheless, Pythagoras was said to have had full recall of all his past lives,

---

398. Herodotus II, 123.

the list being given in Diogenes Laërtius as follows: First Aethalides, the presumed son of Hermes, who awarded him the gift of remembering his lives after death. Then he incarnated as Euphorbus, and after that Hermotimis, who visited the Branchidae, and in whose temple he recognized the shield that Menelaus had dedicated to Apollo. After Hermotimus he was Pyrrhus, a fisherman of Delos, and after that he was finally reincarnated as Pythagoras.

Let me briefly divert a moment to the topic of the Branchidae. This was supposed to be a genealogical line of priests who claimed descent from Branchos, a youth beloved of Apollo. Didyma was an ancient Ionian sanctuary of Apollo located at what is now Didim, Turkey. In Greek, *didyma* means 'twin'. Next to Delphi, Didyma was the most renowned oracle of the Hellenic world, first mentioned in the Homeric Hymn to Apollo. Both Herodotus and Pausanias dated the origins of the oracle at Didyma to *before* the Ionian colonization.

To approach it, visitors would follow the Sacred Way to Didyma, about 17 km long. Along the way were ritual stations with statues of members of the Branchidae family, male and female, as well as animal figures. Some of these statues, dating to the 6th century BCE, are now in the British Museum, taken by Charles Newton in the 19th century. The whole scenario seems to have been copied into the Catholic religion's 'Stations of the Cross'. One also can't help wondering about the 'twin' relationship of Apollo and Artemis in respect of the later myths of Jesus that involve 'Thomas Didymas', or 'the twin' and the possibility of a 'wife of Jesus', as in a woman closely associated with the man around whom the Jesus myth was wrapped.

The priestess of the Didymas's sanctuary, *seated above a sacred spring*, would make pronouncements interpreted by the Branchidae. (Does that oracle sitting over a sacred spring in a temple remind you of anything? Like the stones and wells in our discussion of the origins of Judaism and Islam above? Recent excavations by a German team of archaeologists have uncovered a major sanctuary dedicated to Artemis, with the key ritual focus being water.)

The Branchidae were expelled by Darius' Persians, who burned the temple in 493 BCE, but Alexander the Great undertook to restore the temple and the oracle. Apparently, this project was never completed. Pausanias visited Didyma in the later 2nd century CE.[399] Pliny reported[400] the worship of Apollo Didymiae – Apollo of Didymus – in Central Asia, transported to Sogdiana by a general of Seleucus and Antiochus whose inscribed altars there

---

399. Pausanias, *Description of Greece*, 7.2.6.
400. Pliny's *Natural History*, 6.18.

were still to be seen by Pliny's correspondents. Corroborating inscriptions on amphoras were found by I.R. Pichikyan at Dilbergin.[401, 402]

Back to Pythagoras: I've read some rather silly explanations here and there saying that the ancient Pythagorean pentagram, with two legs up, represented the Pentemychos or 'five sanctuaries', derived from the cosmogony of Pherecydes, who claimed to have been Pythagoras' teacher and friend. However, that is rather doubtful. Wikipedia tells us that the Pentemychos was 'the island or cave' where the first pre-cosmic offspring had to be put in order for the cosmos to appear... the divine products of Chronos' seed, when disposed in the five recesses, were called Pentemuxos. The source citations the Wikipedia author gives for this silly claim are Kirk, Raven and Schofield. Believe me, they say nothing that could be construed in that way. Go back to Pherecydes and read about Ortygie. If you see anything there that suggests such a thing (and I quoted the reference pretty much in full, whereas it was selectively edited on Wikipedia!), I must be blind or nuts.

Nevertheless, I've already suggested that the five hidden recesses might represent an early attempt to map the sky, and what we now know as constellations were designated by Pherecydes as 'recesses' or 'caves' etc., and that they were related to the appearance, and disappearance, of comets from below the horizon or off in space. If that is the case, then it deprives the Pentemychos of any occult significance, whether it came from Pherecydes or not, so I'm sure the folks who are into magick and all that nonsense will not be happy with this idea.

I've skipped over the material from the sources that talk about Pythagoras' political activities in Croton. As already mentioned, he and members of his society attained positions of political power throughout southern Italy. Polybius reports that, in the middle of the 5th century, when the Pythagorean meeting places were torched, "the leading men from each city lost their lives." [403] That means that pretty much everybody who was anybody around there was involved with Pythagoras. Were they the white hats or the black hats? I guess it depends on your perspective. To individuals who seek to manipulate and control others for their own selfish interests, anyone who prevents that is a black hat or an enemy. To those who seek liberty and the fraternity of human beings under wise leadership, a true aristocracy – rule by the best qualified by virtue of education, ethics and lack of self-interest – those

---

401. Parke (1986), 'The Temple of Apollo at Didyma: The Building and Its Function'.
402. Haselberger (1983), 'Die Bauzeichnungen des Apollontempels von Didyma'; (1985), 'Antike Planzeichnungen am Apollontempel von Didyma'; (1991), 'Aspekte der Bauzeichnungen von Didyma'.
403. Polybius II, 39. 1-2.

who approach rulership for reasons of greed and power are the black hats. Considering the overall history of the time, it appears to me that Pythagoras' organization may have been one designed to dominate the political scene and achieve power for the good of all, not for personal gain. We are going to see this again in the next volume in a possibly related cult that is going to surprise you, so keep it in mind. In any event, Pythagoras himself is said to have died a refugee after a 'popular revolt' against him and his companions, undoubtedly masterminded by the wealthy seeking power and increase of their wealth, utilizing propaganda and rabble-rousing techniques that were highly developed at that time. After this disaster, we find Pythagoreans in Greece, including Philolaus in Thebes. And then, the stories began to spread.

It is also entirely possible that Plato's famous tale of Atlantis in *Timaeus* and *Critias* was one of the main things stolen from the books of Pythagoras. I'll expound on this when we come to our discussion of Plato.

All of this is much more interesting than the fanciful tales told about the man. One even wonders if the stories were made up to distract attention away from the truth. And, when that is the case, it is usually a decent person or a group with high ideals that have been overthrown by ravening seekers of power for its own sake, and following such acts, they erect a smoke-screen such as the one created by Plato.

> We are oft to blame in this, tis too much proved - that with devotion's visage and pious action, we do sugar o'er the devil himself.[404]

Hecataeus of Miletus

Hecataeus (550-476 BCE) is not a philosopher, proper, but since he has been quoted in relation to Pythagoras by Heraclitus (coming soon!), I'm including him briefly in his proper chronological spot.

Recall what Heraclitus said about him, quoted in the discussion of Pythagoras:

> The learning of many things does not teach understanding; if it did, it would have taught Hesiod and Pythagoras, and again Xenophanes and *Hecataeus*.

Hecataeus was a historian, born in a wealthy family, who occupied a high position in Miletus. He was against a revolt of the Ionians against Persian

---

404. Shakespeare, *Hamlet*, Polonius to Opheila, Act III, Scene 1.

rule and when the Ionians were defeated, he was a member of the embassy that sued for peace. He was the first *known* Greek historian[405] and the first to mention the Celts. What probably raised the ire of Heraclitus was his *Genealogiai*, an account of the traditions and myths of the Greeks. He opened this book with:

> Hecataeus of Miletus thus speaks: I write what I deem true; for the stories of the Greeks are manifold and seem to me ridiculous.[406]

It seems that he was attempting to employ a critical method to separate history from myth, and for this Heraclitus suggests that he should be included with those who certainly had learned many things but just wasn't getting it. My guess is that Heraclitus was condemning him for tossing the baby out with the bathwater.

Anaximenes 585 – 528 BCE

Anaximenes.

The last of the Milesian school was Anaximenes. Like his predecessors, he was a proponent of 'material monism' which identified one, single, underlying, material reality (fire, air, water, whatever) and which has been hailed as the earliest attempt to provide explanations for the world without recourse to anything supernatural, or non-material. This is seen today as the earliest physics along the line of approaching Quantum Theory with its atoms and quarks.

His predecessors, Thales and Anaximander, thought that the underlying material of the world was water and *apeiron*[407] respectively.

Anaximenes had somewhat different ideas: he proposed that air was the primal matter. He observed that when air condenses by cooling, it becomes visible as fog and then rain and then snow. He just took that idea further and supposed that it went on to form earth and stones with more 'condensing'. He also noticed that water evaporates into air and that very hot air 'ignited' and formed fire. So he divided things into 'hot and dry' and 'cold and wet'.

405. Herodotus' dates for comparison: c. 484 – 425 BCE.
406. Shotwell (1939), *The History of History*, p. 172.
407. An ambiguous word meaning unlimited, infinite or indefinite. From a word meaning 'without end or limit'.

He thought that heavenly bodies were *derived from Earth*, that many earthly bodies lie in the regions of the stars, i.e. that the stars are a lot closer than they actually are. This suggests that a firm connection via observation had been made between the 'terrestrial bodies' and stars of some sort, probably comets and fireballs.

Such a theory might have been created to explain meteorites which are often observed to fall directly from the sky, enveloped in a cloud of smoke. His reasoning probably went: 'if they fell down, they must have evaporated up first'.

Xenophanes of Colophon 570 – 475 BCE

At about the same time that the Milesian school was flowering, the Eleatic school was founded in Colophon[408], another Ionian city, by Xenophanes, a satirist, poet, and social-religious *critic*. Supposedly Xenophanes began traveling at the age of 25 and continued to roam about until he was 92! According to some sources, he was infamous (and exiled!) for his attacks on 'conventional military and athletic virtues of the time'. He ended his life in Sicily. He wrote his ideas in the form of poetry, criticizing Homer and Hesiod, saying that myths and such were more or less human projections. He wrote that:

Xenophanes .

> Homer and Hesiod have attributed to the gods all sorts of things that are matters of reproach and censure among men: theft, adultery, and mutual deception.[409]

In short, his main beef seems to have been the anthropomorphizing of the gods or even thinking that there was any physical manifestation at all. Xeno-

---

408. According to Apollodorus and Proclus, the mythical seer Calchas died at Colophon after the end of the Trojan War. Strabo names Clarus as the place of his death, which would later be a cult center in the territory of Colophon. An oracle had it that he would die when he would meet a better seer than himself. As Calchas and the other heroes on their way home from Troy came upon the seer Mopsus in Colophon, the two competed in their mantic qualities. Calchas couldn't equal Mopsus' skills as a seer, being a son of Apollo and Manto, so he died. In Greek antiquity two sons of Codrus, King of Athens, established a colony there. It was the birthplace of the philosopher Xenophanes and the poet Mimnermus.
409. Diels & Kranz (1951), *Die Fragmente der Vorsokratiker, Xenophanes*.

phanes claimed that "God is one, supreme among gods and men, and not like mortals in body or in mind."[410] His conception of god was that s/he/it is abstract, universal, unchanging, immobile and always present; one eternal being, spherical in form, comprehending all things within himself, is intelligent and moves all things, but bears no resemblance to human nature either in body or mind. Because of his development of the concept of a 'one god greatest *among gods* and men', Xenophanes is often seen as one of the first monotheists in the Western philosophy of religion, although we notice that what he actually said was that this 'greatest god' was greatest over other gods.

He examined fossils and concluded that water must have covered the entire Earth at some point. That is, he actually used physical evidence as opposed to declaring ideas with nothing to back them up except 'logic and reason'. He was one of the first during those times who tried to make a distinction between belief and knowledge. But then he shot himself in the foot by saying that you can know something but not really know it, suggesting that there were 'deeper truths' that you could 'just know' but have no evidence to prove.

Xenophanes was among the first to make the explicit claim that he was writing for future generations. Nevertheless, we notice that he, too, was on the short list of well-educated dummies according to Heraclitus, keeping company with Hesiod, whom he criticizes himself!

Xenophanes' cosmology stated that heavenly bodies were transient structures, the result of cloudy exhalations of the Earth. This is similar to the picture of Anaximenes, but Xenophanes said that the clouds *caught fire as they rose*. We can see that this model can easily be used to explain any unexpected events in the heavens, which suggests that such events were not unknown at the time! But he had difficulty using it to explain the regular stars that were fixed in place, so he came up with the idea that they were extinguished every day and fired up the next from new exhalations being constantly produced by the Earth! In short, this was a purely atmospheric theory of stars designed to accommodate the fearful comets, suggesting that they were formed of clouds that caught fire. No wonder Heraclitus thought he belonged on that list.

---

410. Zeller, *Vorsokrastische Philosophie*, p. 530, n. 3.

Heraclitus 535 – 475

Now we come to Heraclitus: This is the guy who said that Hesiod, Pythagoras, Xenophanes and Hecataeus were well educated in certain respects, but in their analyses, apparently didn't have a clue. He also thought that Homer and Archilochus[411] deserved to be beaten.[412] His exact words, as quoted by Diogenes were:

> *Much learning* does not teach understanding; else would it have taught Hesiod and Pythagoras, or, again, Xenophanes and Hecataeus. ... this one thing is wisdom, to understand thought, as that which guides all the world everywhere.[413]

He is certainly acknowledging the high level of learning of the named individuals, but he points out that it is "thought which guides the world everywhere." This strikes me as being possibly a multi-layered remark. It could mean that thought, or ideas, are the substance of the universe. It could also, at the same time, mean that thought – how a man thinks, or how a civilization *en masse* thinks – determines what happens to him. We are reminded of the saying in Proverbs 23:7: "As a man thinketh in his heart, so is he." Scaling this up to the global level seems to suggest that 'as a civilization thinks/is, so the cosmos creates'. Another way of saying it is: men and nations do not attract what they want, *but what they are*; the soul attracts what it harbors in secret.

Let's see if we can figure out what Heraclitus meant by a process of elimination. As we know now, the main thing about Pythagoras seems to be that he was a shamanic teacher of reincarnation and his view of the cosmos was possibly similar to that of Pherecydes, who wrote about the cosmic battles and the five (or seven) recesses which must have been constellations before constellations were described and refined. It seems possible that Pythagoras took this and converted it into some theory of purification a la Orphism unless that is a later astralization created by Plato. It might also have had some-

---

411. Greek lyric poet from the island of Paros in the Archaic period. He is celebrated for his "versatile and innovative use of poetic meters and as the earliest known Greek author to compose almost entirely on the theme of his own emotions and experiences." From: Brown (1997), *Introduction to Gerber's A companion to the Greek Lyric Poets*, p. 49.
412. Aristotle, *Rhetoric*, 3.17.14 18b 28.
413. Diogenes Laërtius, *Lives*, IX, 1.

thing to do with the books of Pythagoras that were bought and utilized by Plato, which may have included a version of the story of Atlantis that Plato wrote in *Timaeus*
and *Critias*.

Heraclitus.

Hesiod, of course, wrote all of that
business about gods in some sort of
Olympic world, a semi-real region
that might be described as hypercosmic or hyperdimensional, but
even if it was fanciful, it captured the action pretty well if one has comet science and the theories of Bailey, Clube and Napier in mind. Xenophanes, as
we have just seen, obviously didn't have a clue so we can agree with Heraclitus
without much ado. Hecataeus wrote that the stories of the Greeks were
ridiculous, which amounts to criticizing both Hesiod and Homer, who
Heraclitus wants to beat with sticks, so how is it that he is included in the
list? All of them wrote about the gods and the heavens, either from mythological points of view, or as rational attempts to explain away the supernatural, and *both* of these approaches were apparently condemned by Heraclitus.
So what other options are left? I think it comes back to that last part of the
statement: "this one thing is wisdom, to understand thought, as that which
guides all the world everywhere."

Before we go deeper into the ideas of Heraclitus, I think a little background
information on him is in order. He is known for the obscurity of his words
and descriptions, and that may be due to certain issues that affected him.

According to Diogenes, Heraclitus was a hereditary prince who abdi-
cated in favor of his brother because he was expected to participate in government and refused, saying that politics was *ponêra*, or evil. He was self-
taught and something of a real crank, which might be understandable considering the environment in which he lived, which we'll be observing here
and there as we go along. He eventually became so misanthropic that he wandered the hills like a madman eating grass and herbs. When he became ill
with what was called dropsy, or severe edema, which was obviously evidence of some systemic failure, according to one source, he attempted to cure
himself by packing his legs with cow manure and baking in the Sun. That
experiment brought his life as a philosopher to an abrupt end. Before that
fatal act, however, he wrote a book that became quite famous and was still
available down to the time of Plutarch and Clement of Alexandria (150-215
CE). His philosophy was full of riddles and he was known as 'The Weeping

Philosopher'[414] because he was so depressed and negative all the time. That should give us pause when we consider that he said: "this one thing is wisdom, to understand thought, as that which guides all the world everywhere." Maybe he saw something coming as a result of the thinking and behavior of humanity during his times? Theophrastus, quoted by Diogenes, suggests that it was melancholy that prevented him from finishing his works. No kidding!

Reading what little is available about him gives the impression of an incredible, sublime intellect that wasn't quite grounded, but then, that is rather common for geniuses who really *see*. The question is: did he see anything useful and if so, do we have a clue what it was since I must repeat the usual refrain: nearly all of his works are lost.

Heraclitus proposed that the Universe contains a *divine artisan-fire* which foresees everything and, extending throughout the Universe, must produce everything via the unity of opposites: "the path up and down are one and the same."[415, 416] This 'divine fire' later very much attracted Zeno, the founder of Stoicism (we'll meet him shortly), but what it suggests to me is electricity or, more precisely, plasma. It could also be what is called the quantum vacuum, but not simply a physical one. His ideas have the taste of something rather like 'Chi' or even Reich's 'orgone energy'.

This divine fire, or *aether*, is also 'logos' – that is, the basis for all activity in the Universe; it is both the source of passive matter, and the artisan creating with, and enlivening it, which neither increases nor diminishes itself.[417] His cryptic words that "all entities come into being in accordance with this Logos" has been the subject of endless speculation.

In addition to seeing it as the most fundamental of the four elements and the one that is quantified and determines the quantity (Cosmic Mind) of the other three, he presents fire as the cosmos, which was *not made by any of the gods* or men, but "was and is and ever shall be ever-living fire." I don't know about you, but that gives me chills! For Heraclitus, fire is both a substance and a motivator of change, it is active in altering other things quantitatively and performing an activity Heraclitus describes as "the judging and convicting of all things." (If that's true, our civilization is in big trouble!) It is "the thunderbolt that steers the course of all things." There is no reason to interpret the judgment, which is actually 'to separate' (as in wheat from

---

414. The main source for the life of Heraclitus is Diogenes Laërtius, although some have questioned the validity of his account.

415. Diogenes Laërtius, vii. 148.

416. Sextus Empiricus, adv. Math. ix. 104, 101; Cicero, *de Natura Deorum*, ii. 8.

417. Cicero, *de Natura Deorum*, ii. 9, iii. 14.

tares, sheep from goats, etc.), outside of the context of "strife is justice."[418] His term 'strife' had a special meaning as the conflict/unity between opposites. What is intriguing is his apparent allusion to the idea that the cosmos itself can respond to humankind with "the thunderbolt" that steers all things. In an interesting way, this connects us to the ideas of Fred Hoyle and Chandra Wickramasinghe, who proposed that life was brought to Earth by comets, i.e. panspermia. (Thunderbolt = comet.)

He had some other very advanced ideas that are common currency in modern physics. Heraclitus is famous for insisting that the universe is all about *change*. He said, "No man ever steps in the same river twice." If objects are new from moment to moment so that one can never touch the same object twice, then each object must dissolve and be generated continually moment by moment. That reaches right down into Quantum Theory and possibly beyond. No wonder the guy was wandering the hills like a madman!

In respect of ethics, Heraclitus declared that people should not live according to their own judgment but to find out and follow the divine law. His concept of god didn't include any manifestations of what *humans* would call justice. That is, humans are neither made in the image of God nor is God particularly interested in them individually or as a whole. "To God all things are fair and good and just, but people hold some things wrong and some right."[419] God's ways are wise, but human customs are foolish.[420] At the same time, both humans and God are childish (inexperienced): "human opinions are children's toys" and "Eternity is a child moving counters in a game; the kingly power is a child's."[421] Wisdom is *"to know the thought by which all things are steered through all things,"*[422] which must not imply that people are or can be wise. Only Zeus, the wielder of the thunderbolt, is wise.[423]

Some scholars see all of this as mysticism, but clearly it is not: it is pure physics, though the terminology is archaic. And certainly, his mental state was affected by seeing these things and thinking these thoughts because he also declared in despair, "The fairest universe is but a heap of rubbish piled up at random."[424]

---

418. Diels-Kranz (1951), *Die Fragmente der Vorsokratiker*.
419. DK (Diels-Kranz) B51
420. DK B78.
421. DK B70; DK B52.
422. DK B41.
423. DK B32.
424. DK B124.

I think that, in the above, we find the cranky reason that Heraclitus made his list of idiots; he made it clear when he said the universe was *not made by any of the gods* or men, but "was and is and ever shall be ever-living fire." No wonder the guy was melancholy and had nobody to talk to! That's an idea that is hardly comprehensible to the average person even in today's world when people still have to have a creator (whether it's an old bearded guy or the 'god' of evolution who set off the Big Bang is immaterial) to blame for things existing. Not only that, his ideas would be almost impossible for a mind living at that time to even bear. To me, what Heraclitus was saying sounds rather like an early version of Information Theory! [425]

In any event, Diogenes tells us that his treatise *On Nature* was divided into three discourses, one on the universe, another on politics, and a third on theology. He deposited the book in the temple of Artemis and, "according to some, made it the more obscure in order that none but adepts should approach it." This book is going to come back to haunt us.

Anaxagoras of Clazomenae 500 – 428 BCE

Now we come to the Ionian school. Yet again, we find our early Greek philosopher born in Western Turkey, part of the Ionian league [426], though, like several others, he moved to Athens as a young man. Anaxagoras started as a pupil of Anaximenes and wrote a work that began: "All things were together; then came Mind and set them in order." Not very bright, but going in the right direction! It's rather the reverse of what Heraclitus was saying, which was that the 'Cosmic Mind' preceded all.

Anaxagoras was born to a noble and wealthy family and handed his inheritance over to his relations because he couldn't be bothered with it, rather like Heraclitus. His ideas were that the Sun was a mass of red-hot metal and was larger than the Peloponnesus. He also declared that there were *hills and valleys and dwellings on the Moon*. (Remember this!) He said that the whole universe was composed of minute bodies and his moving principle was Mind.

In the beginning, the stars moved in the sky as in a revolving dome, so that the celestial pole which is always visible was vertical. But at some point, the pole took its inclined position. The Milky Way was said by him to be a reflection of the light of stars which are not shone upon by the Sun; comets

---

425. A branch of applied mathematics, electrical engineering and computer science involving the quantification of information.

426. Confederation formed at the end of the Meliac War in the mid-7th century BCE comprising twelve Ionian cities located in today's Western Turkey.

were conjunctions of planets which then emitted flames; meteorites were sparks thrown off by the air, thunder was clouds banging together, lightning is their violent friction, and earthquakes were the result of the sinking of air into the Earth, sort of like terrestrial burps.

He also predicted the weather based on observation and was once asked if some hills would ever become sea and he answered "yes, it only needs time." A veritable flaming genius, this guy.

Anaxagoras was said to be the first who said that Homer was giving examples of virtue and justice in his epics, not just telling wild tales for pure entertainment, which was a clever observation and, as far as I can see, is well supported by modern analyses.[427]

Then there is the story that he predicted that a meteoric stone would fall and it did. The date is a little iffy but most of the experts agree that it was in 467 BCE at Aegospotami, in the Galipoli Peninsula (in Eastern Thrace).[428] Anaxagoras described this comet as an "object of extraordinary grandeur" and many years later, the Roman historian, Seneca, having original sources that are now lost, described it as having been the size of a "great beam". That is when Anaxagoras declared that the whole of the heavens was made of stones and that the rapidity of its rotation is the only thing that kept the stones in place and if this were relaxed, it would fall.

Oh boy! Did he ever get in big trouble! Different accounts are given: 1) He was indicted by Cleon on a charge of impiety because he declared the Sun to be a mass of red-hot metal; he was defended and given a small fine. 2) He was charged by Thucydides with treasonable correspondence with Persia as well as impiety and the sentence was death. 3) He was ill, weak and wasted when he came into court and was acquitted from sympathy. 4) He was defended mightily by Pericles and released, but then committed suicide because of the indignity he had suffered.

That's about it for Anaxagoras. I've only given him this much space because of the charges brought against him *after he declared that the heaven was not as secure as it was claimed to be.* That strikes me as a most peculiar thing. Especially with so many philosophers all around during those times theorizing and claiming this or that, and nobody thinks much about it at all until this guy pipes up and says that stones can – and possibly will – fall from the sky. Of course, his explanation as to why it would happen was silly, but that's not the point. It seems that there was, definitely, a conscious decision made

---

427. See Louden (2011), *Homer's Odyssey and the Near East.*
428. North East Greece.

by the ruling powers of the time that nobody was to say anything at all about stones falling from the sky, and if you want to be a philosopher, you best get with the party line which says that nothing is going on up there at all; never has, and never will. Obviously, the elite rulers were on top of things and didn't want any of that kind of talk stirring up the masses. So, let me paraphrase Queen Gertrude in *Hamlet*: *Methinks they did protest too much!*

Socrates 469 – 399 BCE

Ten years after the death of Confucius, Socrates was born in Athens during the century which has been called the golden age of Athens. The Greeks had stopped the Persians at Marathon in 490 and turned them away for good in 480 at Salamis and in 479 at Plataea. With security from foreign encroachment, the way was prepared for Aeschylus, Sophocles, Euripides, Aristophanes, Pericles, the sophists, and Socrates. The future looked bright, but it was not to last through Socrates' lifetime, as we will see.

Very little is known of his actual life and teachings because everything is filtered to us through Plato, Xenophon and Aristophanes, his students and a critic. His critic, Aristophanes, *depicts him as a clown who taught his students how to bamboozle their way out of debt*. While this is often thought to be a parody, it is true that no one knows how Socrates made his living since he devoted himself exclusively to discussing philosophy. Aristophanes also portrays Socrates as a paid teacher who was running a sophist school, but Plato and Xenophon, his students, explicitly deny that he ever accepted payment for teaching. Later sources claim that he was a stone-mason. Plato refers to his military service: in the *Apology*, Socrates compares his military service to his legal troubles that led ultimately to his death, portraying Socrates as saying that anyone on the jury who thinks he ought to retreat from philosophy must also think soldiers should retreat when it seems likely that they will be killed in battle.

Diogenes reports that Socrates was alleged to have been a student of Anaxagoras and when the latter was condemned to death for impiety, he became a pupil of Archelaus, the physicist. It strikes me as extraordinary that Anaxagoras and Socrates, two in a row, should be condemned to death. But Socrates did live during the time of the Peloponnesian War and the Thirty Tyrants, so I should give you, the reader, a quick run-down on that situation. (Believe me, I do *not* like writing about wars, as you may notice, so this is going to be the Peloponnesian War reduced to just a couple of pages!)

The Thirty Tyrants

The Peloponnesian War was fought between 431 and 404 BCE. The main combatants were the city-states Athens *vs* Sparta. Each of these cities had its own set of alliances that included nearly all of the other city-states. The fighting spread over the entire Greek world. Socrates was about 38 when it began, and it went on for almost 30 years in the background of all his philosophizing! Some "Golden Age!"

The Athenians were, basically, at the head of an empire that was mainly naval. Sparta, in the other corner of the ring, was at the head of a number of independent states that included the land powers (strong army) plus the smaller sea power of Corinth. The Athenians were richer because they collected tribute from the members of their empire.

It all began when Athens violated a treaty that had been made back in 445. The Spartans accused Athens of aggression and threatened war. Pericles, who we met defending Anaxagoras, was the most influential leader and he advised Athens to *not back down*. Diplomacy failed, and the Spartan ally, Thebes, attacked an Athenian ally, Plataea, and after that it was a free-for-all.

After just two years of fighting back and forth, the cosmos apparently made a comment on the behavior of the peoples: The Plague came. The epidemic killed about a third of the population on its first round, and that percentage could also probably be applied to the loss to the army/navy as well. It is believed to have entered Athens through Piraeus, the city's port and sole source of food and supplies coming from Africa (according to Thucydides). Sparta, and much of the Eastern Mediterranean, was also struck by the disease. Thucydides himself contracted the illness, and survived. He was therefore able to accurately describe the symptoms of the disease along with his history of the war.

> As a rule, however, there was no ostensible cause; but people in good health were all of a sudden attacked by violent heats in the head, and redness and inflammation in the eyes, the inward parts, such as the throat or tongue, becoming bloody and emitting an unnatural and fetid breath.
>
> These symptoms were followed by sneezing and hoarseness, after which the pain soon reached the chest, and produced a hard cough. When it fixed in the stomach, it upset it; and discharges of bile of every kind named by physicians ensued, accompanied by very great distress. In most cases also an ineffectual retching followed, producing violent spasms, which in some cases ceased soon after, in others much later.
>
> Externally the body was not very hot to the touch, nor pale in its appearance, but reddish, livid, and breaking out into small pustules and ulcers. But

internally it burned so that the patient could not bear to have on him clothing or linen even of the very lightest description; or indeed to be otherwise than stark naked. What they would have liked best would have been to throw themselves into cold water; as indeed was done by some of the neglected sick, who plunged into the rain-tanks in their agonies of unquenchable thirst; though it made no difference whether they drank little or much.

Besides this, the miserable feeling of not being able to rest or sleep never ceased to torment them. The body meanwhile did not waste away so long as the distemper was at its height, but held out to a marvel against its ravages; so that when they succumbed, as in most cases, on the seventh or eighth day to the internal inflammation, they had still some strength in them. But if they passed this stage, and the disease descended further into the bowels, inducing a violent ulceration there accompanied by severe diarrhea, this brought on a weakness which was generally fatal.

For the disorder first settled in the head, ran its course from thence through the whole of the body, and even where it did not prove mortal, it still left its mark on the extremities; for it settled in the privy parts, the fingers and the toes, and many escaped with the loss of these, some too with that of their eyes. Others again were seized with an entire loss of memory on their first recovery, and did not know either themselves or their friends.[429]

Titus Lucretius Carus (99-55 BCE) gives a second historical description that must have been based on another account since, while his account matches the description of Thucydides closely, he identifies a further symptom of the disease, which, he states, accompanies the ulceration, setting in around the eighth or ninth day.

> If any then had 'scaped the doom of that destruction, yet
> Him there awaited in the after days
> A wasting and a death from ulcers vile
> And black discharges of the belly, or else
> Through the clogged nostrils would there ooze along
> Much fouled blood, oft with an aching head.[430]

Thucydides' account of the plague graphically details the complete disappearance of social morals during the epidemic. He said that people ceased fearing the law since they felt they were already living under a death sentence.

---

429. Translation by M.I. Finley in *The Viking Portable Greek Historians*, pp. 274-275.
430. Bailey (1947), *Prolegomena, Lucretius' De Rerum Natura*.

They also started spending their money like crazy since they figured they wouldn't live long enough to enjoy the fruits of investing. It is also recorded that people stopped behaving decently because most did not expect to live long enough to enjoy a good reputation for it. [431, 432] Athenian women were temporarily liberated from the strict bounds of social custom and Athens was forced to appoint a magistrate called *gynaikonomos* to control them. [433]

Of most interest to us here is the religious turmoil that was caused at the time. Since the disease struck without regard to a person's piety, the people felt abandoned by the gods and there seemed to be no benefit to worshiping them. The Athenians – probably wiser than their leaders – pointed to the plague as evidence that the gods favored Sparta and this was supported by an oracle that said that Apollo himself (the god of plague) would fight for Sparta if they fought with all their might. An earlier oracle had stated that "War with the Dorians [Spartans] comes and at the same time death." [434]

The plague returned twice more, in 429 BCE and in the winter of 427/6 BCE. Pericles was killed by the disease in 429 BCE and, according to Thucydides, Athens was afterward led by a succession of incompetent or weak leaders. That knocked them back for a bit, but they came back for another round. Thucydides said that it was not until 415 BCE that the Athenian population had recovered sufficiently to embark on their disastrous Sicilian expedition. (You'd think they would have figured out that the Cosmos wants people to play nicely together!) At one point, Sparta seemed to be losing until other Athenian subject states decided to revolt as well. This led to a Spartan victory and a temporary peace that lasted 6 years. Then, Athens launched the above mentioned massive attack against Sicily (part of the Athenian empire that revolted) and they were off for another 11 years. In the end, the Athenians were utterly destroyed militarily.

So, now it is 411, Athens is in turmoil, democracy has been overthrown by an oligarchical party which was then overthrown by what was said to be a more moderate regime, and by the end of the year the rebuilt navy helped to restore democracy. However, the peace offers from Sparta were refused and they all sent their little boats out to have at it again! The final end came in 405 when the Athenian fleet was destroyed at – you'll be surprised – Aegospotami.

---

431. Thucydides. II.53.
432. The same breakdown of social controls was reported during the Black Death in the Middle Ages.
433. That certainly reminds us of the 'plague of witches' hunted down by the Inquisition following the Black Death of the Middle Ages!
434. Thucydides, II.53; Thucydides, II.54.

Indeed. The very place where, in 467, our dear departed Anaxagoras predicted and witnessed a meteoric rock to fall and made a theory about it for which he may have been condemned to death.

It really makes you just stop and wonder what the heck is really going on here.

Anaxagoras supposedly died in 428 BCE as a result of his claims about the meteorite and that was just a couple of years *after* the start of this war nonsense. And there was a plague? And more warring? Isn't this exactly the sort of thing that Bailey, Clube and Napier posit occurs during times of increased comet flux with attendant fireballs and meteorites? Why the concocted story in the sources about some possible "treasonable correspondence" with the Persians when, *at that time*, i.e. 467 BCE, the Persians weren't the issue, the Spartans were? [435] Why are the dates of the meteorite – or whatever it really was – so uncertain? The sources suggest 470, 467 and 442, with the choice falling on 467 BCE. Let's take a quick look at our catalogue. [436]

> 470 BCE, China: a broom star comet was seen. (Ho, 12)
>
> 467 BCE, China, Greece: A broom star comet was seen. This event is often but incorrectly, attributed to comet Halley. This is the comet that Plutarch noted appearing prior to the falling of the meteorite at Aegospotami, Greece. (Ho, 13), (Barrett, 4)
>
> 433 BCE, China: a broom star comet was observed. (Ho, 14)
>
> 426 BCE, Winter, Greece: a comet appeared in the north around the time of the winter solstice. (Barrett, 4)

Obviously, either of the latter two comets could have been associated with the Aegospotami falling rock. I would say, based on the date of the death of Anaxagoras, if it really was due to his impiety in talking about rocks falling from heaven, it couldn't have been the 426 sighting, but could definitely have been the 433 event associated with the falling rock(s?). And if that is the case (as is the case in many other instances throughout history), the plague may very well have been a comet borne 'expression of the gods' wrath.' (We'll discuss this even more extensively in Volume IV in the case of the Justinian Plague, for which we have much more data.)

Well, just another sample of the perils of history. You go along and think

---

435. The Persians aided Sparta further on in the war.
436. Most comet references from Yeomans (1991), *Comets: A Chronological History of Observation, Science, Myth, and Folklore.*

things are settled, but then you keep your eyes open, ask a few questions, bring in a little science, especially about comets and such, and everything just falls apart. Meanwhile, back to the Thirty Tyrants.

So the famous Lysander whipped the Athenians (with help from Persia, which, by the way, raises a whole lot of questions about Anaxagoras, as I just mentioned), and the city was put under siege and starved into submission. The most culturally advanced Greek city-state just acted all the way through as though they had fallen out of the stupid tree and hit every branch on the way down. Their arrogance and greed led to their downfall and clearly they weren't reading Heraclitus! Too bad modern-day governments and nations don't learn from history.

As noted, Athens' great strength had been her navy. Also, they had built massive defensive walls. According to the terms of Athens' surrender to Lysander, Sparta assumed command of Athens. Immediately, the Long Walls and fortifications were destroyed, the Athenian fleet was handed over, exiles were recalled, and the chief leaders of Athens' "democracy" were imprisoned. Then a body of thirty local men were nominated to rule Athens and frame a new, oligarchic constitution. It is a mistake to think that all Athenians were unhappy. Many in Athens favored oligarchy over democracy. Later, the pro-democratic faction did restore democracy, but only *through force*.

The Athenians of the time referred to them simply as 'the oligarchy' or 'the Thirty' and it was only later historians who referred to them as the 'Thirty *Tyrants*'. The 'historical' perspective on this event was that the Thirty severely reduced the rights of Athenians, including imposing a limit on the number of citizens allowed to vote. This is seen as an act of the wealthy elite who objected to being subject to the votes of the 'rabble' in a broad-based democracy where all free adult males could vote. Participation in legal functions – which had previously been open to all Athenians – was restricted by the Thirty to a select group of 500 persons.

But let's get some perspective here. It seems to me that it was the people in charge to begin with who got Athens and everybody else into the whole mess of almost 30 years of war and those people who had been in charge, who one must assume were the 'wealthy elite', were imprisoned by Lysander. Further, one of the leading members of the Thirty was Critias, the great-uncle of Plato and *a close associate of Socrates*. As one of the new rulers, he personally black-listed many Athenians who were then executed and *their wealth* confiscated. In short, it looks like the wealthy had been the tail wagging the democratic dog for some time and these were measures designed to deal with that problem. What they did may look like a gang of evil, wealthy elites having their way, but there is, certainly, another way to look at it.

The next thing the Thirty did was to begin a purge of important leaders of the popular party during the Peloponnesian War. Keep in mind that these people had brought on the war and continued it, leading to the deaths of tens or hundreds of thousands of citizens, all to protect their greed, their empire. So what we see are hundreds of wealthy elite former rulers being condemned to execution by drinking hemlock, while thousands more were exiled from Athens. One of the most famous men who escaped from Athens during this reign of terror was the *wealthy* Lysias, who was mentioned in Plato's *Republic*. So it was, indeed, the wealthy who were the target of the new Oligarchy.

But no group of thirty men can be placed in power without there being a few bad apples in the barrel. The difficulty is trying to see what was really going on through the mist of a couple of millennia. Many consider Socrates the wisest of the Greeks, and he fought on the side of Athens against Sparta during the Peloponnesian War, so his possible involvement with the Spartan-backed Thirty Tyrants is surprising. Unfortunately, he didn't write, so historians are left with only what Plato had to say about the matter.

In Plato's *Apology*, which could have been written for personal propagandistic reasons (to make peace with the regime he lived under, i.e. bootlicking), Socrates recounts an incident in which the Thirty once ordered him (and four other men) to bring before them Leon of Salamis, a man known for his justice and upright character, for execution. While the other four men obeyed, Socrates refused, not wanting to partake in the guilt of the executioners. By disobeying, Socrates knew he was placing his own life in jeopardy, and claimed it was only the disbanding of the oligarchy soon afterward that saved his life.[437] That sounds like a bit of after-the-fact damage control because, in point of fact, it was the regime that came to power *after* the Thirty that condemned Socrates to death! Again, something is really wrong with the picture we are given by standard intepretations.

The Thirty appointed a Council of 500 to serve the judicial functions formerly belonging to all the citizens. (In democratic Athens, juries might be composed of hundreds or thousands of citizens without a presiding judge, which sounds like justice by mob rule, not an orderly democracy.) They appointed a police force and granted only 3,000 citizens a right to trial and to bear arms.

A year later, a group of exiles led by the wealthy elite general Thrasybulus, overthrew the Thirty in a coup that killed Critias. The wealthy elitist Lysias was with the exiles who returned. Lysias is considered to be one of the Ten Attic Orators; in short, he was good at making speeches and rabble-rous-

---

437. *Apology*, 32c-d.

ing, which is really what Athenian democracy seems to have been all about. After his return, he wrote *Against Eratosthenes* as an indictment against Eratosthenes, one of the Thirty, for the murder of his brother, Polemarchus. This speech is still considered to be one of the world's most famous orations and is identified by some historians as Lysias's personal best. And it was most likely little more than emotion driving propaganda.

Let us make note of Anytus, for example. He was from a nouveau riche family and became a powerful, wealthy, elite politician in Athens. He had served as a general in the P-War during which he lost Pylos to the Spartans and was charged with treason. He was acquitted by bribing the jury, according to Aristotle. He was a leading supporter of the democratic movement in opposition to the Oligarchy. What else did he do? As we will see, he was one of the prosecutors of Socrates.

The return of 'democracy' to Athens only seems to have made things worse. The changes that could have been made by the Thirty will never be known because Athens resumed its downward slide that led to its takeover by Philip of Macedon and his son Alexander.

It never ceases to amaze me that, with death and destruction everywhere, comets in the skies, probably fireballs and meteorites, probably crazy weather, and certainly pestilence, the wealthy elite never stop their drive to stay in power and destroy the social body they have infected like a virus, only, in the end, to be tossed in the garbage-pit of history with said body, and burned. They never seem to get it.

Well, that's cheerful! I think it is time to return to our philosophers now that we have a little better idea of the world they were living in. I just want to point out that we did the whole Peloponnesian War in just a few pages so I'm sure that's some kind of record!

The Socratic Split

It is actually at this point, the time of Socrates, that we can note an interesting divergence in philosophical thought, or so it appears to me. The issue of Archelaus being the teacher of Socrates, as I have indicated, is a bit controversial because he is never mentioned by Xenophon, Plato, or Aristotle; thus it is assumed that the story was told in order to connect the famous philosopher to the Ionian school. Nevertheless, Diogenes Laërtius, our main source, does invoke the authority of Ion of Chios, a contemporary of Socrates, that Socrates went with Archelaus on a trip to Samos.[438]

---

438. Diogenes Laërtius, ii. 23.

Archelaus

Archelaus (5th century) was a student of Anaxagoras who, it is said, first brought natural philosophy from Ionia to Athens (and look what it got him!). Diogenes says that he was called "The Physicist" to denote the fact that with him, *natural philosophy came to an end* as soon as Socrates introduced ethics. (But is that really true or only apparent because all we know about Socrates came through Plato? Maybe Plato realized the danger of natural philosophy after the executions of Anaxagoras and Socrates?)

Archelaus asserted that the principle of motion was the separation of hot from cold. On this basis, he tried to build his Theory of Everything. He was also the first who explained that sound was the movement of air. He also taught that the Sun is the largest of heavenly bodies and that the universe is unlimited. That is the sum and substance of what we know about him since, repeat after me one more time: no fragments of his work survive!

Socrates Redux

As I've already stated, we know nothing about Socrates that hasn't been filtered through somebody else, mainly Plato. The problem with that is, while Plato *may* have represented many ideas of Socrates fairly accurately, it is widely acknowledged, and we have already touched on this, that he *used the figure of Socrates* to promulgate his own ideas the same way he used Pythagoras, undoubtedly altering their material to suit some agenda as yet unknown. There are evident conflicts and inconsistencies that exist between Plato's accounts and the reports of others such as Xenophon, as well as between some of the earlier vs. the later writings of Plato himself.

Diogenes' account is rather scattered so I've assembled a few snippets about Socrates by theme below just to give you a quick overview of his life, and then I will focus in on a couple of items that strike me as being revelatory of the Secret History behind Socrates. I'm not going to cite book and page for every snippet but rather, invite you to obtain one of those nice, inexpensive, Loeb Library editions of Diogenes Laërtius' *Lives of Eminent Philosophers*. First, regarding the personal habits of Socrates:

> He took care to exercise his body and kept in good condition. ... He was so orderly in his way of life that on several occasions *when pestilence broke out in Athens he was the only man who escaped infection.* ...
>
> ... in his old age he learnt to play the lyre, declaring that he saw no absurdity in learning a new accomplishment. As Xenophon relates in the *Sym-*

posium, it was his regular habit to dance, thinking that such exercise helped to keep the body in good condition.

I have no idea how the ancient Greeks danced, but I had an image of Antony Quinn as Zorba the Greek when I read this![439] Besides being an all-around fun guy, Socrates was also:

> … a man of great independence and dignity of character, Pamphila in the seventh book of her *Commentaries* tells how Alcibiades once offered him a large site on which to build a house; but he replied, "suppose, then, I wanted shoes and you offered me a whole hide to make a pair with, would it not be ridiculous in me to take it?" … Often when he looked at the multitude of wares exposed for sale, he would say to himself, "how many things I can do without."
>
> He showed his contempt for Archelaus of Macedon and Scopas of Cranon and Eurylochus of Larissa by refusing to accept their presents or to go to their court.
>
> There is, he said, only one good, that is, knowledge, and only one evil, that is, ignorance; wealth and good birth bring their possessor no dignity, but on the contrary evil …

That he was not an ivory-tower philosopher, but, on the contrary, fully engaged in life as the means by which one learns and grows, is attested by the following:

> Someone asked him whether he should marry or not, and received the reply, "Whichever you do you will repent it."

Which was based on his personal experience; his wife, Xanthippe, being a famous shrew:

> He said he lived with a shrew, as horsemen are fond of spirited horses, "but just as, when they have mastered these, they can easily cope with the rest, so I in the society of Xanthippe shall learn to adapt myself to the rest of the world."

He was also a man of great heart and generosity:

---

439. Do check out Anthony Quinn doing Zorba's dance here: http://www.youtube. com/watch?v=jeNsr_nQEfE
A great performance here: http://www.youtube.com/watch?v=Ip-XQ1FJ3rE
and here: http://www.youtube.com/watch?v=AlNtTMJAQpg
You can spend hours watching different versions and imagining Socrates in the scene!

Aeschines said to him, "I am a poor man and have nothing else to give, but I offer you myself," and Socrates answered, "Nay, do you not see that you are offering me the greatest gift of all?"

He also must have made many people angry by pointing out their lies and hypocrisies:

> He used to express his astonishment that the sculptors of marble statues should take pains to make the block of marble into a perfect likeness of a man, and should take no pains about themselves lest they should turn out mere blocks, not men. ...

The social control system run by the wealthy elite and their Authoritarian followers went into overdrive against Socrates. Then, as now, one of their weapons was ridicule. Aristophanes, known today as the 'Father of Comedy', was a comic playwright during the time of Socrates. His powers of slanderous ridicule were feared and acknowledged widely, and Plato claimed that his defamatory play, *The Clouds*, was a powerful contributing factor to the trial and execution of Socrates. Aristophanes claimed to be writing for an intelligent and discriminating audience, and used psychological intimidation tactics to coerce them to his view by declaring that they would be judged according to their reception of his plays. He regularly boasted of his originality as a dramatist, yet his plays reveal little more than his conservative, authoritarian perspective by consistently espousing opposition to new influences in Athenian society such as that of Socrates.[440] Aristophanes' depiction of Socrates as *"a clown who taught his students how to bamboozle their way out of debt"* is an interesting remark as we move into the ideas of the Cynics and Stoics, all of whom come across as very Gurdjieffian[441] and against whom similar charges were made.

Aristophanes also attacked Socrates in his plays for "making the worse appear the better" through his art of argumentation. Demetrius of Byzantium does, indeed, tell us that, frequently, due to his vehemence in argument, other men would attack him in rage, hitting him with their fists and tearing his hair out. I'm not so sure that this had to be due to vehemence in argument as to being so obviously right that the hypocrites he was exposing fell into foaming-at-the-mouth fury! One is certainly reminded of the story of Jesus de-

---

440. Aristophanes, *The Clouds*, trans. Dover, Intro. page XIV.
441. Karl Popper treats the Socratic problem in his first book of *The Open Society and Its Enemies* (1945).

fending the woman accused of adultery by writing on the ground with a stick. He was probably listing the similar crimes of her accusers as Socrates would have done. Demetrius further reports that Socrates was despised and laughed at, yet bore all this ill-use patiently. What we can extract from this is that Socrates was apparently one of the most formidable rhetoricians who ever lived, though we have no surviving texts. We are told by Diogenes that during the reign of the Thirty, he was ordered to stop teaching "the art of words", but I think he was confused. It was *after* the Thirty were overthrown by Anytus and his pals that he was ordered to stop teaching and was subsequently executed for refusing to do so. It does indeed sound like what happens when people try to speak truth plainly. And speaking the truth is, apparently, then and now, what the wealthy elite and their control system cannot tolerate.

> Anytus could not endure to be ridiculed by Socrates, and so in the first place stirred up against him Aristophanes and his friends; then afterwards he helped to persuade Meletus to indict him on a charge of impiety and corrupting the youth.
>
> The indictment was brought by Meletus, and the speech was delivered by Polyeuctus, according to Favorinus in his *Miscellaneous History*. The speech was written by Polycrates the sophist, according to Hermippus; but some say that it was by Anytus. Lycon the demagogue had made all the needful preparations.
>
> The affidavit in the case, which is still preserved, says Favorinus... ran as follows:
>
> "This indictment and affidavit is sworn by Meletus, the son of Meletus of Pitthos, against Socrates, the son of Sophroniscus of Alopece; Socrates is guilty of *refusing to recognize the gods recognized by the state, and of introducing other new divinities*. He is also guilty of corrupting the youth. The penalty demanded is death." (Emphases, mine.)

Since we've already noted that Athenian 'democracy' was actually a mob ruled by propaganda produced and promulgated by the wealthy (as it is in our own day), the outcome of the trial is not a surprise. Plato was not even allowed to speak in Socrates' defense. The mob was worked up and...

> Sentence of death was passed... he was put in prison... To one who said, "you are condemned by the Athenians to die," he made answer, "So are they, by nature. (But some ascribe this to Anaxagoras.) ... When his wife said, "you suffer unjustly," he retorted, "Why, would you have me suffer justly?"
>
> ... and a few days afterwards drank the hemlock, after much noble dis-

course which Plato records in the *Phaedo*. When he was about to drink the Hemlock, Apollodorus offered him a beautiful garment to die in: "What," said he, "is my own good enough to live in but not to die in?"

So he was taken from among men... He died in the first year of the 95th Olympiad at the age of seventy. ... Of those who succeeded him and were called Socratics, the chief were Plato, Xenophon, Antisthenes ... and not long afterwards the Athenians felt such remorse that they shut up the training grounds and gymnasia. They banished the other accusers but put Meletus to death ... and no sooner did Anytus visit Heraclea than the people of that town expelled him on that very day. Not only in the case of Socrates but in very many others the Athenians repented in this way... Euripides upbraids them thus in his *Palamedes*: "Ye have slain, have slain, the all-wise, the innocent, the Muses' nightingale."

Ancient and modern commentators have formulated two possible motivations for Anytus' role in Socrates' trial:

1) Socrates constantly criticised the democratic government of which Anytus was a leader. Anytus may have been concerned that Socrates' criticism was a threat to the newly reestablished democracy.[442]
2) Socrates taught Anytus' son and Anytus perhaps blamed Socrates' teachings for poisoning his son's mind or taking him away from the career path his father had set for him. Xenophon has Socrates forecast that the boy will grow up vicious if he studies a purely technical subject such as tanning. Xenophon also tells us that the son became a drunk.[443]

Delian Divers

Going in another direction now for a moment, Diogenes mentions a curious exchange in his *Life of Socrates*.

Unlike most philosophers, he had no need to travel, except when required to go on an expedition. The rest of his life he stayed at home and engaged all the more keenly in argument with anyone who would converse with him, his aim being not to alter his opinion but to get at the truth. They relate that Euripides gave him the treatise of Heraclitus and asked his opinion upon it, and that his

---

442. Burnet (1924), *Plato: Euthyphro, Apology of Socrates, Crito*.
443. Xenophon, *Apology* 29-31.

reply was, "The part I understand is excellent, and so too is, I dare say, the part I do not understand; but *it needs a Delian diver* to get to the bottom of it." [444]

Then, in his *Life of Heraclitus*, he writes:

The story told by Ariston [445] of Socrates, and his remarks when he came upon the book of Heraclitus, which Euripides brought him, I have mentioned in my *Life of Socrates*. However, Seleucus the grammarian [446] says that a certain Croton relates in his book called *The Diver* that the said work of Heraclitus was first brought into Greece by one Crates, who further said it required a *Delian diver* not to be drowned in it. The title given to it by some is *The Muses*, by others *Concerning Nature*; but Diodotus calls it 'A helm unerring for the rule of life'; others 'a guide of conduct, the keel of the whole world, for one and all alike'.[447]

What, one might ask, is a "Delian diver"? Is it as simple as assuming that Heraclitus' work was so deep that it needed an experienced swimmer to dive to the depths to obtain the pearls therefrom? Or is there something more here? Is this a hidden allusion to something that may be important about the relationships between these individuals? Or about their ideas?

First, let's consider one of the charges brought against Socrates; "…refusing to recognize the gods recognized by the state, and of introducing other new divinities." At his death, Diogenes tells us that:

… according to some, he composed a paean beginning: "All hail, Apollo, *Delos'* lord! Hail *Artemis*, ye noble pair!"

Were Apollo and Artemis 'new divinities'? I don't think so. Thus there must be something else here that is not immediately apparent.

Apollo was recognized as a god of light and the Sun, truth and prophecy, healing, plague, music, etc. He was the son of Zeus and had a twin sister, the virginal huntress, Artemis. He was known to the Etruscans as *Apulu*. (We'll discuss the Etruscans in the next volume.) He was the patron of Delphi – the prophetic deity of the Oracle. The lyre was one of his symbols,

---

444. Diogenes Laërtius, II 21-23.
445. Father of Plato.
446. Seleucus of Alexandria, a Roman-era Grammarian. He was nicknamed 'Homeric'. He commented on most of the ancient poets, wrote a number of exegetical and miscellaneous works, the titles of which are given by Suidas but there's not much else to go on.
447. Diogenes Laërtius, IX 11-13.

as it was a symbol for Orpheus. It was long assumed that, as early as the 3rd century BCE, he became identified among Greeks with Helios and Artemis became identified with the Moon. However, scholar Joseph Fontenrose declared that there was no evidence of this conflation earlier than the 3rd century CE! [448]

The Homeric hymns represent Apollo as a Northern intruder and his arrival must have occurred during the Dark Ages. His conflict with Earth was represented by the legend of his slaying her daughter, the serpent Python. Apollo and Artemis can bring death with their arrows. The idea that disease and death come from 'invisible arrows' fired by supernatural beings was common to Germanic and Norse mythology. The Vedic Rudra has similar functions to Apollo and the terrible god is called 'The Archer'. The bow is an attribute of Shiva. Rudra could also bring diseases with his arrows. There are other dragons and serpents slithering around in all these stories, so we can see the cometary connections immediately. [449, 450]

It seems that the oracular cult goes back to Mycenaean times, and in historical times the priests of Delphi were referred to as 'the double axe men' which relates them to the Minoans as well. The double axe was the holy symbol of the Cretan labyrinth and is probably due to cometary plasmoid manifestations.

The non-Greek origins of Apollo have long been acknowledged by scholars, but it was assumed that he came from Anatolia where oracular shrines, symbols, etc. have been found and purification and exorcism texts appear on old Assyro-Babylonian tablets. A Hittite text mentions that the king invited a Babylonian priestess to come and perform a certain purification. A similar story is told by Plutarch who writes that the Cretan seer Epimenides assisted Solon (c. 638 BCE-558 BCE) in the purification of Athens after the pollution brought by the Alcmaeonidae, a powerful and corrupt noble family who came to power in the 7th century. (Pericles and Alcibiades, who we will meet very quickly, belonged to the Alcmaeonidae.) [451]

Homer depicts Apollo *on the side of the Trojans* against the Achaeans during the Trojan War, thus he is pictured as a terrible god who is not to be trusted by the Greeks. In the late Bronze Age (1700 to 1200 BCE), the Hittite and Hurrian god *Aplu* was a god of plague who was invoked during times of pestilence to end same. *Aplu* means 'son of' and was the title given to Ner-

448. Bowden (2005), *Classical Athens and the Delphic Oracle: Divination and Democracy*.
449. Nilsson (1992), *Die Geschicthe der Griechischen religion*, Vol. I, p. 543.
450. Hall (2005), 'Getting Shot of Elves: Healing, Witchcraft and Fairies in the Scottish Witchcraft Trials'.
451. Nilsson, op. cit., pp. 563-564.

gal. Apollo's cult was already fully established in both Delos and Delphi by about 650 BCE and the frequency of 'godly names' given to children, such as Apollodorus or Apollonios, testify to his popularity.

In conclusion, we can say that, no, Apollo and Artemis were *not* 'new divinities' being introduced by Socrates, so the claim must apply to something else, perhaps a new interpretation of who and what these gods actually were and did... like comets, perhaps? Perhaps he came to these views after reading the works of Heraclitus and Pythagoras? We recall regarding Heraclitus' work:

> ... his treatise *ON NATURE* was divided into three discourses, one on the universe, another on politics, and a third on theology. He deposited the book in the *temple of Artemis* and, "according to some, made it the more obscure in order that *none but adepts* should approach it."

The claim that only an adept can penetrate the work of Heraclitus immediately brings to mind the Delian diver as a descriptive name of such an adept. The temple of Artemis and the title of the book may suggest that my interpretation is correct; it was about who the gods *really were* and what they did and could do, and might do again in time.

Referring back to the apparent northern origin of Apollo leads me to this point: Pythagoras was associated with 'Hyperborean Apollo' also, and one of the links between Socrates and Pythagoras is that they both practiced a form of divination. In reference to Socrates, Diogenes writes:

> He used to say that his supernatural sign warned him beforehand of the future...

Considering the several connections between Apollo and pestilence/plague, one is reminded of the special point that Diogenes made of mentioning that Socrates was unaffected by the plague that struck Athens during the Peloponnesian wars. Another curious thing is the remark by Diogenes that "Unlike most philosophers, he had no need to travel, except when *required* to go on an expedition", followed later by:

> Ion of Chios relates that in his youth he visited Samos in the company of Archelaus; and Aristotle [said also] that he went to Delphi...

So, he never traveled unless required, but two trips are mentioned. Was a visit to the hometown of Pythagoras 'required' as an expedition of some sort?

What about the expedition to Delphi? Was this also 'required' for some reason? Additionally, a fragment by Heraclitus states the following:

> The Sibyl with raving mouth utters things *mirthless and unadorned and unperfumed*, [in short, no BS!] and her *voice carries through a thousand years* because of the god who speaks through her.[452] The lord whose oracle is in Delphi neither declares nor conceals, but *gives a sign*. [Emphasis, mine.][453]

This reminds us that Pythagoras was said to have been taught by the Delphic priestess, Themistoclea. And despite the fact that Heraclitus put Pythagoras on his short list of people who weren't able to figure everything out, he acknowledged that he was, indeed, possessed of a great deal of knowledge.

So, just what is this "Delian diver" business about? Are we seeing here messages given in some sort of code, a puzzle that needs to be assembled? Who is Croton and what is his book *The Diver* about? Who is Crates, said to have brought Heraclitus' book to Greece and to have given the *same opinion* of it, using the same term, as Socrates himself? (Note that it is said that it was Euripides who gave the book to Socrates, but I'm not even going to go there right now because we have so much else to cover. Obviously, an entire book could be written exploring this topic alone!)

The only Crates we know of is the Stoic philosopher, Crates of Thebes, who lived between 365 and 285 BCE, much too late to have brought the book to Greece during the time of Socrates. There is no other Crates to be found. There is no 'Crates' or 'Croton' mentioned as persons in the *Suda*. In fact, the *Suda* fuses both of Diogenes Laërtius' versions of this Delian diver story into one, giving the impression that the author of the remark is *only* Socrates; that they assumed Crates and So-crates (shades of Bill and Ted!) were one and the same person. Does that suggest that the second version of the remark in Diogenes' biographies was put there for a reason, as a sort of hint or code?

The only thing respecting Croton that occurs to me is that it was the city that Pythagoras moved to in 530 BCE, where he and his followers were apparently welcomed and became active in the local politics until they were destroyed, probably by the wealthy elite[454], who may have rejected their principles of sharing and mutual support extended to all the people.

---

452. DK 22 B 92.
453. DK 22 B 93.
454. Also, while it cannot possibly have any relationship, I am reminded of Virginia Dare and the lost colony of Roanoke. The only clue to the colonists' fate was the word 'Croatoan' carved into a post of the fort, and the letters 'Cro' carved into a nearby tree.

What about the Delian diver? Why a diver from Delos and not just any other place? During classical times, divers from this island were not considered to have any special abilities nor to perform any special tasks that might distinguish them from divers living on any other island. So the term underscores the difficulty of penetrating what Heraclitus wrote and, as I noted above, can be compared to being an adept, which might suggest some sort of secret society or Mystery cult.

At this point, I want to refer back to something I wrote in Volume I of this *Secret History* series which marvelously brings several of these elements together, including bringing in Hecataeus, one of the others on Heraclitus' short list of wise people who were close but didn't quite go the distance. Diodorus Siculus tells a very strange story about the Hyperboreans that is an extract from the work of Hecataeus:

> Of those who have written about the ancient myths, Hecateus and certain others say that in the regions *beyond the land of the Celts* (Gaul) there lies in the ocean an island no smaller than Sicily. This island, the account continues, is situated in the north, and is inhabited by the Hyperboreans, who are called by that name because their home is beyond the point whence the north wind blows; and the land is both fertile and productive of every crop, and since *it has an unusually temperate climate* it produces two harvests each year.
>
> The Hyperboreans also have a language, we are informed, which is peculiar to them, and are most friendly disposed towards the Greeks, and especially towards the Athenians and the Delians, who have *inherited this goodwill from most ancient times*. The myth also relates that *certain Greeks visited the Hyperboreans* and left behind them costly votive offerings bearing inscriptions in Greek letters. And in the same way Abaris, a Hyperborean, came to Greece in ancient times and renewed the goodwill and kinship of his people to the Delians. [Emphasis, mine.] [455]

Diodorus' remark about the relations between the Hyperboreans and the Athenians and *Delians* is extraordinary in the specific terms that it was "inherited from most ancient times." What gets my antennae quivering is the statement that something costly and inscribed was taken to the Hyperboreans and left with them. (As I said, just following these clues would take an entire book and maybe I'll wrap this series up with just that!) That this story

---

455. *Diodorus of Sicily*, trans. C. H. Oldfather, Volumes II (1935) and III (1939). All quotes from Diodorus are from the same translation.

was common enough is demonstrated by the fact that Herodotus *also* wrote about the relationship of the Hyperboreans to the Delians:

> Certain sacred offerings wrapped up in *wheat straw* come from the Hyperboreans into *Scythia*, whence they are taken over by the neighbouring peoples in succession until they get as far *west* as the Adriatic: from there they are sent south, and the first Greeks to receive them are the Dodonaeans. Then, continuing southward, they reach the Malian gulf, cross to Euboea, and are passed on from town to town as far as Carystus. Then they skip Andros, the Carystians take them to Tenos, and the Tenians to Delos. That is how these things are said to reach Delos at the present time.[456]

One question I have here is this: why is Scythia depicted as being east of the Adriatic? I suspect there are clues here, but I don't have time to stop and go in ten different directions on that. We have to follow this particular thread to the end. The legendary connection between the Hyperboreans and the Delians leads us to another interesting remark of Herodotus, who tells us that Leto, *the mother of Apollo, was born on the island of the Hyperboreans.* That there was regular contact between the Greeks and the Hyperboreans over many centuries is the claim here, but for modern historians, it is highly questionable. Here, we don't know if we are talking about real people who have been assimilated to comet myths or not. But my thought is that it suggests an origin for the peoples who came down into Greece and Anatolia at some point in the distant past, at the time of a great cometary bombardment, and those people could be the later Mycenaeans and/or the Hittites, but formerly the Trojans who were the people of Apollo who was Hyperborean! That, of course, leads to the idea, long theorized by a number of scholars, that Troy was not in the Mediterranean. But again, we don't have time to pursue that here.[457] Herodotus has another interesting thing to say about the Hyperboreans and their sending of sacred offerings to Delos:

> On the first occasion they were sent in charge of two girls, whose names the Delians say were Hyperoche and Laodice. To protect the girls on the journey, the Hyperboreans sent five men to accompany them ... the two Hyperborean girls died in Delos, and the boys and girls of the island still cut their hair as

---

456. Herodotus, *The Histories*, Book IV, trans. Aubrey De Selincourt, p. 226.
457. See Iman Wilkens' book *Where Troy Once Stood* for details, but keep in mind that he is working without taking cometary bombardment into account and is assuming that the Trojan War was actually a human-fought conflict.

a sign of mourning for them... There is also a Delphic story that before the time of Hyperoche and Laodice, two other Hyperborean girls, Arge and Opis, came to Delos by the same route. ...*Arge and Opis came to the island at the same time as Apollo and Artemis...*[458]

It does sound like something of a migration took place and there are some mysterious elements that offer shadowy allusions to *objects of power and exodus*. Herodotus mentions at another point, when discussing the lands of the 'barbarians', "All these *except* the Hyperboreans, were continually encroaching upon one another's territory." Without putting words in Herodotus' mouth, it seems to suggest that the Hyperboreans were not greedy, power-hungry and warlike.

A further clue about the religion of the Hyperboreans comes from the myths of Orpheus. It is said that when Dionysus invaded Thrace (coming from the South to the North), Orpheus did not see fit to honor him but instead *preached the evils of sacrificial murder* to the men of Thrace. He taught "other sacred mysteries" having to do with Apollo, whom he believed to be the greatest of all gods. Dionysus became so enraged that he set the Maenads[459] on Orpheus at Apollo's temple where Orpheus was a priest. They burst in, murdered their husbands who were assembled to hear Orpheus speak, tore Orpheus limb from limb, and threw his head into the river Hebrus where it floated downstream still singing. It was carried on the sea to the island of Lesbos.

Another version of the story is that *Zeus killed Orpheus with a thunderbolt* (comet imagery) for divulging divine secrets. He was responsible for instituting the Mysteries of Apollo in Thrace, Hecate in Aegina, and Subterrenean Demeter at Sparta. And this brings us to a further revelation of Diodorus regarding the Hyperboreans:

> And there is also on the island both a magnificent sacred precinct of Apollo and a notable temple, which is adorned with many votive offerings and is *spherical in shape*. Furthermore, a city is there which is sacred to this god, and the majority of its inhabitants are players on the cithara; and these continually play on this instrument in the temple and sing hymns of praise to the god, glorifying his deeds... They say also that the moon, as viewed from this island, appears to be but a little distance from the earth and to have upon it *prominences*, like those of the earth, which are visible to the eye. The account

---

458. Herodotus, *The Histories*, pp. 226-227.
459. This word reminds me of Alcmaeonidae.

is also given that *the god visits the island every nineteen years, the period in which the return of the stars to the same place in the heavens is accomplished*, and for this reason the Greeks call the nineteen-year period the "year of Meton". At the time of this appearance of the god he both plays on the cithara and *dances continuously the night through from the vernal equinox until the rising of the Pleiades*, expressing in this manner his delight in his successes. And the kings of this city and the supervisors of the sacred precinct are
called Boreades, since they are descendants of Boreas, and the succession to these positions is always kept in their family.

First of all, it appears obvious that this *spherical* temple may be Stonehenge. Well, Stonehenge is actually circular now, but who knows what it looked like in ancient times? Perhaps it was made to appear spherical with its finishings? The second thing is the music which was so important to the Orphics and Pythagoreans. We also note that after reading Heraclitus' book, Socrates apparently took up playing the lyre! The third thing is the reference to the prominences on the Moon which reminds us that Anaxagoras declared that there were hills and valleys and dwellings on the Moon. Was he researching in these areas and – perhaps – mixing things up just a bit, but most dangerous of all, talking about it publicly, leading – ultimately – to his death? Finally, the dancing of the god brings us to consider something rather important. Diodorus is suggesting that the 19-year lunar calendar is a product of the Hyperboreans and that it relates to a period in which the 'return of the stars' is accomplished. This is easily understood as the Metonic cycle[460], but there is more to this than just that: there is the *god dancing through the night from the vernal equinox until the rising of the Pleiades*! As mentioned, I wrote about this in Volume I,

460. A period of very close to 19 years, which is nearly a common multiple of the solar year and the synodic (lunar) month. The Greek astronomer Meton of Athens (5th century BCE) observed that a period of 19 years is almost exactly equal to 235 synodic months, and rounded to full days counts 6,940 days. The difference between the two periods (of 19 years and 235 synodic months) is only a few hours.

where I looked at the problem in a particular way. Now though, with so much more additional information, another key has been revealed. The date that I gave to this event there still stands and now, as we will see in the next volume, has even more support and meaning! The pieces of the puzzle actually fall into place during the time of Julius Caesar. So hang on, we are getting there!

Could this knowledge of cycles of destruction and certain perspectives on the impersonal nature of the universe, and the attempt to share it widely, be the key to the executions of both Anaxagoras and Socrates? Could this knowledge of comet cycles have been the same knowledge possessed by Heraclitus and Pythagoras? Could it be that Anaxagoras did, actually, predict a period of cometary bombardment as suggested, which then actually occurred during the Peloponnesian wars? Was there a Tunguska-like event at the time of the final defeat of the Athenians? Such knowledge would be terrifying to the wealthy elite and their need to control and dominate populations of people which would explain why individuals who knew such things went underground and gave out the clues in a sort of code about 'Delian divers'. Tatian, (c. 120-180 CE) the early Assyrian Christian, writes along this line:

> I cannot approve of Heraclitus, who, being self-taught and arrogant said, 'I have explored myself.' Nor can I praise him for hiding his poem in the temple of Artemis, in order that it might be *published afterwards as a mystery*; and those who take an interest in such things say that Euripides the tragic poet came there and read it, and, gradually learning it by heart, carefully handed down to posterity this darkness.[461]

Well, certainly, as a Christian, he would think that the physics of Heraclitus was demonic, but it seems that he was offended by more than just that. The Christians had a very good reason to conceal the possibilities of cyclical cosmic destruction that was not under the control of their god, as we will soon see with plenty of evidence!

Now, what about Delos, itself? We find the answer with Pherecydes and his *Pentemychos* Recall the lines from the *Odyssey*:

> There is an island called Syrie – perhaps you have heard of it – above Ortygie, where are *the turnings of the sun*.

Compare it to Diogenes' report about Pherecydes:

---

461. Tatian, *Oratio ad Graecos and Fragments*, III.

> There is preserved of *the man of Syros* [Pherecydes] the book ... and there is preserved also *a solstice-marker in the island of Syros.*

Obviously, if this marker was known to Homer, it was there long before Pherecydes! Also, as it happens, the former name of Delos was Ortygie. The name, Delos, alludes to the concept of brilliance, clarity and transparency. The myth tells us that Apollo, in gratitude, changed the name of the island on which he was born, formerly called Ortygia, to Delos, 'visible', 'manifest', 'clear'.[462] Further, according to Diogenes Laërtius, Pythagoras included in his list of former incarnations a *Delian* fisherman named Pyrrhus. No, it's not a 'Delian diver', but one who *fishes from the surface*, and afterward he was reincarnated as Pythagoras. Was he, in this last incarnation, a true 'Delian diver'? Additionally, the name Pyrrhus was also given to the son of the warrior Achilles who *died in the Trojan war*. Naturally, we suspect that the Trojan war itself was a cometary event.

So, the question is: was there some sort of knowledge passed on to such as Socrates, from Heraclitus and Pythagoras, and others, Delian divers all? And did that knowledge include ideas relating to periodic cometary bombardments and destruction of society? Were those ideas predicated in terms of the behaviors of society attracting or repelling destruction? Is that the sort of thing that would have gotten both Anaxagoras and Socrates executed because it was seen as disruptive to the public order because it challenged the very existence of a wealthy elite?

As mentioned already, we are going to return to a number of these connections in the next volume with some amazing revelations, so keep all this in mind. Also keep in mind that both Socrates and Pythagoras were 'handled' by Plato after their deaths, possibly for reasons having to do with self-preservation. Their ideas and teachings were modified and 'Platonized' and, in the end, whether it was conscious and deliberate to keep on the right side of the authorities, or simply ego, it still amounts to a systematic cover-up of the truth. But we don't really know if it was the truth or just competing ideas, although we hope to figure it out in the course of this work.

Alcibiades 450 – 404 BCE

Now we are going to approach our problem from an oblique angle. Remember the mention of Alcibiades above? That he was a member of the clan of

---

462. "Delos, celebrated for its temple of Apollo... According to the story, Delos for a long time floated adrift ... Aristotle has recorded that it owes its name to its having suddenly appeared emerging from the water..." Pliny, *Natural History*, 4.66.

Alcmaeonidae, the powerful 'noble' family of ancient Athens? The first no-table Alcmaeonid was named Megacles and he and his followers violated the temple of Athena by massacring suppliants and they, and their descendants, were thereby considered to be stained, or polluted. The reasons we are dis-cussing him are twofold: 1) this is about where he fits chronologically and his story contributes to our background knowledge of the times; 2) the problem of Alcibiades introduces an important topic that we will deal with more as we go along: that of psychopathy.

We've already discussed Authoritarian types, who are mostly 'followers of authority'. Some of them can even be leaders if they have an authority to back them up, such as the rules of a particular regime or god. But there is another type of leader who very often taps into the mighty, almost oceanic, mob of authoritarian followers, and uses them to fulfill their own drives which may appear, on the outside, to be merely ambitions for wealth and power. But the fact is, they are not that at all, as we will discuss further on. Such individuals are referred to in the psychiatric literature as psychopaths and we need to understand that they are not ravening cannibals or 'Windigo' types exclusively; over the centuries, they have actually become quite refined in a certain sense, in that they are better and better able to disguise their true natures in order to get what they are driven to get, which is dominance over others in a purely animalistic sense.

Alcibiades is mentioned in the *Life of Socrates* where Diogenes tells us about the latter's military service in the Peloponnesian war, writing as follows:

> At all events, he served on the expedition to Amphipolis; and when in the bat-tle of Delium Xenophon had fallen from his horse, he stepped in and saved his life. For in the general flight of the Athenians he personally retired at his ease, quietly turning round from time to time and ready to defend himself in case he were attacked. Again, he served at Potidaea, whither he had gone by sea, as land communications were interrupted by the war; and while there he is said to have remained a whole night without changing his position, and to have won the prize of valour. But *he resigned it to Alcibiades, for whom he cher-ished the tenderest affection, according to Aristippus*[463] in the fourth book of his treatise *On the Luxury of the Ancients*.[464]

---

463. Founder of the Cyrenaic school of Philosophy. He was a pupil of Socrates, but adopted a very different philosophical outlook, teaching that the goal of life was to seek pleas-ure by adapting circumstances to oneself and by maintaining proper control over both adversity and prosperity.

464. Diogenes Laërtius, II 21-23.

Alcibiades, for whom Socrates "cherished the tenderest affection" – doesn't it just warm the cockles of your heart? Well, in the case of Alcibiades, Socrates' supernatural warning system apparently malfunctioned majorly or this was another confusion of Diogenes, similar to his stating that 'the Thirty' forbade Socrates to teach when, in fact, it was after the deposition of the Thirty and the return to power of Anytus and his wealthy pals. In fact, there is a story about Anytus and Alcibiades that suggests that my interpretation is correct.

Plutarch's *Life of Alcibiades* preserves stories of Anytus' tumultuous relationship with the young Alcibiades. Alcibiades seems to have treated Anytus with great contempt: on one occasion when Anytus had invited him to dinner, Alcibiades arrived late and drunk. Seeing the table laid with gold and silver dishes, Alcibiades ordered his slaves to take half of the dishes back to his own house. Having played this prank, Alcibiades departed immediately, leaving Anytus and his other guests greatly surprised. When the guests began to rebuke Alcibiades, Anytus excused him, saying that he loved the boy so much that he would have suffered Alcibiades to take the other half of the dishes, too.

In his seminal work on psychopathy, *The Mask of Sanity*, psychiatrist Hervey Cleckley wrote a short section devoted to Alcibiades the psychopath. I'll save my comments for after you read this remarkable analysis that I am quoting in full, since nobody can tell it like Cleckley! So, without further ado, here is Cleckley's 'The Psychopath in History':

*   *   *

Over a period of many decades psychiatrists, and sometimes other writers, have made attempts to classify prominent historical figures - rulers, military leaders, famous artists and writers – as cases of psychiatric disorder or as people showing some of the manifestations associated with various psychiatric disorders. Many professional and lay observers in recent years have commented on the sadistic and paranoid conduct and attitudes reported in Adolf Hitler and in some of the other wartime leaders in Nazi Germany. Walter Langer, the author of a fairly recent psychiatric study, arrives at the conclusion that Hitler was "probably a neurotic psychopath bordering on schizophrenia," that "he was not insane but was emotionally sick and lacked normal inhibitions against antisocial behavior." A reviewer of this study in *Time* feels that Hitler is presented as "a desperately unhappy man ... beset by fears, doubts, loneliness and guilt [who] spent his whole life in an unsuccessful attempt to compensate for feelings of helplessness and inferiority."

Though the term psychopath is used for Hitler in this quotation it seems to be used in a broader sense than in this volume. Hitler, despite all the unusual, unpleasant, and abnormal features reported to be characteristic of him, could not, in my opinion, be identified with the picture I am trying to present. Many people whose conduct has been permanently recorded in history are described as extremely abnormal in various ways. Good examples familiar to all include Nero and Heliogabalus, Gilles de Rais, the Countess Elizabeth Báthory and, of course, the Marquis de Sade. I cannot find in these characters a truly convincing resemblance that identifies them with the picture that emerges from the actual patients I have studied and regarded as true psychopaths.

Let us turn now to a much earlier historical figure, a military leader and statesman who is not likely to be forgotten while civilization as we know it remains on earth. I first encountered him during a course in ancient history when I was in high school. I had not at that time heard of a psychopath. The teacher did not try to classify him medically or explain his paradoxical career in psychological terms. I felt, however, that this gifted teacher shared my interest and some of my bewilderment as the brilliant, charming, capricious, and irresponsible figure of Alcibiades unfolded in the classroom against the background of Periclean Athens. None of my immature concepts of classification (good man, bad man, wise man, foolish man) seemed to define Alcibiades adequately, or even to afford a reliable clue to his enigmatic image.

The more I read about him and wondered about him, the more he arrested my attention and challenged my imagination. All reports agreed that he was one of the chief military and political leaders of Athens in her period of supreme greatness and classic splendor during the fifth century BCE. This man led me to ponder at a very early age on many questions for which I have not yet found satisfactory answers. According to my high school history book:

> He belonged to one of the noblest families of Athens, and was a near kinsman of Pericles. Though still young, he was influential because of his high birth and his fascinating personality. His talents were brilliant in all directions; but he was lawless and violent, and followed no motive but self-interest and self-indulgence. Through his influence Athens allied herself with Argos, Elis, and Mantinea against the Lacedaemonians and their allies.

The result of this alliance led Athens into defeat and disaster, but Alcibiades on many occasions showed outstanding talent and succeeded brilliantly in many important affairs. Apparently he had great personal charm and easily aroused strong feelings of admiration and affection in others.

Though usually able to accomplish with ease any aim he might choose, he seemed capriciously to court disaster and, perhaps at the behest of some trivial impulse, to go out of his way to bring down defeat upon his own projects. Plutarch refers to him thus:

> It has been said not untruly that the friendship which Socrates felt for him has much contributed to his fame, and certain it is, that, though we have no account from any writer concerning the mother of Nicias or Demosthenes, of Lamachus or Phormion, of Thrasybulus or Theratnenes, notwithstanding these were all illustrious men of the same period, yet we know even the nurse of Alcibiades, that her country was Lacedaemon, and her name Amycla; and that Zopyrus was his teacher and attendant; the one being recorded by Antistheries, and the other by Plato.

In the *Symposium*, one of his most celebrated dialogues, Plato introduces Alcibiades by having him appear with a group of intoxicated revelers and burst in upon those at the banquet who are engaged in philosophical discussion. Alcibiades, as presented here by Plato, appears at times to advocate as well as symbolize external beauty and ephemeral satisfactions as opposed to the eternal verities. Nevertheless, Plato gives Alcibiades the role of recognizing and expounding upon the inner virtue and spiritual worth of Socrates and of acclaiming this as far surpassing the readily discerned attainments of more obviously attractive and superficially impressive men. Plato devotes almost all of the last quarter of the Symposium to Alcibiades and his conversation with Socrates. His great charm and physical beauty are emphasized repeatedly here. The personal attractiveness of Alcibiades is also dwelt upon by Plutarch:

> It is not, perhaps, material to say anything of the beauty of Alcibiades, only that it bloomed with him at all stages of his life, in his infancy, in his youth, and in his manhood; and, in the peculiar character belonging to each of these periods, gave him in everyone of them, a grace and charm. What Euripides says: "of all fair things the autumn, too, is fair" … is by no means universally true. But it happened so with Alcibiades amongst few others. …

Early in his career he played a crucial role in gaining important victories for Athens. Later, after fighting against his native city and contributing substantially to her final disaster, he returned to favor, won important victories again for her and was honored with her highest offices. In the *Encyclopaedia Brittanica* (1949) I read:

Alcibiades possessed great charm and brilliant abilities but was absolutely unprincipled. His advice whether to Athens or to Sparta, oligarchs or democrats, was dictated by selfish motives, and the Athenians could never trust him sufficiently to take advantage of his talents.

And Thucydides says:

> They feared the extremes to which he carried his lawless self-indulgence, and ... though his talents as a military commander were unrivalled, they entrusted the administration of the war to Others; and so they speedily shipwrecked the state.

Plutarch repeatedly emphasizes the positive and impressive qualities of Alcibiades:

> It was manifest that the many wellborn persons who were continually seeking his company, and making their court to him, were attracted and captivated by his brilliant and extraordinary beauty only. But the affection which Socrates entertained for him is a great evidence of the natural noble qualities and good disposition of the boy, which Socrates, indeed, detected both in and under his personal beauty; and, fearing that his wealth and station, and the great number both of strangers and Athenians who flattered and caressed him, might at last corrupt him, resolved, if possible, to interpose, and preserve so hopeful a plant from perishing in the flower, before its fruit came to perfection.

The same writer also cites many examples of unattractive behavior, in which Alcibiades is shown responding with unprovoked and arbitrary insolence to those who sought to do him honor. Let us note one of these incidents:

> As in particular to Anitas, the son of Anthernion, who was very fond of him and invited him to an entertainment which he had prepared for some strangers. Alcibiades refused the invitation, but having drunk to excess in his own house with some of his companions, went thither with them to play some frolic, and standing at the door of the room where the guests were enjoying themselves and seeing the tables covered with gold and silver cups, he commanded his servants to take away the one-half of them and carry them to his own house. And, then, disdaining so much as to enter into the room himself, as soon as he had done this, went away. The company was indignant, and exclaimed at this rude and insulting conduct; Anitas, however, said, on the contrary, that Alcibiades had shown great consideration and tenderness in taking only a part when he might have taken all.

Despite his talents and many attractive features some incidents appear even in his very early life that suggest instability, a disregard for accepted rules or commitments and a reckless tendency to seize arbitrarily what may appeal to him at the moment. Plutarch tells us:

> Once being hard pressed in wrestling, and fearing to be thrown, he got the hand of his antagonist to his mouth, and bit it with all his force; when the other loosed his hold presently, and said, "You bite, Alcibiades, like a woman "No," replied he, "like a lion."

On another occasion it is reported that Alcibiades with other boys was playing with dice in the street. A loaded cart which had been approaching drew near just as it was his turn to throw. To quote again from Plutarch:

> At first he called to the driver to stop, because he was to throw in the way over which the cart was to pass; but the man giving him no attention and driving on, when the rest of the boys divided and gave way, Alcibiades threw himself on his face before the cart and, stretching himself out, bade the carter pass on now if he would; which so startled the man, that he put back his horses, while all that saw it were terrified, and, crying out, ran to assist Alcibiades.

Alcibiades, one of the most prominent figures in Athens, an extremely influential leader with important successes to his credit, became the chief advocate for the memorable expedition against Sicily. He entered enthusiastically into this venture urging it upon the Athenians partly from policy, it seems, and partly from his private ambition. Though this expedition resulted in catastrophe and played a major role in the end of Athenian power and glory, many have felt that if Alcibiades had been left in Sicily in his position of command he might have led the great armada to victory. If so, this might well have insured for Athens indefinitely the supreme power of the ancient world. The brilliant ability often demonstrated by Alcibiades lends credence to such an opinion. On the other hand, his inconsistency and capriciousness make it difficult, indeed, to feel confident that his presence would necessarily have brought success to the Athenian cause. The magnitude of its failure has recently drawn this comment from Peter Green in *Armada From Athens*:

> It was more than a defeat; it was a defilement. There, mindless, brutish, and terrified, dying like animals, without dignity or pride, were Pericles' countrymen, citizens of the greatest imperial power Greece had ever known. In that ... destruction ... Athens lost her imperial pride forever. The shell of splendid self-

confidence was shattered: something more than an army died in Sicily. Athens' imperial pride had been destroyed and her easy self-assertion with it. Aegospotami merely confirmed the ineluctable sentence imposed on the banks of the Assinarus. Pindar's violet-crowned city had been cut down to size and an ugly tarnish now dulled the bright Periclean charisma. The great experiment in democratic imperialism that strangest of all paradoxes-was finally discredited.

If Athens had succeeded in the expedition against Syracuse the history of Greece and perhaps even the history of all Europe might have been substantially different.

Shortly before the great Athenian fleet and army sailed on the Sicilian expedition an incident occurred that has never been satisfactorily explained. Now when Athens was staking her future on a monumental and dangerous venture there was imperative need for solidarity of opinion and for confidence in the three leaders to whom so much had been entrusted. At this tense and exquisitely inopportune time the sacred statues of Hermes throughout the city were mutilated in a wholesale desecration.

This unprovoked act of folly and outrage disturbed the entire populace and aroused superstitious qualms and fears that support of the gods would be withdrawn at a time of crucial need. Alcibiades was strongly suspected of the senseless sacrilege. Though proof was not established that he had committed this deed which demoralized the Athenians, the possibility that Alcibiades, their brilliant leader, might be guilty of such an idle and irresponsible outrage shook profoundly the confidence of the expeditionary force and of the government. Many who knew him apparently felt that such an act might have been carried out by Alcibiades impulsively and without any adequate reason but merely as an idle gesture of bravado, a prank that might demonstrate what he could get away with if it should suit his fancy. Definite evidence emerged at this time to show that he had been profaning the Eleusinian mysteries by imitating them or caricaturing them for the amusement of his friends. This no doubt strengthened suspicion against him as having played a part in mutilating the sacred statues.

On a number of other occasions his bad judgment and his self-centered whims played a major role in bringing disasters upon Athens and upon himself. Though this brilliant leader often appeared as a zealous and incorruptible patriot, numerous incidents strongly indicate that at other times he put self-interest first and that sometimes even the feeble lure of some minor objective or the mere prompting of caprice caused him to ignore the welfare and safety of his native land and to abandon lightly all standards of loyalty and honor.

No substantial evidence has ever emerged to indicate that Alcibiades was guilty of the sacrilegious mutilation of the statues. He asked for an immediate trial, but it was decided not to delay the sailing of the fleet for this. After he reached Syracuse, Alcibiades was summoned to return to Athens to face these charges. On the way back he deserted the Athenian cause, escaped to Sparta, and joined the enemy to fight against his native city.

It has been argued that Alcibiades could not have been guilty of the mutilation since, as a leader of the expedition and its chief advocate, he would have so much to lose by a senseless and impious act that might jeopardize its success. On the other hand his career shows many incidents of unprovoked and, potentially, self-damaging folly carried out more or less as a whim, perhaps in defiance of authority, or as an arrogant gesture to show his immunity to ordinary rules or restrictions. It sometimes looked as though the very danger of a useless and uninviting deed might, in itself, tempt him to flaunt a cavalier defiance of rules that bind other men. If Alcibiades did play a part in this piece of egregious folly it greatly augments his resemblance to the patients described in this book. Indeed it is difficult to see how anyone but a psychopath might, in his position, participate in such an act.

In Sparta Alcibiades made many changes to identify himself with the ways and styles of the enemy. In Athens he had been notable for his fine raiment and for worldly splendor and extravagance. On these characteristics Plutarch comments thus:

> But with all these words and deeds and with all this sagacity and eloquence, he mingled the exorbitant luxury and wantonness in his eating and drinking and dissolute living; wore long, purple robes like a woman, which dragged after him as he went through the marketplace, caused the planks of his galley to be cut away, that he might lie the softer, his bed not being placed on the boards but hanging upon girths. His shield, again, which was richly gilded had not the usual ensigns of the Athenians, but a Cupid holding a thunderbolt in his hand, was painted upon it. The sight of all this made the people of good repute in the city feel disgust and abhorrence and apprehension also, at his free living and his contempt of law as things monstrous in themselves and indicating designs of usurpation.

In contrast to his appearance and his habits in the old environment we find this comment by Plutarch on Alcibiades after he had deserted the Athenian cause and come to live in Sparta and throw all his brilliant talents into the war against his native land:

> The renown which he earned by these public services, not to Athens, but to

Sparta, was equaled by the admiraton he attracted to his private life. He captivated and won over everybody by his conformity to Spartan habits. People who saw him wearing his hair cut close and bathing in cold water, eating coarse meal and dining on black broth, doubted, or rather could not believe that he had ever had a cook in his house or had ever seen a perfumer or had ever worn a mantle of Milesian purple. For he had, as it was observed, this peculiar talent and artifice of gaining men's affection, that he could at once comply with and really embrace and enter into the habits and ways of life, and change faster than the chameleon; one color, indeed, they say, the chameleon cannot assume; he cannot himself appear white. But, Alcibiades, whether with good men or with bad, could adapt himself to his company and equally wear the appearances of virtue or vice. At Sparta, he was devoted to athletic exercises, was frugal and reserved: in Ionia, luxurious, gay and indolent; in Thrace, always drinking; in Thessaly, ever on horseback; and when he lived with Tisaphernes, the king of Persia's satrap he exceeded the Persians themselves in magnificence and pomp. Not that his natural disposition changed so easily, nor that his real character was so variable, but whether he was sensible that by pursuing his own inclinations he might give offense to those with whom he had occasion to converse, he transformed himself into any shape and adopted any fashion that he observed to be agreeable to them.

At Sparta Alcibiades seemed to strive in every way to help the enemy defeat and destroy Athens. He induced them to send military aid promptly to the Syracusans and also aroused them to renew the war directly against Athens. He made them aware of the great importance of fortifying Decelea, a place very near Athens, from which she was extremely vulnerable to attack. The Spartans followed his counsel in these matters and, by taking the steps he advised, wrought serious damage to the Athenian cause. The vindictive and persistent efforts of this brilliant traitor may have played a substantial part in the eventual downfall of Athens. Even before he left Sicily for Sparta Alcibiades had begun to work against his native land in taking steps to prevent Messina from falling into the hands of the Athenians.

Eventually a good many of the Spartans began to distrust Alcibiades. Among this group was the king, Agis. According to Plutarch:

> ... While Agis was absent and abroad with the army, [Alcibiades] corrupted his wife, Timea, and had a child born by her. Nor did she even deny it, but when she was brought to bed of a son, called him in public, Leotychides, but amongst her confidants and attendants, would whisper that his name was Alcibiades, to such a degree was she transported by her passion for him. He,

on the other side, would say in his valiant way, he had not done this thing out of mere wantonness of insult, nor to gratify a passion, but that his race might one day be kings over the Lacedaemonians.

It became increasingly unpleasant for Alcibiades in Sparta despite his great successes and the admiration he still evoked in many. Plutarch says:

> But Agis was his enemy, hating him for having dishonored his wife, but also impatient of his glory, as almost every success was ascribed to Alcibiades. Others, also, of the more powerful and ambitious among the Spartans were possessed with jealousy of him and prevailed with the magistrates in the city to send orders ... that he should be killed.

Alcibiades, however, learned of this, and fled to Asia Minor for security with the satrap of the king of Persia, Tisaphernes. Here he found security and again displayed his great abilities and his extraordinary charm. According to Plutarch:

> [He] immediately became the most influential person about him; for this barbarian [Tisaphernes], not being himself sincere, but a lover of guile and wickedness, admired his address and wonderful subtlety. And, indeed, the charm of daily intercourse with him was more than any character could resist or any disposition escape. Even those who feared and envied him, could not but take delight and have a sort of kindness for him when they saw him and were in his company, so that Tisaphernes, otherwise a cruel character, and above all other Persians, a hater of the Greeks, was yet so won by the flatteries of Alcibiades that he set himself even to exceed him in responding to them. The most beautiful of his parks containing salubrious streams and meadows where he had built pavilions and places of retirement, royally and exquisitely adorned, received by his direction the name of Alcibiades and was always so called and so spoken of.
>
> Thus, Alcibiades, quitting the interest of the Spartans, whom he could no longer trust because he stood in fear of Agis, the king, endeavored to do them ill offices and render them odious to Tisaphernes, who, by his means, was hindered from assisting them vigorously and from finally ruining the Athenians. For his advice was to furnish them but sparingly with money and so wear them out, and consume them insensibly; when they had wasted their strength upon one another, they would both become ready to submit to the king.

It is not remarkable to learn that Alcibiades left the service of the Persians. It does seem to me remarkable, however, after his long exile from Athens, his allegiance to her enemies and the grievous damage he had done her, that *he was enthusiastically welcomed back to Athens, that he again led Athenian forces to brilliant victories, and that he was, indeed, given supreme command of the Athenian military and naval forces.* His welcome back to Athens was enthusiastic. According to Plutarch, "The people crowned him with crowns of gold, and created him general, both by land and by sea." He is described as "coming home from so long an exile, and such variety of misfortune, in the style of revelers breaking up from a drinking party." Despite this, many of the Athenians did not fully trust him, and apparently without due cause, this time, he was dismissed from his high position of command. He later retired to Asia Minor where he was murdered at 46 years of age, according to some reports for "having debauched a young lady of a noble house."

Despite the widespread admiration that Alcibiades could so easily arouse, skeptical comments were made about him even before his chief failures occurred. According to Plutarch, "It was not said amiss by Archestratus, that Greece could not support a second Alcibiades." Plutarch also quotes Tinton as saying, "Go on boldly, my son, and increase in credit with the people, for thou wilt one day bring them calamities enough." Of the Athenians attitude toward Alcibiades, Aristophanes wrote: "They love and hate and cannot do without him."

The character of Alcibiades looms in the early dawn of history as an enigmatic paradox. He undoubtedly disconcerted and puzzled his contemporaries, and his conduct seems to have brought upon him widely differing judgments. During the many centuries since his death historians have seemed fascinated by his career but never quite able to interpret his personality. Brilliant and persuasive, he was able to succeed in anything he wished to accomplish. After spectacular achievement he often seemed, carelessly or almost deliberately, to throw away all that he had gained, through foolish decisions or unworthy conduct for which adequate motivation cannot be demonstrated and, indeed, can scarcely be imagined. Senseless pranks or mere nose-thumbing gestures of derision seemed at times to draw him from serious responsibilities and cause him to abandon major goals as well as the commitments of loyalty and honor.

Apparently his brilliance, charm, and promise captivated Socrates, generally held to be the greatest teacher and the wisest man of antiquity. Though Alcibiades is reported to have been the favorite disciple and most cherished friend of the master it can hardly be said that Socrates succeeded in teaching him to apply even ordinary wisdom consistently in the conduct of his life or to avoid follies that would have been shunned even by the stupid.

According to the *Encyclopaedia Brittanica* (1949), "He was an admirer of

Socrates, who saved his life at Potidaea (432), a service which Alcibiades repaid at Delium; but he could not practice his master's virtues, and there is no doubt that *the example of Alcibiades strengthened the charges brought against Socrates of corrupting the youth."*

When we look back upon what has been recorded of Alcibiades we are led to suspect that he had the gift of every talent except that of using them consistently to achieve any sensible aim or in behalf of any discernible cause. Though it would hardly be convincing to claim that we can establish a medical diagnosis, or a full psychiatric explanation, of this public figure who lived almost two and a half thousand years ago, there are many points in the incomplete records of his life available to us that strongly suggest Alcibiades may have been a spectacular example of what during recent decades we have, in bewilderment and amazement, come to designate as the psychopath.

During this brief period Greece, and Athens especially, produced architecture, sculpture, drama, and poetry that have seldom if ever been surpassed. Perhaps Greece also produced in Alcibiades the most impressive and brilliant, the most truly classic example of this still inexplicable pattern of human life.[465]

*   *   *

Reading something like that gives history an all-new perspective, doesn't it? Not only may psychopaths have been generated in mutations caused by cometary bombardment, it seems that during times of increasing comet flux, repeatedly through history, as we will see, they become very active. Difficult times, as I have said, refine both the best and the worst in humanity. We'll be coming back to this topic, so hang on, we've got a little bit more ground to cover.

Plato 427 – 347 BCE

Plato was related through his mother to Critias, one of the Thirty who ruled Athens following the end of the Peloponnesian war, and who was subsequently killed in the retaking of the city by the wealthy elite. Diogenes tells us that Plato was, essentially, the product of the rape of his mother by his father and his followers were fond of pointing out that he was born on the birthday of Apollo. His birth name was actually Aristocles, but was renamed Plato because of his 'robust' build. One gets the impression that he

---

465. Cleckley (1941, 1988), *The Mask of Sanity.*

was built like a Sumo wrestler. (He was, in fact, a wrestler.) He was also noted for having a weak, high voice. Based on just this description, which compares to that of many ancient descriptions of a eunuch, one cannot help but wonder...

Supposedly he studied under Heraclitus, but that is unlikely since Heraclitus probably never went to Athens. We are also told that Heraclitus "hated the Athenians and his fellow Ephesians..." and went off to wander in the mountains. Plato became the student of Socrates at the age of 20 and Socrates died when he was 28. So actually, very little of his intellectual life was even involved with Socrates, though he has become the chief purveyor of what Socrates may have thought or intended or said. It's surprising that more people don't have a problem with that. He did some traveling about, including visiting the Pythagoreans in Italy, in particular Philolaus and Eurytus. Following this, he went to Egypt in the company of Euripides, probably picking his brain all the way.

As mentioned in the discussion of Pythagoras, Diogenes Laërtius reports that Satyrus[466] and others said that Plato wrote to Dion in Sicily, instructing him to purchase three Pythagorean books from Philolaus for 100 minae.[467] In the same paragraph (the obvious connection being things Sicilian), he tells us that Alcimus reports that Plato "derived great assistance from Epicharmus the Comic poet, for he transcribed a great deal from him..." This Alcimus is either the Greek rhetorician from around 300 BCE or a Sicilian historian about whom almost nothing is known.[468] I would suggest the latter since the subject is a Sicilian comic poet who wrote in a Sicilian dialect, and only another Sicilian might be qualified to recognize the plagiarism. This statement is followed by an example from Alcimus where he, apparently in humor, wrote about "objects of sense and objects of thought" and pointed out the plagiarism. Diogenes then – via Alcimus – presents a comic dialogue, evidently by Epicharmus. Further example is given comparing things Plato said to the words of Epicharmus who, we must remember, was writing comedy! Diogenes patches over this at the end of the discussion by saying: "That Epicharmus himself was fully conscious of his wisdom can also be seen from the lines in which he foretells that he will have an imitator":

---

466. A peripatetic philosopher and historian, whose biographies of famous people are frequently referred to by Diogenes Laërtius and Athenaeus. The Peripatetic school was a school of philosophy in Ancient Greece. Its teachings derived from its founder, the Greek philosopher, Aristotle, and Peripatetic is a name given to his followers.
467. Four minae was the average annual wage of an agricultural worker.
468. Schmitz (1867), 'Alcimus', in William Smith, *Dictionary of Greek and Roman Biography and Mythology*, 1, p. 102.

And as I think – for when I think anything I know it full well – that my words will some day be remembered; someone will take them and free them from the metre in which they are now set, nay, will give them instead a purple robe, embroidering it with fine phrases; and, being invincible, *he will make every one else an easy prey.*[469]

Plato made three trips to Sicily and on his first trip, apparently, was 'forced' to become the lover of the king Dionysius. Plato allegedly called him a tyrant and said other nasty things, at which point Dionysius had him arrested. So the story goes. He was brought to trial and barely escaped death, though he was condemned to be sold as a slave. Someone paid the price and sent him home to his friends, probably telling them to keep him out of trouble. I think, based on how he later wrote about tyrants being against pederasty, and how he himself was an avowed 'lover of young boys', that the charges were more likely to have been along that line; possibly he rejected the advances of Dionysius because he wasn't young enough.

Then Diogenes says something rather curious. One variation of the story that he gives is that the ruler, Dionysius, asked Pollis, a visiting Spartan admiral and ambassador, to take Plato off his hands. Pollis took Plato to the slave market on the island of Aegina, and put him up for sale. Plato was miraculously redeemed and then we learn:

> Pollis, however, is stated to have been defeated by Chabrias and afterwards to have been drowned at Helice, *his treatment of the philosopher having provoked the wrath of heaven...* Dionysius, indeed, could not rest. On learning the facts he wrote and enjoined upon Plato not to speak evil of him. And Plato replied that he had not the leisure to keep Dionysius in his mind.[470]

Regarding this event of the drowning of Pollis, we find that something very interesting was going on. It seems that there was a terrible earthquake and tsunami in 372/373 BCE and the entire city of Helike (Helice) disappeared, submerged in the sea! The much later 2nd century historian, Aelian, records only that a tsunami swallowed up ten Spartan triremes (galley ships).

The entire story looks very suspicious and from our Chronicle of Comets we read:

373-372 BCE, Winter, Greece. A comet was seen in the west at the time of

---

469. Alcimus, quoted by Diogenes Laërtius, III. 17-19.
470. Diogenes Laërtius.

the great earthquake and tidal wave at Achaea, Greece. From the Greek descriptions of the comet's motion, Pingre infers that its perihelion was located in Virgo or Libra and that its perihelion distance was quite small. Pingre considers this comet to be the one the Greek Ephorus reported to have split into two pieces. The accounts given by Aristotle and Seneca suggest the comet was seen in the winter of 373-372 BCE while the account of Diodorus Siculus, an historian of the second half of the first century BCE, suggests the comet was seen in the following year. (Barrett, 5) [471]

Aristotle mentions four comets in his book *Meteorologica*, written around the year 330 BCE. Apparently, only one of them stood out enough to be called the 'Great Comet'.

> The great comet, which appeared about the time of the earthquake in Achaea and the tidal wave, rose in the west ... The great comet ... appeared during winter in clear frosty weather in the west, in the archonship of Asteius: on the first night it was not visible as it set before the sun did, but it was visible on the second, being the least distance behind the sun that would allow it to be seen, and setting immediately. Its light stretched across a third of the sky in a great band, as it were, and so was called a path. It rose as high as Orion's belt, and there disappeared. [472]

Since the discussion is mainly about the risings of the comet, how on the first night it was too close to the Sun, and on the second was the least distance from the sun to be seen, it's obvious that he is recording the progress of its risings until, finally, "it rose as high as Orion's belt and then disappeared." What this can mean is uncertain. Diodorus' description tells us that:

> ... there was seen in the heavens during the course of many nights a great blazing torch which was named from its shape a flaming beam. Some of the students of nature ascribed the origin of the torch to natural causes, voicing the opinion that such apparitions occur of necessity at appointed times, and that in these matters the Chaldeans in Babylon and the other astrologers succeed in making accurate prophecies ... this torch had such brilliancy... and its light such strength that it cast shadows on the earth similar to those cast by the moon. [473]

---

471. Yeomans, op. cit.
472. Aristotle, *Meteorologica*, Book I.
473. Seargent (2009), *The Greatest Comets in History: Broom Stars and Celestial Scimitars.*

It is noteworthy that a few scholars think that this event is what inspired Plato to write the 'myth of Atlantis'.[474, 475, 476, 477] I have a different view, however. I think that Plato got his background for the myth of Atlantis from the lost books of Pythagoras and possibly from discussions with Socrates regarding the work of Heraclitus that required a "Delian diver" to plumb.

It looks like a historical cover-up in the story of Plato's drama in Sicily. (We will shortly come to another 'slave story' that bears a remarkable resemblance to Plato's experience according to Diogenes). I also notice that the destruction of the Temple of Apollo in Delphi, which happened at the same time, is not included in the tale. The bottom line seems to be that there probably was no 'admiral Pollis', but the word was used in the other sense: Polis, a city was drowned fifteen years after Plato's supposed brush with perpetual servitude! This sort of historical prestidigitation[478] is just a little foretaste: we are going to find that the term 'wrath of heaven' was used quite often to describe what can definitely be supposed to be Tunguska-like overhead comet explosions that also cause earthquakes. In the above comet sighting from Yeoman's book, notice that the comet was seen to split and that its "perihelion distance was quite small." Of course, it wouldn't even have to be a Tunguska-like event; a good sized comet coming close could cause any number of things according to plasma cosmology principles. But since there are no other reports from that year, even in the Far East, I'm putting my money on the airburst. Goodness, the things you find when you read history carefully!

Plato and Atlantis

Plato was 23 years old at the end of the Peloponnesian war. He had seen many things during his most impressionable years, including the violent overthrow and death of his uncle, and soon would witness the execution of his teacher. If Pythagoras, Heraclitus, Anaxagoras and Socrates, as well as Critias and other members of the Thirty, were "Delian divers" who made certain 'cosmic connections', and Plato realized that those who talked about these things came to a bad end, usually death, no doubt he would have had the idea to handle this information, these ideas, very carefully.

And so, 15 years after his trip to Sicily, after having gone to the trouble to obtain the three books of Pythagoras, after studying Heraclitus, he must

---

474. Caven (1990), *Dionysios I: War-Lord of Sicily*.
475. Ellis (1998), *Imagining Atlantis*.
476. Forsythe (1980), *Atlantis: The Making of a Myth*.
477. Taylor (1928), *A Commentary on Plato's Timaeus*.
478. A show of skill or deceitful cleverness.

have known the score about the earthquake and destruction of Helice. But his hands were tied. Who could he tell? Maybe his story of Atlantis was the only way he could figure out to pass this knowledge on to others: as a sort of fairy tale.

In the previous volume of this *Secret History* series, I discussed Plato's account of the destruction of Atlantis from a different perspective. With all the additional information that has become available since that time, my view has been somewhat expanded. As we now know from the scientific work presented in this volume, the global cometary disasters that destroyed Plato's Atlantis did actually occur pretty close to the date he gave for them. So, in light of all that, and other things we have uncovered, I think we can safely say that Plato had something to base his story on, but it probably was not an 'Egyptian priest'. *Timaeus* and *Critias*, written by Plato some time around 360 BCE (39 years after the death of Socrates and 12 years after the great comet of 373/2) are the only existing written records which specifically refer to *Atlantis*. Up to that point in time, the great epic destruction stories were the *Iliad* and *Odyssey*, and the city was Troy.

Let's look at the main characters of the dialogues. First, there is Plato's teacher who died under a repressive regime. Then there is Hermocrates, who was a Syracusan general during the Athenians' Sicilian expedition that ended so disastrously. Hermocrates is referenced in Thucydides where he gave a speech before the beginning of the war, demanding that the Sicilian Greeks stop their quarreling. In 415, it was he who formed the coalition that included even non-Sicilian cities, in alliance against the aggressor, Athens. Francis Cornford writes:

> It is curious to reflect that, while Critias is to recount how the prehistoric Athens of nine thousand years ago had repelled the invasion from Atlantis and saved the Mediterranean peoples from slavery, Hermocrates would be remembered by the Athenians as the man who had repulsed their own greatest effort at imperialist expansion.[479]

Timaeus, the character who gives his name to the title of the dialogue, was a Pythagorean philosopher living c. 420-380. He is credited with a lost work entitled *On the Soul of the Universe*. Considering what Heraclitus wrote about the 'Cosmic Mind', that is certainly suggestive.

The final main character is Plato's great uncle, Critias, who was killed in the overthrow of the Thirty. According to Polybius, he asserted that "reli-

---

479. Cornford (1937), *Before and after Socrates*, p. 2.

gion was a deliberate imposture devised by some cunning man for political ends." [480] This reminds us of two things: 1) Thucydides' description of how the Athenians, during the plague at the beginning of the Peloponnesian war, felt abandoned by the gods and fell away from their religious practice, which was one of the things the wealthy elite used to control their behavior. The Athenians clearly understood the plague as evidence that they were in the wrong, despite the fact that their elite rulers were demanding the prosecution of the war for reasons of greed and power; 2) After the overthrow of the Thirty, who had been his friends and associates, Socrates constantly criticised the democratic government. It has been suggested that Socrates' criticism was a threat to the newly reestablished democracy and it certainly may have been in a very particular context if he agreed with his friend Critias that "religion was a deliberate imposture devised by some cunning man for political ends." Speaking the truth about the Natural History of the Earth as revealed by Heraclitus and Pythagoras may very well be what got Socrates killed.

I would suggest that, by the very selection of the main players in the dialogues, Plato is trying to convey a message: the very message that was contained in the works of Pythagoras and Heraclitus.

In response to a prior talk by Socrates about ideal societies, Timaeus and Critias agree to entertain Socrates with a tale that is "not a fiction but a true story." The story is about the conflict between the ancient Athenians and the Atlanteans 9,000 years before Plato's time. Knowledge of the ancient times was apparently forgotten by the Athenians of Plato's day, and the form the story of Atlantis took in Plato's account was that Egyptian priests conveyed it to Solon. Solon passed the tale to Dropides, the great-grandfather of Critias. Critias learned of it from his grandfather, also named Critias, son of Dropides, and was now going to tell it. Basically, the story tells how, in a long-ago war made by greedy, power-mad Atlanteans, the Athenians were the good guys. The story abruptly ends with Zeus – the god of gods – seeing the corruption of the Atlanteans, determined to chastise them. Zeus begins to speak; but what he says, and everything that follows in the *Critias*[481], has been lost. Well, why are we not surprised?

One thing that I find fascinating is that Herodotus, during the second half of the 5th century BCE, almost a hundred years before Plato wrote about Atlantis, reported in the second book of his history that certain Egyptian priests asserted that within historical ages and since Egypt became a king-

---

480. Rosenmeyer (1949), 'The family of Critias'.
481. One of Plato's later dialogues.

dom, "four times in this period (so they told me) the sun rose contrary to his wont; twice he rose where he now sets, and twice he set where he now rises."

So, I think we may assume that Plato took the cue from Herodotus and made up the name and the details of the civilization, and the moral of the story was that a wonderful civilization that began so well could go so wrong and bring cosmic destruction upon its head.

A few of the details that Plato included are:

There have been, and will be again, many destructions of mankind arising out of many causes; the greatest have been brought about by the agencies of fire and water, and other lesser ones by innumerable other causes. There is a story, which even you have preserved, that once upon a time Phaeton, the son of Helios, having yoked the steeds in his father's chariot, because he was not able to drive them in the path of his father, burnt up all that was upon the earth, and was himself *destroyed by a thunderbolt*. Now this has the form of a myth, but really signifies *a declination of the bodies moving in the heavens around the earth, and a great conflagration of things upon the earth, which recurs after long intervals*; at such times those who live upon the mountains and in dry and lofty places are more liable to destruction than those who dwell by rivers or on the seashore …

When, on the other hand, the gods purge the earth with a deluge of water, the survivors in your country are herdsmen and shepherds who dwell on the mountains, but those who, like you, live in cities are carried by the rivers into the sea. … The fact is, that wherever the extremity of winter frost or of summer does not prevent, mankind exists, sometimes in greater, sometimes in lesser numbers. …

Whereas just when you and other nations are beginning to be provided with letters and the other requisites of civilized life, *after the usual interval, the stream from heaven, like a pestilence, comes pouring down*, and leaves only those of you who are destitute of letters and education; and so you have to begin all over again like children, and know nothing of what happened in ancient times. …

In the first place you remember a single deluge only, but there were many previous ones; in the next place, you do not know that there formerly dwelt in your land the fairest and noblest race of men which ever lived, and that *you and your whole city are descended from a small seed or remnant of them which survived*. And this was unknown to you, because, for many generations, *the survivors of that destruction died, leaving no written word*. For there was a time, Solon, before the great deluge of all, when the city which now is Athens was first in war and in every way the best governed of all cities, is said to have performed the noblest deeds and to have had the fairest constitution of any of which tradition tells, under the face of heaven....

Many great and wonderful deeds are recorded of your state in our histories. But one of them exceeds all the rest in greatness and valour. For these histories tell of a mighty power which unprovoked made an expedition against the whole of Europe and Asia, and to which your city put an end. This power came forth out of the Atlantic Ocean... This vast power, gathered into one, endeavoured to subdue at a blow our country and yours and the whole of the region within the straits; and then, Solon, your country shone forth, in the excellence of her virtue and strength, among all mankind. She was pre-eminent in courage and military skill, and was the leader of the Hellenes. And when the rest fell off from her, being compelled to stand alone, after having undergone the very extremity of danger, she defeated and triumphed over the invaders, and preserved from slavery those who were not yet subjugated, and generously liberated all the rest of us who dwell within the pillars....

But afterwards there occurred violent earthquakes and floods; and in a single day and night of misfortune all your warlike men in a body sank into the earth, and the island of Atlantis in like manner disappeared in the depths of the sea. ...

I have told you briefly, Socrates, what the aged Critias heard from Solon and related to us. And when you were speaking yesterday about your city and citizens, the tale which I have just been repeating to you came into my mind, and I remarked with astonishment how, by some mysterious coincidence, *you agreed in almost every particular with the narrative of Solon*; but I did not like to speak at the moment. For a long time had elapsed, and I had forgotten too much; I thought that I must first of all run over the narrative in my own mind, and then I would speak. [Emphasis, mine]

Here we find another interesting clue. Critias has just told us that Socrates was discussing the very things that are included in this story – that *everything Socrates had been saying the previous day* "agreed in almost every particular with the narrative of Solon."

And so I readily assented to your request yesterday, considering that in all such cases the chief difficulty is to find *a tale suitable to our purpose*, and that with such a tale we should be fairly well provided. And therefore, as Hermocrates has told you, on my way home yesterday I at once communicated the tale to my companions as I remembered it; and after I left them, during the night by thinking I recovered nearly the whole it. Truly, as is often said, *the lessons of our childhood make wonderful impression on our memories*; for I am not sure that I could remember all the discourse of yesterday, but I should be much surprised if I forgot any of these things which I have heard very long ago. I listened at the time with childlike interest to the old man's narrative; he was very ready to teach me, and I asked him again and again to repeat his words, so that like an indelible picture they were branded into my mind.

As soon as the day broke, I rehearsed them as he spoke them to my companions, that they, as well as myself, might have something to say. And now, Socrates, to make an end my preface, I am ready to tell you the whole tale. I will give you not only the general heads, but the particulars, as they were told to me.

The city and citizens, which you yesterday described to us in fiction, we will now transfer to the world of reality. It shall be the ancient city of Athens, and we will suppose that the citizens whom you imagined, were our veritable ancestors, of whom the priest spoke; they will perfectly harmonise, and there will be no inconsistency in saying that the citizens of your republic are these ancient Athenians. Let us divide the subject among us, and all endeavour according to our ability gracefully to execute the task which you have imposed upon us. Consider then, Socrates, if this narrative is suited to the purpose, or whether we should seek for some other instead.[482]

And we come to the final understanding that conveys to us the secret of the story of Atlantis: that it did not actually come from an Egyptian priest, but that this was a story that was created to "execute the task which you [Socrates] have imposed upon us," which was to veil in fiction something that was Truth. Does this mean that they were 'making it up'? No, indeed. It means that Plato was attempting to find a vehicle for the history that would ensure its preservation. I may be giving Plato too much credit, he may have merely wanted to capitalize on the Pythagoreans for his own aggrandizement, but the facts of the dialogues suggest otherwise. It was political commentary, history, and ethics in relation to the cosmos, all rolled into one. Another clue is Herodotus.

Herodotus wrote around 450/60 BCE. He had calculated that the Egyptians were claiming that their nation had existed 11,000 years before his time. That is amazingly close to 12,900 years ago, i.e. 10900 BCE, at which point we are fairly certain the cometary event occurred which was remembered as the Flood of Noah, discussed in detail by Firestone, West and Warwick-Smith and others since. But we know from the work of other scientists, including Baillie, Bailey, Clube and Napier, that there were other, periodically repeating events – some greater, some localized – like Tunguska

---

482. Plato, *Timaeus*, translated by Jowett (2012).

or a number of Tunguska-like events. We also know that there are myths and legends about these events that survived amazingly intact into the early 20th century, and may survive still. So surely, there must have been a general awareness of these things in the times of the ancient Greeks by at least a certain set of people, if not amongst the wider public with their penchant for myths and legends. This is the sort of thing that Herodotus was collecting in his 'history'. Since Herodotus often speaks of Pythagoras, it may very well be that he was quite aware of what may have brought about the downfall of the Pythagoreans, and thus brought the topic up in a way that would protect him from their fate, i.e. putting it in the mouth of an Egyptian priest as a fantastic claim. I would even suggest that Plato, by doing the same thing, utilizing an Egyptian priest as the source, was *explicitly referencing what Herodotus had written*, that is, "four times in this period (so they told me) the sun rose contrary to his wont; twice he rose where he now sets, and twice he set where he now rises." Obviously, we are not talking about a pole flip here, but a blazing, sun-like, destructive comet approaching the Earth from the West, a comet as bright as the Sun, or even brighter, sending out thunderbolts, shedding flaming rocks and dust, and roaring with the sound of a thousand crashing seas; Zeus as the representation of the 'Cosmic Mind' "setting things in order" because humanity had lost their moral compass.

So Plato may have been telling us that this sort of civilization-destroying event had occurred four times within a certain historical period. Counting the Flood event as a fifth event – actually the main onslaught of the Giant Comet, probably the most destructive – we have a recurrence of the 'Big One' about every 2,500 years. Yet, as we noted already, the dates that the various researchers have given to large events that can be discerned in the scientific records (tree rings and ice cores) are 12,800 years ago (or 10900 BCE), 8200, 7000, 5200, 4200, 3000, 2354, 1628, 1150, 500, 208 BCE and 550, 850 and 1300 CE.[483] (These can be adjusted as more precise dating methods are developed or applied.) That's a lot more than "four times". But certainly, each of those events would not have been accompanied by the "sun rising in the west," i.e. a comet approaching very close from that direction, so obviously Plato and the gang didn't have the whole scientific banana. (Neither do we!) What Plato had, which seems to shine through the philosophical threads we have followed, was the idea that humanity could *bring this sort of destruction on themselves*, as suggested by Heraclitus, though it was simply a natural reaction of forces, not necessarily anything that was conscious and deliberate on the part of some god. Also, as I pointed out already, simple

---

483. Ice core, peat bog and tree-ring dates combined.

math demonstrates that the time distance between those numbers is as follows: 4,600, 1,200, 1,800, 1,000, 1,200, 646, 726, 478, 650, 292, 758, 300 and 450 years. Is the decreasing time period indicative of the increasing corruption of humanity? And can we define 'corruption of humanity' as a failure to deeply study nature, learn its natural laws, and live in accordance with them?

So, what did Plato get for his efforts? So far, we've found him being accused of plagiarizing all over the place, making fun of people by using the dialogues of a comic to formulate 'philosophy', probably nearly getting put to death for pederasty, and covering up a significant historical event. These accusations may or may not be true. We certainly realize from his dialogues, *Phaedrus* and the *Symposium*, that what Plato wrote and thought and felt bears very little resemblance to what we may think of as 'Platonic Love', which is supposedly beyond the reach of most humans. Any person who reads what Plato actually said about love would never, in a skinny minute, allow him to babysit or preside in a classroom of young children. If you doubt that, just read *Phaedrus* and the *Symposium* carefully and forget that this guy is supposed to be the arbiter of philosophical values, the author of great poetry and whatnot. The words he put into the mouth of Socrates just boggle the mind. Like Socrates, the guy who gave his life for Truth with a capital T, would ever have been interested in this garbage? Or 'ravished' by it? What is utterly soul-chilling is that Plato did this to his teacher, cast him in the role of lending authority to filth. Not only are women physically excluded in Plato's world, but the goddess who supposedly inspires his rapturous pedophilia (for it can't be called anything else) has no woman as an ancestor and is therefore, what? Apparently, barbarians are unable to see the superiority of pederasty which is equated with philosophy and gymnastics and together all three somehow stand against tyranny? Men who don't go after pubescent boys are "poor in spirit"?! We are next told that "so great is the encouragement which all the world gives a boy-lover or lover-boy-child" that his raptures excuse literally any anti-social act or absurd and immature behavior. It sounds as though he is defending the psychopathy of Alcibiades. And, even though the lover of boys, or the boy choosing a lover, can go through all kinds of concatenations in the process of swearing and proving eternal devotion, we learn that this doesn't have to be sincere! But darn those parents who object to their children being sex objects for perverts:

> But when parents forbid their sons to talk with their lovers, and place them under a tutor's care, who is appointed to see to these things, and their companions and equals cast in their teeth anything of the sort which they may

observe, and their elders refuse to silence the reprovers and do not rebuke them – any one who reflects on all this will, on the contrary, think that we hold these practices to be most disgraceful.[484]

In other words, Athenian society wasn't exactly as welcoming to Plato's 'philosophy' as he wanted it to be. Shame on those bad people who want to protect their children from predators!

In case you think I'm quoting out of context, read it yourself. And sure, you will read that "the soul of the young boy should be loved more than the body", but it is entirely unclear how that is accomplished since the mode is purely sexual. He talks out of both sides of his mouth at once. As for fidelity, it is clear from the literature that this was not what actually happened in these pedophilic relationships. They discarded their beloved children the instant they began to look like men.

It seems that, toward the end of his life, Plato concluded that the noblest love denies *any* bodily contact. I suppose that was an easy enough conclusion to come to once his libido had run out. Then, he finds any sexual exchange to be unworthy of a philosopher. In short, after a lifetime of pederasty, abusing hundreds, if not thousands of young boys, Plato finally denied the flesh. And for over two thousand years our civilization has been speaking in awed and hushed tones about this guy? And what is astonishing is the fact that when Plato talks about love, he is *talking about pederasty exclusively* and women are not even a part of the picture! The question is, of course, what effect has this message had on our society as a whole? It seems to me that the influence has been profound, particularly since Christianity was shaped by the influences of Plato in its formative stages. And the result is that the problem in our world is not homosexuality, a private matter between *adults*, but *anti*-sexuality, that is, the obviation of women *in toto*, and we have Plato to thank for this. Thanks to Plato, by way of Christianity, the chief effort has been to inculcate disgust toward sex in general, and women in particular.

Inspired by Plato, St. Augustine found the sexual organs to be shameful and denounced those parts as the loathsome instruments of original sin. Sexual desire was evil and horrible. He scorned humanity because we are born *"inter faeces et urinam"*. What is more, he agonized over this stuff almost endlessly! Then, over the centuries, the tendency to define as 'the flesh' all that is trivial, evil or vile, continued to grow and develop, particularly in relation to women. Those rascally guys who wrote *Malleus Maleficarum*, the

484. Plato, *The Symposium*, ibid., pp. 541-94.

Witches' Hammer[485], made believers out of everyone when their inquisition road-show came to town: woman, in contrast to man, is by nature a vicious liar, the embodiment of fraud and iniquity:

> What else is woman but a foe to friendship, and unescapable punishment, a necessary evil, a natural temptation, a desirable calamity, a domestic danger, a delectable detriment, an evil of nature painted with false colors!

Sounds rather like the other side of Plato's coin, eh? What he didn't write in his dialogues, but wished he could have! Nowadays, things are worse, even with the changing of attitudes, because now the sex pendulum has swung to the extreme opposite and sex is completely divorced from love or any sense of spiritual, emotional, or psychological nobility.

Additionally, when one combs through Plato's formulations of the physical world – his 'natural philosophy' – it sounds like little more than the book of Genesis in fancier words. In fact, I'm sure that Plato influenced the writers of Genesis considerably (as we will discuss in Volume III). He probably did plagiarize. He probably did utilize comedy to convey a few truths, and he probably wasn't such a great genius at anything. But he managed to stay alive and tell a story about cosmic destruction; that's something; even if he added so much nonsense to it that generations of believers have been searching for a truly mythical Atlantis that never existed in the terms that Plato described it at all.

Certainly, there were ancient peoples with significant knowledge and abilities: the megaliths that blanket the Earth give mute testimony to that. But just as the Mesopotamian empires, and the later Roman Empire, could be vast political bodies of extraordinary complexity, though not based on high material technology as we understand it, so were the more ancient empires. In fact, I think that my interpretation of what being a 'high civilization' in those ancient times could have been, as I wrote in the first volume of this series, *Secret History*, still stands. It was based on a completely different interpretation of the Laws of Nature and that explains how there can be, at one and the same time, examples of extraordinary construction abilities, craftsmanship and artistic expression, side-by-side with what we consider to be primitive stone tools and weapons.

What was the ultimate meaning of it? As we read above in the discussion of Archelaus, he was called "The Physicist" to mark the fact that with him,

---

485. The *Malleus Maleficarum* is a treatise on the prosecution of witches, written in 1486 by Heinrich Kramer, a German Catholic clergyman.

natural philosophy came to an end as soon as Socrates introduced ethics. I think we can come to a somewhat different view of things now. First of all, I suspect that Socrates was executed because of his teachings about natural philosophy based on his own understanding, as a "Delian diver", of the works of Pythagoras and Heraclitus.

Secondly, what we notice overall is that most of the original so-called philosophers didn't seem to be very bright about 'natural philosophy' but were rather good at being put in charge of growing colonies, which suggests that their philosophy had a different objective than explaining the order of the universe. Their ideas are just barely cogent enough to be sold to masses of ignorant people and that is probably what they were designed to be used for. The sky was quieting down, and perhaps there was awareness of terrible things that had been done in the past to kings and ruling classes as a result of the popular perception that the gods were angry. And so, things needed to be put on a different footing. Thus 'wise men' were put in charge of colonies, made laws, justified those laws based on 'cosmic principles' that they were busy making up, which definitely separated men from the gods, thus putting the cosmos into an order where nothing 'out there' could ever have anything to do with things 'down here'.

Thirdly, with the rise of the idea of natural philosophy, that things needed explaining, some really bright people turned their minds to the study of the world and ancient knowledge, coming to some rather different conclusions; people like Pherecydes and Pythagoras and especially Heraclitus. Anaxagoras got into trouble pushing this idea of 'finding out the truth' and so did his student, Socrates, and both lost their lives for it. I don't, for a minute, think that natural philosophy died with Socrates; rather it was Plato who buried it so that he could stay alive during times that were not exactly as "golden" as we have been told. He enjoyed his popularity and built a satisfying life for himself by twisting and re-interpreting the work of giant intellects. And then, when he began to get older, when the fires of his flesh began to die away, when the tenor of the times changed somewhat and his own reputation demanded of him something more, he wrote the dialogues detailing the story of Atlantis. He was honest enough to put the discussion in the mouths of those who probably did discuss periodic cataclysms and cleansings, though he felt the necessity of putting the Athenians in the position of the good guys, and casting the bad guys 'out there' beyond the Pillars of Hercules. There may even have been information accessible to him that there was a vast continent across that ocean that suffered the most terrible destruction imaginable, the same event to which the Carolina Bays bear witness. But beyond that, I doubt that there was much more, and so the name Atlantis, and the description of it and its people and lifestyle, were purely figments of his imagination or based on legends and stories of the Hyperboreans. The line of philosophers who followed Plato were thus lost without the keys.

But it seems that the keys may have been passed down along another line. This is speculative and I didn't come to the idea in advance, but rather through a strange discovery made while researching the life and times of Constantine the Great. I found a dangling thread and began to pull on it, following where it led, and it kept going back, and back, and back to Pythagoras and Heraclitus, and the main line it followed to end up there was that of the Stoic philosophers, the counterweight to the Platonic line.

It seems that the Stoics, in a line from Socrates, did carry on the tradition of natural philosophy, though very carefully; they did carry on the ideas of Socrates, Heraclitus, Pythagoras and Pherecydes. Not only does it appear that they carried the torch down through the next couple of centuries with less distortion, but more remarkable discoveries were made during that time that validated the interpretations of ancient myths as stories of comets and destruction. These discoveries were encoded in a newly created Mystery Religion that was formulated and formed by a Stoic philosopher for the express purpose of supporting political changes for the benefit of humanity, to prevent the 'Cosmic Mind' from running amok as it appeared it was about to do. This Mystery Religion actually competed with Christianity for a time and, had it not been for a particular comet impact, might have changed the world for the better. But Christianity prevailed, and the destruction came, and all our history since then has been an attempt to cover up this fact: that the ruling elite brought on destruction by the very fact of their unjust social hierarchy and warmongering. What is worse, that same ruling elite continue in dominance and if the patterns I have seen hold true, it may come again, much sooner and far worse than can be imagined. So, if we want to get there, to be witnesses to this remarkable Secret History, we'd best get on with it. Even though I'm endeavoring to make history as concise and interesting as possible, you do need to read attentively since you never know when the smallest clue will unlock the door to the secrets.

CHAPTER EIGHT

CYNICS AND STOICS

Antisthenes c. 445 – 365 BCE

Another of Socrates' devoted students was Antisthenes, who has been designated as the first *Cynic* philosopher.

Cynics advocated living an ascetic life in accordance with virtue, which is obviously quite different from the life that Plato described. Plato was all about airy-fairy beauty and abstraction, love and pleasures of the flesh (until he got older), disguised in philosophical nonsense about 'ideals' and 'beauty', etc. On the other side, the Cynics and Stoics were eminently pragmatic and down to earth.

Antisthenes' father was an Athenian and his mother a Thracian, which may have connected him to the Orphic and Pythagorean traditions. At one point during the Peloponnesian war he distinguished himself in battle and Socrates remarked that "if both his parents had been Athenian, he would not have turned out so brave."

That's another clue as to how Socrates felt about Athens in respect of that disastrous, wasteful war of unbridled greed.

Diogenes Laërtius tells us that he was first the student of a rhetorician named Gorgias and only later became a student of Socrates. It was from Socrates that "he learned his hardihood, emulating his disregard of feeling." That's a far cry from the portrait of Socrates we get from Plato! Antisthenes was present at Socrates' death and stories were later told about how he was instrumental in seeing that those that condemned him to death were punished. He was said to have been responsible for the exile of Anytus and the execution of Meletus.

I'd say that's pretty practical!

Like Socrates, his teaching style was to simply have dialogues and the Greek historian and rhetorician, Theopompus, even said that *Plato stole many of his ideas.*[486] (Antisthenes was the only one of the Socratic students who was praised by Theopompus.[487]) He was, apparently, possessed of great wit and was often sarcastic, utilizing wordplay to make his points. He is quoted as saying that he would rather fall among crows (*korakes*) than flatterers (*kolakes*), for the one devour the dead, but the other the living.[488] Some of his dialogues were energetic attacks on certain contemporaries including, interestingly, Alcibiades. As I've already suggested, perhaps Socrates wasn't as fond of Alcibiades as Plato and his dialogues might suggest, and Antisthenes knew it.

Antisthenes developed Socrates' fundamental ethical idea that virtue, *not pleasure*, is the object of life, and doing the *right* thing, as opposed to the thing that is pleasing to the self, is virtue. He is reported to have considered pain and even being defamed as a blessing if it comes as a result of virtue.[489] However, he also praised the pleasures of the soul and good friendship, those things that were produced by virtue and right action and relationships.[490] His asceticism appears to be somewhat Pythagorean because he is reported to have said: "Those who would fain be immortal must… live piously and justly."

He made another very interesting remark in view of Heraclitus' theories about the 'Cosmic Mind' as well as Cleckley's idea that Alcibiades was a psychopath. Antisthenes said: *States are doomed when they are unable to distinguish good men from bad.* … "It is strange," said he, "that we weed out the darnel from the corn and the unfit in war, but do not excuse evil men from the service of the state."

A few snips from Diogenes Laërtius about Antisthenes:

> When asked what learning is the most necessary, he replied, "How to get rid of having anything to unlearn."
>
> One day he visited Plato, who was ill, and seeing the basin into which Plato had vomited, remarked, "The bile I see, but not the pride."

---

486. Athenaeus, xi. 508c-d, retrieved here: http://penelope.uchicago.edu/Thayer/E/Roman/Texts/Athenaeus/home.html
487. The works of Theopompus were chiefly historical, and are much quoted by later writers. They included an Epitome of Herodotus's *History*, the *Hellenics*, the *History of Philip*, and shorter pieces. The *Attack on Plato* and the treatise *On Piety*, which are sometimes referred to as separate works, were perhaps only two of the many digressions in the *History of Philip*. The *Three-headed*, an attack on the cities of Athens, Sparta and Thebes, was published under the name of Theopompus by his enemy, Anaximenes of Lampsacus.
488. See: http://lucianofsamosata.info/wiki/doku.php?id=cynics:cynic_lives
489. Diogenes Laërtius, vi. 3
490. Xenophon, *Symposium*, iv. 41.

Phanias, in his work on the Socratics, tells us how some one asked him what he must do to be good and noble, and he replied, "you must learn from those who know that the faults you have are to be avoided."

It is better to be with a handful of good men fighting against all the bad, than with hosts of bad men against a handful of good men. Pay attention to your enemies, for they are the first to discover your mistakes.

Are there any clues that Antisthenes carried forward any information about cyclical catastrophes or insights derived from Heraclitus, Phrecydes and Pythagoras? I've combed through what is available and there isn't much except the above remarks about weeding out evil men from government. His lost work on Natural Philosophy (*Physicus*) contained *a theory of the nature of the gods*, in which he argued that there were many gods believed in by the people, but only one *natural* God.[491] He also said that God *resembles nothing on Earth*, and therefore could not be understood from any representation[492], which is similar to Heraclitus.

Among the titles of his lost books there is nothing that suggests that he wrote on the topics that interest us here, so if there was a certain knowledge possessed by Socrates, and passed to him, we find no hints of it except the following remarks from Diogenes Laërtius:

> It would seem that the most manly section of the Stoic School owed its origin to him. Hence Athenaeus the epigrammatist writes thus of them:
>
> Ye experts in Stoic story, ye who commit to sacred pages *most excellent doctrines – that saves man's life and cities*. But that Muse that is one of the daughters of Memory approves the pampering of the flesh, which other men have chosen for their aim.

"Saves cities"? I know it is a bit premature to draw a general conclusion about this, but considering the conjectures made thus far, it appears to me that the idea of the ancients, that the conduct of human beings en masse, is directly related to punishment by the 'gods', as in destruction by comets, continued to run as a golden thread through the line of the Cynics and Stoics and emerged, apparently, in a dramatic way at the time of Caesar (as I've already suggested). So when I notice something like the above, it can be interpreted in a number of ways, of course, but the most parsimonious is that what was meant was exactly what was said: the Stoics taught doctrines that could *save*

---

491. Cicero, *De Natura Deorum*, i. 13.
492. Clement of Alexandria, *Stromata*, v.

the lives of men and cities. Notice that the second part of the epigram suggests that people forget the truth in their search of pleasure. This is true on many levels, even to the level of brain chemistry that scientific studies show can cause pain if a person considers something that is unpleasant.

In conclusion, Antisthenes, the student of Socrates, appears to have developed ideas that were foundational to Cynicism, and these ideas were passed along to Diogenes of Sinope and thence to Crates and from him to Zeno, the founder of the Stoics. Some have argued that a connection between Antisthenes and Diogenes was impossible and that the Stoics invented it to acquire a link to Socrates; others argue the other way.[493, 494, 495] It is possible that Zeno could simply have studied the works of Heraclitus and others and formulated the Stoic conceptions on his own. But, all things considered, I favor the definite link because there are just too many parallel lines of thought coming down from Pherecydes, Heraclitus, *Pythagoras and Socrates* that end up in Zeno's formulations, as we will see. Plus, there are (antagonistic) links between Plato and the next philosopher that we will discuss, Diogenes, that strengthen the likelihood of the connection. And lastly, the style of the Cynics was such that it was designed to try to *shock people awake* and make them think and change their ways in order that society might become more virtuous, thus "saving the lives of men and cities."

Diogenes of Sinope 412 – 323 BCE

Are there any clues that Diogenes of Sinope knew anything about ancient cataclysms? Nothing direct at all that I can find. However, his story provides such interesting clues in respect of Socrates, Plato, and the bogus 'Golden Age', that I think it is worth including some of these details.

Sinope was a city on the shores of the Black Sea in the general area where Pythagoras' former slave supposedly was busy duping the ignorant barbarians with tales of reincarnation. If such ideas were being spread, as Herodotus suggested in his histories, Diogenes shows no sign of having been initiated into those mysteries! That, of course, makes me wonder if Herodotus was being quite straightforward in the telling of that tale. On the other hand, so much has been destroyed and re-written, you have to pick through it very carefully to find anything at all.

---

493. Dudley (1937), *A History of Cynicism from Diogenes to the 6th Century A.D.*
494. Navia (2005), *Diogenes the Cynic: The War Against the World.*
495. Long (1996), 'The Socratic Tradition: Diogenes, Crates and Hellenistic Ethics', in Branham & Goulet-Caze (Eds.), *The Cynics: The Cynic Movement in Antiquity and Its Legacy.*

For me, Diogenes is one of the most interesting characters in the history of philosophy because he was like a wild-man philosopher. He didn't start that way, of course, but he sure took it to the limits! His father was a banker and Diogenes was exiled for defacing the currency as a young man.[496] Though he said he did it on the advice of the oracle, one can see in this action a rebellion against the false standards of society, which seems to be the theme of Diogenes' life and the impetus for the development of his particular way of 'teaching'. In any event, after he was exiled from his home and moved to Athens, he began a lifelong practice of challenging established customs and values in a very public way. One suspects that he did it in the manner he did because it made him look crazy enough that the elite thought he could be safely ignored.

Diogenes' teaching style was that of action. He was pretty much the direct opposite of Plato, who used endless high-sounding words while his actions belied his virtue. Diogenes made his very public avoidance of earthly pleasures a commentary on contemporary Athenian behaviors. For example, he lived in a large jar – an ancient homeless person – and destroyed the single wooden bowl he possessed after seeing a peasant boy drink from the hollow of his hands. It was contrary to Athenian customs to eat in public, such as in the marketplace, and when Diogenes was rebuked for exactly that, he explained that it was during the time he was in the marketplace that he felt hungry. I can't help but be reminded of Jesus and his disciples being reprimanded for picking corn on the Sabbath![497] Diogenes Laërtius writes:

> He used to say that he followed the example of the trainers of choruses; for they too set the note a little high, to ensure that the rest should hit the right note.[498]

In other words, he lived his life as an exaggerated commentary on the world around him. He used to stroll about in full daylight with a lighted lamp; when asked what he was doing, he would answer, "I am just looking for a man."[499] Modern sources often say that Diogenes was looking for an "honest man",

---

496. This appears to be corroborated by archaeology: large numbers of defaced coins (smashed with a large chisel stamp) have been discovered at Sinope, dating from the middle of the 4th century BCE, and other coins of the time bear the name of Hicesias as the official who minted them. See: Seltman (1938), *Diogenes of Sinope, Son of the Banker Hikesias.*

497. Matthew 12.

498. Diogenes Laërtius, VI: 34-36.

499. Laërtius, *Lives* VI:41, trans. Hicks (1925).

but it is clear from the original was that he was looking for a "human" (anthrôpos); his point being that the unreasoning behavior of the people around him revealed that they did not qualify as human.[500]

The behavior described so far certainly does remind us of Socrates, who was a 'gadfly' according to Plato. This was a description of a person who upsets the *status quo* by being an irritant and asking upsetting questions. Plato quoted Socrates as saying, during his trial: "If you kill a man like me, you will injure yourselves more than you will injure me," because his role was that of a gadfly, "to sting people and whip them into a fury, all in the service of truth." [501]

According to one story, Diogenes was captured by pirates "under the command of Scirpalus" while traveling to Aegina and subsequently sold as a slave *in Crete*. This story is suspicious to me because it was the same place where Plato was taken by the mythical "Pollis" to be sold as a slave, but was allegedly rescued in the nick of time. It seems that Diogenes was also 'nearly rescued'.

> Cleomenes in his work entitled *Concerning Pedagogues* says that the friends of Diogenes wanted to ransom him, whereupon he called them simpletons; for, said he, lions are not the slaves of those who feed them, but rather those who feed them are at the mercy of the lions: for fear is the mark of the slave, whereas wild beasts make men afraid of them.[502]

Having two such similar incidents in the lives of two associated philosophers is astonishing. In fact, there are a couple of items in Diogenes Laërtius' account that may bear on this, both of them in relation to Plato:

> Plato saw him washing lettuces, came up to him and quietly said to him, "Had you paid court to Dionysius, you wouldn't now be washing lettuces," and that he with equal calmness made answer, "If you had washed lettuces, you wouldn't have paid court to Dionysius." [503]

This is a curious exchange in view of the supposed sexual encounter between Plato and Dionysius of Sicily who, following Plato's attack on him, allegedly tried to have Plato sold as a slave on the island of Aegina. If one connects

---

500. Ibid., VI:32.
501. Apology, 30e.
502. Diogenes Laërtius, VI: 74-76.
503. Diogenes Laërtius, VI: 58-60.

Diogenes sitting in his jar. Painting by Jean-Léon Gérôme (1860).

this to the fact that Diogenes was sold as a slave on the island of Aegina, together with the exchange cited above about "paying court to Dionysius", it makes one wonder just what happened to who? Were the two of them traveling together at the time? Was it actually Diogenes who refused the attentions of Dionysius, which resulted in his being sold as a slave (not captured by pirates), and was Plato actually involved with the ruler sexually in exchange for favors exactly as he describes should be the case between male lovers in *Phaedrus*? If this is a plausible scenario, Diogenes would have been 24 and Plato 39 at that time. There is also this:

> When Plato styled him a dog, "Quite true," he said, "for I come back again and again to those who have sold me." [504]

Notice that he says that he keeps coming back to "those who have sold me" as opposed to "those who have bought me". Most curious. Then there is this:

> Being reproached with begging when Plato did not beg, "Oh yes," says he, "he does, but when he does so, he holds his head down close, that none may hear." [505]

One wonders if that was a reference to Plato's relationship with Dionysius. Diogenes certainly made it very, very clear that he did not approve of the

504. Diogenes Laërtius, VI: 38-40.
505. Diogenes Laërtius, VI: 66-68.

lifestyle of Plato in many anecdotes about the former that I'm not interested in following here.

Anyway, according to the accounts, being put up for sale, having been asked his trade, Diogenes replied that he knew no trade but that of governing men, and that he wished to be sold to a man who needed a master. He was then sold to a Corinthian named Xeniades who bought him to be a tutor to his two sons. Then it is said that he spent the rest of his life in Corinth teaching the doctrines of virtuous self-control. Some stories say that he was set free by Xeniades after a time, and others say "he grew old and died at Xeniades' house in Corinth." He is even said to have lectured to large audiences at the Isthmian Games, which is pretty amazing for a slave! [506, 507, 508]

It is actually difficult to reconcile his teaching activities with those of a slave unless he truly was master of the one who purchased him. In another account relating to Aegina [509], which seems to be the point around which all this business circles, Diogenes Laërtius tells a story that may reflect this relationship:

> A certain Onesicritus of Aegina is said to have sent to Athens the one of his two sons named Androsthenes, and he having become a pupil of Diogenes stayed there; the father then sent the other also, Philiscus, in search of him; but Philiscus also was detained in the same way. When, thirdly, the father himself arrived, he was just as much attracted to the pursuit of philosophy as his sons and joined the circle – so magical was the spell which the discourses of Diogenes exerted. Amongst his hearers was Phocion surnamed the Honest, and Stilpo, the Megarian and many other men prominent in political life. [510]

On the other hand, the story may not even be about Diogenes since it sounds more like Socrates. Not only that, but it is situated in Athens, not Corinth, which is where Diogenes was said to have spent the rest of his days. It was in Corinth that a meeting between Alexander the Great [511] and Diogenes is

---

506. Laërtius, op. cit., VI:29, 30-31.
507. Dio Chrysostom, *Discourses*, Or. 8.10, trans. Cohoon (1932).
508. Lucian, *Historia*, 3.
509. Aegina is an island about 17 km from Athens. During and after the Peloponnesian wars, it declined significantly. Its prosperity depended on slave labor though Aristotle's estimate that the population of slaves was 470,000 is doubted. It's acknowledged that the number of slaves did exceed the number of free men and that Aegina's fate anticipated the fate of Greece as a whole.
510. Diogenes Laërtius, VI, 74-77.
511. Keep in mind that Alexander's teacher was Aristotle of the Platonic Academy line of philosophers.

supposed to have taken place. Plutarch and Diogenes Laërtius recount that they exchanged only a few words: while Diogenes was relaxing in the sun, Alexander, thrilled to meet the famous philosopher, asked if there was any favor he might do for him. Diogenes replied, "Yes, stand out of my sunlight." Alexander then declared, "If I were not Alexander, then I should wish to be Diogenes." In another account of the conversation, Alexander found the philosopher looking attentively at a pile of human bones. Diogenes explained, "I am searching for the bones of your father but cannot distinguish them from those of a slave."[512] I have doubts about these stories. After all, Alexander's tutor was Aristotle, who was from the 'other school', and Alexander therefore would have been unlikely to resonate with the telling of such hard Truths.

Along with Antisthenes and Crates of Thebes, Diogenes is considered one of the founders of Cynicism. The ideas of Diogenes, like those of most other Cynics, must be arrived at indirectly because Cynic ideas are inseparable from Cynic practice; therefore what we know about Diogenes is contained in the anecdotes concerning his life, which include sayings attributed to him in a number of scattered classical sources.

Diogenes maintained that all the artificial growths of society were incompatible with happiness and that morality requires a return to the simplicity of nature. In his words, "Humans have complicated every simple gift of the gods." Although Socrates had previously identified himself as belonging to the world, rather than a city, Diogenes is credited with the first known use of the word 'cosmopolitan'. When he was asked where he came from, he replied, "I am a citizen of the world". This was a radical claim in a world where a man's identity was intimately tied to his citizenship in a particular city state.[513]

Diogenes had nothing but disdain for Plato and his abstract philosophy. Diogenes viewed Antisthenes as *the true heir to Socrates*, and shared his love of virtue and indifference to wealth, together with a disdain for the opinions of society at large. This is certainly interesting if, in fact, it is true that Plato was inclined to claim the ideas of others as Theopompus had said about him in relation to Antisthenes.

---

512. Laërtius, VI:38; Cicero, *Tusculanae Quaestiones*, 5.32.; Plutarch, *Alexander*, 14, *On Exile*, 15; Dio Chrysostom, Or. 4.14. There is a similar anecdote in one of the dialogues of Lucian (Menippus, 15) but that story concerns Menippus in the underworld.
513. Laërtius, VI:44; Cicero, *Tusculanae Quaestiones*, 5.37.; Plutarch, *On Exile*, 5.; Epictetus, *Discourses*, i.9.1. Laërtius, VI:63,. Compare: Laërtius, VI:72, Dio Chrysostom, Or. 4.13, Epictetus, *Discourses*, iii.24.66.

As Plato was conversing about Ideas and using the nouns "tablehood" and "cuphood," he said, "Table and cup I see; but your tablehood and cuphood, Plato, I can nowise see." "That's readily accounted for," said Plato, "for you have the eyes to see the visible table and cup; but not the understanding by which ideal tablehood and cuphood are discerned."

On being asked by somebody, "What sort of a man do you consider Diogenes to be?" "A Socrates gone mad," said he.[514]

The fact that Plato himself described Diogenes as "a Socrates gone mad" suggests that he was fully aware that the philosophical line he was taking was not Socratic. Either that, or some of the anecdotes about Diogenes really belong to Socrates, as suggested by the Alexander and 'slave bones' story above. It seems obvious, from the anecdotes Diogenes Laërtius recounts, that Diogenes deliberately sought out Plato to embarrass him by challenging his interpretations of Socrates and sabotaging his lectures. Diogenes also called the school of Euclides – another former student of Socrates – "bilious", and said Plato's lectures were a waste of time. Considering the direction that Plato and his followers took, I'm inclined to agree with Diogenes.[515]

Many anecdotes of Diogenes refer to his dog-like behavior, and his praise of a dog's virtues. Diogenes believed human beings live artificially and hypocritically and would do well to study the dog. Besides performing natural bodily functions in public with ease, a dog will eat anything, and make no fuss about where to sleep. Dogs live in the present without anxiety and have no use for the pretensions of abstract philosophy. In addition to these virtues, dogs are thought to know instinctively who is friend and who is foe. Unlike human beings who either dupe others or are duped, dogs will give an honest bark at the truth. Diogenes stated that "other dogs bite their enemies, I bite my friends to save them."[516]

The term 'Cynic' itself derives from the Greek word *kynikos*, 'dog-like' from *kyôn*, 'dog'. One reason offered in ancient times for why the Cynics were called dogs was because Antisthenes taught in the Cynosarges gymnasium at Athens. The word Cynosarges means the 'place of the white dog'.[517] Later Cynics also sought to turn the word to their advantage, as a later commentator explained:

---

514. Diogenes Laërtius, VI. 52-54.
515. Laërtius, op. cit. VI:24; Plato, *Apology*, 41e.; Xenophon, *Apology*, 1. Laërtius, VI:54 ; Aelian, *Varia Historia*, 14.33.
516. Diogenes of Sinope, quoted by Stobaeus, *Florilegium*, iii. 13. 44.
517. Laërtius, VI:13. Cf.: *The Oxford Companion to Classical Literature*, 2nd edition, p. 165.

There are four reasons why the Cynics are so named. First because of the indifference of their way of life, for they make a cult of indifference and, like dogs, eat and make love in public, go barefoot, and sleep in tubs and at crossroads. The second reason is that the dog is a shameless animal, and they make a cult of shamelessness, not as being beneath modesty, but as superior to it. The third reason is that the dog is a good guard, and they guard the tenets of their philosophy. The fourth reason is that the dog is a discriminating animal which can distinguish between its friends and enemies. So do they recognize as friends those who are suited to philosophy, and receive them kindly, while those unfitted they drive away, like dogs, by barking at them.[518]

Diogenes is discussed in a 1983 book by German philosopher Peter Sloterdijk, *Critique of Cynical Reason*, in which he is used as an example of the *kynical*, in which personal degradation is used as a caricatured form of censuring society. (Like self-immolation lite.) Calling the practice of this tactic *"kynismos,"* Sloterdijk explains that the *kynical actor* actually embodies the message he/she is trying to convey. The goal is typically dramatically acted out regression that mocks authority, particularly when authority is considered to be corrupt, suspect or unworthy.[519] Thus, the very existence of this style of philosophy during the so-called 'Golden Age of Greece' says quite a bit about the true conditions that prevailed at the time. A few samples from Diogenes Laërtius:

> Once he saw the officials of a temple leading away someone who had stolen a bowl belonging to the treasurers, and said, "The great thieves are leading away the little thief."...
>
> Dionysius the Stoic says that after Chaeronea[520] he was seized and dragged off to Philip, and being asked who he was, replied, "A spy upon your insatiable greed." For this he was admired and set free. ...
>
> Perdiccas[521] having threatened to put him to death unless he came to him, "That's nothing wonderful," quoth he, "for a beetle or a tarantula would do the same."

---

518. See the 7th March lecture, Michel Foucault, *The Courage of the Truth Lectures at the Collège de France* (2011).
519. Long, A. A. (1996), 'The Socratic Tradition: Diogenes, Crates, and Hellenistic Ethics'.
520. The Battle of Chaeronea was fought in 338 BCE, near the city of Chaeronea in Boeotia, between the forces of Philip II of Macedon and an alliance of Greek city-states including Athens and Thebes. The battle was the culmination of Philip's campaign in Greece (339–338 BCE) and resulted in a decisive victory for the Macedonians.
521. One of Alexander's generals.

When someone was extolling the good fortune of Callisthenes [522] and saying what splendor he shared in the suite of Alexander, "Not so," said Diogenes, "but rather ill fortune; for he breakfasts and dines when Alexander thinks fit."

When he was dining in a temple, and in the course of the meal loaves not free from dirt were put on the table, he took them up and threw them away, declaring that nothing unclean ought to enter a temple.

When Alexander stood opposite him and asked, "Are you not afraid of me?" "Why, what are you?" said he, "a good thing or a bad?" Upon Alexander replying "A good thing," "Who then," said Diogenes, "is afraid of the good?"

When asked what was the most beautiful thing in the world, he replied, "Freedom of speech." [523]

There is another discussion of Diogenes and the Cynics in Michel Foucault's book *Fearless Speech*. There Foucault discusses Diogenes' public dramas in relation to speaking of truth in the ancient world. Foucault later expands this to establish *an alternative conception of militancy and revolution* through a reading of Diogenes and Cynicism.[524] One can see hints of the idea of non-violent protest such as that advocated by Gandhi here as well.

When you think about it, Diogenes of Sinope sounds an awful lot like Jesus, now doesn't he, right down to the interactions with the 'money changers' at the beginning of his career? Considering that New Testament scholar Burton Mack has identified the earliest layers of the sayings of the individual around whom the Jesus myth was formed, to have been based on Cynic philosophy, Diogenes and his colleagues may be as close as we can get to picturing the 'real Jesus' with any accuracy (with Socrates and his death for telling the truth thrown in).

There are conflicting accounts of Diogenes' death at the age of nearly 90. He is alleged variously to have held his breath; to have become ill from eating raw octopus; or to have suffered an infected dog bite.[525]

When asked how he wished to be buried, he left instructions to be thrown

---

522. Historian and great nephew of Aristotle by his sister Arimneste. Through the influence of Aristotle, who had been tutor to Alexander, Callisthenes was appointed to travel with Alexander on his Asiatic expedition as a professional historian. During the first years, Callisthenes did nothing but praise Alexander. As time went by, Callisthenes' tone changed. He sharply criticized Alexander's adoption of Persian customs, including his desire that people prostrate themselves before him. He then became involved in a plot against Alexander, was imprisoned, and died of either torture or disease there.

523. Diogenes Laërtius, VI.

524. Foucault (2001), *Fearless Speech*.

525. Laërtius, op. cit. VI:76, 77; Athenaeus, 8.341.

outside the city wall so wild animals could feast on his body. When asked if he minded this, he said, "Not at all, as long as you provide me with a stick to chase the creatures away!" When asked how he could use the stick since he would lack awareness, he replied, "If I lack awareness, then why should I care what happens to me when I am dead?" In other words, even as he was dying, Diogenes made fun of people's excessive concern with the 'proper' treatment of the dead and their general inability to think critically.

The Corinthians erected to his memory a pillar on which rested a dog of Parian marble and a statue of Diogenes with his symbolic dog was erected at his home town, Sinop.[526]

As I noted at the beginning of this discussion, we don't seem to find any clues that Diogenes knew or passed on ideas respecting periodic destructions via comets or anything else. None of the writings listed as being his by Diogenes Laërtius survive. Perhaps we will find a clue in the life of the student who is the link between Diogenes and Zeno; Crates. But before we get to Crates, let's divert to investigate a contemporary of Diogenes of Sinope, a certain Eudoxus, who is going to play a role in further developments.

Diogenes.

Eudoxus 410 – 347 BCE

Eudoxus first studied mathematics with Archytas, who we met in our discussion of Pythagoras. Recall that it wasn't until after Plato spent time with Archytas at Tarentum that his formerly rather cool view of Pythagoras warmed up and he (allegedly) acquired the three books of Pythagoras. There are surviving fragments from the work of Archytas that strongly suggest that it was he, not Pythagoras, who formulated many of the *scientific and mathematical ideas* attributed to Pythagoras by Plato. So we note that Archytas was a Pythagorean who was also a scientist and mathematician.

Archytas was famous for founding mathematical mechanics. He was also reputed to have built the first artificial, self-propelled flying device. Archytas dealt with several mathematical formulations that were important to later

---

526. Cicero, *Tusculanae Quaestiones*, 1.42.; Laërtius, VI:78; *Greek Anthology*, 1.285.; Pausanias, 2.2.4.

mathematical works. Politically and militarily, Archytas was the dominant figure in Tarentum in his generation. (Remember Tarentum? It was 20 miles from Metapontum, where Pythagoras allegedly ended his days.) The Tarentines elected him *strategos* (general), seven years in a row – violating their own rule against successive appointments. He was allegedly undefeated as a general. So it seems that some Pythagoreans had resumed their role in politics. Archytas had a reputation for virtue as well as efficacy and some scholars have argued that Archytas was one of the models for Plato's philosopher-king, and that he influenced Plato's political philosophy as expressed in *The Republic*.

Following his studies under Archytas, Eudoxus studied medicine with Philiston and then, around 387 BCE, at the age of 23, Eudoxus traveled to Athens to study with the followers of Socrates. He eventually became the pupil of Plato, with whom he studied for several months, but *due to a disagreement they had a falling out*, after which he traveled to Heliopolis, Egypt, to pursue his study of astronomy and mathematics. From Egypt, he then traveled north to Cyzicus, located on the South shore of the Sea of Marmara, then south to the court of the famous king of Caria, Mausolus. During his travels he gathered many students of his own. I can't determine any particular reason for his intinerary since I find no clues relating to either Cyzicus or Mausolus.[527]

Nearly 20 years after he had left Athens, Eudoxus returned with his students in tow. According to some sources, around 367 he assumed headship of the Academy during Plato's period in Syracuse (during which time, apparently, Archytas attempted to rescue Plato from Dionysius II in the rather curious story of Plato being sold as a slave when it is altogether likely that something quite different occurred)[528] and taught Aristotle. He eventually returned to his native Cnidus, where *he served in the city assembly*. While in Cnidus, he built an observatory and continued writing and lecturing on theology, astronomy and meteorology.

He died either in 355 or 347 BCE. Much, much later, in the 16th century, when Europe finally began to emerge from the Dark Age of Catholicism, Eudoxus was 'rediscovered'.

Listing and describing all his many mathematical achievements here is not necessary, but we are interested in his astronomy, astrology and mathematics relating to same. In mathematical astronomy, Eudoxus' fame is due

---

527. The name that became 'mausoleum' because his wife built him a really fantastic tomb.
528. Dionysius also appears in Dante's *Inferno*, in which he is referred to as 'Dionysius of Sicily' in Canto 12. He is among the many souls named by Chiron that boil in blood for violence against others.

to the introduction of the *astronomical globe* [529] which is going to play an important role in the solution of a mystery in the next volume, and his early contributions to understanding the movement of the planets. He is also said to have introduced *the first descriptions of the full classical set of constellations*. In any event, the works of Eudoxus are among those studied by Zeno who we will meet shortly.

What is going to become important is this question: where did Eudoxus get his constellations? It is going to become very, very clear, further on, that he tapped into some very ancient source. And I do mean ancient; I doubt it was from Egypt, which was almost astronomically illiterate until the Greeks came.

Crates of Thebes 365 – 285 BCE

Crates was the son and heir of a wealthy Theban family, but he renounced his life of ease to become a pupil of Diogenes. He was known to refer to himself as "a fellow-citizen of Diogenes, who *defied all the plots of envy.*" [530] What could *that* mean?

Considering what we have learned about Diogenes' 'in your face' activities *vis-à-vis* the authorities of the time, it suggests that there was a sort of brotherhood of social activists who were attracted to the Cynic way of protest. What we should like to know is: what is it that could attract a rich kid to such a life? Crates is also described as being the student of Bryson the Achaean [531], and of Stilpo who was also mentioned as possibly being a student of Diogenes, though as I mentioned in reference to that anecdote, it sounded more like Socrates, unless a whole lot of Diogenes' life has been erased. [532]

Crates is said to have been deformed, a hunch-back with a lame leg who, nevertheless, lived a life of cheerful simplicity. [533] He was nicknamed the Door-Opener [534] because he would enter any house and people would receive him gladly:

> He used to enter the houses of his friends, without being invited or otherwise called, in order to *reconcile members of a family*, even if it was apparent that they were deeply at odds. He would not reprove them harshly, but in a soothing way, in a manner which was non-accusatory towards those whom he was

---

529. i.e., awareness that the earth was a globe came from somewhere.
530. Diogenes Laërtius, vi. 93.
531. Diogenes Laërtius, vi. 85.
532. Seneca, *Epistles*, 10.1.
533. Julian, *Orations*, 6.201b.
534. Plutarch, *Symposiacs*, 2.1.

correcting, because he wished to be of service to them *as well as to those who were just listening.*[535]

Despite his physical deformities, he was apparently something of a babe-magnet. One of his students, a certain Metrocles of Maroneia, had a sister named Hipparchia who is said to have fallen in love with Crates, his lifestyle and teachings. She abandoned her wealthy and pampered life and married him. According to accounts, the marriage was remarkable in those times for being based on mutual respect and equality between the couple. Stories about Hipparchia appearing in public everywhere with Crates are told mainly because respectable women did not behave as she did. They had at least two children, a girl and a boy named Pasicles.

Crates was the teacher of Zeno of Citium[536] and was undoubtedly the biggest influence on Zeno in his development of Stoic philosophy, so one has to wonder what Crates passed to him when we consider the direction that Zeno took. Zeno always regarded Crates with the greatest respect, and some of the accounts we have of Crates have probably come down to us via Zeno's writings.[537]

Crates wrote a book of letters on philosophical subjects, the style of which is compared by Diogenes Laërtius to *that of Plato*[538]; but these no longer survive. Several fragments of his thought survive, however. He taught a simple asceticism, which seems to have been milder than that of his predecessor Diogenes:

> And therefore Crates replied to the man who asked, "What will be in it for me after I become a philosopher?" "You will be able," he said, "to open your wallet easily and with your hand scoop out and dispense lavishly instead of, as you do now, squirming and hesitating and trembling like those with paralyzed hands. Rather, if the wallet is full, that is how you will view it; and if you see that it is empty, you will not be distressed. And once you have elected to use the money, you will easily be able to do so; and if you have none, you will not yearn for it, but you will live satisfied with what you have, not desiring what you do not have nor displeased with whatever comes your way."[539]

---

535. Julian, Orations, 6.201b, from Reale (1980), *The Concept of First Philosophy and the Unity of the Metaphysics of Aristotle*, p. 34. See also: Apuleius, *Florida*, xiv, who makes a similar statement.
536. Diogenes Laërtius, i. 15, vi. 105, vii. 2.
537. Diogenes Laërtius, vi. 91. Cf. vii. 4
538. Diogenes Laërtius, vi. 98
539. Teles, Fragment 4a, from O'Neill (1977), *Teles: The Cynic Teacher*.

Again we are reminded of the figure of Jesus and his 'sayings' and little so-cial dramas. Crates' philosophy was imbued with humor that was both gen-tle and subtle. He jokingly suggested that people should not eat anything but lentils because luxury and extravagance were the chief causes of sedi-tions and insurrections in a city.[540] This joke would later feature as a satire in book IV of Athenaeus' *Deipnosophistae*, where a group of Cynics sit down for a meal and are served a lengthy 'feast' of bowl after bowl of lentil soup.[541]

One of Crates' poems was a parody of a famous hymn to the Muses writ-ten by Solon in which the latter prayed for prosperity, a good reputation and "justly acquired possessions." Crates' parody humorously typified Cynic de-sires:

> Glorious children of Memory and Olympian Zeus,
> Muses of Pieria, listen to my prayer!
> Give me without ceasing food for my belly
> Which had always made my life frugal and free from slavery ...
> Make me useful to my friends, rather than agreeable.
> As for money, I do not wish to amass conspicuous wealth,
> But only seek the wealth of the beetle or the maintenance of the ant;
> Nay, I desire to possess justice and to collect riches
> That are easily carried, easily acquired, and are of great avail to virtue.
> If I may but win these, I will propitiate Hermes and the holy Muses,
> Not with costly dainties, but with pious virtues.[542]

Crates also parodied Homer, writing a poem describing the ideal Cynic state in counter-point to Homer's description of Crete. Crates' city is called *Pera*, which in Greek is the beggar's wallet which every Cynic carried:

> There is a city Pera in the midst of wine-dark Tuphos,
> Fair and fruitful, filthy all about, possessing nothing,
> Into which no foolish parasite ever sails,
> Nor any playboy who delights in a whore's ass,
> But it produces thyme, garlic, figs, and bread,
> For which the citizens do not war with each other,
> Nor do they possess arms, to get cash or fame.[543]

---

540. Plutarch, *Moralia*.
541. Athenaeus, *Deipnosophists*, iv. 157.
542. Julian, *Orations*, 6.199d-200a, from Navia (1996), *Classical Cynicism: A Critical Study*.
543. Crates, Fragment 6, from Gutzwiller (2007), *Guide to Hellenistic Literature*, p. 136.

The word *tuphos* in the first line is one of the first known Cynic uses of a word which literally means mist or smoke. It was thereafter used by the Cynics to describe the mental confusion in which most people live their entire lives. The Cynics sought to clear away this fog and to see the world as it really is.

He is said to have died at a great age and was buried in Boeotia.[544]

Any clues there? None that I can see on the surface. I'm still wondering about that "fellow-citizen of Diogenes, who *defied all the plots of envy*." Did he mean that he, himself, defied all the plots of envy, or that Diogenes did? What were the plots, and who was doing the envying and was in a position to plot against them? Is this a reference to being able to 'get away with' something? If so, what?

What we see in the Cynics is a small group of social activists, at least as far as the surface appearance goes. But perhaps that was a deliberate act, as was about everything they did? One of the Cynics, Monimus, is even described as having faked madness so as to be released from service to his banker master. Obviously, considering the style of their lives, which included abandoning wealth and property, living in the sparest and most frugal way, going out in public and agitating and inviting ridicule, they were seriously dedicated to something! We have examples in our modern times of fundamentalists who believe in some dire end that will come to people if they are not persuaded to change their ways. Was such an idea behind the behavior of the Cynics? Were they convinced that Zeus was going to "correct and straighten out" society at large if they didn't come into line with the laws of nature? Was this a hidden part of their doctrine that they dared not speak aloud because they understood well the fate of Anaxagoras and Socrates? Was this what was meant by having "defied all the plots of envy"? That they managed to teach and acquire followers, and spread the word, in spite of the machinations of those in power?

Obviously, too much is lost to be able to determine for sure what was really going on. And it is really interesting that Burton Mack has identified the earliest layer of the alleged Jesus sayings in the gospels as being distinctively Cynic. We know that he was also talking about the 'coming of the lord' who was going to 'correct and straighten out' all things on Earth. So perhaps a parallel can be drawn here. In any event, times were changing and we come to the founding of the Stoics, from whom we have a tiny bit more in the way of clues.

---

544. Diogenes Laërtius, vi. 98.

Zeno c. 334 – 262 BCE

Stoicism proper was founded in Athens by Zeno of Citium. Zeno was born on the island of Cyprus, was of Phoenician descent and the story is, from the *Lives* by Diogenes Laërtius, that Zeno was a merchant who came to philosophy in Athens after surviving a shipwreck! He studied under Crates of Thebes, who was the most famous Cynic philosopher living in Greece at that time, followed by other teachers of other schools.

Engaging in a little speculation, it may have been due to his merchant background that Zeno decided to imitate the Platonic Academy and take things to the next level by founding a more formal school of Cynic philosophy which he modified somewhat to become 'Stoicism'. Modeling the curriculum on the Academy, he divided the new philosophy into three parts: Logic (which included rhetoric, grammar, and theories of perception and thought); Physics (not just science, but the divine nature of the universe as well); and Ethics, the end goal of which was to achieve happiness through the right way of living *according to Nature*. Because Zeno's ideas were built upon by Chrysippus and other later Stoics, it is difficult to determine exactly what he thought at the very beginning, but his general views were probably foundational and can thus be inferred from what was written later.

The Universe, in Zeno's view, is God: a divine reasoning entity, where all the parts belong to the whole. Into this pantheistic system he incorporated the physics of Heraclitus.

We recall here that Heraclitus proposed that the Universe contains a *divine artisan-fire*, which foresees everything, and, extending throughout the Universe, must produce everything via the unity of opposites; "the path up and down are one and the same." [545, 546] This "divine fire" was fundamental to everything else Zeno thought. Cicero, a pompous ass if ever there was one, wrote:

> Zeno, then, defines nature by saying that it is artistically working fire, which advances by fixed methods to creation. For he maintains that it is the main function of art to create and produce, and that what the hand accomplishes in the productions of the arts we employ, is accomplished much more artistically by nature, that is, as I said, by *artistically working fire*, which is the master of the other arts. [547]

---

545. Diogenes Laërtius, vii. 148.
546. Sextus Empiricus, adv. Math. ix. 104, 101; Cicero, *de Natura Deorum*, ii. 8.
547. Cicero, *de Natura Deorum*, ii. 22.

I think that Cicero was rather out of his depth, though his remarks that this divine fire "advances by fixed methods" is interesting. If the methods are fixed, that means someone is thinking about cycles and periodic activity.

According to classical scholar Anthony Long, "the importance of Heraclitus to later Stoics is evident most plainly in Marcus Aurelius." Explicit connections of the earliest Stoics to Heraclitus showing how they arrived at their interpretation are missing but they can be inferred from the Stoic fragments that Long concludes to have been "modifications of Heraclitus." [548]

Zeno and his fellow Stoics were intensely interested in Heraclitus' treatment of this mysterious 'fire'.

> The primitive substance of the universe is a divine essence (pneuma) which is the basis of everything which exists. The separation of force from matter produces a divine fire (aether) which, as the basis of all matter, is differentiated into elements and shaped by the tension caused by the pneuma working according to the divine reason (logos) of the universe. *These processes are responsible for the formation, the development, and ultimately, the destruction of the universe in a never-ending cycle* (palingenesis). ... The Stoics also recognised the existence of other gods and divine agents as manifestations of the one primitive God-substance.
>
> The cycle of its transformations and successive condensations constitutes the life of the universe. The universe and all its parts are only different embodiments and stages in the change of primitive being which Heraclitus had called a progress up and down. ...
>
> But *this process of differentiation is not eternal*; it continues only until the times of the restoration of all things. For the world which has grown up will in turn decay. ...to be consummated in a general conflagration (*ekpyrôsis*) when once more the world will be absorbed in God. Then in due order a new cycle of the universe begins, reproducing the previous, and so on forever.[549]

As a consequence of this idea that the world is regularly born and dies, *Zeno focused on the idea of world ages, or cosmic cycles.* They obviously understood the idea that when things in the world, probably including human behavior on social and individual scales, had decayed sufficiently, God would bring a purging fire on the land and 'correct' things, and set them straight.

For the Stoics, God is everywhere as the ruler and upholder, and at the same time the law of the universe. Zeno declared *cult images, shrines, tem-*

---

548. Long (2001), *Stoic Studies*, Chapter 2.
549. Hicks (1911), *Stoics*, Encyclopædia Britannica (11th edition).

ples, sacrifices, prayers and worship to be of no avail. That's pretty much in line with what Critias was reported to have said and probably what Socrates also thought and taught. For Zeno, a really acceptable prayer can only emerge from a virtuous and devout mind. The Stoics, however, defended *the stories of the gods* because divinity could be ascribed to *such manifestations as the heavenly bodies,* which were conceived as the *highest of rational beings.*

Divinity could also be seen as the *forces of nature*: divinity could inspire certain men such as heroes and great and holy intellects; thus *the cosmos was teeming with divine agencies* and they *could communicate with one another,* and if one of them was unhappy, others might react. It seems obvious that Zeno realized that the 'gods' were the agents of 'correction' and that this was what was being described in myth and legend as having happened over and over again.

It was said that Zeno was of an earnest, if not gloomy, disposition; that he preferred the company of the few to the many; and that he was fond of *burying himself in investigations.*[550] I would suggest that he may have become obsessed with the idea of figuring out the cosmic cycles of destruction.

One of Zeno's close associates and students was Aratus the poet, author of a work entitled *Phaenomena,* which was a description of the constellations and other celestial phenomena, partly based on the work of Eudoxus of Cnidus, the astronomer-mathematician of the Pythagorean school who introduced the astronomical globe and the full set of astrological constellations into the Hellenic world of his day.

Aratus c. 315 – 240 BCE

Aratus is not terribly important to us except as the transmitter of the astronomy of Eudoxus. What is important is that he had access to the works of Eudoxus, which might mean that this work was also available to others around him, and discussed by them, at least for a period of time.

Aratus was a native of Soli in Cilicia, a town about 20 miles from Tarsus from whence the apostle Paul also hailed. There are several accounts of Aratus' life by Greek writers, and the *Suda* and Eudocia[551] also mention him. He is known to have studied with Menecrates in Ephesus and Philitas

---

550. Diogenes Laërtius, vii. 14, 15, 16, and compare 26. Also: Sidonius Apollinaris, *Epistles,* ix. 9.
551. Aelia Eudocia Augusta (c. 401-460) was the wife of Theodosius II, and a prominent historical figure in understanding the rise of Christianity during the beginning of the Byzantine Empire. Her father was a philosopher named Leontius who taught Rhetoric at the Academy. He taught her rhetoric, poetry and philosophy. We'll deal with her in a subsequent volume.

in Cos. As a disciple of the Peripatetic philosopher Praxiphanes, in Athens, he met the Stoic philosopher Zeno. About 276, he was invited to the court of the Macedonian king, Antigonus II Gonatas, whose victory over the Gauls in 277 BCE Aratus set to verse. It was here, also, that he wrote his most famous poem, *Phaenomena* ('Appearances'). He then spent some time at the court of Antiochus I Soter of Syria, but subsequently returned to Pella in Macedon, where he died sometime before 240/239 BCE. His chief pursuits were medicine (which is also said to have been his profession), grammar and philosophy.[552]

The *Phaenomena* appears to be based on two prose works – *Phaenomena* and *Enoptron* ('Mirror', presumably *a descriptive image of the heavens*) – by Eudoxus of Cnidus. We are told by the biographers of Aratus that it was the request of Antigonus to have them turned into verse, which gave rise to the *Phaenomena* of Aratus. It appears from the fragments of the work preserved by Hipparchus (we'll meet him soon), that Aratus closely imitated parts of them both, but especially the first, which is a good thing because it preserved a great clue to several mysteries!

The purpose of the *Phaenomena* is to give an introduction to the constellations, with the rules for their risings and settings; and of the circles of the sphere, amongst which the Milky Way is reckoned. The immobility of the Earth, and the revolution of the sky about a fixed axis, is asserted and the path of the Sun in the zodiac is described. However, though the planets are introduced, they are mentioned as merely bodies having a motion of their own, without any attempt to define their periods, nor is anything said about the Moon's orbit.

There are numerous problems with the descriptions in the work which later scholarship has shown be due to the fact that the risings and settings were accurate for an epoch *as far back as 3400 BCE*. What this means is that *Eudoxus was working with astronomical information that was extremely ancient*. As I asked in the discussion of Eudoxus above, one definitely wonders from where he got his constellations and his other astronomical information. It was most likely Babylonian because it certainly wasn't Egyptian.

The second half of the work, *Diosemeia*, consists of *forecasts of the weather from astronomical phenomena*, with an account of its effects upon animals. It appears to be an imitation of Hesiod's *Works and Days* combined with Aristotle's *Meteorologica* and Theophrastus' *On Weather Signs*. Nothing is said in either poem about Hellenistic astrology.

Authors of twenty-seven commentaries are known; those written by

552. Mair & Mair (trans.) (1921), *Callimachus and Lycophron; Aratus*.

Theon of Alexandria, Achilles Tatius and Hipparchus of Nicaea survive, as well as an Arabic translation that was commissioned in the 9th century by the Caliph Al-Ma'mun. He is cited by Vitruvius, Stephanus of Byzantium and Stobaeus.[553, 554, 555]

So much for Aratus, as Herodotus would say.

Cleanthes c. 330 BCE – c. 230 BCE

Cleanthes was the successor to Zeno as the head of the Stoic school in Athens. He was originally a boxer who came to study philosophy and made a living by carrying water at night. His power of patient endurance, or perhaps his slowness, earned him the title of 'the Ass' from his fellow students, a name which he was said to have rejoiced in because it meant that his back was strong enough to bear whatever Zeno put upon it. He preserved and developed Zeno's teachings and originated new ideas of his own in Stoic physics which amounted to developing Stoicism along the lines of materialism and pantheism.

We are somewhat interested in Stoic ethics because, as we've already noted, Heraclitus and the other old-timers suggested strongly that how human societies behaved might have a bearing on where, when and how they were 'chastened' by Zeus and his 'thunderbolts'. But I'm not going to get into it deeply. I will mention here that Cleanthes 'materialized' the soul and taught a form of reincarnation, that souls live on after death, but that the intensity of the soul's existence would vary according to the strength or weakness of the particular soul.[556] This sounds remarkably like the ideas of Gurdjieff!

Zeno had said that the goal of life was "to live consistently," the implication being that no life but the passionless life of reason could ultimately be consistent with itself.

Cleanthes is credited with having added the words "with nature," thus completing the well-known Stoic formula that the goal is "to live consistently with nature."[557]

For Cleanthes, this meant, in the first place, living according to the dictates of the universe; for *the universe is under the governance of reason*, and everyone has the possibility to learn about the world-course, to recognize

553. Mair & Mair, op. cit., p. 363.
554. Kidd (Ed.) (1997), *Phaenomena*.
555. Martin (Ed.) (1998), *Aratos; Phénomènes*.
556. Plutarch, Plac. Phil. iv. 7.
557. Stock (1908), *Stoicism*.

it as rational and cheerfully to conform to it. This, according to him, is true freedom of will: not acting without motive, or apart from set purpose, or capriciously, but *humbly acquiescing in the universal order* and, therefore, in everything that befalls one.[558]

The direction to follow Universal Nature can be traced in his famous prayer:

> Lead me, Zeus, and you too, Destiny,
> To wherever your decrees have assigned me.
> I follow readily, but if I choose not,
> Wretched though I am, I must follow still.
> Fate guides the willing, but drags the unwilling.[559]

This is also remarkably similar to the ideas presented in the New Testament book of Romans, written by another native of Tarsus, the apostle Paul:

> For God's wrath and indignation are revealed from heaven against all un-godliness and unrighteousness of men, who in their wickedness repress and hinder the truth and make it inoperative. For that which is known about God is evident to them and made plain in their inner consciousness, because God has shown it to them. For ever since the creation of the world His invisible nature and attributes, that is, His eternal power and divinity, have been made intelligible and clearly discernible in and through the things that have been made.[560]

Cleanthes regarded the Sun as being divine; because the Sun sustains all living things, it resembled the *divine fire* which (in Stoic physics) animated all living beings, hence it too must be part of the vivifying fire or aether of the universe.[561]

The earliest Stoics, such as Cleanthes, Aristo and Sphaerus, all wrote commentaries on the work of Heraclitus, which suggests strongly that, under Zeno, they were all involved in the same search for the key to understanding the cosmic cycles.[562]

The earliest surviving Stoic work, the *Hymn to Zeus* of Cleanthes, though

---

558. Davidson (1907), *The Stoic Creed*, p. 143.
559. Epictetus, *Enchiridion*, 53; Seneca, *Epistles*, cvii, 11. The fifth line is not found in Epictetus.
560. Romans 1: 18, 19, 20. Amplified, Zondervan.
561. Cicero, *de Natura Deorum*, ii. 15.
562. Diogenes Laërtius, vii. 174, ix. 5, 15

not explicitly referencing Heraclitus, is clearly influenced by that work. Cleanthes *physicalized and modified* the Heraclitean logos, as I just mentioned. Additionally, he asserted that Zeus ruled the universe with law, and the weapon he utilized to ensure that things conform to the laws of the cosmos was *the 'forked servant', the "fire" of the "ever-living lightning."* Cleanthes then says, "Zeus *uses the fire to straighten out the common logos that travels about mixing with the greater and lesser lights"* This is Heraclitus' logos, but now it is confused with the common *nomos*, which Zeus uses to make the wrong right and "order the disordered." [563] In short, if you act naughty, not only will Santa bring you a lump of coal, Zeus might smite you with lightning.[564]

The *Hymn to Zeus* is extremely interesting considering our background subject: cometary cataclysms that recur at intervals. If you recall, the image of Ninurta I included on page 204, showed him holding a stylized lightning bolt. This lightning bolt closely resembles plasmoid phenomena observed both in the laboratory and in space, as was covered in the discussion of plasma physics (see p. 98). So here, it almost seems as if Cleanthes is saying that recurring cataclysms straighten things out in the cosmos.

In short, to Cleanthes, these things are not just abstract principles of things going on in noumenal worlds, the 'hypercosmos', as was the interpretation of the Platonists and their predecessors; Cleanthes is saying that these things happen in the real world on a more mundane level and he probably included scale in his speculations: a single human could be 'straightened out', or a group, a city, a nation; they could be straightened out by coming into conformity with Nature, or they could be straightened out by being reduced to primal substance (ashes). For Cleanthes, the Logos is quick and powerful, and sharper than any two-edged sword. Tension itself Cleanthes defined as a fiery stroke; in his *Hymn to Zeus*, lightning is the symbol of divine activity.

I should also mention that the Christian fathers of the early church had a great deal to say about this 'Logos' business because it was of paramount importance to them to distance themselves from their pagan roots. The Stoic modification of Heraclitus' idea of the Logos was also influential on Jewish philosophers such as Philo of Alexandria, who connected it to 'Wisdom personified' as God's creative principle. Philo uses the term *Logos* throughout his treatises on Hebrew Scripture, in a manner clearly influenced by the Stoics.

Cleanthes died at the age of 99, c. 230 BCE. We are told that an ulcer forced him to fast and even though the ulcer improved, he continued his fast, say-

---

563. The ancient Greek can be found in Blakeney (1921), *The Hymn of Cleanthes*.
564. Sorry folks, but sometimes you just have to lighten this stuff up a bit.

ing that, as he was already half-way on the road to death, he would not trouble to retrace his steps.

Cleanthes' pupil was Chrysippus, who became one of the most 'important' Stoic thinkers and succeeded him as the leader of the school.

Chrysippus c. 279 BCE – c. 206 BCE

Chrysippus, like Aratus, was a native of Soli, just 20 miles from Tarsus. He was a prolific writer who focused on the topics of logic, the theory of knowledge, ethics and physics. He created an original system of propositional logic in order to better understand the workings of the universe and role of humanity within it, etc. Chrysippus expounded on the idea that the behavior of human beings is significant in respect of the fate of individuals, cities, nations, and the world itself. He asserted that all things happen according to fate: what seems to be accidental has always some hidden cause. The unity of the world consists in the chain-like dependence of cause upon cause. Nothing can take place without a sufficient cause. According to Chrysippus, every proposition is either true or false, and this must apply to *future* events as well[565]:

> If any motion exists without a cause, then not every proposition will be either true or false. For that which has not efficient causes is neither true nor false. But every proposition is either true or false. Therefore, there is no motion without a cause. And if this is so, then all effects owe their existence to prior causes. And if this is so, all things happen by fate. It follows therefore that whatever happens, happens by fate.[566]

As it was with Heraclitus, and was now being developed explicitly, the Stoic view of fate is based on a view of the universe as a whole. If his opponents argued that, if everything is determined by destiny, there is no individual responsibility and it doesn't matter what anyone does, Chrysippus responded that there is simple and complex predestination. Becoming ill may be fated whatever happens but, if a person's recovery is linked to consulting a doctor, then consulting the doctor is fated to occur together with that person's recovery, and this becomes a complex fact. All human actions – in fact, our destiny – are decided by our relation to things, or as Chrysippus put it, events are "co-fated" to occur.

The non-destruction of one's coat, he says, is not fated simply, but co-fated

---

565. Zeller (1880), *The Stoics, Epicureans, and Sceptics.*
566. Cicero, *On Fate*, pp. 20–21.

with its being taken care of, and someone's being saved from his enemies is co-fated with his fleeing those enemies; and having children is co-fated with being willing to lie with a woman. ... For many things cannot occur without our being willing and indeed contributing a most strenuous eagerness and zeal for these things, since, he says, it was fated for these things to occur in conjunction with this personal effort. ... But it will be in our power, he says, with what is in our power being included in fate.[567]

It seems to me that Chrysippus was taking things a bit too far with his pre-deterministic approach to human life and experience. It was to be a very long time before Hugh Everett formulated the 'Many-worlds' interpretation of quantum mechanics, which suggests that there is a very large – perhaps infinite – number of universes, and everything that could possibly have happened in our past, but did not, has occurred in the past of some other universe or universes. It seems to me, however, that branching universes could be implied in Heraclitus' cosmology, which Chrysippus has now tossed out with the bath-water and gone down a path that was to be taken by Christian ethicists sometime later. For Chrysippus, ethics depended on understanding the nature of the universe; for the Christians, ethics depended on one's relationship with god and obeying his commands.

Chrysippus took his speculations about pre-destination into the realm of prophecy. He attempted to reconcile divination with his own rational doctrine of strict causation. Omens and portents are *symptoms* of certain occurrences, he asserted, and further that human beings probably miss most signs of the intent of the universe because only a few are known to humanity. In response to the argument that divination became superfluous in a foreordained universe, he responded that both divination and our actions in response to same are included in the chain of causation.

Whoah! Talk about circular reasoning! And this guy was said to have rarely passed a day without writing at least 500 lines! In total, he wrote more than 700 works. He was diffuse and obscure in his utterances, but he became the chief authority for the school.[568] Interestingly, Chrysippus also taught a therapy of extirpating the unruly passions and due to his efforts to systematize things in this way, giving people practical things that promised to transform them, Stoicism became one of the most influential philosophical movements in the Greek and Roman world for centuries!

Chrysippus was succeeded as head of the Stoic school by his pupil Zeno

567. Diogenianus in Eusebius, *Praeparatio Evangelica*, vi. 8.
568. Diogenes Laërtius, vii.

of Tarsus. Of his 700 plus written works, none have survived except as fragments embedded in the works of later authors like Cicero, Seneca, Galen, Plutarch, etc. Further fragments of two works by Chrysippus are preserved among the charred papyrus remains discovered at the Villa of the Papyri at Herculaneum. These are *Logical Questions* and *On Providence*. A third work discovered there may also be by him.[569]

Zeno of Tarsus c. 200 BCE

Diogenes says that this Zeno was a pupil of Chrysippus, and that he "left few writings, but many disciples."[570] From what little is known about his philosophical views, he was an orthodox Stoic, but according to Eusebius, the later Christian historian, Zeno *doubted the doctrine of the conflagration of the universe.*[571] If this is even true, it was a considerable modification of the physical theory of the Stoics. It is not known when he died. He was succeeded as head of the Stoic school by Diogenes of Babylon.

Diogenes of Babylon c. 230 – c. 150/140 BCE

Diogenes of Babylon[572] was born in Seleucia on the Tigris in Babylonia and studied in Athens under Chrysippus; he succeeded Zeno of Tarsus as head of the Stoic school, though it is not certain when. Among his pupils were Panaetius and Antipater of Tarsus, both of whom succeeded him in turn. He seems to have *closely followed the views of Chrysippus*, especially on dialectic, in which he is said to have instructed Carneades.[573]

Together with Carneades and Critolaus, he was sent to Rome to appeal a fine of a hundred talents imposed on Athens in 155 BCE for the sack of Oropus. They delivered their speeches first in numerous private assemblies,

---

569. Fitzgerald (2004), 'Philodemus and the Papyri from Herculaneum', in Fitzgerald et al. (Eds.), *Philodemus and the New Testament World Philosophy*.

570. Diogenes Laërtius, VII. 35.

571. Eusebius, *Praeparatio Evangelica*, 15. 18.

572. Also known as Diogenes of Seleucia.

573. A Skeptic of the Platonic Academy. By the year 159 BCE, he had started to refute all previous doctrines, especially Stoicism, and even the Epicureans whom previous skeptics had spared. As head of the Academy, he was one of three philosophers sent to Rome in 155 BCE where his lectures on the uncertainty of justice caused consternation among the leading politicians. He left no writings and many of his opinions are known only via his successor Clitomachus. He seems to have doubted the ability, not just of the senses but of reason too, in acquiring truth. His Skepticism was, however, moderated by the belief that we can, nevertheless, ascertain probabilities of truth, to enable us to live and act correctly. Cicero, *Academica*, ii. 30; *De Oratore*, ii. 38.

then in the Senate. Diogenes pleased his audience chiefly by his sober and temperate mode of speaking.[574]

Cicero called Diogenes "a great and important Stoic." [575] In the works of the Epicurean philosopher Philodemus, found in carbonized papyrus rolls recovered from the ruins of the Villa of the Papyri at Herculaneum, Diogenes is discussed more frequently than any philosopher besides Epicurus himself.[576]

Cicero speaks of him as deceased by 150 BCE, and since Lucian claims that he died at the age of 80, he must have been born around 230 BCE.[577, 578] He wrote many works, but none of his writings survive, except as quotations by later writers.[579]

He was succeeded by Antipater of Tarsus.

Diogenes, being from Babylon, may very well have imported important astronomical information into the line of the Stoic school, though it would not be necessary since we have the input of Eudoxus by way of Aratus.

Antipater of Tarsus d. 130/129 BCE

Very little is known about his life except that he was the disciple and successor of Diogenes of Babylon as leader of the Stoic school in Athens, and that he was the teacher of Panaetius.[580] Plutarch speaks of him, along with Zeno, Cleanthes and Chrysippus, as one of the principal Stoic philosophers, and Cicero mentions him as being remarkable for acuteness. Apparently, he spent quite a bit of his time debating with members of the rival Platonic Academy. It appears that there were constant disputes recurring between the two schools[581, 582], but we don't know the nature of them. Since the Platonists were the originators of the airy-fairy astralizing interpretation of about everything, and the Stoics appear to have been rather pragmatic, one cannot help but wonder if the topic of cometary catastrophe was ever debated

---

574. Aulus Gellius, *Attic Nights*, vii. 14; Cicero, *Academica*, ii. 45.
575. Cicero, *De Officiis*, iii. 12.
576. Obbink (2004), 'Craft, Cult, and Canon in the Books from Herculaneum', in *Philodemus and the New Testament World*, p. 73-84.
577. Cicero, *De Senectute*, 23.
578. Lucian, *Macrobii*, 20.
579. Tiziano Dorandi, Chapter 2: 'Chronology', in Algra et al. (1999), *The Cambridge History of Hellenistic Philosophy*, pp. 50-1.
580. Cicero, *de Divinatione*, i. 3, *de Officiis*, iii. 12.
581. Plutarch, *De Stoicorum Repugnantiis*.
582. Cicero, *de Officiis*, iii. 12.

between them. We cannot know because the writings of the Stoics have not survived, while the works of Plato and Aristotle have.

There is one noteworthy thing that I found about Antipater: he taught belief in God as "a Being blessed, incorruptible, and of *goodwill* to men," and blamed those who ascribed to the gods "generation and corruption," *which is said to have been the doctrine of Chrysippus*.[583] In other words, he didn't buy into Chrysippus' idea that everything was cause and effect, including when bad things happen. However, "generation and corruption" may refer to the tendency of cometary bodies to break up and disintegrate catastrophically put in terms of sex as did Hesiod.

According to Antipater, God is only good, so that must mean that he thought that when bad things happen, there is some other cause than God, such as human beings bringing it on themselves, perhaps? It's such a small clue that not much can be made of it.

Antipater wrote a treatise on the gods and two books on divination, which emerges again as a common topic among the Stoics, suggesting that they were still engaged in trying to determine cycles of destruction or causal links. Antipater's view was that divination worked simply because of the foreknowledge and benevolence of God: God knew what was going to happen and sometimes he gave hints! He also asserted that dreams were supernatural intimations of the future, and collected stories of *divination attributed to Socrates*.[584]

Now, this last is most interesting. We already know that Socrates claimed to have 'signs' that guided his actions and this may confirm his interest in, and practice of, divination. Perhaps Antipater was trying to get back to the roots of things and counter the slow drift away from original principles that had been taken by Chrysippus? He also seems to not have had a very high opinion of his own teacher, Diogenes of Babylon.[585] He was succeeded by his pupil, Panaetius.

Hipparchus c. 190 BCE – c. 120 BCE

Before we discuss Panaetius, the next Stoic in the line, we are going to make a diversion and have a look at Hipparchus – who was not a Stoic – because this is about where he fits in the chronology. It seems that, just as the Stoic school was losing its mojo, other things were happening in the intellectual

---

583. Plutarch, *De Stoicorum Repugnantiis*.
584. Cicero, *de Divinatione*, i. 3, 20, 39, 54.
585. Cicero, *de Officiis*, iii. 12, 13, 23.

environment that will lead us to the solution of a major mystery that we will be discussing in the next volume. (Yes, I know I've mentioned it several times; I'm just highlighting the various interconnections!)

Hipparchus is considered to have been the greatest ancient astronomer of antiquity. He was also a geographer, and a mathematician who is credited with establishing the foundations of trigonometry. However, as we know, he is most famous for his *incidental* discovery of precession of the equinoxes. As it happens, Aratus' preservation of the work of Eudoxus plays a part in all this.

Hipparchus was born in Nicaea, Bithynia (now Iznik, Turkey), and probably died on the island of Rhodes where he lived much of his life. He is known to have been a working astronomer at least from 162 to 127 BCE. He was the first astronomer whose quantitative and accurate models for the motion of the Sun and Moon survive. For this he certainly made use of the observations and perhaps the mathematical techniques accumulated over centuries *by the Chaldeans from Babylonia*. Additionally, there is a line in Plutarch's *Table Talk* where he states that Hipparchus counted 103049 compound propositions that can be formed from ten simple propositions; 103049 is the tenth Schröder–Hipparchus number[586] and this line has led to speculation that Hipparchus knew about *enumerative combinatorics*, a field of mathematics that developed independently in *modern* mathematics.[587, 588]

Hipparchus developed trigonometry and solved several problems of spherical trigonometry. With his solar and lunar theories and his trigonometry, he may have been the first to develop *a reliable method to predict solar eclipses*. His other achievements include the compilation of the first comprehensive star catalog of the western world, and possibly *the inventions of the astrolabe and the armillary sphere*[589], which he used during the creation of much of the star catalogue. It would be three centuries before Claudius

---

586. In number theory, the Schröder-Hipparchus numbers form an integer sequence that can be used to count the number of plane trees with a given set of leaves, the number of ways of inserting parentheses into a sequence, and the number of ways of dissecting a convex polygon into smaller polygons by inserting diagonals. These numbers begin 1, 1, 3, 11, 45, 197, 903, 4279, 20793, 103049, …

587. Stanley (1997), 'Hipparchus, Plutarch, Schröder and Hough'.

588. Acerbi (2003), 'On the shoulders of Hipparchus: A reappraisal of ancient Greek combinatorics'.

589. An armillary sphere (variations are known as spherical astrolabe, armilla, or armil) is a model of objects in the sky (in the celestial sphere), consisting of a spherical framework of rings, centred on Earth, that represent lines of celestial longitude and latitude and other astronomically important features such as the ecliptic.

Ptolemaeus' synthesis of astronomy would supersede the work of Hipparchus and it is heavily dependent on it in many areas.

Relatively little of Hipparchus' direct work survives into modern times. Although he wrote at least fourteen books, *only his commentary on the popular astronomical poem by Aratus was preserved by later copyists*. Most of what is known about Hipparchus comes from Ptolemy's (2nd century CE) *Almagest*, with additional references to him by Pappus of Alexandria and Theon of Alexandria (c. 4th century CE) in their commentaries on the *Almagest*; from Strabo's *Geographia*, and from Pliny the Elder's *Naturalis historia*.

Hipparchus is thought to be the first to calculate a *heliocentric system*, but he is *said* to have abandoned his work because the calculations showed the orbits were not perfectly circular as was believed to be mandatory by the Aristotelian science of the time.

Earlier Greek astronomers and mathematicians were influenced by Babylonian astronomy to *some* extent, for instance the periodic relations of the Metonic cycle and Saros cycle[590] came from Babylonian sources. But Hipparchus seems to have been *the first to exploit Babylonian astronomical knowledge and techniques systematically*. Except for Timocharis and Aristillus, he was the first Greek known to divide the circle in 360 degrees of 60 arc minutes (Eratosthenes before him used a simpler sexagesimal system dividing a circle into 60 parts). He also used the Babylonian unit *pechus* ('cubit') of about 2° or 2.5°.

Hipparchus probably compiled a list of Babylonian astronomical observations; G. J. Toomer, a historian of astronomy, has suggested that Ptolemy's knowledge of eclipse records and other Babylonian observations in the *Almagest* came *from a list made by Hipparchus*. Hipparchus' use of Babylonian sources has always been known in a general way, because of Ptolemy's statements. However, Franz Xaver Kugler demonstrated that the synodic and anomalistic periods that Ptolemy attributes to Hipparchus had already been used in Babylonian ephemerides.[591]

Hipparchus also studied the motion of the Moon and confirmed the accurate values for two periods of its motion that *Chaldean astronomers* certainly possessed before him. The traditional value from Babylonian System B for the mean synodic month is 29 days; 31,50,8,20 or 29.5305941... sexagesimal days. Expressed as 29 days + 12 hours + 793/1080 hours, this value was later used in the Hebrew calendar. The Chaldeans also knew that 251

---

590. The saros is a period of 223 synodic months (approximately 6585.3213 days, or nearly 18 years 11 days), that can be used to predict eclipses of the Sun and Moon.
591. Kugler & Strassmaier (1900), *Die Babylonische Mondrechnung*.

synodic months = 269 anomalistic months. Hipparchus used a multiple of this period by a factor of 17, because that interval is also an eclipse period. The Moon also is close to an integer number of years: 4267 moons : 4573 anomalistic periods : 4630.53 nodal periods : 4611.98 lunar orbits : 344.996 years : 344.982 solar orbits : 126,007.003 days : 126,351.985 rotations. The 345-year eclipses reoccur with almost identical time of day, elevation, and celestial position. Hipparchus could confirm his computations by comparing eclipses from his own time with eclipses from Babylonian records from 345 years earlier.

Pliny tells us that Hipparchus demonstrated that lunar eclipses can occur five months apart, and solar eclipses seven months (instead of the usual six months); and the Sun can be hidden twice in thirty days, but *as seen by different nations*. The result that two solar eclipses can occur one month apart is important, because this cannot be based on observations: one is visible on the northern and the other on the southern hemisphere – as Pliny indicates – and the latter was inaccessible to the Greeks.[592] Thus it is clear that Hipparchus was capable of calculating things that he could not observe. It also makes it clear that, by this time, at least some individuals understood that the Earth was a sphere, following Eudoxus. Prediction of a solar eclipse, i.e. exactly when and where it will be visible, requires a solid lunar theory and Hipparchus must have been the first to be able to do this. He may have discussed these things in *On the monthly motion of the Moon in latitude*, a work mentioned in the *Suda*. But this, like nearly everything from antiquity that might have conveyed accurate information, has been lost to us thanks to Christianity.

Before Hipparchus, Meton, Euctemon and their pupils at Athens had made a solstice observation (i.e. timed the moment of the summer solstice) on June 27th, 432 BCE (Julian calendar). Aristarchus of Samos is said to have done the same in 280 BCE, and Hipparchus also had an observation by Archimedes to hand. Next, Hipparchus himself observed the summer solstice in 135 BCE, but he found observations of the moment of equinox more accurate.

Between the solstice observation of Meton and his own, there were 297 years spanning 108,478 days. D. Rawlins noted that this implies a tropical year of 365.24579... days = 365 days;14,44,51 or 365 days + 14/60 + 44/602 + 51/603 in sexagesimal calculations, and that this exact yearlength has been found on one of the few Babylonian clay tablets which explicitly specifies the System B month.[593]

---

592. Pliny the Elder, *Naturalis Historia*, II.X.
593. Rawlins (1982), 'An Investigation of the Ancient Star Catalog'.

Before Hipparchus, astronomers knew that the lengths of the seasons are not equal. Hipparchus made observations of equinox and solstice and, *according to Ptolemy*[594], determined that spring (from spring equinox to summer solstice) lasted 94½ days, and summer (from summer solstice to autumn equinox) 92½ days. This is inconsistent with a premise of the Sun moving around the Earth *in a circle at uniform speed*. Hipparchus' solution was to place the Earth not at the center of the Sun's motion, but at some distance from the center. Indeed, this model *can* describe the *apparent* motion of the Sun.

He apparently made many observations between the years 162 BCE and 128 BCE. It was these observations that led to the discovery of precession. Hipparchus measured the longitude of Spica and Regulus and other bright stars. Comparing his measurements with data from his predecessors, Timocharis and Aristillus, he concluded that Spica had moved 2° relative to the autumnal equinox. Taking that in conjunction with the issues of the lengths of the tropical year (the time it takes the Sun to return to an equinox) compared to the sidereal year (the time it takes the Sun to return to a fixed star), Hipparchus concluded that the equinoxes were moving – 'precessing' – through the zodiac, and that the rate of precession was not less than 1° in a century. The idea that this motion may have been due to the helicoidal movement of the solar system around the galaxy, and the galaxy through space, doesn't seem to have occured to him or many others since.

As we have discussed above, Eudoxus of Cnidus in the 4th century BCE had described the stars and constellations in two books called *Phaenomena* and *Entropon*, which Aratus memorialized in a poem with the same title. The only work of Hipparchus that has come down to us is his commentary on this poem. This amounted to, mainly, many stellar positions and times for rising, culmination and setting of the constellations based on his own measurements, which revealed the glaring 'errors' of the material from Eudoxus, which – as we have already noted – he must have obtained elsewhere, along with his astronomical globe. Hipparchus' discovery of precession appears to be related to his commentary on the *Phaenomena* by Aratus, recording the information of Eudoxus, since precession would have explained the conflicts he found between what was written there and his own observations. He may have written the commentary as a form of comparison and from that exercise realized that he was dealing with a description of the sky over 3,000 years earlier, which may have prompted further investigations and conclusions that would have been beneficial to science had all his work not been consigned to the trash-bin of history.

---

594. *Almagest*, III.4.

Late in his career (possibly about 135 BCE), Hipparchus compiled his star catalog. *He also constructed a celestial globe depicting the constellations, based on his observations.* This celestial globe may have been the model for the Atlas Farnese Globe. The peculiar thing about this globe is the fact that all the constellations are shown *in reverse*, as they would be seen by someone outside of the cosmic system, i.e. the 'hypercosmic' perspective. Or, perhaps, it was intended to be viewed in a mirror for some reason.

The image above is a representation of the constellations on the Farnese Globe. As you can see, all the figures are reversed. (The missing areas are due to damage to the original.)

Hipparchus' interest in the fixed stars may have been inspired by the observation of a supernova (according to Pliny), or by his discovery of precession, according to Ptolemy, who says that Hipparchus could not reconcile his data with earlier observations made by Timocharis and Aristillus, or it could have been a search for comets. We'll never know. Virtually all Hipparchus' writings are lost, including his work on precession. They are mentioned by Ptolemy, who explains precession as the rotation of the celestial sphere around a motionless Earth.

The exact dates of his life are not known, but Ptolemy attributes to him astronomical observations in the period from 147 BCE to 127 BCE, and some of these are stated as made in Rhodes; earlier observations since 162 BCE might also have been made by him. His birth date (c. 190 BCE) was calculated based on clues in his work. Hipparchus must have lived at least some time after 127 BCE because he analyzed and published his observations from that year.

Hipparchus clearly obtained much information from Alexandria as well as Babylon, but it is not known when or if he visited these places. It is not known what Hipparchus' economic means were, nor how he supported his scientific activities. His appearance is likewise unknown; there are no contemporary portraits. In the 2nd and 3rd centuries, coins were made in his honor in Bithynia that bear his name and show him with a globe; this supports the tradition that he was born there. He is believed to have died on the island of Rhodes, where he seems to have spent most of his later life.

In any case, the work started by Hipparchus has had a lasting heritage, and was much later updated by Al Sufi (964 CE) and Copernicus (1543 CE). Ulugh Beg reobserved all the Hipparchus stars he could see from Samarkand in 1437 to about the same accuracy as Hipparchus'. The catalog was superseded only in the late 16th century by Brahe and Wilhelm IV of Kassel thanks to the use of better measuring instruments (even before the invention of the telescope). As a consequence of the durability of his work, Hipparchus is considered the greatest observational astronomer from classical antiquity until Brahe.[595] The Astronomer's Monument at the Griffith Observatory in Los Angeles, California, USA, features a relief of Hipparchus as one of six of the greatest astronomers of all time and the *only one* from Antiquity.

Panaetius c. 185 – c. 110/09 BCE

Panaetius was born in *Rhodes* and was a pupil of Diogenes of Babylon and Antipater of Tarsus in Athens. He was apparently in Rhodes in 149 BCE when he was chosen by the people of Lindos on Rhodes to be the priest of Poseidon Hippios and it is not impossible that he knew, and associated with, Hipparchus. Probably through Gaius Laelius, who had attended the lectures of Diogenes and then of Panaetius, he was introduced to the Roman general Scipio Africanus, and – like Polybius before him – gained his friendship. Both Panaetius and Polybius accompanied him as part of a Roman delegation to the Hellenistic east in 139-138 BCE.[596, 597, 598, 599]

He moved to Rome with Scipio where he introduced Stoic doctrines. In 129 BCE, after the death of Scipio, he returned to head the Stoic school in Athens. With Panaetius, Stoicism became much more eclectic, so that even

---

595. Bobrick (2005), *The Fated Sky*, p. 151.
596. Cicero, *de Finibus*, ii. 8.
597. Suda, *Panaitios*, comp. Polybios.
598. Cicero, *de Finibus*, iv. 9, *de Officiis*, i. 26, *de Amicitia*, 27, comp. pro Murena, 31, Velleius i.13.3
599. Cicero, *de Re Publica*, vi. 11, in Astin (1959), *Classical Philology*, and Astin (1967), *Scipio Aemilianus*, pp. 127, 138, 177.

among the Neoplatonists he passed for a Platonist! He assigned the first place in philosophy to Physics, not to Logic, and appears not to have undertaken any original treatment of the latter.[600, 601]

In Physics *he gave up the Stoic doctrine of the conflagration of the universe.*[602] He simplified the division of the faculties of the soul and doubted the reality of divination.[603] In Ethics he insisted that moral definitions should be laid down in such a way that they might be applied by the man who had not yet attained to wisdom.[604] In short, he was turning the School into 'Stoics for Dummies'.

Astrology had been important in Stoic thought until the time of Diogenes the Babylonian. Panaetius, under the influence of the Platonic Academy, was said to have rejected the astrology of the early Stoics completely. His rebellion within the school didn't last because his own successor, Posidonius, reinstated the role of astrology. We'll come back to Posidonius in a moment.

What, No Planets?

It is interesting that none of the above philosophers/cosmologists had much to say about planets. This fact is so conspicuous by its absence that one is justified in wondering whether planets were considered important at all. Among the pre-Socratic Greeks, the earliest indicators point to Pythagoras as being the one to *notice* the planets, but even here there is no

A streaking comet shares the sky with the luminous band of the Milky Way.

mention of the names of the planets until about the 4th century BCE. Aristotle, writing later in the *Meteorologica*, mentioned that the Italian Pythagoreans considered comets to be "rare *apparitions of one of the planets.*" A similar view was said to be held by the mathematician Hippocrates of Chios (430 BCE) and his pupil, Aeschylus.

---

600. Proclus, in Plato's *Timaeus*.
601. Diogenes Laërtius, vii. 41.
602. Cicero, de *Natura Deorum*, ii. 46, comp. 142; Stobaeus, Ecl. Phys. i.
603. Cicero, *de Divinatione*, i. 3, ii. 42, 47, *Academica*, ii. 33, comp. Epiphanius, adv. Haeres. ii. 9.
604. Clement of Alexandria, *Stromata*, ii; Plutarch, *Demosthenes*.

On the other hand, in two hundred years, at least seven distinct *theories of comets* came from early Greek philosophers and this is noteworthy. It seems that there was a serious reason among the Greeks to *explain something that required a resolution.* In these explanations, we see the powerful urge to normalize things, to abandon any explanation for something that might suggest that cosmic bodies – gods – could and would smite the Earth.

Clube and Napier make note of something interesting about Aristotle's cosmological thesis that gives a clue to what must have been going on at the time. It seems that Aristotle believed that *the Milky Way also lay in the sublunary zone,* i.e. in the plane of the ecliptic, between the Moon and the Earth, and he *claimed that it was a hot accumulation of the disintegra-*

Zodiacal light.

tion products of many comets. A number of other pre-Socratic sages also held similar views about the Milky Way. Some of the Pythagoreans taught that the Milky Way and comets were both produced by the same optical illusion: a reflection of sunlight. From the various descriptions Clube and Napier have collected, it seems that the earliest philosophers of this period knew, either from direct experience, or from that of their forebears, that comets disintegrated and formed a luminous dust cloud in the plane of the ecliptic and that this was the earlier 'Milky Way', as opposed to the later one, the edge-on view of our galaxy. Clube notes that this viewpoint is entirely consistent with Aristotle's otherwise inexplicable remark in his *Meteorologica,* where he speaks of an earlier time when much dust had been deposited in the tropical zone of the Zodiac "because of a decline in the number of comets!" [605]

In short, we have here a direct report of an association between comets and the zodiacal light or belt, a white glow that can be seen in the night sky from the vicinity of the Sun along the ecliptic just after sunset and before sunrise in spring and autumn when the zodiac is at a sharp angle to the hori-

---

605. *Meteorologica*, 345a, 6-11.

zon. This cloud must have been very pronounced then, though in our own day, it has been so diminished that moonlight or light pollution can make it difficult to discern. Still, on very dark nights it can still be observed as a band completely around the ecliptic, forming a thick, pancake-shaped cloud in the solar system. It is composed of comet dust that spirals slowly into the Sun, thus it is clear that it was deposited fairly recently, in cosmic terms, to be there at all. The light itself is caused by sunlight reflecting off the dust particles.[606, 607]

In later formulations, the 'milky way' was described as the path that the soul took to and from the heavens, and since we strongly suspect that this milky way was actually the zodiacal light, we can infer that another role of comets began to be theorized during the 1st millennium BCE, to wit, that the souls of the dead were ferried from earth to heaven (and vice versa) on comets. This might be due to the fact that interactions with comets and their effects were often deadly on a wide scale.

Finally, it should be noted that the ancient names that are now attached to planets once had strong cometary associations and descriptions (Mars, Jupiter, Saturn), as we have already discussed earlier. Later, planetary names came to be associated with fixed zodiacal longitudes, suggesting that the names were originally associated with observed comets that became associated with certain regions of the sky – the Pherecydes, known as constellations later – as well as certain times of year when the Earth intersected their fixed meteor streams in the zodiac. The attaching of the names to the planets themselves was a relatively late development due to the gradual disappearance of the brighter, Earth-crossing, cometary bodies which originally bore the names. Naturally, we may assume that these disappearances could have included not just breaking up into dust and smaller chunks, but a number of devastating impacts as well.

All of this tends to confirm that the Dark Age from which the ancient Greek civilization arose coincided with a period of intense meteoric and cometary flux in the sky and the constant presence of a vast cloud of reflective comet dust. This could very well be what gave rise to of Anaximander's picture of the heavens as "vast wheels of fire." It might also explain many other things, such as the fact that Aristotle's *Meteorologica* was not about 'meteorological' phenomena, but was really concerned with *meteoric* phenomena – or at least explaining it away! Additionally, the fact that the Greeks went to

606. Nesvorný et al. (2010), 'Cometary Origin of the Zodiacal Cloud and Carbonaceous Micrometeorites. Implications for hot debris disks'.
607. Jenniskens (2006), *Meteor showers and their parent comets*, p. 108.

the trouble of classifying comets suggest that such phenomena were active in those days and contributed to the anxiety and restlessness of the population (and we've found a few instances of possible impacts even during those times). Describing cometary phenomena as being related to Earth processes also suggests that the actions they were describing were things they found it necessary to explain: storms and whirlwinds in relation to fiery objects in the sky were not just the products of their imaginations. They were using logic to deal with a frightening phenomenon.

The realistic understanding of the action of gods-as-comets, the very real destruction wrought by same, and the perceived powerful need of the populace to get and stay on the right side of the right gods in order to forestall destruction, had been gradually displaced by, on the one side, Greek scientific rationality which divorced the gods and their intentions from natural phenomena – which was right enough in principle – but on the other side, the gods and associated beliefs were retained in 'astral' religions that projected the gods into some nebulous 'heaven' – an invisible, hypercosmic astral world in the sky (definitely not on Earth!) – that no longer had anything at all to do with the very *real* skies above our heads. I would even suggest that astral religions made human responsibility to the Earth and others a nebulous proposition.

Nevertheless, the astral religions at least preserved, though distorted, a version of the traditional understanding that the natural world was a purpose-driven system of larger-than-life forces which could, in the blink of an eye, turn on human beings and destroy them unless the proper rites were performed and life was lived according to the dictates of the various 'gods'. Obviously, in the physics of Heraclitus, the rites and worship of gods is irrelevant, but human behavior, as part of the 'Cosmic Mind', *was very relevant*. It appears that Socrates and his circle came to agree with this conception and may have even died because of it, and that, later in his life, Plato presented it obliquely in his story of Atlantis. But his followers either did not know, or rapidly forgot in the same way the followers of the early Stoics lost their way. I've toyed with the idea that Plato didn't know, that he wasn't let in on the discussions, but discarded it because his studious avoidance of the topic, and his determined procedure in a very different direction, suggests that he knew which side his bread was buttered on and just wasn't going to go there.

This very early *mechanization of reality* eventually became a perfect creation of a god who was definitely *outside* the system – no more gods allowed in except as psychic influences – and is actually the beginning of the division between science and religion. It is, in fact, the crux of the 'Horns of Moses', which are – in the deepest meaning – the horns of a dilemma: two

completely different approaches to reality and all within it. One perspective takes on the outer form of rationality, but underneath is desperately irrational in its *belief* that the material world is all that exists. The other is a perspective that totally rejects rationality in favor of the belief that those same unknown forces – which could, and should, be explored and explained by science – can't be explained and must not be explored in a rational way – belief is all that matters! And both of them insist on a soulless, mechanical cosmos born *ex nihilo*, either as a result of the Big Bang or by divine fiat.

CHAPTER NINE

GOOD VERSUS EVIL – THE COSMIC CONNECTION

Thus far, we have not only assembled a great deal of scientific information on the topic of cyclical cometary cataclysms, we have also covered the possible transformative effects such interludes may have on our world, especially humanity and the societies that human beings construct. In particular, we have made an overview of the emergent Greek civilization, which is the bedrock of our own, and also took a look at the road not traveled: Stoicism. Well, that's not entirely the case since a great many Stoic ideas were borrowed by Christianity, but they were combined in an unhealthy way with the astralizing influences of Platonic philosophy filtered through Judaism, and then dressed up in the garb of Roman Particularism. Further, it was only in the context of massive destruction of human society that Christianity was able to rise up from the ruins and pretend that it had been there all along and no one was the wiser. But before all that could happen, as is the way with cosmic and socio-political phase transitions, several steps along the road to disaster were taken and that is what the next volumes will cover.

What I can see after wading through literally tons of material is that the same patterns repeat over and over again. It seems to me that we can have some idea of what is before us only if we understand what is behind us, and make some effort to pinpoint where we are on the cycle of transition. We have touched on the question of causation here several times: *is there a dynamic relationship between the global behaviors of a people and the disasters that fall on them, or is it simply random?* I don't think we can adduce any certain proof for the former proposal – and certainly, the materialists want us to believe the latter – but from where I sit, the circumstantial evidence that the moral condition of humanity at large is related to its fate is more than sufficient to convict. What I want to do in this series is convey this to the reader in as efficient and interesting a way as possible.

Being a student of the ideas of George Gurdjieff for the past near-thirty years, and having followed a system of self-development rather similar to his for at least the past 20 years, I was certainly gratified to discover that many of his ideas respecting psychology are confirmed and expanded in modern, scientific, cognitive psychology. Still, it was something of a surprise to discover, during the course of this study, that many of his ideas were obviously drawn directly from the philosophy of the Stoics, and further, that the modern, scientific study of the human brain/mind and personality appears to support these ideas. Perhaps there are still existent Stoic-based esoteric schools in the area of the world where Gurdjieff grew up; as he said himself, many of his ideas were "esoteric Christianity".

Be that as it may, the Stoic philosophical system may be very important for our study of phase transitions in our world that include – or are predicated on – cyclic cometary disasters, so let me set out a few things about it here.

First of all, the Stoics proposed that everything in the cosmos derives from two principles, one active and one passive. I would like to adjust those terms to more modern understanding and call them positive and negative polarities, on/off, yes/no. For the Stoic, the active/positive principle was the rational, divine, governing, and informing idea; what the Sufis would call the 'Names of God' and what we would call something akin to Information Theory. In physics, it has been proposed that bits of *information* are the universe's basic building blocks. Claude Shannon, a mathematician considered to be the 'father of information theory', calculated that the information content of any event was proportional to the logarithm of its inverse probability of occurrence. What that means is that an unexpected, infrequent event contains much more information than a more regular, repeating, event.[608] The cumulative effect of regularly repeating events can lead to something that is seemingly unexpected and infrequent, but really isn't if one is paying close attention and extracting the signal from the noise. Information Theory is possibly the bridge between *ex nihilo* creation and the theory of evolution. Information can – and does – exist in a non-physical state and some of that information could very well transition into matter, which might then dynamically interact with additional information to get the evolution ball rolling. This appears to me to be what was behind the ideas of the Stoics and led to their basic cosmic economy, which goes as follows:

(a) The world is rationally organised, and so explicable and understandable. The pattern is complete throughout.

---

608. Vedral (2010), *A Quantum Calculation*.

(b) Within the organisation, different elements and parts are dynamic and governing, others are passive in function.

(c) The world is purposefully providential; so there is also a design as well as a pattern, and the good end is discoverable by the rational understanding of this.

(d) The divine element is completely and only immanent.[609]

(e) As the system is an organic whole, the understanding of any part contributes to the understanding of the whole, and vice versa. Even the operation of any part is relevant to the operation of the whole. (Think fractals here.)

(f) The operational law of cause and effect runs right through the behavior of phenomena and of living creatures.

(g) The understanding and explanation of its operation lies within, and only within, itself.

There are several things that follow logically from the above. The first is that we can learn about the world in any number of ways by examining the parts and applying principles of scale (as long as our analysis is objectively encompassing of the selected part). In other words, it is a more fully explicated version of 'as above, so below'. Secondly, since we are operating with physical senses, we can only infer information/concepts from function and behavior of material things. Thirdly, god, per se, is not only the guiding force of the universe *in the form of information*, but is the prime constituent. As the Sufis say: everywhere you look, there is the Face of God. Finally, the purest form of godliness is rationality; that is, coming as close as possible to the information that informs, and forms, matter.

Thus far, I have not discussed one of the most important of the Stoics: Posidonius[610], so it is time to move in that direction. He is going to play an interesting role in the next volume when we recount what was going on in Rome while Greece was busy explaining comets away. But before we get to him, historically speaking, some of his ideas are important to present at this juncture.

---

609. Immanence refers to philosophical and metaphysical theories of divine presence, in which the divine is seen to be manifested in the material world. It is often contrasted with theories of transcendence, in which the divine is seen to be outside the material world.

610. Posidonious c. 135 BCE – 51 BCE was acclaimed as the greatest polymath of his age. None of his vast body of work can be read in its entirety today, as it exists only in fragments.

Posidonius defined the all-pervading goodness of the world as a triad: god, nature and fate; three aspects of the same thing. God was the governing principle of the system (information that was not 'matterized'), Nature was the field of action, the physical continuum, i.e. matterized God; and Fate described the laws of operation. Since the system is an organic whole and the operational law of cause and effect was a part of the system, it logically followed that *the operation or state of any part could be relevant to the operation of the whole.* This meant that forms of divination were valid means of scientific exploration, though certainly not in isolation. What followed from this was that, since it was possible to predict such things as tides from the position of the Moon, it should also be possible to predict the future behavior of other phenomena, including human events, from patterns and signs in the heavens and on Earth. I don't think that we need to assume that Posidonius took this to unreasonable lengths, as Augustine claimed, since the evidence that he was an 'astrologer' in the usual sense is just not there. But what seems to have been on his mind was the scientific exploration of signs and seasons and trying and testing various methods of relating major events on the planet in the socio-political sphere to the cosmos at large and discovering their dynamic interaction. In other words, as a rationalist who believed that a rational law permeated the universe, Posidonius inferred that all events follow an unbroken chain of causation, even if we, at the human level, cannot always see the cause for a specific effect. But, theoretically, the world should be rationally comprehensible if we study the world and all within it, and learn the patterns of cause and effect at one scale, and then apply them to other scales. Like a fractal, the cosmic patterns always follow through to real world events and we can follow the chain backward by way of scientific observations and analyses. In Posidonius' view, cosmic design was imposed rationally from the top down, but we can only partially reveal it and check the facts that will lead to understanding this design, from the bottom up.

Certain moral principles flow naturally from such a construction of the cosmos, and the human being could be seen as a mini-universe with the potential for top-down rationality in the design of their lives also. Obviously, since the human being was a universe among many within the larger universe, this capacity for controlling their lives was limited in extent. But still, the place from which it manifests is the rational mind, the counterpart, or fragment of, the divine designer (information) of the universe. This conception puts philosophy of mind, or psychology, squarely within the field of science, though there are certainly points that cross over into arts. Human free will, constrained by the just-mentioned multiplicity of fellow humans existing within the larger system, depends on the individual studying and knowing and mastering their own brain/mind so that they can respond rationally to the events and dynamics over which they have no control.

A rational universe can be conceived of by considering an individual human being. The human body has many components and it seems that the driving force within a person is to maintain life at an optimum level. Anything that can harm the body or terminate life is considered 'bad'. A human being who acts in ways that bring danger or damage to the body is not behaving rationally. One doesn't decide that the body doesn't need feet or hands or vital organs, and remove them and expect to continue at an optimal level of life. One cannot take harmful substances into the body, or disrupt the complex chemical systems, without reducing the quality of life for the body as a whole. Therefore, a rational human, as the model for a rational universe, always seeks those things for its body that optimize life, i.e. are conducive to health and general well-being. I'm not going to draw this analogy out too far, but obviously, health and well-being can include having creative work, congenial relations with family and friends, and so on.

The analogy can be taken to the socio-political scale. In a society, the various parts of the 'body politic' can be seen to hold similar relations to one another as the parts of the body of a single individual. There are individuals in a society that form the bones, those that form sinew and muscle, those that constitute the functionality of various organs, including the brain, the guidance system. Obviously, a society that does not care for all parts of itself can be likened to a human being who is not engaged in an optimal life. Worse, a society that harms any part of itself is behaving irrationally and out of accord with cosmic rationality. This can be described as an insane person who believes that his arm is a snake and chops it off with an axe. He may think his foot is a giant rat, and batter it with a club. Obviously, that sort of behavior will lead, ultimately, to the death of the body. This analogy can include such things as parasitic infestations, and even parts of the body that have 'lost their mind', such as cancer, etc. and these parts can be played by humans or groups of humans whose behavior and actions within a society or nation destroy the health of the body as a whole, even causing death.

Historically speaking, over and over again it appears that the body of humanity has been either self-mutilating or weak and prone to disease in these analogic ways, and even worse. Very often, the 'brain' of social systems, i.e. the ruling elite, becomes diseased and believes that it can exist without a body at all and it ties a noose around its own neck while it teeters on a stool with a broken leg. While it is true that the brain requires a higher percentage of nutrients for proper function, extreme economic inequity amounts to virtual starvation of the rest of the body and the ultimate death of the brain itself. Sometimes these conditions are brought on by infections or by other areas of the body being weakened and becoming cancerous, and this spreads to and affects the brain. *Thus, the primary duty of the rational brain is to discover what the rest of the body needs for optimum health and performance, and see that it is supplied.* The same is true for any governing/ruling class. It is only rational to see that it is not merely advisable, but absolutely mandatory, to nurture and provide for the masses of humanity as one would care for one's own body because, in point of fact, that is the case on the larger scale.

Moving to the planetary scale, there is the Gaia Hypothesis. Going in that direction, it seems to me that humankind and its interactions with the flora and fauna of the planet constitute some sort of bio-geological force, or even just a *capacitor* of some sort, in electrical terms, and the potentials of this large-scale, possibly cosmic, embodiment are rarely taken into account, even in such things as the 'Gaia Hypothesis' of scientist James Lovelock.[611] Lovelock proposes that all organisms and their inorganic environment are closely integrated to form a self-regulating complex system that maintains the conditions for life on Earth. He is concerned mainly with the stability of global temperature, ocean salinity, oxygen in the atmosphere and other factors of habitability. His main proposition is that the Earth is a self-regulating complex system of tightly coupled biosphere, atmosphere, hydrospheres, and so forth. The conclusion is that Gaia seeks a physical and chemical environment that is optimal for life and that human beings affect this by their physical presence and activities.

The Gaia Hypothesis was upgraded to a theory when, in 2001, a thousand scientists at the European Geophysical Union meeting signed the *Declaration of Amsterdam*[612], which began with: "The Earth System behaves as a single, self-regulating system with physical, chemical, biological, and human components." That was on the 13th of July, 2001. Two months later: 9-11 and all that has followed came upon us. And since 9-11, the fireball activity on the Earth has increased dramatically.[613]

So, despite the fact that many scientists are working in that direction, it is insufficient to counter the sickness that has invaded humanity at the present time. The question we need to ask is this: *is there a connection between*

---

611. Lovelock (2000), *Gaia: A New Look at Life on Earth.*
612. Retrieved here: http://www.grida.no/news/press/2187.aspx
613. See the American Meteor Society's statistics on fireball reports here: http://www.amsmeteors.org/fireballs/fireball-report/

9-11 and all that has followed and the increasing instability of our planet? Is there a feedback loop between human beings and the planet, the planet and the solar system, the solar system and the galaxy, in terms of *information*? And if so, what can that mean for our future? And if we don't like the information that will be sent back to us via possible cometary bombardment, how can we change our signal?

In looking at the historical periods before, during and after alleged cometary events, there definitely does appear to be a certain set of correlations. We've already noted what Victor Clube had to say about it:

> Even before the Black Death came, then, a human catastrophe of great proportions was under way in late medieval times. Indeed, the cold snap lasted well beyond the period of the ... plague. *A number of such fluctuations are to be found in the historical record*, and there is good evidence that **these climatic stresses are connected not only with famine but also with times of great social unrest, wars, revolution and mass migrations.**[614]

Though he was speaking about a later event, nevertheless the same patterns repeat over and over again in the socio-political sphere. It is this that causes my unease in just blithely dismissing the human factor as being in no way involved in what happens on earth *vis-à-vis* the cosmos. Just as in physics where it has been noted that consciousness is involved in a dynamic way in quantum events, so may *it be possible that large-scale planetary events are related to the mass consciousness of great numbers of humans on the surface of planet Earth in some sort of cosmic feed-back loop.* As Bailey, Clube and Napier note, there is a sequence of events that follows a set pattern:

> Every 5-10 generations or so[615], for about a generation, mankind is subject to an increased risk of global insult through a 'Shoemaker-Levy type' train of cometary debris resulting in sequences of terrestrial encounters with sub-km meteoroids.
> 1. While the resulting risk is ~ 10%, the global insults take the form of:
>   (a) multiple multi-megaton bombardment,
>   (b) climatic deterioration through stratospheric dust-loading, not excluding ice-age, and
>   (c) consequent uncontrolled disease/plague.
> 2. The sequence of events affecting involved generations is potentially

---

614. Clube (1990), op. cit.
615. 150 to 300 years.

debilitating because, *whether or not the risk is realised, civilization commonly undergoes violent transitions e.g. revolution, migration and collapse.*

3. Subsequently perceived as pointless, such transitions are commonly an embarrassment to national elites, even to the extent that historical and astronomical evidence of the risk are abominated and suppressed.

The thing that keeps coming to my mind is: prior to 9-11 – which is certainly *a violent transition in human civilization that is now in progress* – there were no global insults from space or climatic deterioration via dust-loading that I could detect. It has only been since 9-11 that all of these factors have begun to manifest, increasing year by year, until now the weather on planet Earth – to take just one factor – has become overtly threatening to human life and survival. Famine and economic collapse stare us in the face and if the events follow the pattern, I expect a global plague of some sort to break out any day. And it could very well come from comet dust because the reports of noctilucent clouds (caused by comet dust loading the upper atmosphere) appearing further and further south come in several times a month now. What else is in that dust?

For the few years leading up to the year 2000 there was, indeed, a great deal of what I called 'Millennial Fever'. And the impacts of Comet Shoemaker-Levy on Jupiter may have made an impression on the minds of humanity but apparently did not deliver the message that could have gotten through! Having lived through all that nonsense and observed it in real time, what I noted about that was that it was all focused on a date: the year 2000, and a number of 'prophecies', mainly Nostradamus'. Parallel to the 'Millennialist' types, the followers of Nostradamus, or fundamentalist Christians looking for Jesus to come, were those who promoted the 2012 variation based on the alleged 'ending' of the Mayan calendar. But, again, please notice that none of this was *precipitated* by any sorts of global insults from space or noticeable climate deterioration at that point, unless we can surmise that the expectation of the end of the world brought on the comets that struck Jupiter as a precursor, which is something to be considered. It seems that the system might actually be tightly-coupled, and the Shoemaker-Levy event and Millennial Fever combined to produce 9-11: the wealthy elite themselves became frightened that they might lose control and began a program to cement their hold on humanity. This then added more energy to the coupled system and began the spiral of more intense deterioration. It was only after 9-11 that increasing fireball flux began and climate change became a really hot topic! And, as time has passed, fireballs, meteorites, and even a dozen or so actual small impacts, have increased dramatically. Earthquakes, volcanic eruptions, hurricanes, tsunamis, giant sinkholes, outgassings, strange electrophonic groanings in the sky, and so on and so forth, are piling up like crazy.[616] *It's as though the actions of the global elite, supported by the oceanic mass of authoritarian followers, brought these sorts of things upon us.* And the more these kinds of things happen, the more we see evidence of what Victor Clube described:

> Confronted on many occasions in the past by the prospect of world-end, national elites have often found themselves having to suppress public panic... an institutionalized religion is expected to oppose predestination and to secure such general belief in a fundamentally benevolent deity as can be mustered. ...
>
> ... the Christian, Islamic and Judaic cultures have all moved since the European Renaissance to *adopt an unreasoning anti-apocalyptic stance*, apparently unaware of the burgeoning science of catastrophes. History, it now seems, is repeating itself: it has taken the Space Age to revive the Platonist voice of reason but it emerges this time within a modern anti-fundamentalist, anti-apocalyptic tradition over which governments may, as before, be unable to exercise control. ... **Cynics (or modern sophists), in other words, would say that we do not need the celestial threat to disguise Cold War intentions; rather we need the Cold War to disguise celestial intentions!** [Emphasis in the original.] [617]

As noted, we could find our cosmic insult event in the impacts of Shoemaker-Levy on Jupiter in 1994, which caused a great shock within the scientific community. Comet Hyakutake came in 1996, then Hale-Bopp in 1997, neither of which should have, or would have, created such a stir had they not arrived in the lead-up to the year 2000. There was the death of Princess Diana in 1997, weird weather, including massive floods in Europe that year, and then the suicide of the Heaven's Gate cult in relation to Hale-Bopp in 1998. The Christian, New Age and UFO fundies were all going bananas, so to say, in reaction to these things. But again, would they have caused such a frisson of fear had it not been that the end of the millennium was approaching and something was 'expected'?

The point I am endeavoring to make is this: along the line of the Gaia Hypothesis, perhaps humankind is involved in something greater than just the homeostasis of the planet in a "tightly coupled system of biosphere, atmosphere, hydrosphere." Perhaps there are tightly coupled systems that include relationships between the Sun, the Earth-coupled biospheres and its

---

616. See Sott.net for daily updates on these occurances.
617. S. V. M. Clube (1996), op. cit.

neighbors and cosmic visitors? Perhaps the socio-political development of humankind is more intimately involved in cosmo-planetary events than has been previously supposed? Perhaps what happens 'out there' is a reflection of what is happening on Earth? Perhaps the ancients actually learned something in those interactions with comets when they formulated Judicial Astrology? Perhaps the decency of the rulers, the correctness of the behavior of the populace, actually *was* a significant factor in avoiding destruction? And, conversely, perhaps corruption in high places, authoritarian followers supporting and feeding energy into a corrupt system was/is a significant factor in actually bringing on destruction, even in terms of global, cosmic cataclysm? Perhaps, also, the extent and severity of the destruction depends on the depth and extent of the corruption?

Those of you who have read the first volume of *Secret History* are aware of the parallels between the scientific descriptions of the global cosmic disaster 13,000 years ago with the ancient descriptions of the great Flood, and how closely the descriptions of this event matched ancient materials relating to the semi-legendary story of Atlantis and its fall. The story Plato told was of a global empire that sought to rule the world and was making war everywhere when the end came. He got the idea from somewhere, even if the details are made up. As I pointed out, before Atlantis, the great tale of a destroyed nation was that of Troy. In that tale, the war began because of the abduction of a woman, Helen, *a violation of the rules of hospitality*. The story in the Bible – borrowed from Mesopotamian myths – records that the destruction came, more or less *as a result* of the 'Sons of God' mating with 'the daughters of men' and producing giants and 'men of renown' who obviously weren't the good guys because that statement is immediately followed by:

> The Lord saw that the wickedness of man was great in the earth, and that every imagination and intention of all human thinking was only evil continually. And the Lord regretted that He had made man on the earth, and He was grieved at heart.
>
> So the Lord said, I will destroy, blot out, and wipe away mankind, whom I have created from the face of the ground—not only man, [but] the beasts and the creeping things and the birds of the air—for it grieves Me and makes Me regretful that I have made them.[618]

So, obviously, all of these tales are drawn from the same well-spring of something real and terrible that happened, as Firestone et al. have demonstrated,

---

618. Genesis 6: 5-7.

and which Bailey, Clube and Napier further support with clear scientific astronomical evidence of what must have caused the Deluge and massive death and destruction on our planet. And all of the tales point to conditions of moral degeneracy of one sort or another prior to the event. Connection?!

Getting back to the Stoics, they determined, possibly by a similar process to what I have just outlined, that the cosmic rational principle is providential toward the good of humanity. But – and this is a very big 'but' – it must be human rationality that meets and reflects cosmic providence, setting goals and pursuing them, and that includes inculcating right conduct and understanding of moral good. In that way, human beings can fulfill their natural part in the grand cosmic scheme for good, not evil.

However, all men are not good. In fact, as the Stoics noted, despite the possibilities of being good by following the principles of cosmic rationality, some men are vicious. So, how did they explain this? There were different explanations from different Stoic philosophers, with Posidonius organizing and refining the ideas.

In terms strikingly similar to modern cognitive science, Posidonius stated that the mind had numerous capacities or faculties depending on the individual's *inborn temperament*. These were various combinations of rationality, emotions and desire (drives). In describing this, he made use of Plato's metaphor of the charioteer of reason driving two horses (emotion and desire). In Gurdjieff's system, this became the horses, carriage, driver and master, or emotions, body, brain and soul. In the end, Posidonius explained that good could only come when the emotions and drives were under the control of the rational factor (which applies at all scales). Despite the fact that all three aspects are 'natural', only rationality had absolute value because "Some people are deceived into thinking that what belongs to the irrational powers of the soul as natural goals, are natural goals without qualification; what they don't know is that *pleasure and power over one's neighbor are goals of the animal aspect of our soul*, while wisdom and all that is good and moral together are the goals of the rational and divine aspect."[619] He argued that emotions and reason have different sources (true) and that emotions are the *motions of irrational faculties*, which seems to be borne out by cognitive science.[620]

Regarding vicious men, it is only thanks to Galen[621] who quoted and dis-

619. Posidonius quoted by Galen in *De Placitis Hippocratis et Platonis*, V. 472, p. 452.3-10 M, p. 330.1-6.

620. See Kahneman's *Thinking Fast and Slow* and Wilson's *Strangers to Ourselves*.

621. Aelius Galenus or Claudius Galenus (CE 129 – c. 200/c. 216), better known as Galen of Pergamon (modern-day Bergama, Turkey), was a prominent Roman (of Greek ethnicity) physician, surgeon and philosopher.

cussed Posidonius' views that we have any clue at all as to which direction he was thinking on this matter. The following is from a discussion of Posidonius' refutation of Chrysippus on the topic of 'The Problem of Evil':

> Posidonius too reasonably censures and refutes him. For if it were really true that children had a natural affinity to morality right from the beginning, vice could not arise internally from themselves, but would have to come to them from an external source only. But surely, we see children going wrong in any case, even if brought up in good habits and properly educated.

The argument continues against Chrysippus who claimed that 'naturally good' children could *only* be corrupted by things they are exposed to, either communicated to them by others, or experienced directly. He then enjoins Posidonius' argument against this view:

> I [Galen] am at a loss with both of these... For why don't children, when they see or hear an example of evil, why don't they hate it and run from it, since they have no natural affinity for it? [As proposed by Chrysippus.] And my surprise increases still more in the case of the other 'cause', when although now neither seeing nor hearing any evil, they are deceived by the things themselves. For what necessity is there that children be enticed by pleasure as a bait if they have no affinity to it, or turn themselves and flee from pain if they are not naturally alienated from it too? Why should children have to fling themselves at and delight in praise and honours, be distressed and run from condemnation and dishonor, if it is true that they actually do not have natural affinity and alienation towards these? [Chrysippus implies] that he recognized some kind of natural affinity and alienation in us towards each of the foregoing. For when he says that perversion in regard to good and evil in morally imperfect men arises through the persuasiveness of appearances and through communication from others, he must be asked the cause or explanation why pleasure proffers a persuasive appearance of good, and pain of evil. And so too why are we so readily persuaded when we hear winning at the Olympics and the erection of one's statue praised and glorified by the majority as good, and defeat and disgrace as evils? Yes that too is criticized by Posidonius.
>
> And Posidonius tries to show that the causes of all false suppositions, when they occur in the contemplative sphere, they arise because of the emotional pull; this pull is preceded by false opinions when the rational faculty has become weak in regard to judgment. For he said that while a creature's impulse was sometimes born in the judgmental decision of the rational faculty, most often it occurs in the movement of the emotional faculty. ... different physi-

cal temperaments each produce 'emotional movements' peculiar to themselves; 'emotional movements' was the term habitually applied to them by Posidonius. But Aristotle straight out calls all such settled states of mind in animals 'characters' and explains in what way they are composed in their different mixtures.

This is the reason, I believe, why the cure of mental disturbance is also in some people welcome and easy because their emotional movements are not strong, and the rational is not weak by nature, nor void of understanding; it is rather through ignorance and bad habits that such men are compelled to live by emotions. But with some people the cure is harsh and rough, when the movements of emotion which necessarily occur through their physical state, are in fact big and violent, and the rational is by nature weak and uncomprehending. For two things are necessary if one is going to demonstrate improvements in a man's character: (a) the rational aspect must grasp knowledge of the truth, and (b) the movements of emotion must be blunted by habituation to good practices.[622]

In the above, we see strong implications of the 'nature vs. nurture' argument about psychopathy and other personality disorders. Since we are going to be encountering quite a few individuals whose behavior will be as astonishingly inexplicable as that of Alcibiades, as analyzed by Cleckley above, we might as well get this topic out of the way now.

Psychopathy and Historical Considerations

History, in its purest form, is simply a recitation of events, what really happened at a certain point in time and at a certain place. Historians, (and archaeologists, in some instances) do their best in analyzing and trying to sort out causes and effects. Some of them try to figure out what drives key individuals to do some significant thing and, as far as I have been able to see after reading history for over 40 years, many historians do a rather mediocre job of it (though there are exceptions). The reason for this, as should be clear by this point in the present text, is because they do not take environment and good psychopathology into account, as needs to be done. They also rarely – if ever – take their own psychology into account! Before historians – or anybody, for that matter – write narratives about what they think really happened, they should have already taken their own tendency to lie to themselves *all the time* into account.[623]

---

622. Galen, op cit., V. 459-65, pp. 437.1-444.11M, pp. 316.21-322.26.
623. See, for example: Wilson (2004), *Strangers to Ourselves: Discovering the Adaptive Unconscious*; Kahneman (2011), *Thinking Fast and Slow*; Trivers (2011), *Deceit, Fooling Yourself the Better to Fool Others*.

The problem is, I think, a failure to understand that groups, societies and nations ought to be looked at as – more or less – 'living systems', with all the problems that a living being is heir to, including birth, growth, maturity, old age, death and, most importantly, sickness. What this means is that the failure of most analysts in this field is that they do not factor in the complexity of human psychology, considering that the human being is the primary unit of any sociological system just as a cell is the primary unit in a body. Most social, religious and governmental systems are predicated on a very simplified view of human beings that does not take into account the complexity and variety of human types and how they interact together, very much like organs in a body. This applies to any ideology which attempts to over-simplify psychological reality, whether it be one utilized by a totalitarian system or by democracy as well. People are different and whatever is qualitatively different and remains in a state of permanent evolution cannot be equal.

Just as Toynbee[624] noted that empires fall due to internal and external causes, so is it that human beings – very often the pivots of history – act as they do based on internal and external causes as the Stoics propose. A human being is a pattern-seeking and reading organism that seeks its own survival at the most basic level. Added to that is the fact that, as an organism subject to sexual reproduction and the recombination of DNA that this entails, human beings are *not* created equal or at all the same, by any stretch of the imagination, and some of them seek their own survival at the expense of others or even require the suffering of others to feel satisfied; it's hard-wired absence of conscience, as psychopathy experts generally agree. What is more, those types of individuals tend to rise to the top because there are no emotional considerations to distract them from their pursuit of power. Does that mean they are truly rational, as they like to think? No. It means that *they are dominated by their animal drives* to the exclusion of true rationality and generally have only the most primitive emotions.

I have written on this topic rather extensively both in print and on the Internet so here I'm going to pass over it rather quickly, with source citations for the reader unfamiliar with this body of work.

According to Hervey Cleckley[625], Robert Hare[626], Martha Stout[627], Anna

---

624. Arnold Joseph Toynbee CH (14 April 1889 – 22 October 1975) was a British historian whose twelve-volume analysis of the rise and fall of civilizations, *A Study of History, 1934-1961*, was a synthesis of world history, a metahistory based on universal rhythms of rise, flowering and decline, which examined history from a global perspective.
625. Cleckley (1988), *The Mask of Sanity*.
626. Hare (1999), *Without Conscience*.
627. Stout (2006), *The Sociopath Next Door*.

Salter[628], Sandra L. Brown[629], Andrzej M. Lobaczewski[630], Paul Babiak[631] and many other experts in psychopathy, a diagnosis of psychopathy cannot be made on the basis of visible behavioral symptoms *to the exclusion of interpersonal and affective symptoms* because such a procedure essentially makes psychopaths of many people who are simply injured by life or society, and allows the true psychopaths who have a well-constructed 'mask of sanity' to escape detection. Based on a growing body of literature, many (or most) psychopaths grow up in stable, well-to-do families and become white collar criminals who, because of money and position, never have their *private destructive behaviors* exposed to public view and repeatedly avoid contact with the justice system. These types, who do untold damage to society at large, are not 'classified' under present diagnostic systems. There are others who never break any laws at all, they simply destroy people around them emotionally and psychologically. In other words, the most dangerous psychopath is educated, wealthy and socially skilled.

The issues of nature vs. nurture are a hot topic in psychopathy studies. There is the school that says all people are pretty much the same, and that people who are badly treated as children grow up to treat others badly; they learn from the adult examples set for them; they identify with the aggressors; this is the nurture school. The nature school says there is *wide variation in inherited dispositions* and that many people who are treated badly do not grow up to treat others badly, that those who do would have done so anyway, even if treated well, because they were born 'bad'. They also point out the not inconsiderable evidence that there are many psychopaths that do not have the abusive backgrounds postulated by the nurture school. Robert Hare, psychopathy expert, says that there are varying components of nature and nurture involved, but that *nature* – heritability – is the *strongest* factor. This appears to be exactly what Posidonius was saying. Opponents of this idea oppose it for the very simple reason that being inherited would mean that there is no cure. Well, there is no cure for a lot of physical and mental conditions, so why should psychopathy be such a bone of contention?[632] Perhaps it is the nature of the beast, an individual who looks and behaves (mostly) completely human, but lacks those very characteristics that are said to be what make humans human, as opposed to just two-legged animals with opposable thumbs. They all look human, so they must all BE human and the same, right? Wrong.

628. Salter (2004), *Predators, Pedophiles, Rapists.*
629. Brown (2010), *Women Who Love Psychopaths.*
630. Lobaczewski (2007), *Political Ponerology.*
631. Babiak & Hare (2007), *Snakes in Suits.*
632. Frankenstein (1959), *Psychopathy: A Comparative Analyisis of Clinical Pictures.*

Clinical psychologist Andrzej Lobaczewski refers to neuroanatomical structures as the human "instinctive substratum". He points out that the instinctive substratum of the human being has a slightly different biological structure than that of animals.

> Energetically speaking, it has become less dynamic and become more plastic, thereby giving up its job as the main dictator of behavior. It has become more receptive to the controls of reasoning, without, however, losing much of the rich specific contents of the human kind.
>
> It is precisely this phylogenetically developed basis for our experience, and its emotional dynamism, that allow individuals to develop their feelings and social bounds, enabling us to intuit other people's psychological state and individual or social psychological reality. It is thus possible to perceive and understand human customs and moral values. From infancy, this substratum stimulates various activities aiming at the development of the mind's higher functions. In other words, our instinct is our first tutor, whom we carry inside all our lives. Proper child-rearing is thus not limited to teaching a young person to control the overly violent reactions of his instinctual emotionalism; it also ought to teach him to appreciate the wisdom of nature contained and speaking through his instinctive endowment.

Nearly all creatures other than man have well-developed and powerful instinctive drives that dominate their life experiences in place of the more plastic human system where the self-reflective, rational, frontal cortex has taken over the rule of the roost. Some animals can stand and walk within a short period of birth; they can find their way to a source of food; all kinds of marvelous 'hard-wired' behaviors exist in myriads of creatures that are only hinted at in man because of this plastic substratum that relies more on training than hard-wired behaviors to help man survive. As a result of this plasticity, human infants are the most helpless creatures on Earth. Nevertheless, science has demonstrated that human infants are born with basic temperaments and, in some cases, a bit more (or less) than usual.

Suppose a condition – either trauma or genetically caused – that either prevents the proper development of the human instinctive substratum, or restricts it to a more dynamic, less plastic role, or even – via genetic recombination – produces in a human being a neuroanatomical system that is an atavistic throwback to one of our animal cousins on the evolutionary tree? Imagine the emotional nature of a crocodile in a human being? It gives an all-new meaning to the 'Reptilian Brain', doesn't it?

Given a retarded or damaged instinctive substratum, it is highly possible –

even probable – that psychological deviations will manifest. Such cases are likely beyond the ability of current medical science to help and – in many cases, *though not all* – can lead to anti-social, violent and/or criminal behavior. Keep in mind here that a normal instinctive substratum for an animal is not normal for a human being and, if an essentially animal substratum is the cause of deviant behavior in certain cases (as I strongly suspect), we can only infer what is inside from that behavior. What strikes me as important here is that the apparent behavior of many psychopaths is dynamically similar to the emotional behaviors of certain animals in certain states, driven by instinct. And notice that I am focusing on emotions here, not intelligence!

When considering a grown up psychopath, there are highly complex neurological circuits that have developed apace in the process of learning what works to get his needs and demands met. A complex and even brilliant intelligence can be harnessed in service of a dominating animalistic drive-system combined with a restricted, deviant or even absent, human-oriented emotional nature. For all *human* intents and purposes, psychopaths *behave* as though the core of their being is little more than a hunger at the center of a bundle of neurological inputs and outputs; just a sort of black hole that wants/needs to suck everything into it. Under the influence of this internal structure – this ever-present, never fulfilled hunger – the psychopath is not able to appreciate the wants or needs of other human beings, the subtle shades of a situation, or to tolerate ambiguity. The entire external reality is filtered through – made to conform to – this rigid and primitive internal structure, *in the service of primitive drives.*

When psychopaths are frustrated, i.e. when they do not get what they want, when satisfaction of the hunger is denied or delayed, what they seem to feel is that everything in the world 'out there' is against them while they are only good. This may, of course, translate into actual thought loops of being good, long-suffering and only seeking the ideal of love, peace, safety, beauty, warmth and comfort that *comes with satiation* (never mind that they can never achieve it), but the most fundamental thing about it is that when a psychopath is confronted with something displeasing or threatening to his hunger, that object (person, idea, group, whatever) is placed in the 'all bad' category and their destruction is thus justified. And, of course, with a psychopath, their rage has numerous possibilities (including utilizing a very complex brain) for sustaining itself for a very long time: as long as necessary for *that object* of the rage to be incorporated as was originally desired.

If the brain of the psychopath is forced to face mounting evidence that some choice or act of his/hers has created a problem or made a situation worse, this must be denied by the brain as being in any way part of the self and projected as coming from 'out there'. The internal structure of the psychopath will admit to no wrong (it cannot), nothing bad, no errors, and so, anything that is defined as 'bad' is naturally – structurally – projected onto someone or something else. And keep in mind that this is *not because they choose to do that*; **it is because they cannot do otherwise.** There is nothing at the core but a hunger connected to neural inputs and outputs, wrapped up in grandiosity and eternal perfection; that is the way they are made.

As a consequence of having such a primitive core structure coupled with a complex – and in some cases, brilliant – brain, psychopaths become masters of projective identification.[633] That is, they project onto and into others everything that is bad (remembering that 'bad' changes according to what the psychopath wants at the moment – that's part of the structure), and seek in manipulative ways to induce in that other person what is being projected, and seek to control the other person who is perceived as manifesting those 'bad' characteristics. In this way, the psychopath gains enjoyment and feels 'in control' which amounts to getting 'fed' or 'nurtured' in some way. Keep in mind also that what the psychopath considers to be good has nothing to do with truth, honor, decency, consideration for others, or any such thing, other than what the psychopath wants at any given moment. In this way, any violation of the rights of others, any foul, evil deed, can be perpetrated by a psychopath and he will still sleep like a baby (literally) at night because he has done nothing wrong!

One of the main barriers to understanding psychopathy is due to the fact that psychopaths rise to the top and have done so since time immemorial, and the social structures and belief systems that are inculcated in us from birth are due to their machinations and for their benefit. You could say that it is projective identification at the social level. What is more, we are most like the psychopath when we project onto psychopaths our own internal

---

633. "A process whereby parts of the ego are thought of as forced into another person who is then expected to become identified with whatever has been projected. The projector strives to find in the other, or to induce the other to become, what they deny in themselves. Projective identification differs from simple projection in that projective identification can become a self-fulfilling prophecy, whereby a person, believing something false about another, relates to that other person in such a way that the other person alters their behavior to make the belief true. The second person is influenced by the projection and begins to behave as though he or she is in fact actually characterized by the projected thoughts or beliefs, a process that may happen outside the awareness of both parties involved. The recipient of the projection can suffer a temporary loss of insight, a sense of experiencing strong feelings...[of] being manipulated so as to be playing a part, no matter how difficult to recognise, in somebody else's phantasy." Laing (1969), *Self and Others*, pp. 37 and 111.

states of goodness and decency and believe that, because they look human, they are like us; we are conditioned to the belief that all humans are all created equal, and "all have sinned and come short of the glory of God" and that just a bit more effort, more forgiveness, and a little repentance means anybody can be saved. It just ain't so. The knowledge of psychopathy and ponerology is what 'opens the cage door', yet it seems the heavily conditioned psychologists and psychiatrists of the mainstream are too afraid to 'go there' – to step out of the cage and really see where this knowledge could lead them. Thus there are endless attempts and theories to fit the square peg of psychopathy into the round hole of 'humanist dogma' that insists on the uniform nature of the core self for every single human-looking being. Sometimes this wishful thinking can fuel a more egotistical attitude. Lobaczewski refers to this as the "egotism of the natural world view."

> [W]e often meet with sensible people endowed with a well-developed natural world view as regards psychological, societal, and moral aspects, frequently refined via literary influences, religious deliberations, and philosophical reflections. Such persons have a pronounced tendency to overrate the values of their world view, behaving as though it were an objective basis for judging other people. They do not take into account the fact that such a system of apprehending human matters can also be erroneous, since it is insufficiently objective. Let us call such an attitude the "egotism of the natural world view". ...
>
> Today, however, the world is being jeopardized by a phenomenon which cannot be understood nor described by means of such a natural conceptual language; this kind of egotism thus becomes a dangerous factor stifling the possibility of objective counteractive measures. Developing and popularizing the objective psychological world view could thus significantly expand the scope of dealing with evil, via sensible action and pinpointed countermeasures.[634]

What we have here is similar to the old saying about the devil: his greatest defense is that nobody believes in him. Well, we do have a devil in our midst, only he isn't some kind of supernatural creature, he is an intra-species predator that looks like us and, unless you are able to peel away the mask by close, personal association over time, acts like us. In fact, as Hervey Cleckley points out, the psychopath is so normal with his mask on that he epitomizes all that neurotic, self-doubt plagued normal humans would love to be.

Psychopaths seem to have in abundance the very traits most desired by normal persons. The untroubled self-confidence of the psychopath seems almost

---

634. Lobaczewski, op. cit.

like an impossible dream and is generally what 'normal' people seek to acquire when they attend assertiveness training classes. In many instances, the magnetic sexual attraction of the psychopath seems almost supernatural.

Cleckley's seminal hypothesis concerning the psychopath is that he suffers from a very real mental illness indeed: a profound and incurable affective deficit. If he really feels anything at all, they are emotions of only the shallowest kind. Cleckley also gives grounds for the view that psychopathy is quite common in the community at large. He has collected some cases of psychopaths who generally function normally in the community as businessmen, doctors, and even psychiatrists. Some researchers see criminal psychopathy – often referred to as anti-social personality disorder – as an extreme of a 'normal' personality dimension (or dimensions).

We would characterize criminal psychopaths as 'unsuccessful psychopaths'. The implication, of course, is that many psychopaths may exist in society who cope better than do those who come to the attention of the judicial and welfare systems.

Being very efficient machines, like a computer, they are able to execute very complex routines designed to elicit from others support for what they want. In this way, many psychopaths are able to reach very high positions in life. It is only over time that their associates become aware of the fact that their climb up the ladder of success is predicated on violating the rights of others. "Even when they are indifferent to the rights of their associates, they are often able to inspire feelings of trust and confidence."

In a world driven by conscienceless individuals, even those who would otherwise behave in more pro-social ways tend to shut down their conscience in order to survive or protect those they love.

An external event can act on a dozen different individuals by inducing in them a dozen variations of organismic response. The external environment is constantly acting on human beings and that environment includes social conditioning from childhood to planetary environment, which may include influences of which science is not yet aware or, if they are aware, do not fully understand, including solar radiation and cosmic rays and EM emanations of all sorts from the planet, the atmosphere and the cosmos. All of these – and probably more – can condition the response of the organism which is already born with particular tendencies to greater or lesser sensitivity to those inputs.

Further, there is a statistically significant percentage of individuals born with damaged or deficient psychological apparatus in the same way individuals can be born with physical handicaps. As many psychologists and neuroscientists of our modern day have noted, and more vigorously in recent years, these types of individuals can have profoundly influential effects on human society, usually negative. Since current events are just history in the making, and we are aware of these factors acting in the social and political environment now, we must take those factors into consideration when reviewing historical events. A historian who looks at a particular development in history and attributes motives to the characters based on inadequate psychological knowledge only confounds the issues.

This idea leads to the primary reason for the failure of such systems of analysis: when considering a human population, what is left out of the equation is the fact that, in every society on Earth, there is a certain percentage of individuals that are extremely deviant from the masses of normal people, and this small group is generally very active in ways that can affect hundreds, thousands, even millions of other human beings in negative ways. The analogy of a disease pathogen in a body serves very well to convey the proper perspective.

Deviant personalities, being in a minority and knowing that they are a minority, feel driven to take power over their environment in order to alleviate the stress of this feeling of being abnormal. This drive enables them to easily 'rise to the top', and then to interpenetrate the entire social structure with a ramified network of mutual and multiple pathological conspiracies in a way similar to how a disease takes over a body.

It is said that power corrupts, and absolute power corrupts absolutely. What this view does not convey is that power attracts deviants and the corruption of everything else is then a result of pathological persons – who are innately attracted to gaining power over others – spreading their corruption and making it easy for other corrupt persons to join them 'at the top'. This is the primary driver of all the so-called 'cycles of history'.

Just as a disease organism seeks its own survival and to propagate, pathologically deviant persons want power over others and they are not inhibited by considerations of conscience or feeling for others. An analogy of this is that the disease pathogen is totally uncaring of the damage it may do to the organ systems it invades. It only wants to survive and propagate. The bacteria or virus has evolved many unique characteristics that enable it to take over a body when that body is weak. Thus, when societies are weakened for any of a number of reasons, deviant personalities are able to utilize their specifically evolved methods and means to achieve that power that normal people with normal morals simply cannot comprehend because it is not part of their reality and most human beings tend to assume that everyone else is like themselves, because they are conditioned to do so by pathologically devised social and religious "norms".

And so, networks of pathological deviants rise to power again and again, imposing their distortions on the masses of normal people like a disease, until the masses wake up and get rid of the deviants (bring in the therapies), normalize human relations, and begin to take care of the body of society, thus restoring health. For a while.

The problem of deviants coming to power again and again is due to the same factor mentioned above: that human beings tend to believe that others that look like them, talk like them, walk like them, are in fact like them, even inside. They are not. There are vast differences between human beings. All people are not created equal in ability, though they certainly ought to be equal in terms of opportunity and legal rights.

If people would begin to look at various social structures as organic systems and analyze them in the context of a 'body', then there would be greater success in establishing proper social hygiene so as to maintain optimum health. It ought not to be considered a Utopian dream for societies to gain and prolong a state of good health since many people do it in their individual lives.

Just as a few disease pathogens of exceptional virulence can take down a human system and incapacitate it, or even kill it, so can a few deviant personalities and their networks of propagated pathogenic cohorts, participate in the genesis of a kind of evil which envelops an entire nation. The psychological substructure of the deviants, like the evolutionary propagating mechanisms of a pathogen, drives them with dreams of obtaining power and imposing their will upon society. What is worse is that such deviants, like germs, do not realize that they, too, will be buried in the earth or tossed into the fire with the very body they have destroyed. That's another historical fact, repeated many times, that is there for anyone to see.

We need to remember that psychopaths and other personality-disordered individuals really have no choice but to be what they are; they are like forces of nature. But normal human beings *do* have a choice as to whether they will abuse others or accept abuse or not. By abusing or accepting abuse, they give power to the psychopaths to abuse others, so it is not just a matter of self-preservation; it is a matter of making sure that our children have a future. It seems that, in a world where the people cannot or will not rise up against psychopathy in power, the Cosmos will do it for them and take them out as well for their silence and acquiesence. The bottom line is, nobody and no event is going to 'save' anyone. It is only human beings, individually and collectively, who have the power to BE their own salvation.

It certainly gives one pause and it appears that this very topic was one which interested Posidonius intensely and was the impetus for much of his research.

Posidonius

Returning to Posidonius and the Stoics, I'll discuss his mathematics and astronomy when we come to him in the chronicle of the next volume where he figures as an important player; at the moment, I want to lay the groundwork for understanding my own approach since, as it happens, it is practically identical to that of this extraordinary man who lived over 2,000 years ago.

As we've already learned, the main thrust of the Stoics was that human beings should strive for rational control of moral action as defined by the rational – as objective as possible – understanding of the human constitution and *cosmic design as related to humans.* Posidonius explained a moral 'mistake' as being due to a person being inadequately educated, either in rational understanding or life habits, who was ruled by his or her emotions. Such a person would give more value to objects of emotion and desire (drive) which would cause them to so distort their rational thoughts that they ended up making a choice that actually overrode moral reason. Posidonius insisted that the root of evil or vicious action is internal, a seed lying in the natural pathology of our own make-up. He agreed that the seed could be nurtured and grown by external agencies, but in the end, right or wrong is our individual, personal responsibility.

So, what to do? Posidonius had a very practical approach. He proposed that an individual should be trained along two pathways simultaneously. The first one was theoretical study of the natural world and the second was training by having moral rules that define appropriate acts to follow. He denied the idea of the perfect wise man being like a body that never, ever got sick. There was no such thing as unassailable health. For Posidonius, the ordinary person was generally healthy but 'prone to sickness' when making good choices and sick but with potential for recovery when making wrong decisions. That was why both courses of education were needed: one aimed at developing and strengthening the rational mind with knowledge and awareness, and the other directed at overcoming mental pathology, bad habits, wrong reactions and overactive emotions.

According to Posidonius, the rational aspect of a person was amenable to infusion of knowledge and training *when he was sane.* He could then be taught that he needed to follow, in everything, *reason, which is similar to the rationality that infuses the cosmos.* And the way to find that out was to study the cosmos itself, i.e. the world and everything in it. One should understand fully and completely that it is a deviation from true humanness to be swept along by our irrational aspects like an animal. Thus, such a course of study would include natural philosophy and logic so as to come to an understanding of the structure and operation of the cosmos and our positive, responsible function within it, and from this to acknowledge that our rationality, not our emotional impulses, was our true directing force. In other words, ætiology, the study of causation, should be one of our chief occupations.

However, when the ordinary man is *insane due to excessive emotionality*, different training methods needed to be used since irrational states do not respond to rational discussion. He observed that emotions arise and then abate over time. He also observed that sometimes, emotions could be 'run-out' by being deliberately triggered and driven. This was compared to gaining control of a runaway horse by allowing it to run until it was exhausted.

It should be noted here that in no way did the Stoics think that eradicating emotions was proper. As Posidonius noted, they are a necessary part of our natural and normal mental make-up. But like a horse, they needed to be trained and not allowed to pull the carriage over a cliff. Seneca tells us that Posidonius elaborated a whole system of ethics for training and it included different methods of persuasion, exhortation and many examples. All this is lost.

We come now to Posidonius' interest in History. For Posidonius, *history was one of the main means by which the seeker came to know and understand the cosmos.* History teaches us a *respect for the facts*, understanding that emerges from putting those facts together and explaining causes, and the labor of searching for proofs teaches consistency and logic. More than this, History is a collection of descriptions of the behavior of many individuals, societies and the planet itself, over long periods of time, which gives the student much material for rational analysis so as to recognize the patterns and understand, thereby, the causes.

Posidonius wrote 52 books of history. The range and scope of his undertaking was staggering and, from the few fragments that survive the destruction of his work, we can note that he, too, sought to include facts, major and minor events, things of global and local importance, and social and environmental phenomena.

> Its account consistently displays that although external circumstances, both human and environmental, may be contributory factors to action, real motive is not imposed from without, but from *internal character*, an analysis in direct, and surely deliberate, opposition to other historians like Polybius. *This view is illustrated not only in individuals of power, but in national character.* The migratory invasions of the Cimbri, a major and disruptive historical

event of the period, was not to be explained merely by the natural phenomena of floods pushing them back from their native Jutland, but by their own inherent piratical and nomadic character. ...

To drive this point home, Posidonius was willing to expand an incident beyond its mere historical importance. His brilliant, vividly detailed and lengthy account of the brief career of Athenion, the Athenian tyrant of 88 BCE, far outruns what was a comparatively insignificant event in the Mithridatic Wars. But Posidonius was intent on unmasking in detail the disastrous effect, and how it came about, of an immoral so-called philosopher tyrant on the silly Athenian mob, however briefly.

This indicates another notable moral preoccupation of the *History*: its reiterated interest in the relationship between ruler and ruled, in all permutations, whether in a voluntary subordination, or as ruler and slaves; it involves the character of both ruler and ruled, and their relationship. And of course, this reflects in the historical medium the working out of the moral axiom of the element of rational rule controlling the subordinate, or its failure to do so.

There is much else, of course, including a sustained attack on popular legend and superstition in favour of rational explanation through cause and effect. So the *History*, like the sciences and mathematics, is a necessary investigation for his philosophy. ...

Posidonius' place in intellectual history does not derive from the scattered riches of a polymath, but from *an audacious panoptic attempt to understand, and hence explain in its complete context, our material world by the rationality of its operation, checked where we can by observation of the facts, and so define our own behavior in it.* ...

[Posidonius'] willingness to explore to the limits the thesis that the common rationality of the cosmic order and the function of our own comprehension is the only possible means of explanation and understanding, and hence that our behavior, morality and happiness in the end should depend on that alone, is the drawing together under the formal cloak of Stoicism, some of the most important and stimulating threads running through the whole of Greek philosophy. But his most important contribution was to enlist and integrate with philosophy the whole range of intellectual disciplines open to human investigation.[635]

My own aims with writing this history are similar to those of Posidonius: an *attempt to understand, and explain in its complete context, our material world by the rationality of its operation, checked where we can by observation*

---

635. Kidd (1999), *Posidonius*, Vol. III, Introduction, pp. 23-27, excerpts.

of the facts, and so define our own behavior in it. And, like Posidonius, I will discuss details of certain things that strike me as important to our exploration of cause and effect, and sometimes pass rather quickly over other things with barely a mention.

Referring back to the Dark Interlude section where I discussed our problems with trying to figure out truth in terms of our basic reality and how finding out the truth of our history – past and current events – is one of the few things we have to practice on, so to say; there are also issues with our sources which, in the end, is a result of the influence of Moses via Christianity acting on Western civilization in a most particular way right up to our present time. As Robin Lane Fox noted:

> No generation can afford to ignore whether Christianity is true and, if it is not, why it has spread and persisted and what is the proper response to it.[636]

The transition from the pagan Western reality to the absolute domination of Christianity took some time. That is in the way of macrocosmic quantum jumps as I have described them earlier in this text. But, as with any phase transition, it may be possible to find the demarcation point, the influence that amounted to the straw that broke the camel's back, so to say. I think it was cosmic disaster in the true sense of the word: dis-aster = 'evil star' and we will be chronicling the approach of this 'evil star' through history all the while noting what it might be in that history that acts as an attractor.

I have chosen to approach the topic this way because the truth is, I wasn't really able to understand the Moses problem itself until I could thoroughly understand more recent historical problems of the same sort. And, while talking about the Dark Ages is problematical at best due to the dearth of information (that's why it's called a Dark Age, after all!), we do at least have some materials to work with.

The problem is that, as far as I can see, no one has ever gone to the trouble of trying to untangle the knotted mess and tease out the various threads and lay them all side by side in a condensed way so that we can get a real overview.

In short, we will be creating our own chronicle, recovering our history as best we can. Only when we fully have an idea of where we have been, can we understand where we are and, possibly, see where we are going. And if we don't like it, possibly change course.

---

636. Fox (1987), *Pagans and Christians*, p. 8.

Celestial Intentions

As I read through the piles of books on the archaeology, history (assumed and reasonably reconstructed from data), and especially the input from the sciences such as astronomy, geology and genetics that should accurately parallel the archaeology and history, but usually doesn't for all the reasons we've discussed so far, in order to collect the material for this series of volumes, the one thing that became increasingly apparent was that, over and over and over again this planet has been bombarded by various types of impacts, the most common being the overhead comet fragment airburst of the Tunguska type. These events have repeatedly brought cultures, nations, even civilizations, to their knees. Dark Ages are inevitably the result, and then, when human society begins to recover, myths are created, religions are born, or re-born with twists and distortions, and always and ever, the facts of the previous era of destruction are covered up in veils of metaphor and allegory.

Why? What sort of madness is this?

It is actually very simple. Historically, when a people begin to perceive atmospheric, geological, climatic disruption and all the ills that these bring on a society, including famine, plague and pestilence, they individually and collectively look to their leaders to fix things. That is where the concept of the Divine King came from to begin with: the king was supposed to be able to intercede for his people with the gods. If the king was unsuccessful with his intercession, a solution had to be found. Sacrifices were made, rituals were performed, and of course, if that didn't work, if the gods remained angry, then *the king had to die*. This is possibly due to a similar brain switch that drives people to seek whatever relieves the stress on their brain: if the gods are angry, find a scape-goat. And when it is the nation that is threatened, the most obvious guilty person or persons are those in charge, the king and his elite. What's more, they know their vulnerability to this reaction instinctively. Then again, given that human history appears to be defined by a succession of more or less corrupt ruling elites, and if we are to assume that such corruption (and its spread throughout society) is the mechanism by which a civilization attracts cosmic catastrophe, blaming and deposing the elite is a good solution. The problem, however, is that the underlying mechanism is not understood by the people, which means that they lack the knowledge that, if they are to prevent further destruction, they must, at all costs, prevent the establishment of any future corrupt elite.

In the end, the people and the elite both seek a paradigm that downplays cyclical catastrophes, but they do it for different reasons. The people want to relieve the enormous stress of a certain but unpredictable major catastrophe, while the elite want to remain in power. The compromise that serves both objectives is the illusion of an elite that is able to protect the people from any disaster. This illusion can take various forms: rituals to appease the gods, revision of history displaying a uniformitarian, uneventful evolution of humanity, and lots and lots of propaganda.

This lie works well during the periods of calm between two major catastrophes. However, history shows that when famines, earthquakes and plagues have struck and taken a heavy toll, when volcanoes erupt or comets blaze across the sky or meteor storms and weather anomalies increase, the illusion collapses, the *raison d'être* of the elites (i.e. protecting the people) collapses and the target has always and will ever be, ultimately, the ruling classes. And they know it. Thus, when such as Anaxagoras or Socrates or Critias mention these uncomfortable facts, they are silenced by ridicule and defamation, and even death.

The symptoms of an increased cometary activity are systematically covered up by the elites as man-made phenomena. The jet contrails due to higher concentrations of atmospheric cometary dust are depicted as 'chemtrails', sprayed by government agencies, the ever more frequent overhead cometary explosions are presented as missile tests, the weather changes due to a de-

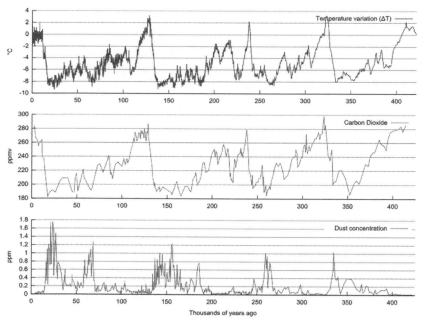

Vostok ice cores. Temperature, CO_2 and dust variations for the past 425,000 years show a positive correlation between dust concentration, CO_2 reduction and temperature drop. (After Petit et al.)

386

creased solar activity triggered by the approaching Sun's companion and its accompanying cometary swarm is labeled 'anthropogenic global warming'.

By attributing the cause of those cosmically induced events to men, the elites maintain the illusion that they are in control. 'Chemtrails' can be stopped if the 'sprayings' end, missile tests can be stopped if the military can be coerced to do so, global warming can be reduced by controlling man-made greenhouse gas emissions.

However, contrails triggered by increased cometary activity, overhead cometary explosions, and cosmically induced solar and weather disruptions can't be changed by the elite. Not only that, if the public realizes this, they may also begin to think that the 'gods are angry' and try to find the real reason, settling ultimately on the corruption and violence of the elite in their efforts to get and maintain greater power.

If the masses of humanity were to recognize the real causes of such phenomena, that would entail recognizing the powerlessness of the elite and therefore the end of their 'mandate from heaven'.

Mike Baillie comments:

> The Chinese believed that an emperor could reign only while he enjoyed the Mandate of Heaven, that is, while he 'looked after his people'; if for any reason he failed to look after their well-being, Heaven would withdraw its Mandate and the emperor and probably his ruling dynasty would be deposed. ... Heaven would have been seen to withdraw its Mandate when the sky darkened, the crops failed and famine ensued bringing death to large numbers of people. The emperor, guilty or not, gets the blame for failing his people. In the aftermath of a calamitous dust-veil event the political upset could easily lead to the deposing of the ruling regime.[637]

Of course, in the beginning of such times of trouble, people *want* to believe that their government – their kings and ruling elite – are powerful enough, or pure enough, to control nature such that the floods, wildfires, earthquakes and volcanic eruptions cease and all returns to normal. And the ruling elite take advantage of this during such times by trying to find likely scapegoats in other nations, some minority group in their own country, or their personal enemies – including those who are pointing out that it just might be their corruption that is bringing on all the evils – so as to distract the larger populace from their own possible sins of commission or omission. This means that such a period can include protracted wars and the accompanying nec-

---

637. Baillie (1999), p. 62.

essary burden of taxes, persecutions of this group or that group, generally increasing social hysteria and unrest, until finally, one day, the people, as a whole, wake up and see that their rulers have behaved very badly and *all* the blame gets dumped on them. This is ironic because an anthropocentric worldview where man believes he is in control stops people – even people in power – from being aware of the realities of our existence on this

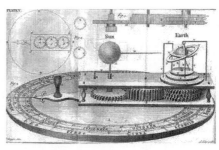

The astral movements by Newton. A mechanistic world view where life is a linear system in which all events can be reduced to and explained as matter in motion.

planet which include civilization destroying cosmic events.

Victor Clube writes in *The Cosmic Winter*:

> Even before the Black Death came, then, a human catastrophe of great proportions was under way in late medieval times. Indeed, the cold snap lasted well beyond the period of the ... plague. *A number of such fluctuations are to be found in the historical record*, and there is good evidence that **these climatic stresses are connected not only with famine but also with times of great social unrest, wars, revolution and mass migrations.**[638]

The Horns of Moses: Creeping Mechanization

What we see in this non-exhaustive examination of the development of the ideas that underpin Western Civilization is a creeping tendency to mechanize everything. While viewing the world as really 'real' – really physical, the basis of the scientific approach – academia subtly, step-by-step, downgraded the Cosmos and all within it to little more than a self-propelling *system* that was, oddly, not really affected by this acknowledged really real outside world! How bizarre is that? The world became an evolutionary *thing* driven from evolution itself, inside the system, *with no relationships to anything other than this mindlessness*, especially not anything outside of the Earth!

The development of these ideas in ancient Greece during that chaotic period of empire formation, together with a tendency to regard philosophers as 'useless', put a period to free inquiry. A few ideas came along during that

---

638. Clube (1990).

time, including a heliocentric cosmology by Philolaus[639], Heracleides of Pontus[640] and Aristarchos of Samos[641], but these ideas (correct ones, as it happens) went no further and the Aristotelian school of thought was promoted to the exclusion of everything else.

Certainly, Aristotle was a clever guy in many respects, but his astronomy and cosmology (not to mention his ideas about differences between the sexes) were abysmally ignorant. He stated that "exhalations" or evaporations of two kinds are continuously given off by the Earth: wet or steamy, or dry and smoky. This is all that is needed to explain everything that goes on in the atmosphere and skies. He then adds that: "Our remote ancestors have handed down remnants to their posterity in mythical form to the effect that these [heavenly bodies] are gods and that the divine encompasses the whole universe." In other words, he is denying what may be the truth and then positing that the primary substances are divine and are located in the heavens, but then the fiery substances that rise to become these atmospheric phenomena, are exclusively of the Earth!

Needless to say, after Aristotle, cosmological speculation fell into decline. The Aristotelian view was adopted by the Alexandrian school[642] and, as already noted, reigned unchallenged for almost two thousand years.

The Plan

We are going to go comet hunting through history in the next volumes. I am going to create a chronology that includes – even emphasizes – the extremely important elements of the environment, particularly the astronomical environment, on the events of our history. What this chronology will include will be as comprehensive a listing of environmental, astronomical, geological and climatological events as I can assemble. Among these are records of Chinese astronomers revealing that a lot was happening in the skies that somehow either nobody in Europe was recording, or if

---

639. (c. 470 – c. 385 BCE), Greek Pythagorean and Presocratic philosopher.
640. (c. 390 BCE – c. 310 BCE), Greek philosopher and astronomer who lived and died at Heraclea Pontica (modern Turkey). In addition to being one of the originators of the heliocentric theory, he also proposed that the Earth rotates on its axis, from west to east, once every 24 hours.
641. (c. 310 BCE – c. 230 BCE), Greek astronomer and mathematician. He proposed a heliocentric model and was the first one to put the planets in their correct order of distance around the Sun.
642. Term used to describe the religious and philosophical developments in Alexandria after the 1st century. The doctrine was a synthesis of Platonism, Stoicism and the later Aristotelianism.

they did, those records were 'lost' – accidentally or deliberately, with few exceptions. I will alternate this type of material with selected social and political events so that, at the end, we can evaluate whether or not there is a relationship between things that happen on Earth and things that happen in the heavens.

My first target in the next volume is going to be the Roman Empire, victim of our most recent Dark Age, which archaeology reveals was a devastating reduction in population and the termination of the so-called civilized processes for a very long time – within historical times.

As we go along, we will be assembling and assessing evidence that there is, indeed, a secret history (in more ways than one), and I will share some very interesting discoveries I have made in the process of collecting the materials for this chronology. I think that what I have discovered will make the case for deliberate expunging of certain records including the knowledge of what really brought on the Dark Ages. We've already seen what Greeks, in the service of rationality and politics, did to the knowledge of our reality; I think I can show, *through the history itself,* that what was later done *on that foundation* was an extraordinary process of retrogression, dominated by that singular figure in the history of Western Civilization: Moses.

The very fact that a primitive, obscure, Middle Eastern tribal god managed to acquire so much space in the consciousness of the founders of Western Civilization is as astonishing as the fact that a primitive pathological deviant rose to power in mid-twentieth century Germany and nearly brought the entire planet to its knees. In fact, the two events may have certain things in common. Hitler – and current-day oppressors working toward the same goal – would not have been able to do what they have done if it had not been for Moses and the twisted world-view that resulted from the combination of Middle-Eastern models of imperialism combined with the delusional results of the Greek Platonic astralizers and Roman ego.

I will be drawing on a significant selection of the ancient sources that we *do* have for the periods in question but, as you will see, rather selectively as to topic. The fact that I did it this way actually led to a startling revelation about one of these sources, as well as the solution to a 2,000 year-old mystery. I actually think that you are going to enjoy this way of looking at history, because trying to figure out What Really Happened when there are all kinds of competing agendas about truth, past and present, is actually as much fun as playing detective!

So, put on your Sherlock Holmes hat and let's travel back in time!

BIBLIOGRAPHY

Acerbi, F. (2003). 'On the shoulders of Hipparchus: A Reappraisal of Ancient Greek Combinatorics', *Archive for History of Exact Sciences,* 57: 465–502.

Adam, Adela Marion (Ed.) (1925). Plato, *Apology of Socrates,* Cambridge University Press.

Ahbel-Rappe, Sara (2010). *Damascius' Problems and Solutions Concerning First Principles,* Oxford University Press.

Akurgal, Ekrem (1962). *The Art of the Hittites,* Abrams Publishers.

Alexander, Hartley B. (1964). *The Mythology of All Races, Vol. 11: Latin-America,* Cooper Square Publishers.

Alford, John & Funk, Carolyn & Hibbing, John (2008). 'Twin Studies, Molecular Genetics, Politics, and Tolerance: A Response to Beckwith and Morris', *Faculty Publications: Political Science,* Paper 32, University of Nebraska.

Alford, John & Hibbing, John (2005). 'Are Political Orientations Genetically Transmitted?', *American Political Science Review,* 99 (2): 153–67.

Alfvén, Hannes (1966). *Worlds-Antiworlds: Antimatter in Cosmology,* Freeman.

—— (1988). 'Has the Universe an Origin?', *Trita-EPP,* 7: 6.

Allan, D. S. & Delair, J. B. (1997). *Cataclysm! Compelling Evidence of a Cosmic Catastrophe in 9,500 B.C.,* Bear & Company.

Al-Tabari, Abu Ja`far Mohammad ibn Jarir (1881-1882). *Annals of the Apostles and Kings,* Brill.

Altemeyer, Robert (1981). *Right-Wing Authoritarianism,* University of Manitoba Press.

—— (1988). *Enemies of Freedom: Understanding Right-Wing Authoritarianism,* Jossey-Bass.

—— (2006). *Atheists: A Groundbreaking Study of America's Nonbelievers,* Prometheus.

—— (2006). *The Authoritarians,* University of Manitoba.

Altemeyer, Robert & Hunsberger, Bruce (1997). *Amazing Conversions: Why Some Turn to Faith and Others Abandon Religion,* Prometheus.

Alvarez, Luis W. & Alvarez, Walter & Asaro, Frank & Michel, Helen V. (1980). 'Extraterrestrial Cause for the Cretaceous-Tertiary Extinction: Experiment and Theory', *Science*, 208 (4448): 1095–1108.

Anthony, David W. (2010). *The Horse, The Wheel and Language: How Bronze-Age Riders from the Eurasian Steppes Shaped the Modern World*, Princeton University Press.

Apuleius (1909). *The Apologia and Florida*, Greenwood Press Reprint.

Aristotle (2010). *Rhetoric*, ReadaClassic.com.

Arrizabalaga, Jon & Garcia-Ballester, Luis & French, Roger & Cunningham, Andrew (Eds.) (2010). *Practical Medicine from Salerno to the Black Death*, Cambridge University Press.

Ashe, Geoffrey (1999). *The Book of Prophecy: From Ancient Greece to the Millennium*, Blandford Publishing.

Astin, A. E. (1959). 'Cicero de Re Publica VI', *Classical Philology Journal*, 54: 221–2.

—— (1967). *Scipio Aemilianus*, Oxford University Press.

Attridge, H. W. & Oden, R. A. Jr. (1981). 'Philo of Byblos: The Phoenician History: Introduction, Critical Text, Translation, Notes', *Catholic Biblical Quarterly Monograph Series*, Catholic Biblical Association of America.

Azéma, Marc & Rivère, Florent (2012). 'Animation in Palaeolithic art: a pre-echo of cinema', *Antiquity Journal*, 86 (332): 316–324.

Babbitt, Frank Cole (Trans.) (1931). Plutarch, *Moralia: Rules for the Preservation of Health, Vol. III*, Loeb Classical Library.

Babiak, Paul & Hare, Robert (2007). *Snakes in Suits*, Harper Business.

Bailey, Cyril (1947). 'Titi Lucreti Cari De Rerum Natura Libri Sex', edited with Prolegomena, in *Critical Apparatus, Translation, and Commentary*, Clarendon Press.

Bailey, M. E. & Clube, S. V. M. & Napier, W. M. (1990). *The Origin of Comets*, Pergamon Press.

Baillie, Mike (1999). *Exodus to Arthur: Catastrophic Encounters with Comets*, Batsford.

—— (2006). *New Light on the Black Death: The Cosmic Connection*, Tempus.

Baillie, Mike & McCafferty, Patrick (2005). *The Celtic Gods: Comets in Irish Mythology*, Tempus.

Bartlett, Robert C. (Ed.) (2006). Xenophon, *The Shorter Socratic Writings: Apology of Socrates to the Jury, Oeconomicus and Symposium*, Cornell University Press.

Beloe, William (Trans.) (2010). Gellius, *The Attic Nights*, Nabu Press.

Berger, Peter & Luckmann, Thomas (1967). *The Social Construction of Reality: A Treatise in the Sociology of Knowledge*, Anchor.

Black, Jeremy & Green, Anthony (1992). *Gods, Demons and Symbols of Ancient Mesopotamia: An Illustrated Dictionary*, University of Texas Press.

Blakeney, E. H. (1921). *The Hymn of Cleanthes: Greek Text Translated into English: with Brief Introduction and Notes*, Society for Promoting Christian Knowledge.

Bobrick, Benson (2005). *The Fated Sky*, Simon & Schuster.

Bond, Alan & Hempsell, Mark (2008). *A Sumerian Observation of the Köfels' Impact Event*, Alcuin Academics.

Bowden, Hugh (2005). *Classical Athens and the Delphic Oracle: Divination and Democracy*, Cambridge University Press.

Bowman, Glenn (1998). 'Mapping History's Redemption: Eschatology and Topography in the Itinerarium Burdigalense' in Levine, Lee. I. (Ed.), *Jerusalem: Its Sanctity and Centrality to Judaism, Christianity and Islam*, Continuum Press.

Brightman, Robert A. (1988). 'The Windigo in the Material World', *Ethnohistory*, 35 (4): 337–379.

Brown, Christopher G. (1997). Introduction to Douglas E. Gerber's *Companion to the Greek Lyric Poets*, Brill.

Brown, Norman O. (Trans.) (1953). Hesiod, *Theogony*, Pearson.

Brown, Sandra L. (2010). *Women Who Love Psychopaths*, Mask Publishing.

Bryce, Tevor R. (2002). *Life and Society in the Hittite World*, Oxford University Press.

Burke, John G. (1991). *Cosmic Debris: Meteorites in History*, University of California Press.

Burkert, W. (1972). *Lore and Science in Ancient Pythagoreanism*, Harvard University Press.

Burnet, J. (1892). *Early Greek Philosophy*, A.& C. Black.

—— (1924). *Plato's Euthyphro, Apology of Socrates and Crito*, Clarendon.

Bury, R. G. (Trans.) (1949). Sextus Empiricus, *Against the Professors*, Loeb Classical Library.

Caven, B. (1990). *Dionysios I: War-Lord of Sicily*, Yale University Press.

Cherniss, Harold (Trans.) (1976). Plutarch, *Moralia, Vol. XIII*, Loeb Classical Library.

Cicero (2008). *De Senectute*, BiblioLife.

—— (2012). *The Tusculan Questions of Marcus Tullius Cicero in Five Books*, Forgotten Books.

Clay, Albert Tobias (1915). *Babylonian Texts, Yale Oriental Series Vol. I*, New Haven.

Cleckley, Hervey M. (1988). *The Mask of Sanity: An Attempt to Clarify Some Issues About the So Called Psychopathic Personality*, William A. Dolan.

Clement of Alexandria (2004). *The Stromata, or Miscellanies, V5*, Kessinger Publishing.

Clube, S. V. M. 'Narrative report on the hazard to civilization due to fireballs and comets', addressed to the European Office of Aerospace Research and development, June 4, 1996, Oxford University.

Clube, S. V. M. & Hoyle, F. & Napier, W. M. & Wickramasinghe, N. C. (1996). 'Giant Comets, Evolution and Civilization', *Astrophysics and Space Science*, 245 (1): 43-60.

Clube, S. V. M. & Napier, W. M. (1982). *The Cosmic Serpent*, Universe Publisher.

—— (1990). *The Cosmic Winter*, Blackwell.

Cohoon, J. W. (Trans.) (1932). Dio Chrysostom, *Discourses 1–11*, Harvard University Press, Loeb Classical Library.

Cornford, Francis MacDonald (1937). *Plato's Cosmology: The Timaeus of Plato*, Hackett.

Gutzwiller, K. (Ed.) (2007). Crates, 'Fragment VI' in *Guide to Hellenistic Literature*, Blackwell.

Cruttenden, Walter (2005). *Lost Star of Myth and Time*, St. Lynn's Press.

Cusick, David (1828). *Sketches of Ancient History of the Six Nations*, Turner & McCollum.

Dalley, Stephanie (1989). *Myths from Mesopotamia: Creation, the Flood, Gilgamesh, and Others*, Oxford University Press.

Dalton, O. M. (1915). *The Letters of Sidonius*, Clarendon Press.

Davidson, William Leslie (1907). *The Stoic Creed*, Clark.

Davies, Philip R. (1987). *Behind the Essenes: History and Ideology in the Dead Sea Scrolls*, Scholars Press.

—— (1992). *In Search of "Ancient Israel": A Study in Biblical Origins*, T&T Clark.

—— (1996). *Sects and Scrolls*, University Of South Florida.

—— (1998). *Scribes and Schools: The Canonization of the Hebrew Scriptures*, Westminster John Knox Press.

—— (2000). *Qumran: Cities of the Biblical World*, Lutterworth Press.

—— (2004). *Whose Bible is it Anyway?* 2nd Edition, T&T Clark.

—— (2008). *Memories of Ancient Israel: An Introduction to Biblical History–Ancient and Modern*, Westminster John Knox Press.

—— (2009). *The Origins of Biblical Israel*, T&T Clark.

—— (2011). *On the Origins of Judaism*, Equinox Publishing.

—— (2011). *The Complete World of the Dead Sea Scrolls*, Thames & Hudson.

Davis, Marc & Hut, Piet & Muller, Richard A. (1984). 'Extinction of species by periodic comet showers', *Nature*, 308: 715–717.

De Lacy, Phillip H. (Trans.) (1984). Galen, *De Placitis Hippocratis et Platonis*, Akademie.

De Lacy, Phillip H. & Einarson, Benedict (Trans.) (1959). Plutarch, *Moralia*, Vol. VII, Loeb Classical Library.

De Selincourt, Aubrey (Trans.) (1972). Herodotus, *The Histories*, Book IV, Penguin.

Diamond, Jared (1991). *The Third Chimpanzee: The Evolution and Future of the Human Animal*, Hutchinson Radius.

—— (1997). *Guns, Germs, and Steel: The Fates of Human Societies*, W. W. Norton.

—— (2005). *Collapse: How Societies Choose to Fail or Succeed*, Viking.

Diehl, Ernst & Proclus, Ernst (2010). *Procli Diadochi in Platonis Timaeum Commentaria*, Vol. III, Nabu Press.

Diels, H. & Kranz, W. (1951). *Die Fragmente der Vorsokratiker*, Vols. I-III, Weidmann.

Dorandi, Tiziano (2005). 'Chapter 2: Chronology', in Algra et al. (Eds.), *The Cambridge History of Hellenistic Philosophy*, Cambridge University Press.

Dover, K. J. (Trans.) (1968). Aristophanes, *Clouds*, Clarendon Press.

Doyle, Conan (1890). *The Sign of the Four*, Spencer Blackett.

Dozy, Reinhart Pieter Anne & De Goeje, M. J. (1864). *Die Israeliten zu Mekka*, Kessinger Publishing.

Dryden, John (Trans.) (2004). Plutarch, *The Life of Alexander the Great*, Modern Library.

Dudley, Donald R. (1937). *A History of Cynicism from Diogenes to the 6th Century A.D.*, Mayo Press.

Dunn, Christopher (1998). *The Giza Power Plant*, Bear & Company.

Eliade, Mircea (1964). *Shamanism: Archaic Techniques of Ecstasy*, Princeton University Press.

—— (1971). *The Myth of the Eternal Return: Or, Cosmos and History*, Princeton University Press.

Ellis, R. (1998). *Imagining Atlantis*, Alfred A. Knopf.

Epictetus (2008). *The Enchiridion*, Forgotten Books.

Eusebius (2012). *Praeparatio Evangelica*, Amazon Digital Services (Kindle Edition).

Fagles, Robert (Trans.) (1991). Homer, *The Iliad*, Penguin Books.

Finkelstein, Israel & Silberman, Neil Asher (2002). *The Bible Unearthed: Archaeology's New Vision of Ancient Israel and the Origin of its Sacred Texts*, Touchstone.

—— (2007). *David and Solomon: In Search of the Bible's Sacred Kings and the Roots of the Western Tradition*, Free Press.

Finley, M. I. (1977). *The Viking Portable Greek Historians*, Penguin.

Firestone, Richard & West, Allen & Warwick-Smith, Simon (2006). *The Cycle of Cosmic Catastrophes: How a Stone-Age Comet Changed the Course of World Culture*, Bear & Company.

Forsythe, P. Y. (1980). *Atlantis: the Making of a Myth*, McGill – Queen's University Press.

Foucault, Michel (2001). *Fearless Speech*, Semiotext(e).

—— (2011). 'The Courage of the Truth Lectures', at the Collège de France, lecture 7 March, Palgrave Macmillan.

Fox, Robin Lane (1987). *Pagans and Christians*, Alfred A. Knopf.

Frank, Erich (1923). *Plato und die sogenannten Pythagoreer: ein Kapitel sus der Geschichte des griechischen Geistes*, Halle.

Frankenstein, Carl (1959). *Psychopathy: A Comparative Analyisis of Clinical Pictures*, Grune & Stratton.

Franzén, L. G. & Cropp, R. A. (2007). 'The peatland/ice age hypothesis revised, adding a possible glacial pulse trigger', *Geografiska Annaler*, 89A (4): 301–330.

Freud, Sigmund (1967). *Moses and Monotheism*, Vintage.

Garbini, Giovanni (2009). *Myth and History in the Bible*, T&T Clark.

——— (2011). *History and Ideology in Ancient Israel*, SCM Press.

Gellner, Ernest (1995). *Anthropology and Politics*, Blackwell.

Gmirkin, Russell E. (2006). *Berossus and Genesis, Manetho and Exodus: Hellenistic Histories and the Date of the Pentateuch*, T&T Clark.

Goldwurm, Hersh (1982). *History of the Jewish people: The Second Temple Era*, Mesorah Publications.

Gore, Rick (2004). 'Who Were the Phoenicians?', *National Geographic Magazine* (October).

Gould, Stephen Jay (1977). *Ever Since Darwin: Reflections in Natural History*, Norton.

Green, Alberto R. W. (2003). *The Storm-God in the Ancient Near East* (Biblical and Judaic Studies, Vol. VIII), University of California, Eisenbraun.

Grondine, E. P. (2005). *Man and Impact in the Americas.*

Guillaume, A. (1955). *The Life of Muhammad*, Oxford University Press.

Gulick, Charles Burton (Trans.) (1928). Athenaeus, *The Deipnosophists*, Books 3–4, Loeb Classical Library.

——— (1933). *The Deipnosophists*, Books 11–12, Loeb Classical Library.

Gummere, Richard M. (Trans.) (1917). Seneca, *Moral Epistles*, Loeb Classical Library.

Hall, Alaric (2005). 'Getting Shot of Elves: Healing, Witchcraft and Fairies in the Scottish Witchcraft Trials', *Folklore*, 116: 19–36.

Hare, Robert (1999). *Without Conscience: The Disturbing World of the Psychopaths Among Us*, Guilford Press.

Harmon, Austin M. (Trans.) (1913). Lucian, *Macrobii*, Harvard University Press.

Haselberger, Lothar (1983). 'Die Bauzeichnungen des Apollontempels von Didyma', *Architettura*, 13–36.

——— (1985). 'Antike Planzeichnungen am Apollontempel von Didyma', *Spektrum der Wissenschaft* (April), 70–83.

——— (1991). 'Aspekte der Bauzeichnungen von Didyma', *Revue archéologique*, 99–108.

Herodotus (2010). *The Histories*, Vol. II, Nabu Press.

——— (2012). The Histories, Vol. IV, Nabu Press.

Hicks, R. D. (Ed.) (1925). Diogenes Laërtius, *Lives and Opinions of Eminent Philosophers*, Loeb Classical Library.

Hoffner, H. A. (1990). *Hittite Myths*, Society of Biblical Literature.

Holford-Strevens (1997). 'Favorinos: the Man of Paradoxes' in Barnes, J. & Griffin, M. (Eds.), *Philosophia togata*, Vol. II, 188–217.

Hoyle, Fred (1993). *The Origin of the Universe and the Origin of Religion*, Moyer Bell.

Jastrow, Morris (1911). *Aspects of Religious Belief and Practice in Babylonia and Assyria*, G. P. Putnam's Sons.

Jenniskens, Petrus Matheus Marie (2006). *Meteor Showers and Their Parent Comets*, Cambridge University Press.

Jones, W. H. S. (Trans.) (1993). Pausanias, *Description of Greece*, II, VII, Loeb Classical Library.

Jowett, B. (2006). Plato, *Phaedo*, Digireads.com.

—— (2012). *The Dialogues of Plato in Five Volumes. Vol. III: Containing The Republic, Timaeus, Critias*, CreateSpace Independent Publishing Platform.

Juergens, Ralph E. (1973). 'On Celestial Mechanics', *Pensée: Immanuel Velikovsky Reconsidered*, 3 (1): Winter.

—— (1982). 'Electric Discharge as the Source of Solar Radiant Energy (Part I)', *Kronos Press*, 8 (1).

Julian, Orations IV, in Navia, L. (1996), *Classical Cynicism: A Critical Study*, Greenwood Press.

Julian, Orations, VI, in Reale, G. (1980), *The Concept of First Philosophy and the Unity of the Metaphysics of Aristotle*, SUNY Press.

Kahn, Charles H. (2001). *Pythagoras and the Pythagoreans*, Hackett.

Kahneman, Daniel (2011). *Thinking, Fast and Slow*, Farrar, Straus and Giroux.

Keay, Colin S. L. (1980) 'Anomalous Sounds from the Entry of Meteor Fireballs', *Science*, 210: 11–15.

—— (1980). 'Audible Sounds Excited by Aurorae and Meteor Fireballs', *Journal of the Royal Astronomical Society of Canada*, 74: 253–260.

Kennett, James P. & Firestone, Richard B. & West, Allen et al. (2012). 'Very high-temperature impact melt products as evidence for cosmic airbursts and impacts 12,900 years ago', *Proceedings of the National Academy of Sciences*, 109 (44): E2960–E2969.

Kenny, D. (1986). 'A Celtic Destruction Myth: Togail Bruidne Da Derga', *Catastrophism and Ancient History*, 8: 57–64.

Kidd, Douglas (Ed.) (1997). Aratus, *Phaenomena*, Cambridge University Press.

Kidd, I. G. (1999). *Posidonius*, Vol. III, The Translation of the Fragments, Cambridge University Press.

King, L. W. (1912). 'Babylonian Boundary-stones and Memorial-tablets in the British Museum', British Museum, London.

Kirk, G. & Raven, J. & Schofield, M. (2003). *The Presocratic Philosopher*, Cambridge University Press.

Knight-Jadczyk, Laura (2005). *The Secret History of the World and How to Get Out Alive*, Red Pill Press.

—— (2012). *The Noah Syndrome*, Red Pill Press.

Koch, Heinrich (2000). *The Diluvian Impact,* Peter Lang.

Kovacs, Maureen Gallery (1989). *The Epic of Gilgamesh, Translated with an Introduction and Notes*, Stanford University.

Kramer, Samuel Noah (1944). *Sumerian Mythology: A Study of Spiritual and Literary Achievement in the Third Millennium B.C.*, University of Pennsylvania.

Krinov, E. L. (1949). *The Tunguska Meteorite*, Izdatelstvo Akademii Nauk SSSR.

Kugler, Franz Xaver & Strassmaier, Johann Nepomuk (1900). *Die Babylonische Mondrechnung (The Babylonian lunar computation)*, BiblioBazaar.

Kurtz, Paul (1992). *The New Skepticism: Inquiry and Reliable Knowledge*, Prometheus.

Laing, R. D. (1969). *Self and Others*, Penguin.

Laroche, E. (1971). *Catalogue des textes hittites: Études et commentaires*, Paris (abbr. CTH).

Lee, H. D. P. (Trans.) (1952). Aristotle, *Meteorologica*, Loeb Classical Library.

Lefebvre, S. & Kosovichev, A. G. (2005). 'Changes in the subsurface stratification of the Sun with the 11-year activity cycle', *Astrophysics Journal*, 633: L149.

Lemche, Niels Peter (1985). *Early Israel: Anthropological and Historical Studies*, Brill.

—— (1997). *Prelude to Israel's Past: Background and Beginnings of Israelite History and Identity*, Baker Academic.

—— (1998). *The Israelites in History and Tradition*, Westminster John Knox Press.

—— (2003). *Historical Dictionary of Ancient Israel*, Scarecrow Press.

—— (2008). *The Old Testament between Theology and History: A Critical Survey*, Westminster John Knox Press.

Lerner, E. J. (1991). *The Big Bang Never Happened*, Random House.

Lewis, John S. (1997). *Rain of Iron And Ice: The Very Real Threat of Comet and Asteroid Bombardment*, Helix Books.

Lewy, Hildegard (1950). 'Origin and Significance of the Magen Dawld', *Archiv Orientalni* (Journal of the Czechoslovak Oriental Institute), 18 (3).

Lewy, Julius (1937). 'Tablettes Cappadociennes Cuneiform Texts, Vol. XXI', Department of Oriental Antiquities, Louvre Museum, P. Geuthner.

Ling-Israel, P. (1990). 'The Sennacherib Prism in the Israel Museum – Jerusalem', in Klein, J. & Skaist, A. (Eds.), *Bar-Ilan Studies in Assyriology: Dedicated to Pinḥas Artzi*, 213–47, Bar-Ilan University Press.

Lobaczewski, Andrzej M. (2007). *Political Ponerology: A Science on the Nature of Evil Adjusted for Political Purposes*, Red Pill Press.

Long, A. A. (1996) 'The Socratic Tradition: Diogenes, Crates, and Hellenistic Ethics', in Branham, R. Bracht & Goulet-Cazé, Marie-Odile (Eds.), *The Cynics: The Cynic Movement in Antiquity and Its Legacy* (2000), University of California Press.

—— (2001). *Stoic Studies*, University of California Press.

Loomis, Roger Sherman (1927). *Celtic Myth and Arthurian Romance*, Columbia University Press.

—— (1963). *The Grail: From Celtic Myth to Christian Symbol*, Princeton University Press.

Louden, Bruce (2011). *Homer's Odyssey and the Near East*, Cambridge University Press.

Lovelock, James (2000). *Gaia: A New Look at Life on Earth*, Oxford University Press.

Lucian (1902). *Vera Historia*, University of Michigan Library.

Macdonald, C. (Ed.) (1995). Cicero, *Pro Murena*, Bristol Classical Press.

MacKenzie, Donald A. (1915). *Myths of Babylonia and Assyria*, Gresham.

Mair, A. W. & Mair, G. R. (Trans.) (1921). Callimachus, *Callimachus, Lycophron, Aratus*, Loeb Classical Library.

Malkowski, Edward F. (2005). *Before the Pharaohs: Egypt's Mysterious Prehistory*, Bear & Company.

Martin, Jean (Ed.) (1998). Aratus, *Phénomènes*, Collection Budé.

Martin, N. G. & Eaves, L. J. & Heath, A. C. & Jardine, R. & Feingold, L. M. & Eysenck, H. J. (1986). 'Transmission of social attitudes', *Proceedings of the National Academy of Science*, 83: 4364–8.

Masaudi, Ali ibn al-Husayn (1877). *Les prairies d'or*, IV, Imprimerie impériale.

Master, S. (2001). 'A Possible Holocene Impact Structure in the Al Amarah Marshes, Near the Tigris-Euphrates Confluence, Southern Iraq', *Meteoritics & Planetary Science*, 36: A124.

Matsumoto, David (Ed.) (2009). *Cambridge Dictionary of Psychology*, San Francisco State University.

Matthews, Robert (2001) 'Meteor clue to end of Middle East civilisations', *The Sunday Telegraph* (4 November).

May, Herbert G. (1935). *Material Remains of the Megiddo Cult*, University of Chicago Press.

McCarter Jr., & Kyle, P. (1980). 'The Balaam Texts from Deir 'Alla: The First Combination', *Bulletin of the Schools of Oriental Research*, 239: 49–60.

McRaney, David (2012). *You Are Not So Smart: Why You Have Too Many Friends on Facebook, Why Your Memory Is Mostly Fiction, and 46 Other Ways You're Deluding Yourself*, Gotham.

Mehren, M. A. F. (Ed.) (1866). Al-Dimashqi, Muhammad ibn Ibrahim, *Kitab al-nukhbat al-dahr fi 'ajaib al-barr w'al-bahr*, St. Petersburg.

Melott, A. L. & Bambach, R. K. (2010). 'Nemesis Reconsidered', *Monthly Notices of the Royal Astronomical Society Letters*, 407: L99–L102.

Miller, Walter (Trans.) (1913). Cicero, *De Officiis*, Loeb Classical Library.

Morris, Ian (2010). *Why the West Rules – for Now: The Patterns of History, and What They Reveal About the Future*, Farrar, Straus and Giroux.

Mullen, William (1997). 'Natural Catastrophes during Bronze Age Civilisations', 2nd SIS Cambridge Conference, Fitzwilliam College, organised by The Society for Interdisciplinary Studies (July 11–13).

Navia, Luis E. (2005). *Diogenes the Cynic: The War Against the World*, Humanity Books.

Nesvorný, David & Jenniskens, Peter & Levison, Harold F. & Bottke, William F. &

Vokrouhlický, David & Gounelle, Matthieu (2010). 'Cometary Origin of the Zodiacal Cloud and Carbonaceous Micrometeorites. Implications for hot debris disks', *Astrophysical Journal*, 713 (2): 816.

Neugebauer, Otto (1945). 'Mathematical Cuneiform Texts', *American Oriental Series*, Vol. 29. New Haven: American Oriental Society.

Neusner, Jacob (1979). *Tosefta, Translation from the Hebrew*, Vol. III, Ktav Publishing

——— (1991). *The Mishnah: A New Translation*, Yale University Press.

Nilsson, Martin (1992). *Die Geschicthe der Griechischen religion*, Vol. I, C. H. Beck.

Oakley, Barbara (2008). *Evil Genes*, Prometheus.

Oldfather, C. H. (Trans.) (1935). *Diodorus of Sicily*, Vol. II, William Heinemann.

——— (1939). *Diodorus of Sicily*, Vol. III, Harvard University Press.

——— (1925). Epictetus, *Discourses*, Vols. I-II, Loeb Classical Library.

Ouspensky, P. D. (1949). *In Search of the Miraculous: Fragments of an Unknown Teaching*, Mariner Books.

Paliga, Sorin (1997). 'La divinité suprême des Thraco-Daces', *Dialogues d'histoire ancienne*, 20 (2): 137–150.

Parke, H. W. (1986). 'The Temple of Apollo at Didyma: The Building and Its Function', *Journal of Hellenic Studies*, 106: 121–131.

Paton, W. R. (Trans.) (1918). *The Greek Anthology*, Loeb Classical Library.

Polybius (1922). *The Histories*, Vol. II, Loeb Classical Library.

Paul, R. A. (1994). 'Freud, Sellin and the Death of Moses', *International Journal of Psychoanalysis*, 75: 825–837.

Pearson, Lionel & Sandbach, F. H. (Trans.) (1965). Plutarch, *Moralia*, Vol. XI, Loeb Classical Library.

Peiser, Benny J. & Pamer, Trevor & Bailey, Mark E. (1998). *Natural Catastrophes During Bronze Age Civilizations: Archaeological, Geological, Astronomical, and Cultural Perspectives*, Archaeopress.

Peratt, Anthony L. (1986). 'Evolution of the Plasma Universe: II. The Formation of Systems of Galaxies', *IEEE Trans. on Plasma Science*, PS-14: 763–778.

——— (1992). *Physics of the Plasma Universe*, Springer.

——— (2003). 'Characteristics for the Occurrence of a Hight-Current, Z-Pinch Aurora as Recorded in Antiquity', *ICCC Transactions on Plasma Science*, 31 (6).

——— (1995). 'Introduction to Plasma Astrophysics and Cosmology', *Astrophysics and Space Science*, 227: 3–11.

Peratt, Anthony L. & Green, J. (1983). 'On the Evolution of Interacting, Magnetized, Galactic Plasmas', *Astrophysics and Space Science*, 91: 19–33.

Peratt, Anthony L. & Green, J. & Nielson, D. (1980). 'Evolution of Colliding Plasmas', *Physical Review Letters*, 44: 1767–1770.

Petrie, William Flinders (1883). *Pyramids and Temples of Gizeh*, Kessinger Publishing.

Pherecydes of Syros, *Encyclopedia Britannica*, 9th edition, Vol. 18, R. S. Peale & Co.

Philodemus (2004). 'Craft, Cult, and Canon in the Books from Herculaneum' & 'Philodemus and the Papyri from Herculaneum', in Fitzgerald, John T. & Obbink, Dirk & Holland, Glenn Stanfield (Eds.), *Philodemus and the New Testament World*, Brill.

Plato (2012). *Phaedrus*, CreateSpace Independent Publishing Platform.

—— (2012). *The Symposium*, CreateSpace Independent Publishing Platform.

Popper, Karl (1945). *The Open Society and Its Enemies, Vol. 1: The Spell of Plato*, Routledge.

—— (1963). *Conjectures and Refutations: The Growth of Scientific Knowledge*, Routledge.

Porphyry & Plotinus & Iamblichus & Diogenes Laërtius (2012). *Life of Pythagoras*, Nabu Press.

Rackham, H. (Trans.) (1933). Cicero, *De natura deorum*, Loeb Classical Library.

—— (1942). Cicero, *De Fato, De Oratore*, Loeb Classical Library.

—— (1952). Pliny, *Natural History*, Loeb Classical Library.

Raup, David M. & Sepkoski, Jr., J. John (1984). 'Periodicity of extinctions in the geologic past', *Proceedings of the National Academy of Sciences*, 81 (3): 801–5.

Rawlins, D. (1982). 'An Investigation of the Ancient Star Catalog', *Proceedings of the Astronomical Society of the Pacific*, 94: 359–373.

Redford, Donald B. (1992). *Egypt, Canaan, and Israel in Ancient Times*, Princeton University Press.

Reid, James S. (Ed.) (2007). *The Academica of Cicero*, Evergreen Review.

Rogers, John H. (1998). 'Origins of the ancient constellations: Part I. The Mesopotamian Tradition', *Journal of British Astronomical Association*, 108 (1): 9–28.

—— (1998). 'Origins of the ancient constellations: Part II. The Mediterranean Tradition', *Journal of British Astronomical Association*, 108 (2): 79–89.

Rosenmeyer, Thomas G. (1949). 'The Family of Critias', *American Journal of Philology*, 70 (4): 404–410, Johns Hopkins University Press.

Rudder, Ben (1999). 'Fire, Flood and Comet', *New Scientist Book Review* (9 January).

Russell, Bertrand (1967). *History of Western Philosophy*, Simon & Schuster/Touchstone.

Sagan, Carl & Druyan, Ann (1985). *Comet*, Ballantine Books.

Sallaska, Georgia (1969). *Three Ships and Three Kings*, Doubleday.

Salter, Anna (2004). *Predators, Pedophiles, Rapists, And Other Sex Offenders*, Basic Books.

Sand, Shlomo (2009). *The Invention of the Jewish People*, Verso Books.

Schaeffer, Claude (1948). *Stratigraphie Comparée et Chronologie de l'Asie Occidentale (Compared Stratigraphy and Eastern Asian Chronology)*, Cumberlege.

Schibli, Hermann S. (1990). *Pherekydes of Syros*, Oxford University Press.

Schlafly, Roger (2011). *How Einstein Ruined Physics: Motion, Symmetry and Revolution in Science*, DarkBuzz.

Schmitz, Leonhard (1867). 'Alcimus', in William Smith (Ed.), *Dictionary of Greek and Roman Biography and Mythology*, Vol. 1 (1844), Taylor and Walton.

Schott, A. & Schaumberger, J. (1947). 'Vier Briefe Mâr-Ishtars an Asarhaddon über Himmelserscheinungen der Jahre -670/688', *Zeitschrift für Assyriologie*, 47.

Schumaker, John F. (1995). *The Corruption of Reality: A Unified Theory of Religion, Hypnosis, and Psychopathology*, Prometheus.

Seargent, David (2009). *The Greatest Comets in History: Broom Stars and Celestial Scimitars*, Springer.

Sellin, Ernst (1924). *Geschichte des Israelitische-Jüdischen Volkes*, Verlag Von Quelle & Meyer.

Sellin, Ernst & Watzinger, Karl O. (1973). *Jericho, die Ergebnisse der Ausgrabungen Dargestellt*, Zeller Verlag.

Seltman, C. T. (1936). 'Diogenes of Sinope, Son of the Banker Hikesias', Transactions of the International Numismatic Congress.

Shipley, Frederick W. (Trans.) (1924). Velleius, Marcus Paterculus, *Compendium of Roman History*, Loeb Classical Library.

Shotwell, James T. (1939). *The History of History*, Columbia University Press.

Shrimpton, Gordon S. (1991). *Theopompus The Historian*, McGill-Queen's University Press.

Silagadze, Z. K. (2003). 'Tunguska genetic anomaly and electrophonic meteors', *Acta Physica Polonica*, B 36: 935.

Stanley, Richard P. (1997), 'Hipparchus, Plutarch, Schröder, and Hough', *The American Mathematical Monthly*, 104 (4): 344–350.

Stiebing, William H. Jr. (2001). 'When Civilization Collapsed: Death of the Bronze Age', *Archaeology Odyssey Magazine* (September/October).

Stobaeus (2010). *Ioannis Stobaei Florilegium*, Vol. III, Nabu Press.

Stock, St. George William Joseph (1908). *Stoicism*, Constable.

Stout, Martha (2006). *The Sociopath Next Door*, Three Rivers.

Stoyanov, Yuri (2000). *The Other God: Dualist Religions from Antiquity to the Cathar Heresy*, Yale University Press.

Taylor, A. E. (1928). *A Commentary on Plato's Timaeus*, Oxford University Press.

Teles (1977). 'Fragment 4a', from O'Neill, E., *Teles: The Cynic Teacher*, Scholars Press for the Society of Biblical Literature.

The Amplified Bible, Zondervan (1995).

The Bible, King James Version.

Thompson, Thomas L. (1992). *Early History of the Israelite People: From the Written and Archaeological Sources*, Brill.

—— (2000). *Bible in History*, Random House.

—— (2000). *The Mythic Past: Biblical Archaeology and the Myth of Israel*, Basic Books.

—— (2002). *The Historicity of the Patriarchal Narratives: The Quest for the Historical Abraham*, T&T Clark.

—— (2005). *The Messiah Myth: The Near Eastern Roots of Jesus and David*, Basic Books

Thornhill, Wallace & Talbott, David (2007). *The Electric Universe*, Mikamar Publishing.

Toomer, G. J. (Trans.) (1998). Ptolemy, *Almagest*, Princeton University Press.

Trivers, Robert (2011). *Deceit and Self-Deception: Fooling Yourself the Better to Fool Others*, Penguin.

Van Seters, John (1987), *Abraham in History and Tradition*, Yale University Press.

—— (1992). *Prologue to History: The Yahwist as Historian in Genesis*, Westminster John Knox Press.

—— (1994). *The Life of Moses: The Yahwist as Historian in Exodus – Numbers*, Westminster John Knox Press.

—— (1997). 'The Geography of the Exodus', in Silberman, Neil Asher, *The Land That I Will Show You*, Sheffield Academic Press.

—— (2002). *A Law Book for the Diaspora: Revision in the Study of the Covenant Code*, Oxford University Press.

—— (2007). *In Search of History: Historiography in the Ancient World and the Origins of Biblical History*, Eisenbrauns.

—— (2009). *The Biblical Saga of King David*, Eisenbrauns.

—— (2011). *Changing Perspectives I: Studies in the History, Literature and Religion of Biblical Israel*, Equinox Publishing.

Vedral, Vlatko (2010). *A Quantum Calculation*, Oxford University Press.

Velikovsky, Immanuel (1950). *Worlds in Collision*, Macmillan.

Walton, John H. (2003). 'Exodus, date of', in Alexander, T. D. & Baker, David W., *Dictionary of the Old Testament: Pentateuch*, InterVarsity Press.

Warner, Rex (Trans.) (1952). Thucydides, *The History of the Peloponnesian War*, Penguin Classics.

Waterfield, Robin (Trans.) (1998). Herodotus, *The Histories*, Oxford Paperbacks.

Weidner, E. (1922). *Keilschrifturkunden aus Boghazköi*, 4, Berlin (abbr. KUB).

Weiss, Harvey (1997). 'Late Third Millennium Abrupt Climate Change and Social Collapse in West Asia and Egypt' in Weiss, H. & Dalfes, H. N. & Kukla, G. (Eds.), *Third Millennium BC Climate Change and Old World Collapse*, 711-723, Springer.

Weiss, Moritz (1913). 'Kissat Ibrahim. Die Lebensgeschichte Abrahams nach einer anonymen arabischen Handschrift der Königlichen Bibliothek zu Berlin herausgegeben und mit kritischen Anmerkungen versehen' (Dissertation), Kirchhain N.-L., M. Schmersow.

Westen, Drew & Blagov, Pavel S. & Harenski, Keith & Kilts, Clint & Hamann, Stephan (2006). 'An fMRI study of motivated reasoning: Partisan political reasoning in the U.S. Presidential Election', *Journal of Cognitive Neuroscience*, 11 (Nov. 18): 1947-58.

Whitelam, Keith W. (2006). 'General Problems of Studying the Text of the Bible ...', in Rogerson, John William & Lieu, Judith, *The Oxford Handbook of Biblical Studies*, Oxford University Press.

Whitmire, Daniel P. & Jackson, Albert A. (1984). 'Are periodic mass extinctions driven by a distant solar companion?', *Nature*, 308: 713–715.

Whittaker, Molly (Ed.) (1982). Tatian, *Oratio ad Graecos and Fragments*, Oxford University Press.

Wilkens, Iman (1990). *Where Troy Once Stood: The Mystery of Homer's Iliad & Odyssey Revealed*, Rider/Century Hutchinson.

Wilson, Nigel G. (Trans.) (1997). Aelian, *Varia Historia*, Loeb Classical Library.

Wilson, Timothy D. (2004). *Strangers to Ourselves: Discovering the Adaptive Unconscious*, Belknap Press of Harvard University Press.

Woolf, Raphael (Trans.) (2001). Cicero, *De finibus bonorum et malorum*, Cambridge University Press.

Yeomans, Donald K. (1991). *Comets: A Chronological History of Observation, Science, Myth, and Folklore*, Wiley Science Edition.

Zeller, Eduard (2010). *The Presocratic Philosophy*, OGB.

—— (2011). *The Stoics, Epicureans, and Sceptics*, Ulan Press.

—— (2012). *Die Philosophie der Greichen in ihrer geschichtlichen entwicklung*, Ulan Press.

Znamenski, Andrei A. (2007). *The Beauty of the Primitive: Shamanism and Western Imagination*, Oxford University Press.

Zorzos, Gregory (2009). *Suda Lexicon: Letter A–AE*, CreateSpace Independent Publishing Platform.

INDEX

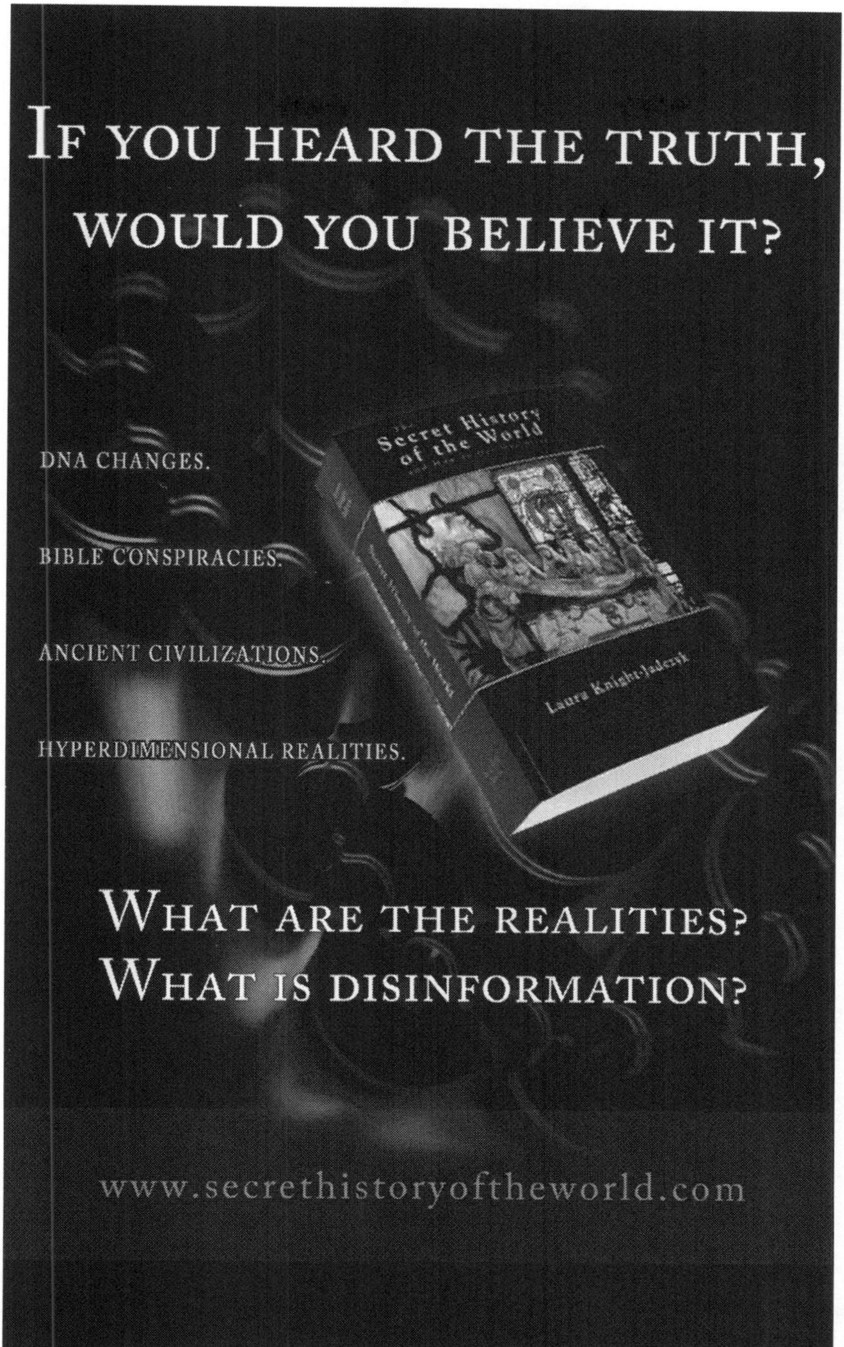
IF YOU HEARD THE TRUTH,
WOULD YOU BELIEVE IT?
DNA CHANGES.
BIBLE CONSPIRACIES.
ANCIENT CIVILIZATIONS.
HYPERDIMENSIONAL REALITIES.
The Secret History of the World
Laura Knight-Jadczyk
WHAT ARE THE REALITIES?
WHAT IS DISINFORMATION?
www.secrethistoryoftheworld.com

Psychopaths rule our World.

Printed in Great Britain
by Amazon.co.uk, Ltd.,
Marston Gate.